A TREATISE CONCERNING ANTICHRIST,

DIVIDED INTO
TWO BOOKS,
THE FORMER, PROVING
THAT THE POPE IS
ANTICHRIST:

THE LATTER, maintaining the same assertion, against all the objections of Robert Bellarmine, Jesuit and Cardinal of the Church of Rome.

By GEORGE DOWNAME, *Doctor of Divinity,*
and lately reader of the Divinity Lecture in Paul's.

Revelation 18:4, 6.
Come out of Babylon my people, that you be not partakers with her in her sins, and that you receive not of her plagues, etc. Render unto her as she has rewarded you, and repay her double according to her works.

AT LONDON Imprinted for Cuthbert Burbie. 1603.

Berith Press
P.O. Box 861, Kansas, OK 74347
(918) 896-2055
www.berithpress.com

A treatise concerning Antichrist divided into two books, the former, proving that the Pope is Antichrist, the latter, maintaining the same assertion, against all the objections of Robert Bellarmine, Jesuit and cardinal of the church of Rome was first published in 1603.

This Berith Press reprint, in which spelling, grammar, and formatting changes have been made, is ©2023 by Berith Press. All rights reserved. With thanks to David Jonescue, Logan West, and Alex Sarrouf of Project Puritas for their endeavors, and to EEBO-TCP for the corpus of texts it has produced. Printed in the U.S.A.

ISBN 979-8-9893238-7-6

Table of Contents

Preface..1
Letter to King James..5

Book 1, proving that the Pope is Antichrist..9
Chapter 1, propounding the state of the controversy, and the grounds of our proofs......10
Chapter 2, of the place or seat of Antichrist 17
Chapter 3, concerning the time of the revelation of Antichrist..........................42
Chapter 4, of the conditions of Antichrist, and his opposition unto Christ.............63
Chapter 5, of the pride and ambition of Antichrist, advancing himself above all that is called *God*, etc...84
Chapter 6, of other vices or sinnes of Antichrist......................................113
Chapter 7, of the miracles, or rather lying signs and wonders of Antichrist...........135
Chapter 8, of the name and mark which Antichrist shall impose upon men of all sorts, with some other effects...158
Chapter 9, those things which Antichrist was and is to suffer..........................174

Book 2, maintaining that the pope is Antichrist....................................179
Chapter 1, answering Bellarmine his first argument concerning the name *Antichrist*...180
Chapter 2, maintaining that Antichrist is not one definite and singular person......187
Chapter 3, concerning the time of Antichrist's coming..................................221
Chapter 4, maintaining against Bellarmine his first demonstration, that Antichrist has come...228
Chapter 5, maintaining against Bellarmine his second demonstration, that Antichrist has already come..238
Chapter 6, answering his third demonstration, concerning Enoch and Elijah 246
Chapter 7, answering his fourth demonstration, concerning the most grievous persecution under Antichrist..259
Chapter 8, answering his fifth demonstration concerning the term of Antichrist's reign, namely: 3 and a half years...274

Chapter 9, answering his sixth demonstration concerning the end of the world..*286*
Chapter 10, concerning the name of Antichrist..*293*
Chapter 11, concerning the marke, which Antichrist shall impose upon men..*305*
Chapter 12, of the generation and nation of Antichrist..............................*321*
Chapter 13, of the seat or See of Antichrist..*336*
Chapter 14, concerning the doctrine of Antichrist.....................................*350*
Chapter 15, of the miracles of Antichrist...*377*
Chapter 16, of the kingdom and battles of Antichrist................................*387*
Chapter 17, being the conclusion of the whole treatise...............................*412*

Appendix - The Historic Reformed Doctrine of the Papal Antichrist....................*417*

Preface

If any reader has come across the works of the Downame brothers John and George, they would recognise a sharp and piercing quality of both brothers to not only quickly address the heart of an issue, but also to give a majestic scope of details that provides a comprehensive treatment of the subject at hand. You may have in mind John Downame's work *The Christian Warfare*, which has been described as the magnum opus of the genre.[1] And John's elder brother George was made much of the same stuff: his work on the Covenant of Grace ran contrary to the prevailing Arminian opinions of Archbishop Laud and his followers – so much so that Laud tried to prevent it circulating, however this was unsuccessful.[2]

Downame's *Treatise Concerning Antichrist* that you have in your hands was initially published in 1603, setting out the historic Protestant and Reformed position, that the office of the papacy is the Antichrist. George Downame was appointed the Bishop of Derry in 1616, and served in this role for 17 years. In 1626 – over twenty years on from his publication of his treatise on Antichrist – Downame "was among the most zealous signatories of the protestation against the toleration of popery."[3]

Indeed, Downame precisely showed how it was all the popes considered in the role within the papacy, rather than any one particular pope, who collectively and successively took up the office of the Antichrist, as the apostle Paul had prophesied in 2 Thessalonians 2. Downame spends his first book proving that that man of sin could be none other than the pope of Rome, and his second book is taken up with refuting Cardinal Robert

---

[1] <https://history.hanover.edu/courses/excerpts/260down.html> [Accessed 11/28/2023]

[2] <https://www.dib.ie/biography/downham-downame-george-a2743.> [Accessed 11/28/2023]

[3] <https://en.wikisource.org/wiki/Dictionary_of_National_Biography,_1885-1900/Downham,_George> [Accessed 11/28/2023]

Bellarmine. The relevance for our day is high, because Bellarmine had popularized the view on Antichrist taught by the Spanish Jesuit priest, Francisco Ribera, about a yet-futuristic Antichrist whose reign would span a mere seven years, and not centuries.

H.C. Martin wrote, "As he attempted to advance the Roman Catholic Counter Reformation, Ribera was embarrassed by the persistent Protestant identification of the Papacy with the Antichrist. To counter this he revived a futuristic interpretation for the Book of Revelation (he placed all but the first three chapters in the future). Antichrist was restored to a person and an individual ruler (not the pope) who would arise in the future. Antichrist would reign for three and one half years and his teaching was embellished with a rebuilding of a temple at Jerusalem, revival of the Levitical Laws and Sacrifices, plus various Jewish aspects in addition to the wholly unfulfilled persecution of the Church. This futuristic interpretation was popularized by Cardinal Bellarmine and became widely accepted within Romanism."[4]

In the scheme advanced by Ribera and Bellarmine, the Antichrist would yet come in the future, and would be accepted by the Jews as their (false) messiah. This myth perpetuates to this day in elements of dispensationalism that also see the Jewish people being ensnared by a false savior who holds to the office of Antichrist for a seven year period. Bellarmine in his commentary on Antichrist displays a fair amount of eschatological agnosticism when he claimed of the mark of the beast: "I believe it is a positive character that will be devised by Antichrist, just as Christ had the sign of the cross made known to all. Yet no one will know what this character will be until Antichrist comes, just as we said on his name."[5]

By contrast, Protestants such as George Downame taught that the distinguishing mark of Antichrist was already present in the world, and that it belonged to the apostate (not apostolic) church of Rome. Bellarmine leans

---

[4] <https://www.lutheranlibrary.org/634-martin-origin-dispensational-futurism/> [Accessed 11/28/2023]

[5] Robert Bellarmine, *Antichrist*, translated by Ryan Grant (USA, 2018), p.84

on the antiquity of the church fathers to seek to prove his point that the Antichrist would sit in a constructed material temple in Jerusalem, and thus the pope – seated in Rome – could not be Antichrist.

Downame provides a sharp contrast with Bellarmine, not leaning on the antiquity of the church fathers themselves, so much of the Scriptures themselves, which are of infinitely greater antiquity and authority. Downame writes in this treatise:

> *To this testimony of Gregory, I might add several other witnesses. But my purpose is not to draw my arguments from the writings – and as it were, the cisterns – of men who lived before the revelation of Antichrist. And therefore unless they themselves had been prophets, they could not fully expound these prophecies – but from the pure fountains of holy Scriptures expounded by the history and event, the best interpreters of prophecies.*
>
> *For as Daniel says of the like (or rather as the papists say of these same prophecies concerning Antichrist) "The words are closed up, and sealed, until the appointed time."*[6]

I hope that in these brief opening remarks, you have been encouraged to see the vast difference between the historic Protestant and Reformed doctrine of the Antichrist that has been carried into the present day via the doctrine of historicism, and the Jesuit teaching of futurism that became popularized through the school of dispensationalism. And indeed, one can trace a line from Ribera and Bellarmine to dispensationalism, because after their day, because Manuel Lacunza, a Jesuit priest writing in the 18th century from Chile, who wrote under the pseudonym Juan Josafat Ben-Ezra, penning a commentary on Revelation entitled: *The Coming of the Messiah in Majesty and Glory.*

---

[6] Daniel 12:9

Edward Irving – a minister from the Church of Scotland who was deposed for heresy – discovered Lacunza's commentary, learned Spanish, and translated the work into English, thus opening up futurism to the English-speaking evangelical world.

This context will help the reader to understand why so many popular dispensational and chiliast ideas correspond with the Jesuitical eschatology of the likes of Ribera and Bellarmine.

This reprint of George Downame's work on Antichrist is most relevant to our day, in which Cardinal Bellarmine's ideas of the Antichrist ruling for 3.5 years and building a temple in Jerusalem, and Enoch and Elijah physically returning to earth perpetuate in dispensationalism still.

In this work, I have maintained most of the original footnotes, Latin, Greek, and Hebrew. May the Lord bless your reading of this most valuable book.

Joseph Weissman, Oklahoma, 2023

TO THE MOST HIGH
AND MIGHTY, MOST
CHRISTIAN AND WORTHY KING,

J A M E S, by the grace of God, King of England,
Scotland, France and Ireland, defender of the
faith, etc. All prosperity and true happiness
in this life, and eternal felicity in
the life to come.

The blessed dispensation of God's most gracious providence towards this land; (for which his holy name is always to be praised in his church) in bringing your Highness unto this kingdom, in the beginning of this seventeenth century after Christ, seems to presage that the happy reformation of the church, restitution of the gospel, consumption of Antichrist, decay of Babylon happily begun in the last century, shall in this age or century receive a notable confirmation and increase, if not a perfect consummation.

For however while the darkness of popery over spread the Christian world, not only the inhabitants of the earth were made drunk with the golden cup of the whore of Babylon's fornications, but the kings also and princes of the earth having drunk of the same cup, committed spiritual whoredom with her, and gave power to support the beast, yet when as it pleased God to enlighten the world with the bright beams of his glorious gospel, then Antichrist began to consume, and Babylon to decay: the preachers discovering Antichrist, the people coming out of Babylon, and the princes which before had assisted Antichrist, setting themselves against him.

This great work of God in the full consumption of Antichrist and confusion of Babylon, the ministers of God, that is to say, princes and Preachers, are to accomplish and bring to pass. The preachers, by preaching the everlasting gospel; at the sound whereof Babylon falls, as once the walls of Jericho at the noise of the trumpets sounded by the priests: and by the ministry whereof as it were the spirit of the Lord's mouth, Antichrist falls into a consumption, as Dagon once did fall before the ark.

The princes, partly by their godly example, going out and in before the people in the sincere profession of the truth, and detestation of popery; partly by their authority, providing faithful ministers, countenancing their ministry, oppugning Antichrist in his religion and in his members, bereaving the whore of Babylon – the pope's concubine – of her means, and lastly sacking her and consuming her with fire. For which cause as I thought it my duty (being called to read a lecture in divinity) when I perceived the papists within these few years (I know not upon what other hopes then of raising their fortunes out of the ruins of this whole island) grown more insolent then in former times, to make the best opposition I could against them, and to that end handled this main controversy concerning Antichrist (whereupon all popery depends) both καταδεικνύοντας proving the affirmative, namely: that the pope is Antichrist, and also αποδεικνύοντας disproving the negative against the objections of Bellarmine the Goliath of the papists: so being now at the instance of many well disposed persons, to publish this treatise, I have thought good to dedicate the same to your majesty, as the chief patron and defender of the faith and gospel of Christ (upon earth) against Antichrist and his adherents.

For hereby not only your royal courage may be stirred up, and your godly resolution in oppugning Antichrist (according to the prophecies of the scripture, foretelling the duty of Christian princes in this behalf) more and more confirmed: but also it may most evidently appear to all men, that upon most just and weighty considerations, you and your people renounce all communion with the pope and church of Rome, and by all good means do set ourselves against them. For if the pope be Antichrist (which is proved in this book) and consequently the church of Rome, the whore of Babylon, and synagogue of Antichrist: the papists (who call themselves *catholics*, and us *heretics*), the limbs of Antichrist; the religion and doctrine of popery, the mystery of iniquity and mere Antichristianism, it follows necessarily that Christian princes are not to tolerate either the religion of papists or their persons within their dominions – the religion of papistry being a catholic apostasy from God, consisting not only in respect of the worship, of manifold superstition and most gross idolatry; but also in respect of the doctrine, of many hundred Antichristian errors and doctrines of devils.

The persons of Catholic-papists, being Catholic heretics and revolters from God, members of Antichrist, palpable idolaters; many of them (especially the Seminary priests and Jesuits) persuaders of others to idolatry and apostasy from God. Not to speak of the treason against Christian princes which is enclosed in the bowels of popery, and bosoms of papists. For they teach that all Christian princes who acknowledge not the pope for their supreme head and lord (as no true Christians do) are schismatics at the least, and consequently that the pope has authority to depose them, and to absolve their subjects from their allegiance: and that the pope when he proceeds to the sentence of excommunication and deposition of them (as he did against your sister of blessed memory Queen Elizabeth, and does, so oft as he dares, against others) he does not err in his definitive sentence. And therefore (whatsoever they pretend to the contrary) it is certain, that they being the marked slaves of Antichrist, wholly devoted to his will, are also willing and ready (when means and opportunity fail not) to put in execution his Antichristian censures, and devilish designs.

In consideration whereof, Christian princes and people, are not only bound to come out of Babylon, and to renounce all communion with the pope and church of Rome, but also they are to reward the where of Babylon, as she has rewarded us, yea to repay her double: and not only to hate her, but also to make her desolate and naked, to eat her flesh and consume her with fire. And hereof Christian princes are to be assured, that as those which join with the pope in persecuting the faithful, do fight under the banner of Antichrist the beast, against Christ the Lamb: so they in oppugning the pope and church of Rome, do fight the battles of Christ against Antichrist. And consequently are to promise to themselves undoubted victory: they fighting under the banner of the Lamb, who shall be sure to overcome, seeing he is the Lord of Lords, and King of Kings: and those also that are with him, though esteemed of Antichrist and his adherents, as schismatics and heretics, yet are they called, elect, and faithful.

Encourage therefore yourself most Christian king (as we doubt not but you do) to maintain forever the truth of Christ, against the falsehood of Antichrist. And doubt you not both of happy success and victory in this life, and of an immortal crown of glory in the life to come. The God of all mercy and power, who in his unspeakable bounty towards us, has placed your highness over us in peace, make both you and us truly thankful to his majesty for this inestimable benefit: and establish your highness and your royal posterity in the throne of this kingdom, to the glory of his great name,
advancement of his kingdom, propagation of the gospel, con-
fusion of popery, consolation of all true Christians,
and your own everlasting comfort.
Amen.

Your Majesty's
most humble
and
dutiful subject

GEORGE DOWNAME.

Book 1

The first book, proving that the pope is Antichrist.

Chapter 1

Propounding the state of the controversy, and the grounds of our proofs.

(1) Whereas the Holy Spirit (2 Thessalonians 2:8) has foreshown that Christ our Savior shall consume Antichrist with the spirit of his mouth, that is, by the ministry of his word, which (Isaiah 11:4) is called the rod or scepter of his mouth, and the spirit of his lips: it cannot therefore be denied, but that it is the duty of all faithful ministers, who are as it were the mouth of christ unto his people, to set themselves against Antichrist; that by their ministry his kingdom may be weakened, and the kingdom of Christ Jesus more and more advanced.

For this cause, I took upon myself in my public readings not long since, to entreat of this main controversy between us and the church of Rome concerning Antichrist. But because my speech could prosite only those that heard me, I have – for several causes – thought good by writing to make the benefit of my labors common: firstly that by this means the papists who are tractable [teachable] may be reclaimed, secondly that those who are obstinate among them may be confounded, thirdly that Protestants and professors of the truth who are sound and resolute may be more and more confirmed, and lastly and especially that those who are weak and wavering may be stayed, and preserved from falling into that fearful judgment, which as the Lord has threatened (2 Thessalonians 2) against unsound professors in these latter times.

So has it within these few years fallen upon very many who, having by the great mercy of God been delivered out of the more-than-Egyptian bondage of Antichrist; and being set in the way toward the celestial Canaan and land of promise, seemed with the unthankful Israelites to be weary of the celestial manna, the food of their souls, and desired to be again among the fleshpots of Egypt. For "seeing they had not received the love of the truth that they might be saved, therefore God has sent upon them the efficacy of error that they should believe lies," (meaning the lies of Antichrist) "that all they might be condemned, which believed not the truth, but delighted in unrighteousness," meaning the mystery of iniquity whereof he had spoken (verse 7), that is to say, Antichristianism or popery.

(2) And that we may proceed in order, we are first to set down the state of this controversy, which indeed is the cheese of all controversies between us and the papists, and of the greatest consequence. For if this were once thoroughly cleared, all others would easily be decided. Our assertion therefore in few words is this:

The pope of Rome, who is as it were the god of the papists, is that grand Antichrist, who according to the prophecies of the Holy Spirit in the Scriptures, was to be revealed in these latter times.

The papists hold the contrary.[7] And whereas we say and prove that their lord god the pope's holiness is Antichrist, they affirm that our assertion is blasphemy, and our arguments dotages [foolishnesses]. But if it were no harder a matter to demonstrate the truth of our assertion than to prove their conceit concerning Antichrist, and the proofs thereof to be mere dotages, I would very easily put this question out of controversy: that **the pope is Antichrist.**

(3) But first our assertion is to be expounded, and afterwards proved. As touching the name we agree (says Bellarmine) in this, that as the name Christ is taken two ways, to wit, commonly and properly, so also the name Antichrist.[8]

---

[7] Rhemists in 2 Thessalonians 2; Bellarmine, Book 3, de Pont. Rom. on the Antichrist, chapter 18
[8] Lib. 3. De Pont. Rom. c.2

The name *Christ* commonly belongs to all that are anointed of God;[9] and that either to the special calling of a king, prophet or priest, or to the general calling of a Christian. And in this sense it is taken either more largely for the whole body of those that profess the name of Christ,[10] whereof some are members of Christ in title and profession only; or more strictly for the society of the elect the citizens of heaven, who have the mark of God,[11] and are not only in show and profession, but also indeed and in truth members of the mystical body of Christ.

Peculiarly and κατ' εξοχήν[12] the name Christ belongs to Jesus the Son of God, who was *anointed with the oil of gladness above all his fellows*,[13] and is the head, after a general manner, of all Christians, but more specially of the elect.

In like sort, the contrary name **Antichrist** belongs commonly to all that are enemies to Christ; and those either open and professed enemies as the Jews, Turks, infidels (in which sense the word is not used in the Scripture) or else covert, professing themselves Christians, and under the name and profession of Christ, oppugning Christ and his truth. And so it is taken either more largely to signify the whole body of heretics (as in the epistles of John)[14] or more strictly the society of them who having made an apostasy from Christ, have received the mark of the beast.

Properly or rather peculiarly and κατ' εξοχήν it belongs to *the man of sin, the son of perdition*:[15] who after a more general manner is the head of all heretics, and more specially of that society, which has the mark, the number and name of the beast.[16] The society or body of those who, having made an apostasy from Christ to Antichrist and the Antichristian state which in the Scriptures is called the whore of Babylon, we hold to be the apostatical

---

[9] Psalm 105:15
[10] 1 Corinthians 12:12
[11] Revelation 9:4
[12] This Greek phrase means *par excellence*
[13] Psalm 45:7
[14] 1 John 2:18, 22
[15] 2 Thessalonians 2:3
[16] Revelation 13:17

church of Rome.[17] The head of this Antichristian body and catholic apostasy, we hold to be the pope of Rome; and consequently that the pope is that grand Antichrist, whom the Holy Spirit in the Scriptures has described unto us. And that he κατ' εξοχήν is called *the Antichrist*, not only because he is the head of the Antichristian body, but also because he being in profession the vicar of Christ, is indeed *Aemulus Christi*, that is, an enemy opposed unto Christ, in emulation of like honor, as if we should say, a counter-Christ, as the word *Antichrist* does also signify.

(4) But when we say that the pope is Antichrist, we mean not this or that pope – however some of them have been more notorious Antichrists than others, as for example Sylvester II, Gregory VII a.k.a. Hildebrand, Boniface VIII. John XXII a.k.a. Alexander VI. etc. – but the whole row or rabble of them, from Boniface III downward. For although the Antichrist is but one person, yet he is not one as Christ the head of the Christian body, is one. Christ because he lives forever has no successors, and therefore is one in nature and number, as being one singular and definite person.

The head of the Antichristian body, which is to continue to the end of the world, is continued not in one singular and definite person, but in a succession of many, who are mortal and momentary; which successively have been, are, or shall be the heads of the catholic apostasy: of any whereof indefinitely, or of all commonly, the word Antichrist is understood.

For even as the pope or vicar of Christ according to the popish conceit is one person not in number and nature, but by law and institution, one at once ordinarily, but many successively; so Antichrist is not one singular person, but a succession of Antichristian popes, which we begin at Boniface III, because he, with much ado, about the year of our Lord 607, obtained from the emperor Phocas – and all his successors since have challenged unto

---

[17] Revelation 17

them – the Antichristian title of *the head of the catholic* or *universal church*, or ecumenical and universal bishop.[18]

This title of blasphemy, as Gregory calls it, befitting him that resembles Lucifer in pride, when as John the Bishop of Constantinople had challenged not long before, to wit, about the year 600, in the time of Maurice, whom Phocas cruelly murdered, Gregory the Great – then pope of Rome – affirmed confidently (for so he says, *Fidenter dico*) that therein he was the forerunner of Antichrist, who was now even at hand. *Omnia enim quae praedicta sunt, fiunt. Rex superbiae prope est,* and *quod dici nefas est, sacerdotum ei praeparatur exercitus*:[19] "For all things," (says he) "which were foretold, do now come to pass. The king of pride," (meaning Antichrist) "is at hand: and that which is horrible to be spoken, an army of priests is prepared for him." Whereby he would also insinuate that he should be the prince of priests.

Now this is a principle in the church of Rome, that the pope (especially such a pope as Gregory the Great, speaking definitively and confidently), cannot err. And if this be true (as they may not deny, the pope being the foundation of all their truth) then must they needs confess that Antichrist was come, almost a thousand years since, and that the pope their prince of priests, who not only succeeds John of Constantinople in that Antichristian title, but also far exceeds him in all Antichristian pride, challenging a sovereign and universal authority not only above all other bishops and priests, but also above all kings and emperors, is that Antichrist.

(5) To this testimony of Gregory, I might add several other witnesses. But my purpose is not to draw my arguments from the writings – and as it were, the cisterns – of men who lived before the revelation of Antichrist. And therefore unless they themselves had been prophets, they could not fully expound these prophecies – but from the pure fountains of holy Scriptures expounded by the history and event, the best interpreters of prophecies.

---

[18] Lib. 4 epist. 32 & 34 & 38
[19] Lib. 4. epist. 38

For as Daniel says of the like (or rather as the papists say of these same prophecies concerning Antichrist) "The words are closed up, and sealed, until the appointed time."[20] And accordingly was it said by Augustine, *prophetias citiùs impleri quàm intelligit*: that "prophecies are fulfilled sooner than understood," and by Irenaeus whom Bellarmine also alleges to the same purpose, *omnes prophetiae* (says he) *priusquam habeāt efficaciam, aenigmata sunt et ambiguitas hominibus*: "All prophecies before they have their complement, are unto men dark and doubtful speeches."[21] And therefore speaking of some part of the prophecies concerning Antichrist,[22] he says, *Certius et sine periculo est sustinere adimpletionem prophetiae, quàm suspicari*, etc: "It is more sure and safe to wait for the fulfilling of the prophecy, then beforehand to deliver uncertain guesses."[23] Omitting therefore the uncertain conjectures of men (for such are several opinions of the fathers concerning Antichrist, as Bellarmine confesses of some)[24] from the sacred Scriptures, the undoubted oracles of God, I frame this demonstration:

- Unto whomsoever the prophecies of holy Scripture describing Antichrist, the head of the Antichristian body, do wholly and only agree, he is that grand Antichrist who is foretold in the Scriptures.
- Unto the pope of Rome the prophecies of holy Scripture concerning Antichrist the head of the Antichristian body, do wholly and only agree.
- Therefore the pope of Rome is that grand Antichrist which is foretold in the Scriptures.

---

[20] Daniel 12:9
[21] Lib. 4 *Against Heresies*, c.43, Bellarmine, *de pont. R*, lib.3 c.10
[22] Revelation 13
[23] Lib. 5 *Against Heresies*
[24] Lib.3 *De Pont.* c.10

The proposition I take for granted. For seeing as the Holy Spirit has purposefully in several places of Scripture taken upon him fully and sufficiently to describe Antichrist, and that to this end, that he might be known; we need not doubt, but that this description of Antichrist is so perfect and so proper unto him, as to whom that description agrees not, he is not Antichrist: and contrariwise whom it wholly and only fits, he must be held and acknowledged to be that Antichrist.

All the controversy therefore is concerning the assumption, namely: whether the descriptions of Antichrist in the Scriptures agree to the pope or not. Antichrist is described by the Holy Spirit, especially in three places, namely: in 2 Thessalonians 2, in Revelation 13:11 to the end, and in Revelation 17. For I omit those places in the prophecy of Daniel which usually are alleged[25] (because they speak properly of Antiochus Epiphanes, who was but a type of Antichrist, as Bellarmine also confesses),[26] and Revelation 9, because it is by some expounded of the Turks.

(7) And that the description of Antichrist in the Scriptures fitly agrees to the pope, it appears by this induction. For all the arguments and notes whereby Antichrist is described in the Scriptures may be reduced to these heads, to wit, the *place* or *seat* where we are to find him; the *time* when we were to look for him; his *condition and qualities*, that he is an adversary opposed unto Christ in emulation of like honor, a man of sin in general, and more particularly a horrible idolator; his *actions and passions*, that is, such things as he shall either do or suffer.

I will make it evident by the help of God (whose all-seeing Spirit I humbly beseech to guide me into the truth) that all and everyone of them do so fitly and properly agree to the pope of Rome, that in the descriptions of Antichrist in the Scripture, the pope may behold himself as it were in a glass.

---

[25] Chapters 7 & 8 & 11 & 12
[26] Lib. 3 *de Pont*, R.c. 18 & 21

Chapter 2
Of the place or seat of Antichrist.

(1) And first as touching the place or seat of Antichrist, I reason thus:

- Mystical Babylon, spoken of in Revelation 17-18, is the seat of Antichrist.
- Rome is Mystical Babylon, spoken of in Revelation 17-18.
- Therefore Rome is the seat of Antichrist.

As touching the proposition, you are to understand that Babylon in the Scriptures is taken sometimes *literally*, and sometimes *mystically*: literally, for Babylon either in Chaldea, or in Egypt. Babylon in Chaldea was the Metropolis or imperial city of the Babylonian and Assyrian monarchy. Babylon in Egypt is called *Babylis* and *Cayrus*, of which some understand Peter to speak in 1 Peter 5:13, Babylon mystical in Revelation, is the seat or chief city of Antichrist,[27] resembling the Assyrian Babylon in pride, idolatry, filthiness, and especially in most cruel persecution of the church of God. And for the same causes, in Revelation 11:8, it is called spiritually, Sodom and Egypt: *Sodom*, for pride and filthiness; *Egypt*, for idolatry and for cruelty towards the Israel of God.

And as the church of Christ in Revelation is called *Jerusalem* mystically, or *the holy city*; so the church and especially the metropolis or chief city of Antichrist, is mystically called *Babylon*. This, as it is the received opinion of the faithful, so may it evidently be gathered out of Revelation 17-18, which without all doubt are prophecies concerning Antichrist, and the Antichristian city and seat, as the papists themselves often confess.[28]

---

[27] 1 Peter 5:13, Revelation 17:5
[28] Bellarm. Lib. 3, de Pont. R.c.2, Sander, demonstr. 13 & 18, etc.

(2) For that which the papists sometimes object that by *Babylon* is meant not any one city or company, but the universal company of the reprobate, it is unworthy of answering. And the argument which our Rhemists bring to prove their assertion is without sense, to wit, in their annotation upon Revelation 18:21, where the angel, throwing a great stone into the sea, says, "with such violence shall that great city Babylon be thrown, and be found no more." "By this," (say they), "it seems clear that the apostle does not mean any one city, but the universal company of the reprobate, which shall perish in the day of judgment." But I answer that the destruction of the universal company of the reprobate on the day of judgment is described afterwards in Revelation 20:11.

And this destruction – as appears plainly by the circumstances of the text, especially in verse 9 and the following verses up to verse 18 – shall be *before* the day of judgment, and therefore is not the destruction of the universal company of the wicked. For if the universal destruction of the wicked were here signified, then none of the wicked should survive after this destruction to lament the same, as there shall (verses 9-10, 17).

And that the universal society of the wicked is not meant by Babylon, evidently appears by the whole discourse in chapters 17 and 18, where the Holy Spirit speaks of a city ruling over the princes of the earth, situated upon seven hills, sitting upon many waters, that is, ruling over many people, nations and languages, with whom all princes and inhabitants of the earth have committed fornication, whose destruction is bewailed of all sorts of the wicked, none of which people or princes, or wicked ones that mourn for her, should be of the universal company of the reprobate (as undoubtedly they are) if Babylon signified the whole number of the wicked.

And whereas they allege Jeremiah 52, where only the history of the Babylonian captivity is recorded to prove that *Babylon* signifies the whole number of God's enemies, it argues that they have not so much as any show of reason to object against the truth of this proposition, namely that mystical Babylon is the seat, or as they speak, the See of Antichrist, and therefore from henceforth until something further be objected, I will take it for granted.

(3) But let us come to the assumption – namely: that Rome is mystical Babylon – which I will prove by three arguments.

1st argument: The description of Babylon, and of the whore of Babylon set down by the Holy Spirit in Revelation 17, agrees in all points to Rome and the Roman state.

But most plainly in these two: {1} Firstly, that the whore of Babylon is that great city which in the apostles' time, had the kingdom over the kings of the earth.[29] {2} And secondly, that this city is situated on seven hills, which two notes most properly describe Rome.[30] And so Propertius describes it, *Septem vrbs alta iugis, toti quae praesidet orbi*, that is: "the city mounted on seven hills, overruling the whole world."[31]

That Rome was the imperial city of the world, and the metropolis of the Roman monarchy, it is out of question, neither is there any of our adversaries either so ignorant or so shameless as to deny it. From hence therefore I reason thus:

- That city which in the apostles' time had dominion over the kings of the earth, is the whore of Babylon.
- Rome is that city which in the apostles' time, and since also under the pope, had dominion over the kings of the earth.
- Therefore Rome is the whore of Babylon.

---

[29] Revelation 17:18
[30] Revelation 17:9
[31] Eleg. 10. *Lib.* 3

And that Rome also was situated on seven hills, it is most manifest. Of her Virgil says,[32]

Scilicet and rerum facta est pulcherrima Roma,
Septem quae vna sibi muro circumdedit arces.

Varro,[33] speaking of a festival day, which among the Romans was called *Septimontium*, he says it was so called, *ab his 7. montibus in quibus vrbs sit a est*, that is, "from the seven hills whereon the city was situated." And Plutarch upon the same occasion calls Rome επτάλοφος, *Septicollem*, that is seven-hilled.[34] Blondus says, *Montes in vrbe septem numerantur*, "The hills within the city are seven in number." And the names of these seven hills are commonly known, and usually named in Roman authors, namely: Palatinus, Capitolinus, Qutrinalis, Coelius, Esquilinus, Viminalis, and Aventinus.

(4) Yea but say our English Rhemists, the angel himself here [depicts] these seven hills to be alone with the seven heads, and the seven kings.[35] And yet the heretics take them literally for seven hills, whereas the number of seven is mystical, signifying universally all of that sort. And they might mark that the prophets' visions here are most by seven, whether he talks of heads, horns (which notwithstanding are not seven but ten) candlesticks, churches, kings, or hills.

For answer whereunto, we must know that the beast whereon the whore of Babylon sits, is generally the Empire of Rome, but more especially *Urbis Romae*, the city of Rome, which was the imperial, and is the papal seat. This beast is said to have seven heads: which the Holy Spirit expounds in two ways.

---

[32] *Georgics* 2, in fine
[33] Lib , *de ling. lat.*
[34] Plutarch, *Roman Problems*, Book 1.65
[35] In Revelation 17:9

Septem capita urbis, the seven heads of the city are seven hills, the seven heads of the empire or people subject to Rome (which also are compared to waters whereon the whore sits)[36] are seven kings, that is seven several regimens, or heads of government, (for so the Holy Spirit elsewhere calls them),[37] whereby the empire or people of Rome has at different times been governed: to wit, kings (which also were seven) consuls, decemvirs, tribunes (not *tribuni plebis*, but *tribunt militum consulari potestate*), dictators, emperors, and popes.

Now the apostle does not say, the seven heads are seven hills, and the seven hills are seven kings: but the seven heads are seven hills, and they (namely: seven heads) are (also) seven kings, as Bellarmine also acknowledges.[38] For this interpretation which they give to the angel, firstly, is inconvenient. For heads do more fitly resemble kings which are the heads of the body politic, than hills do. And secondly, it is false, for if the hills be kings, then the city (which is the woman, verse 18) sits upon the seven kings, for she sits upon the hills (verse 9).[39] Neither is this interpretation of seven heads – that they are seven hills – any interpretation at all, except we understand *hills* properly.

Moreover, both the hills and kings are said to be seven, not because seven is a mystical number, signifying all the kingdoms of persecutors, but because they are seven indeed. Which also may be said of the seven candlesticks and seven churches, as in chapters 1-3 of Revelation, which they bring for an instance. Of the hills there is no question: and it is as true of the kings, and therefore the angel numbers them (verse 10).[40] "Five," (says he) "are fallen, one is, and the other is not yet come" – which is verified of these seven regimens of which I spoke.

---

[36] Revelation 17:1, 15
[37] Daniel 8:21
[38] Lib. 3, *de pont. Rom.*, cap. 5
[39] Revelation 17:9, 18
[40] Revelation 17:10

For the regimens of kings, consuls, decemvirs, tribunes, dictators, were ceased in the apostles' time: One (that is of the Emperors) then was, and the seventh, that is to say, of the popes, was not yet come.[41] And as touching the Roman Empire erected and revived by the pope: it is the beast that was a flourishing imperial state, but is not indeed and in truth the empire of Rome, but rather an image of it (Revelation 13) although it is in name and title the empire of Rome. This beast that was and is not, it is also the eighth head or regimen, and is one of the seven, namely of emperors.[42]

(5) 2nd argument: The fact that Rome is mystical Babylon may be proven by the testimonies of very good authors.

Jerome says, *Romanam urbem in Apocalypsi Ioannis and Epistola Petri Babylonem specialiter appellare,* that the city of Rome is called Babylon especially, in the Revelation of John, and epistle of Peter. Augustine calls Rome *the second Babylon,* and *Babylon of the West.*[43] To these we may add Tertullian, Primasius, Victorinus (who says, the seven heads are the seven hills on which the woman, that is, the city of Rome does sit) Prosper, and many others, Sibylla also oftentimes expressly calls Rome *Babylon.*

(6) 3rd argument: by the confession of our adversaries themselves.

[1] For first to prove that Peter was at Rome, they say that by *Babylon* mentioned in 1 Peter 5:13 is meant *Rome,* although there can be no sufficient reason given, why the apostle, if he had meant Rome, should not rather have used the name of *Rome* than of *Babylon.*

[2] Secondly, the Rhemists – convicted with clearness of truth writing on Revelation 17:18 – confess that if by *Babylon,* it is meant any one city (which before we have proven) it is most likely to be old Rome. And on

---

[41] Revelation 17:8
[42] Revelation 17:11
[43] Jerome on Isaiah 47, Letter to Marcellus, question 11, etc., Augustine, *City of God,* Book 18 Chapter 22 & 27, *Against the Jews* 3, etc.

verse 5, they do confess, that as the persecuting emperors, which (as they say) were figures of Antichrist, did principally sit in Rome; so it may well be, that the great Antichrist shall have his seat there. And again on verse 18, they allege a reason: "For by the authority of the old Roman Empire, Christ was put to death first," applying the prophecy of Revelation 11:8 to Rome, thereby unwittingly confessing that Rome is that great city, which as in Revelation 17 is called *Babylon* mystically, so in that place is termed spiritually *Sodom and Egypt*, where our Lord was also crucified.

[3] Thirdly, the author of *The Wardword*, not knowing how to deny this so evident truth, is content thus far to agree with us that Rome is Babylon. "For not only John," (says he) "in Revelation, but Peter also in his epistle does call Rome *Babylon*, and we do not deny it." Bellarmine also confesses so much,[44] *Per meretricem intelligi Romain*, that by *the whore of Babylon* is to be understood as Rome, and proves the same by the testimony of Tertullian and Jerome. Therefore, seeing as mystical Babylon is the chief city and See of Antichrist, as our adversaries cannot deny with any show of reason, and seeing Rome is mystical Babylon, as has been proven not only by reason and testimonies, but also by the confession of our adversaries, the conclusion must necessarily be inferred that Rome therefore is the seat of Antichrist.

(7) What then? What can the papist answer to this syllogism?

- Mystical Babylon is the seat of Antichrist,
- Rome is mystical Babylon,
- Therefore Rome is the seat of Antichrist.

"It may well be," say the Rhemists, "that the great Antichrist shall have his seat there." "And we do not deny," says the author of *the Wardword*, "but that Rome is Babylon." And Bellarmine does not only say it, but prove it.

---

[44] Lib. 3. *de pont.* R.c. 13

How then? Indeed, when it comes to Rome, we must make distinctions. For Rome is either *heathen* or *christened*. *Heathen Rome* under the persecuting emperors was Babylon, but *Rome christened* is the Apostolic See, and as it were, the Jerusalem of the Christians.

But this evasion of theirs, however they please themselves in it, is frivolous and absurd, as shall appear by these reasons. For first, if Rome is Babylon, as now at the length they confess, and consequently the seat of Antichrist, as they cannot deny with any show of reason, I would be glad to know from them, whether under the heathen emperors Rome could be called the seat of Antichrist, because Antichrist did then sit in Rome, or because he was to sit there after the heathen emperors were removed. If they say "because he sat there then," their answer is ridiculous, and contrary to all that they themselves hold concerning Antichrist. Therefore they must confess that Rome is called Babylon and the seat of Antichrist; not because Antichrist sat there while it was heathen, but because he was to sit there after the emperors were removed.

(8) And that the Holy Spirit by *Babylon* does not mean heathen Rome under the persecuting emperors, either only or principally, but Rome christened under the pope, it may further appear out of the whole discourse of John in Revelation 17-18.

The whore of Babylon is the great city, which in the apostles' time, and since under the popes, reigned over the kings of the earth; called a whore, and the mother of fornications: not only because her self has by spiritual fornications plaid the strumpet, according to that which is said of Jerusalem: *Fidelis civitas facta est meretrix*, "The faithful city is become a harlot" (Isaiah 1:21) – but also infected all kings and nations, subject unto her, with her superstition and idolatry. But heathen Rome, which neither dealt by whorish sleights and allurements, but by martial policy and power, neither had professed herself to be the Church and spouse of Christ, could not so fitly be called a harlot, whereby is signified an adulterous and apostatical state.

And besides, heathen Rome for the most part permitted to every country their own religion: and was so far from enforcing her religion upon other nations subject unto her, that as in her was erected the Pantheon in honor of all the gods (which Boniface IV having obtained from Phocas, consecrated to the virgin Mary and all the saints) so she admitted the idols, religions, and superstitions almost of all other countries, excepting the religions of the Egyptians and the Jews, because they did not forsooth beseem the majesty of the empire.[45]

But popish Rome, of Bethel is become Bethaven (Hosea 4:15), and of a faithful city an harlot (Isaiah 1:21), exceeding all others in whorish enticements, cozenages [deceptions], impudencies, cruelties, and all filthiness: insomuch that we may truly say with Mantuan, *Roma est iam tota lupanar*, "Rome wholly is become a stew;" and with Petrarch, that she is *scelerum aetque dedecorum omnium sentina*: "The sink and sewer of all villainies and shameful practices" – and has not only played the harlot herself, but is become the mother of all fornications, that is, idolatry and superstitions, and the fountain of all other abominations in the Christian world, with which the cup of her fornications inebriates (which more argues the sottishness of the Romish religion) all kings and people that consent unto her, and with fire and sword, obtrudes her superstitions and Idolatrous religion, unto all nations that they can make subject to that See.

(9) Again, if John had spoken of old Rome, which then openly persecuted the saints, then had he not spoken of a mystery (as he does)[46] neither would he so greatly have wondered to see the whore of Babylon's either idolatry or cruelty, against the saints (as he does in verse 6) if by the whore were meant old Rome, whose idolatry and cruelty to John was not strange.

---

[45] Marcellin. Lib. 16, Rosin. Lib. 2 c.9
[46] Revelation 17:5, 7

And further that the Holy Spirit by *Babylon* means popish Rome, it may be proven out of Revelation 17:8 to the end of the chapter, where the angel declares unto John the mystery of the beast, whereupon the woman sits, which has the seven heads and ten horns. For although this beast – as appears by conferring with Revelation 13,[47] may signify in general the Roman state as it is opposed to Christ, which in respect of the regimen – has been subject to seven heads of government, in respect of the imperial city is seated on seven hills, and in respect of the empire was divided in the apostles' time into ten provinces or kingdoms, as Strabo and others testify; yet here the angel speaks especially of the Roman state and empire renewed, and as it were revived by the pope.

To this, as also to the papacy (which is the second beast in Revelation 13) though they are either of them but several heads of the beast (verses 10-11) yet the Holy Spirit gives the name of the beast: "For this beast on which the woman sitteth, was and is not, and shall arise out of the depth," and again, "that it is the beast which was and is not, though it be." And verse 11, having shown that the seven heads of this beast signify both the imperial seat standing on seven hills, and also seven kings, that is, seven chief governments, he says: 'This beast which was and is not, is the eighth." (namely: *head of government,* for he speaks in the masculine: και αυτος ογδοος εστιν) and is one of the seven, namely: of emperors. All of this cannot be understood of the Roman Empire, as it was heathen, but as it is popish. For this head, which had been and after was not (for it lay void from the time of Augustulus unto Charlemagne, the space of 325 years, namely: from the year 475, unto the year 800) was after to arise (for so he says μελλει αναβαινειν) being revived by the pope, who was to put life into the image of the former beast.[48]

For this empire, erected by the pope, although it has the name of the beast ascribed unto it, yet it is but the image of the former beast, and

---

[47] Revelation 13:1-2
[48] Revelation 13

therefore is not, in truth and imperial authority and dominion, the empire of Rome, although in title it be. And further it is said, that this beast is the eighth head, and is one of the seven, which cannot be understood of the heathen emperors but of the popish.

- *If* therefore this beast whereupon the whore of Babylon sits – ruling and guiding the same, as the rider does the beast upon which he sits – is not the old empire but the new, erected by the pope, *then* the whore of Babylon is not old Rome under the heathen emperors, but Rome christened under the pope.
- But the first is true.
- Therefore the last.

(10) Fifthly, "The ten horns (says the angel) which thou sawest are ten kings," that is, the chief governors of the ten provinces or kingdoms, who before the dissolution of the empire in the west, had not as yet received the kingdom; because they still remained as proconsuls or propraetors, that is deputies and lieutenants under the emperor.

But after the empire was dissolved in the west, they received power as kings about the same time with the beast: Antichrist the pope (for so Antichist both in chapters 13 and 17 is considered, {1} as a head of the beast, and {2} as a beast by itself).

For albeit neither he could reign in Rome, nor they in the provinces, by sovereign authority, while the empire stood in the west, and flourished; yet when it was once decayed, (but especially when the emperor also of the east had by the pope's means lost his title in Italy and Rome, and was by him bereaved, as the author of the book called *Fasciculus Temporum* says, of the western empire) then he seized on Rome, and a great part of Italy, and they on the several provinces. And that these ten horns are the heads of ten kingdoms, which together with the beast (meaning Antichrist) shall divide among them the Roman Empire, (for that is signified when it is said that they receive power as kings, that is, sovereign authority, the same hour with the beast) it is the received opinion of the best writers. Yea Bellarmine himself says, *Johannes dicit decem reges, qui sibi diuident Rom. imperium, odio habituros purpuratam meretricem. i. Romam, et eam desolatam facturos*: "John does say that the ten kings which shall divide among them the Roman Empire, shall hate the harlot arrayed with purple, that is (says he) Rome, and shall make her desolate."[49]

And therefore the Holy Spirit in that place speaks not of Rome as it was under the heathen emperors, nor of the empire as it was heathen, for then it was not dissolved; and long before the dissolution, had Rome ceased to be heathen, but of the empire erected and renewed by the pope; which although it neither enjoys Rome itself the imperial seat, nor yet the provinces which in times past belonged to the empire, yet has the name and title thereof. And consequently, he speaks of Rome as she should be, not only after the dissolution of the old empire in the west, but also after the erection of the new, that is to say, of popish Rome.

(11) Of these ten horns, it is further said that they all have one mind, being all of the same popish religion, all of them with one consent wholly devoted to the pope, and sworn unto him.[50] To whom for a time they give over themselves, and their whole power to help and support the beast, thinking themselves bound (as he has persuaded them) to exercise their temporal sword, that is, their civil power, for the church, meaning himself, and at his beck and commandment. And being joined to him and united one with another by holy leagues (as they call them) make holy wars, indeed, against Christ the lamb in his true members.[51]

---

[49] Lib. 3 de Pont. R. cap. 13
[50] Revelation 17:13
[51] Revelation 17:13-14

But when as Christ shall begin to consume Antichrist with the preaching of his word (as he is sure to overcome because he is the Lord of Lords) then these ten horns which before had joined with Antichrist, and had committed spiritual fornication with the whore, shall begin to hate the whore and to leave her desolate and naked.[52]

This cannot be understood of old Rome, but of that which now is, whereof this prophecy already is in part fulfilled. For since the revelation of Antichrist in these latter times, the pope has lost, as Bellarmine complains, *magnā Germaniae partem, Suetiam, Gothiam, Noruegiam, Daniā vniuersam, bonā Angliae, Galliae, Heluetiae, Poloniae, Boemiae ac Pānoniae partem*, that is: "a great part of Germany, all Sweden, Gothland, Norway, Denmark, a good part of England, (but he might as well have said all England, and thereunto added, Scotland and Ireland) a good part of France, Helvetia, Polonia, Boemia, and Pannonia."[53] So several of these ten kings have already forsaken the whore of Babylon, and have bereaved her of a great part of her maintenance, and left her, as much as lies within them, naked – and the rest in God's good time will accomplish his will.

(12) Seventhly, it is apparent that John's treatise of Rome extends until the destruction thereof.[54] If therefore by *Babylon* is meant only heathen Rome under the persecuting emperors; then the destruction – which the Holy Spirit denounces against the whore of Babylon – did befall Rome while it was heathen. But it is absurd to say that this destruction befell heathen Rome. For first this destruction is an utter and final destruction (Revelation 18:21-23). And before this destruction the empire was to be divided into ten kingdoms, which first should join with Antichrist, and afterward oppugn him. Which is utterly false of heathen Rome, but yet is begun to be fulfilled of Rome popish, and will in due time be accomplished.

---

[52] Revelation 17:2
[53] Lib. 3. *De Pont. R.* cap.21
[54] Revelation 17 & 18

And again, it is most plain that John entreats of the state and condition of Rome, as it shall be in the time of Antichrist. But Antichrist – as the papists themselves confess – was not to come while Rome was heathen, but after the dissolution of the Roman Empire. And lastly, Jerome and other fathers, in whose times Rome was not heathen, do notwithstanding call it *Babylon*. Not that then it was, or had been before, but because it should be according to the prophecies of the Holy Spirit, the seat of Antichrist, whose coming, he and other of the fathers supposed not to be far off. And therefore Jerome, in his Epistle to Marcella, uses this argument as the principal to persuade her to come from Rome (which then was not heathen) because it is Babylon.

(13) These arguments might suffice to prove that not heathen Rome under the emperors, but christened Rome under the popes, is mystical Babylon the chief city and See of Antichrist. But yet for better evidence of this truth, and for the clearer manifestation of Antichrist, I will further prove unto you, that Rome – christened and professing herself to be the church of Christ – is the seat of Antichrist. For *if* Antichrist shall sit at all in Rome, *then* shall he sit in Rome christened, professing herself to be the church of Christ. But he shall sit in Rome (as has been proven in part and shall further be cleared) therefore in Rome christened, and professing herself to be the church of God.

The proposition is built upon this foundation: that Antichrist shall sit in the Church of God, and therefore if Antichrist shall sit at Rome, he shall sit in Rome professing herself the church of God.

Now then, that *Antichrist shall sit in the church of God*, I prove by the testimony of Paul, affirming (2 Thessalonians 2:4) that Antichrist shall sit in the temple of God. But because the papists labor by might and main to extort this place from us as serving rather to prove their conceit that *Antichrist shall sit in the temple of God at Jerusalem*, I will therefore deliver the place from their corruptions, and also make good our interpretation.

For first, the temple at Jerusalem, and city itself, as it was a type of the church of Christ: so when the church of Christ was once planted by the preaching of the gospel throughout the world, it was utterly and finally to be abolished, according to the prophecy of our Savior Christ (Matthew 24:14): "And then shall be the end," – namely of the temple and city of Jerusalem. For after the temple was once utterly destroyed by Titus Vespasian, as Christ had shown beforehand, it is never to be rebuilt.[55]

For as Daniel says, according to the vulgar translation, which with the papists is the only authentic text of Scripture (Daniel 9:27) *Et erit in templo abominatio desolationis, & vsque ad consummationem et finem perseverabit desolatio*, "And there shall be in the temple the abomination of desolation, and unto the consummation and end, the desolation shall continue," or as Jerome speaks more plainly, *Vs{que} ad consummationem et finem mundi perseverabit desolatio*: "The desolation shall continue unto the consummation and end of the world." Our Savior Christ also (Luke 21:22, 24) foretold that Jerusalem – being destroyed by the Romans – should be trodden underfoot by the Gentiles, until the times of the Gentiles be fulfilled, that is until the second coming of Christ, which in the next words is described.

Wherefore when, as Julian the Apostate endeavored by the Jews to re-edify the temple that he might convince the preaching of Christ of falsehood – (as Theodoret speaks)[56] which he could not do, unless Christ had taught that it should not be reedified – our Savior Christ by fire first from heaven, and after out of the earth, and by a fearful earthquake hindered this enterprise, thereby approving his Godhead, and showing that he was not pleased, as Sozomen says, with the renewing of the temple.

It seems also to have been the judgment of Cyril, with many others in the primitive church, that the temple should never be rebuilt. And Jerome says[57] that the opinion which is for the restoring of the temple, is a Jewish

---

[55] Matthew 24:2
[56] Lib. 3 cap. 20, Socrat. Lib. 3, cap.20, Sozom. Lib.5. cap.ult
[57] To Marceullus

fable. Whereas therefore the papists teach that Antichrist shall cause this temple to be built, and that he shall have his seat there, which they know shall never be – what do they else but make a mockery of all the prophecies of the Holy Spirit concerning the coming of Antichrist, and with Julian, go about to give the lie to Daniel and our Savior Christ?

(14) Again, if the apostle had by temple meant such a temple as should be built by Antichrist, he would not have called it the Temple of God, but rather of the Devil. *Non enim templum alicuius idoli* (says Augustine)[58] *aut daemonis, templum Dei Apostolus diceret*. "For the temple of some idol or Devil, the Apostle would not call the temple of God."

Neither are we by *the temple of God* to understand a material building, for such (as Bellarmine truly says) are not called the temple of God in the New Testament. And therefore the more gross is he to understand it of a material temple, and of a corporal sitting. For first, material temples in the writings of the apostles are not called the temples of God; but the congregations of God's people are the temple of God. See 1 Corinthians 3:16-17, 2. Corinthians 6:16, Ephesians 2:21, and Revelation 3:12. And according to the Scripture's phrase speaks Lactantius,[59] *Sola* (says he) *catholica Ecclesia est, quae verum cultum retinet, hic est fons veritatis, hoc est domicilium fidei, hoc templum Dei*: "It is the catholic church alone which retains the true worship: this is the wellspring of truth, this is the house of faith, this is the temple of God."

The temple of God therefore signifies the congregation or company of them which profess the name of Christ. In this temple, Antichrist sits, that is, rules and reigns. For we are not to understand it of the corporal gesture, as appears by that which follows, "he shall sit in the temple of God as God," that is, he shall rule and reign as if he were a god, for that is meant by *God's sitting*, who does not sit after a corporal manner. In the temple of God

---

[58] Augustine, *The City of God*, Book 20 Chapter 19
[59] Lactantius, *Institutes*, Lib. 4, Cap.30

therefore, which is his church, Antichrist sits, that is rules and governs, challenging a sovereign and universal dominion over all those that profess the name of Christ, as being the head, husband and lord of the universal church: which agrees most fitly and properly to the popes of Rome.

Neither are we to omit the phrase of *sitting*. For whereas princes are said to *reign* for so many years, the popes are said to *sit*, and the chief place of his dominion is called his *Sedes*, that is See or seat.

(15) And this our interpretation is confirmed by the testimonies of the ancient. "The temple of God," (says Theodoret) "he calls the churches, wherein Antichrist shall challenge to himself the first seat, endeavoring to show himself to be God." And again, *Dei autem templum vocat ecclesias*: "The temple of God he calls the churches." Jerome:[60] *et in templo Dei* (says he) *vel Hierosolymis vt quidam putant, vel in ecclesia vt veriùs arbitramur*: "And he shall sit in the temple of God, either at Jerusalem as some think, or in the church, as we more truly suppose." [In] Chrysostom, it seems that και is put corruptly for εις, for so the Greek scholiast, who usually reports word for word, out of Chrysostom says "in the temple": "He says not *in the temple at Jerusalem,* but *in the churches of God.*"

And likewise Theophylact: "Not in the temple which is at Jerusalem especially, but simply in the churches and in every temple of God."

Augustine of these words says, "But in what temple of God he shall sit as God, it is uncertain; whether in that ruin of the temple which king Solomon built, or else in the church. For the apostle would not call the temple of an idol or devil, the temple of God."[61]

Whereupon some (to whose judgment not only Augustine in this place,[62] but Primasius also subscribes), some I say, by *Antichrist* in this place will have understood not the prince himself, but his whole body after a sort,

---

[60] Jerome, *Ad Algasium*, Question 11
[61] Augustine, *The City of God*, Book 20 Chapter 19
[62] Bellarmine cites it as Augustine's own judgment, chapter 13.

that is the multitude of men pertaining unto him together with the prince himself. And they think it might better be read in the Latin as it is in the Greek, *non in templo Dei, sed in templum dei sedeat, tanquam ipse sit templum Dei quod est ecclesia. Sicut dicimus sedet in amicum. i. velut i. amicus*, etc. He sits not in the temple of God, but as the temple of God, as if he were the temple of God which is the church, even as we say *sedet in amicum*, that is, he sits as a friend. This exposition most fittingly agrees to the pope, and church of Rome who esteem themselves alone to be the catholic church, and all others professing the name of Christ, to be heretics and schismatics. By this which has been said, it is plain that by the temple we are to understand the church of God.

And yet this does no more prove the church of Rome to be the true church of God, then they can prove the temple of Antichrist at Jerusalem, where they say he should sit, to be the temple of God.[63] It is sufficient that the church where Antichrist sits, has been the true church, and still is in title and profession; although in truth it be but an apostate church. For Antichrist, as he was to sit in the church, so he was to be the head of the apostasy, and of those that fall from God: who notwithstanding (according to that exposition in Augustine) shall sit *in templum Dei*, as though they alone were the true church of God.

(16) But the papists confirm their exposition – namely: that the temple of God signifies the temple at Jerusalem – out of Revelation 11:8. Where John shows (they say) that the bodies of Enoch and Elijah, being slain by Antichrist, shall lie in the streets of Jerusalem. Whereunto I answer that John in that place neither speaks of Enoch and Elijah, nor yet of Jerusalem. And whether he speaks of the persecution of Antichrist, there may be some doubt; because he seems in verses 2 and 7 to speak of the same persecution of the holy city that is the church, under the heathen; and namely the

---

[63] Of this, see more in the 2nd Book, and Chapter 13, Sections 4-6.

persecuting emperors, for 42 months, which is mentioned in Revelation 13:5.

But supposing it to be understood of Antichrist his persecution, let us consider the force of their argument:

- Where the two witnesses of God are slain by Antichrist, there is (they say) the seat of Antichrist.
- At Jerusalem the two witnesses of God shall be slain.
- Therefore at Jerusalem shall be the seat of Antichrist.

The proposition they take for granted, which notwithstanding, is not generally true. For the two witnesses of God may be slain in that place by the authority and commandment of Antichrist, where his proper seat is not. For as our Savior Christ was put to death, by the authority of the Roman Empire at Jerusalem, where notwithstanding was not the imperial seat of the emperor, so the witnesses of our Savior Christ might be slain by the authority and commandment of the Antichrist of Rome, either at Jerusalem or elsewhere, where notwithstanding is not the proper seat of Antichrist.

This alone is sufficient to overthrow their whole argument. For if their proposition is not generally true, then their whole argumentation from a particular proposition is mere sophistry.

(17) Notwithstanding, their assumption is also to be denied, because the Holy Spirit speaks not of Jerusalem (as Jerome proves) but of Rome, or rather of the Empire of Rome. Yea but (say they) Christ also was crucified where the two witnesses should be slain: at Jerusalem Christ was crucified, and not at Rome, therefore at Jerusalem the two witnesses should be slain. I answer to the assumption: Christ was crucified at Jerusalem, and in the great city also,[64] that is to say, within the Roman Empire, wherein and by authority

---

[64] Revelation 17:18

where of our Savior Christ was put to death. In which sense the Rhemists seem to apply this prophecy to Rome. If by *the great city* (say they) is meant any one city, it is most likely to be old Rome, for by the authority of the old Roman Empire Christ was put to death first. Whereunto I might add that even in Rome itself, Christ has been crucified in his members, and that within Jerusalem, Christ was not crucified (Hebrews 13:12).

Now that Jerusalem is not here meant, but Rome, or rather, the Roman Empire, I prove: first, because it is called the great city. By which title throughout Revelation is meant Babylon or Rome, as appears by comparing these places. Revelation 14:8 and 16:19. and 18:10, 16, 18-19 & 21, but especially Revelation 17:18, where the woman, that is, the whore of Babylon is said to be the great city which reigns over the kings of the earth. And of this great city is the Empire of Rome (which as it is called Sodom, which is the name of a city, so also Egypt, which is the name of a kingdom) the streets may fitly signify the cities or towns of the several provinces. Once only is this title given to Jerusalem, and then not to the earthly Jerusalem, but to the heavenly (Revelation 21:10).

And so Augustine expounds this place, *In plateis ciuitatis magnae. i. in medio ecclesiae*, "In the streets of the great city, that is, in the midst of the church,"[65] saying that by the name *church*, he must needs understand an adulterous and apostatical church (which elsewhere is called *the whore of Babylon*), because as it follows in the text, it is called spiritually *Sodom* or *Egypt*. For even as in the midst of the church even at Jerusalem, Christ was crucified, so also the two witnesses of Christ were to be slain in the midst of the church, and even in that city which professes herself to be as it were the Jerusalem of Christendom. Secondly, the great city whereof he speaks, is called spiritually *Sodom* or *Egypt*. *Sodom*, for her pride and uncleanness; *Egypt* for her idolatry and cruelty towards the Israel of God.

---

[65] Homily 8 in Revelation

These titles most fitly agree to Rome, which is not inferior either to Sodom in pride and uncleanness, or to Egypt in gross idolatry, and savage cruelty towards the church of God. But they are not in this place ascribed to Jerusalem, which in Revelation and elsewhere in the New Testament, is called *the holy city*, even then when it had crucified our Savior Christ.[66] And not to seek further, even in Revelation 11:2, neither is the city of Jerusalem in Revelation anywhere spoken of in the ill part. This is also Jerome's argument in his Epistle to Marcella. "None of the holy Scripture (he says) can be contrary to itself, and much less the same place of Scripture." For about ten verses before, Jerusalem is called *the holy city*. Now if it be called the holy city even after the passion of our Lord, how is it again called *spiritually Sodom and Egypt*?

But Bellarmine answers that Jerome did not write this in good sooth, by which answer it were easy to elude any testimony: as though Jerome made no conscience to write untruths, especially in so weighty a matter, although in the name of others.

Thirdly, before the time of the Book of Revelation, which was in the latter end of Domitian's reign, the temple and city of Jerusalem were utterly destroyed, and never so to be rebuilt as to become the seat of Antichrist, therefore this place cannot be understood of Jerusalem.

Wherefore these objections notwithstanding, our assertion remains firm and steadfast, that Antichrist was to sit in Rome christened, and professing herself the church of God. Even as the bishops of Germany in Aventin, applying both this prophecy of Paul, and that of John in Revelation 17, to the Antichrist of Rome, "In Babylonia say they, *in temple Dei sedet*: he sits in Babylon in the temple of God."[67]

---

[66] Matthew 4:5, 27:53
[67] Lib. 5. Hist. Boc.

(18) Now let us further consider what other evasions they use to avoid this truth. First they say that Babylon did not signify any one city, but the whole society of the wicked. Secondly, if it signified any one city, then it was old Rome. Now thirdly, if the whore of Babylon does signify Rome christened, that yet notwithstanding, it is not (as Bellarmine is not ashamed to say) the seat of Antichrist.[68]

But if Rome christened, or the Church of Rome, is the whore of Babylon (as we have proved though our adversaries should not confess it) then is it so called because she is an adulterous and apostate church, which has fallen from Christ to Antichrist, whom instead of Christ she acknowledges to be her husband and head: then she is the mother both of all fornications,[69] that is of all superstitious and idolatrous worship, and also of all abominations, as atheism, Machiavellism, sodomy and Antichristian heresies, with whom the kings and inhabitants of the earth have committed fornication,[70] being made drunk and intoxicated with the golden cup of her fornications, that is, of her glorious idolatries and Antichristian heresies, who as she is clothed with scarlet, so is she dyed red, and drunk with the blood of the saints, and with the blood of the martyrs of Jesus:[71] as being that city and church wherein the two witnesses of Christ are put to death (Revelation 11). And can she then be the whore of Babylon, and not the Antichristian city and state?

Especially considering these two things which the papists themselves are forced to confess: first, that the state of Rome is here figured as it shall be in the time of Antichrist; secondly, that Antichrist shall be one of the seven heads, and namely the last head of the Roman beast, and consequently shall have Rome for his principal seat.

---

[68] *De Pont. Rom. lib.* 3, c.13
[69] Revelation 17:5
[70] Revelation 17:2, 4
[71] Revelation 17:4, 6

Let us see then whether the Jesuit be able to bring so much as a show of reason against this truth. For it may be you expect his proof. "Antichrist," says he, making his collection out of Revelation 17:16, "shall hate Rome, and shall fight with her, and shall make her desolate, and burn her. Whereupon it follows manifestly, that Rome shall not be the seat of Antichrist."[72] But it should seem the Jesuit was in a dream when he framed this argument. For it is evident that not Antichrist, but the ten horns, that is the ten kings, shall hate the whore, that is, the Antichristian city and president thereof: and accordingly Tertullian,[73] *Prostituta illa ciuitas, à decemregib. dignos exitus referet*: "That city which has prostituted herself to play the harlot, shall from the ten Kings receive her deserved end."

And so in another place himself being better awaked reasons from that place. "The ten kings" (says he) "which shall divide among them the Roman Empire, and in whose time Antichrist shall come, shall hate the purple harlot that is Rome and make her desolate; how then shall she be the seat of Antichrist?" Whereunto I answer that the very contrary is to be inferred upon that place: where it is said that the ten horns, that is the ten kings, which shall divide among them the Roman Empire, shall indeed for a time join with Antichrist, and give their power unto him. But when Christ shall begin to waste and to weaken him with the spirit of his mouth, then these ten kings shall oppose themselves against the Antichristian city and the head thereof. This event and experience in parte has proved to be true in some of these ten kings, as has before been shown. From that place therefore we may reason thus:

- The purple harlot which the ten kings shall assault is the city of Antichrist.
- Rome is that purple harlot, as the adversary himself confesses.

---

[72] Lib. 3. *De Pont. Rom.* cap.13
[73] Tertullian, *On The Resurrection*, c.25

- Therefore Rome is the city of Antichrist.

(19) Their last refuge is this: that Christian Rome, where the pope sits, does not stand upon seven hills, but is removed from the seven hills into the plain of Campus Martius, and that the pope sits on the other side of the river upon the mount Vatican. Saunders therefore thought it to be but a childish argument to prove from the seven hills that the seat of Antichrist is at Rome. But we would know of him whether it be the same Rome where they say Peter sat or not. If it is the same, then it stands on seven hills; if it is not the same, how is it then the apostolic seat and chair of Peter?

True indeed it is, that in the time of the emperors, the Pomarium of the city was enlarged, so that it enclosed a good part of Campus Martius: and that since some more ancient parts of the city being decayed, the greatest part of private buildings stand in the plain. Yet notwithstanding even to this day, the seven hills are enclosed within the walls of the city, and upon them there do yet remain, besides some of the pope's palaces and courts, several churches and houses of religion and other buildings of note – as that learned divine of blessed memory Dr. Fulke particularly shows in his answer to the Rhemists.[74]

Neither does the enlarging of the city in one part, and the decaying of it in another, prove it not to be the same city. And although the pope does live in the Vatican, or in any other palace of his wheresoever, yet who does not know that Rome is the papal – or as they call it, the "apostolic" – seat, appointed as they say by Christ himself?[75]

Neither can the pope as they teach change his seat: or if he should, he should cease to be the successor of Peter. For: "whosoever is chosen bishop of the city of Rome, he," (say they) "is the successor of St. Peter, the vicar of Christ, and bishop of the world." And as Rome in general is the pope's seat,

---

[74] Rod. Cupers, *De Eccles.* Pag. 37, Num. 1
[75] Cupers, *De Eccles.*, p.226, Num. 16, Cupers, pag. 37, Num. 4, Cupers pag. 106, Num. 11

or See; so more specially the cathedral church of Lateran, whereof more properly the pope is bishop, as the husband of one wife. In which respect they say that as Peter and his successors are the head of the whole church or university of the faithful, so the Lateran church – being referred to other material churches – is the head of all churches of the world. Unto this church was adjoined the chief palace of the pope, which was inhabited by them until the time of Boniface IX as Onuphrius testifies,[76] that is to say 1400 years almost after Christ: howsoever since the time of Leo X who lodged therein, it is within these last hundred years decayed. Now it is well known that the palace and church of Lateran stands on Caelian Hill, in the most remote part of the city, and furthest distance from the Vatican.

So that all these shifts and evasions of the papists notwithstanding, it is evident, that Rome, which we have now proven to be the seat of the pope, is by the former reasons alleged, the seat of Antichrist.

---

[76] *De 7. Vrb. eccl.*

Chapter 3
Concerning the time of the revelation of Antichrist.

(1) As from the place we gather the pope to be Antichrist, because the seat of Antichrist is Rome christened, or professing herself the church of Christ, so the consideration of the time joined with that of the place, does make this truth much more evident. Rome christened is the seat of Antichrist: but when does Antichrist sit, that is, reign there? I answer that he could not exercise Antichristian dominion there, while the emperors had their seat in Rome. But when the emperors were removed and the empire in the West dissolved, then did Antichrist succeed them in the seat, that is, in the government of Rome.

And this may be proved first, by the testimony of Paul (2 Thessalonians 2:8): "And then that outlaw," meaning Antichrist, "shall be revealed." And when is that? "When he that hindereth shall be taken out of the way." And who is that which hinders the revelation of Antichrist for a time, that he might be revealed in his due time? Who this was, the apostle had told the Thessalonians by word of mouth, and therefore forbear for just causes to tell them by writing which they knew already, to wit, that he might not incur the needless hatred of the Romans. But that which he had told them, in all likelihood, was continued in the church. For although this place in itself is most difficult, yet generally it is understood of the empire and emperors of Rome by most of the ancient writers of the church.

Tertullian: "Who shall be taken out of the way, but the Roman state? Whose departure – being divided among ten kings – shall bring in Antichrist."[77]

Ambrose: "After the decay of the Roman Empire, Paul says that Antichrist shall appear."

---

[77] Tertullian, *On The Resurrection of the Flesh*

Chrysostom on these words, "Only he that holdeth, that is," (as he expounds) "hindereth now until he be taken out of the way," says he: "that is, the Empire of Rome, when it shall be taken out of the way, then he (meaning Antichrist) shall come, and worthily. For while men shall be in awe of the empire, none will hastily be brought in subjection to Antichrist. But when the empire shall be dissolved, he shall seize upon the vacancy, and shall challenge to himself the empire or rule both human and divine."

Jerome speaking of these words,[78] "And now what hindereth you know, that he might be revealed in his time: that is," (says he) "what the cause is why Antichrist comes not yet, you know very well. Neither could he plainly say that the Roman Empire is to be destroyed, which the emperors think is eternal. Wherefore according to the Revelation of John, there is written in the forehead of the harlot clothed with purple, a name of blasphemy, that is, *Romae aeternae*: to Rome eternal."

And afterwards these words: "only he which holdeth now must hold until he be taken out of the way, and then that out law shall be revealed," he expounds thus: "Only that the Roman Empire which now holds (that is, governs) all nations, depart and be taken out of the way, and then Antichrist shall come."

Cyril: "Antichrist shall come, when the times of the Roman Empire shall be fulfilled."[79]

Primasius: "The kingdom of the Romans shall be taken out of the way, before Antichrist be revealed."

Theophylact: "When the Roman Empire shall be taken out of the way, then shall Antichrist come."

The Greek scholiast on those words, *that which holdeth* etc., "he means," says he "that which letteth and hindereth." And what is that? Many understand the Holy Spirit, others the Roman Empire, whose judgment is

---

[78] To Algasium, Question 11.
[79] Catech. 15.

the better? For until that be dissolved, Antichrist shall not come. And for this cause blessed Paul spoke so obscurely, because he would not incur unseasonable enmity with the Romans. For when they should hear that the Empire of the Romans shall be dissolved, they would persecute him and all the faithful, as being such as looked for the dissolution of the empire. But if he had spoken of the Holy Spirit, what letted him to have said plainly, that the grace of the Holy Spirit did hinder him that he should not appear?"

To which we may add, that in the sixth verse, the apostle speaks in the neuter gender, and in the seventh in the masculine – the former whereof may signify the empire and the latter the emperor, of whom the Holy Spirit speaks, as of one man (ο αντιχριστος) as he tends to speak sometimes of Antichrist and we of the pope; although both by the one and the other is signified not one man, but a state or succession.

Augustine in deed says of these words, "but he that hinders shall hinder" – "I do confess that I am utterly ignorant of what he says. Some think that this is spoken of the Roman Empire, and that Paul the apostle would not therefore write it plainly, lest he should incur this slander that he was an ill willer to the Roman Empire, which men hoped to be eternal."[80]

Notwithstanding this seems to have been his judgment also, for afterwards he thinks those words may thus be expounded of the empire of Rome, *tantū qui modo imperat, imperet etc.*: "Only he which reigneth must reign (for so κατεχον also may signify, and to the same purpose Primasius expounds those words, *tantū vt qui tenet nunc, sc. imperiū*, only he which holdeth now, to wit: the empire) until he is done, that is taken, out of the way; and then that outlaw shall be revealed, whom no man doubts to signify *Antichrist*."

(2) But what need I to be so diligent in gathering testimonies for the confirmation of this truth, seeing it is not only confirmed by the former

---

[80] Augustine, *City of God*, Book 20, Chapter 19.

assertion (for how could Antichrist reign in Rome while the Roman Emperors remained or reigned there) but also is confessed by Bellarmine himself, namely that by this let, is to be understood the Empire of Rome. Rather let us consider whether the empire that hindered, was taken out of the way, or not. Bellarmine understands this *taking away* to mean an utter abolishing of the Roman Empire, so that there should not remain so much as the name of the emperor or king of the Romans, from whence he would prove that Antichrist is not yet come, because the Roman Empire is not yet abolished.

We confess that the Roman Empire which hindered the revelation of Antichrist was to be dissolved, and also divided among ten, that is many kings (for so this number of ten is often used indefinitely),[81] which is all that can be gathered either out of the Scriptures or fathers. But that there should be such an utter abolishment of the Roman Empire, as that there should not remain so much as the name or title of the Emperor or King of the Romans, we do utterly deny.[82]

It is sufficient that the emperor was so far forth taken out of the way as it hindered the revelation or dominion of Antichrist, And so much the phrase of the apostle seems to import, "εως εκ μεσου γενηται: Until he be done out of the way," (or as the Rhemists themselves do read, "Until he be taken out of the way") as may appear by conference of like places.[83] Let us then consider, in what sense the Roman Empire did hinder, and was to be taken away, and in what sense it hindered not, and was to remain. For the better understanding whereof we are to distinguish between the old empire and the new. The old empire, as it hindered the dominion of Antichrist, was to be taken out of the way, that it might be no more a hindrance thereunto.

The new empire in the west erected by the pope does not hinder the dominion of Antichrist, but rather supports him, and therefore together with

---

[81] Numbers 14:22, Job 19:3, Nehemiah 4:12.
[82] See Book 2, Chapter 5
[83] Matthew 13:49, Acts 17:53 & 23:10; 1 Corinthians 5:2; 2 Corinthians 6:17

Antichrist was to remain. Neither does the apostle speak of the new empire, but of the old, as shall appear by these reasons:

(3) **First reason**: The apostle speaks of the empire which hindered or held then, and of that only: for so he says, "Only he which now letteth will let until he be taken out of the way." And Jerome expounds those words, "and now what hindereth, you know," after this manner: "*quae causa sit vt Antichristus in praesentiarū non veniat optime nostis*, You know very well what the cause is that Antichrist comes not now."[84] But the old empire hindered them and not the new. And therefore the apostle speaks of the taking away of the old empire and not of the new.

Second reason: Again, when he says the empire hindered, he means the imperial authority and dominion, and that at Rome, not the title or name thereof in Germany. For it is not the name or title of an emperor in Germany that can hinder the dominion of Antichrist at Rome, and much less at Jerusalem, where the papists say his seat shall be.

Third reason:, Antichrist appeared and showed himself (and in that sense was revealed) before the erection of the new empire. For the new empire is the image of the former beast: which Antichrist the second beast (Revelation 13) causes to be made. And whereas Antichrist is (as the papists also confess) the seventh head of the beast which has heads, the empire renewed (which is the beast that was and is not though it be) is the eighth in order, though in name it is one of the seven, and in that sense is to be referred to the sixth head, namely the emperors.

Fourth reason: The whore of Babylon, that is the Antichristian state, was to sit upon the beast which afterwards was to ascend, that is, the empire renewed. Therefore with Antichrist, there was to remain an imperial state, though much abased under him.

---

[84] To Algasium, Question 11.

Fifth reason: The empire renewed is the beast whereupon the whore of Babylon sits. And therefore is so far from hindering Antichrist, that it supported him, as the beast does the rider. And to that end indeed was this empire erected in the west, that it might support the church of Rome. For when as the church of Rome was oppressed by the king of the Lombards, it sought aid from the emperors of Constantinople; and when they would not defend the church, the pope translated the empire to the French king: and from him upon the same occasion to the Germans, and that to this end, *vt Rex Teutonicorum foret imperator et patronus sedis Apostolicae*: that "the King of the Almains might be emperor and patron of the Apostolic See." And for the same cause, the emperor is called by them *procurator sieve defensor Romanae Ecclesiae*: the proctor or defender of the church of Rome.

Sixth reason: The papists themselves do hold that the empire which now is, shall continue unto the end of the world. For they say that in Daniel 2 (as many others also have said) a succession of the chief kingdoms or monarchies of the earth is described, which should continue until the end of the world: the last whereof is the Roman Empire.

Seventh reason: The destruction of the Roman Empire (which the fathers say shall go before the revelation of Antichrist), is the dissolution and division thereof among ten kings, which indeed long since happened to the old empire, but cannot happen to the new, unless we can imagine that ten mighty kings shall arise out of the bare name and title of an emperor divided among them. When the papists therefore teach us not to expect Antichrist until the empire that now is either be divided into ten kingdoms, they are ridiculous; or utterly abolished which they say shall continue to the end, they are absurd, and in both impious, making (as it may seem) a scorn of the prophecies concerning Antichrist, which they make to imply impossibilities and contradictions.

(4) By this which has been said it, plainly appears that howsoever the old empire in the west, which hindered the dominion of Antichrist, was to be taken out of the way before Antichrist should be revealed; yet notwithstanding even with, and under Antichrist there was to be an imperial state in name and title, which is the beast whereon the whore of Babylon sits, and therefore is so far from hindering Antichrist, as that it supports him. Let us then consider how the empire which hindered the revelation of Antichrist was taken out of the way, and how afterwards Antichrist was revealed.

Of the taking away of the emperor, as also of the revelation of Antichrist there are two degrees. The Roman emperor was first taken out of the way, when the imperial seat was transferred by Constantine the Great from Rome to Byzantium or Constantinople, and that to this end, as they have set down in the forged *Donation of Constantine*, that he might leave room to the pope.[85] Because indeed, where the princehood of priests, and head of Christian religion was placed by the heavenly emperor, there it is not just that the earthly emperor should have power. Secondly, after the death of Constantine the great, and of Flauius Valerius Constantinus his son, the Roman Empire being divided into two parts – the eastern and the western – and by division being weakened, the western was overthrown in the year of our Lord 475. and Rome itself taken by the Goths. So that neither in Rome any Roman afterwards had his seat of authority, until the pope took upon him the sovereignty: neither in the West was there any Roman Emperor until Charles the Great, that is to say, from the year 475 unto the end of the year 800.

In the meantime, Italy was governed first by the Goths, and afterwards a great part thereof by the Lombards. And howsoever the emperors of the East had recovered Rome, and some part of Italy, which because they governed by exarchs having their seat in Ravenna, was called the Exarchate of

---

[85] Dist. 69.c. Constantinus & de electione c. fundament, in sexto

Ravenna, the Lombards, enjoying the rest: yet before the renewing of the empire in the west, the emperor of the east had lost all Italy and Rome, and that by the pope's means.

For when Leo III called Isaurus, Emperor of Greece, had held a council at Constantinople of 330 bishops, wherein it was decreed that all images within the empire should be destroyed and burnt: and afterwards put the same decree in execution: the popes of Rome first Gregory II and after Gregory III excommunicate him, forbade tributes to be paid him out of Italy and Rome, absolve his subjects from their allegiance unto him, and having stirred up not only the Italians, but Lombards also against him, the exarch of Ravenna is slain, and the emperor deprived of all his dominion and revenues in Italy and Rome. So that howsoever the empire in the east stood all this while: yet according to the prophecy of the apostle, he which hindered the revelation of Antichrist, that is to say, the emperor of Rome, was taken out of the way: firstly, by removing himself from Rome and moving to Constantinople, where Antichrist could not usurp that dominion and sovereignty whiles the emperor had his seat there, which afterwards he did. Secondly, because the empire of the west, which properly was the empire of Rome, was dissolved, and the emperor of the east lost his title and interest in Italy and Rome.

(5) Of the revelation of Antichrist there are also two degrees. The first, of his reigning and showing himself in his colors: the second, of his acknowledgement. Of his reigning, there are two degrees also. The first, when he challenged supreme authority over the universal church of Christ. Which he did when he usurped the title of universal or ecumenical bishop or head of the universal church, which was done as we said about the year 607. About which time besides other prodigious sights there appeared a terrible comet, and then we hold that Antichrist (to wit, the head of the Antichristian body) was born.

True it is that the seeds of Antichristianism were sown before his time: and even from the apostles' time the mystery of iniquity, that is, Antichristianism, was working although more covertly, and preparation was made towards the birth of the great Antichrist, partly by heresies and some declinations in the church of Rome in religion from the purity of the primitive church, partly by the ambition of diverse of the Bishops of Rome, who advancing themselves as Socrates says, beyond the limit of priesthood into foreign dominion, contended to have the primacy above all other churches (and that is the chief scope of many of their epistles decretal) and to the same end forged a canon of the council of Nice, when their ambition was curbed by other general councils. And lastly by the indulgence of devout emperors and princes, who have by great devotions and privileges advanced that church. Notwithstanding, we hold that Antichrist was not revealed, until he showed himself by usurping an universal dominion over the church of God.

(6) But notwithstanding this great title and authority, Antichrist was yet but in his nonage, and under the government not only of the emperor, but also, for a time, of the emperor's lieutenant in Italy the Exarch of Ravenna, by whom the election of the pope (made by the clergy and people of Rome) was of necessity to be ratified and confirmed, until Benedict II, obtained this privilege from the Emperor Constantine IV called Pogonatus, that the election of the pope by the clergy and people of Rome should be good without the confirmation of the emperor – upon which privilege obtained, the pope began to care little for the emperor, holding himself henceforth to be αὐτόνομος or rather as the apostle speaks ανομος, without law,[86] and subject to the judgment of no man, as they profess in several of their canons.

Not long after they began to advance themselves both against and above the emperor. Constantine I suffered the emperor Justinian to kiss his feet,

---

[86] 2 Thessalonians 2:8

about the year of our Lord 710. Within three years after the same, Constantine set himself against the emperor Philippicus Bardanes in defense of images, as did his two successors Gregory II and Gregory III against Leo Isaurus in the same quarrel. In whose three times (that we may know Rome to be the mother of spiritual fornications) were held three councils at Rome, wherein worshiping of images was approved, and the oppugners thereof excommunicated. And we must note that about this time (says the Author of the book called *Fasciculus Temporum*) the popes began above their wont to oppose themselves even in temporal matters against the emperors, because of their unsoundness in the faith (for so he calls their oppugning of images) and to translate the empire from nation to nation, as time required.

As for Gregory II, he was the first which avouched himself superior to the emperor; who also excommunicated Leo III because he sought to abolish the idolatry of his time, which they call worshiping of images. But his successor Gregory III not only excommunicated the said emperor for the same cause, but also forbade any tributes or duties to be paid unto him out of Italy and Rome, and absolved his subjects from their allegiance unto him. Whereupon Rome (being then a duchy) with several other cities in Italy, revolting from the emperor, sware obedience to the pope, who by the defection of the Italians, and help of the Lombards, dispossessed the emperor of all his revenues in Italy; and consequently (as the popish author of the book called *Fasciculus Temporum* says) *totum regnum occidentis ab eo abstulit*, "He took from him the whole kingdom of the west." But when as the Lombards held the Exarchate of Ravenna which the pope intended to himself, and sought to rule over all Italy as the Goths had done, not exempting Rome or those other cities which had revolted to the pope; first, Gregory III when Rome was besieged by Luitprendus, used the friendship of Carolus Martellus to free him from the siege.

Whereupon the pope removed the tuition of the church of Rome from the emperor of Greece unto Carolus Martellus the great master of France, and to his son Pipin after him. Whom that the pope might bind unto him, and find a sufficient defense against his enemies, he (namely Zacharias) having (as themselves testify) deposed Childeric the King of France from his kingdom, and absolved his subjects from their allegiance (because indeed he was too simple to rule), and made him (namely Pepin) King of France. Who afterwards when his help was entreated by the pope Stephen III, against Aistulphus the King of Lombards, enforced the said king to yield up the Exarchate of Ravenna, and Pentapolis, which he gave to the pope.

This donation, his son Charles the great confirmed and enlarged with a plentiful addition (reserving notwithstanding to himself the royalties of those possessions) when he had at the entreaty of Adrian the pope overthrown the kingdom of the Lombards in Italy. For which cause, as also for that he assisted Pope Leo III against the insurrections of the people of Rome, punished his adversaries, and caused the people of Rome to swear allegiance to the pope. The pope (namely Leo III) crowned him Emperor of Rome, translating that title from the emperor of the east to him, and in him renewing the empire of the west, which had been void since the time of Augustulus. And as he made him emperor, so to him was committed by Adrian and Leo, the confirmation of those which were elected to the papacy. This yoke, as the popes following often struggled against it, so at the last, they shook it off.

And whereas, in former times, the pope was subject to the emperor, and being elected was confirmed by him, afterwards it came to pass that as the empire was renewed in Charlemagne, and after revived in Otto the Great, and that to this end that it might support the papacy; so the pope (namely John XII, a.k.a John XIII) caused the emperor to swear unto him to that end, took order for the election of the emperor, appointing seven electors, reserving the coronation of the emperor and confirmation of the election unto himself; and at the length subjected the emperor unto him as his vassal, challenging both swords and usurping an universal dominion and sovereignty over all the Christian world, not only over ecclesiastical persons, as bishops and priests, but also civil, as princes, kings, emperors, whom he esteems as his vassals, and makes them kiss his feet, as we shall show more fully when we come to speak of his Antichristian pride.

Unto this monarchy (as they call it) not only of spiritual but also of temporal power, they long aspired, but never fully attained, until the time of Gregory VII, in whom Antichrist was come to his full growth, wherein he flourished, until our Savior Christ the king of kings and Lord of Lords began to waste and consume him with the breath of his mouth.

This is what Aventin says: "Hildebrand, who also is called Gregory VII, first established the pontifical empire, which his successors for the space of 450 years (that is to Aventin and also Luther's time) so held, in spite of the world, and notwithstanding the emperors, that they have brought all both in heaven and hell into bondage etc., at their pleasure. They cast men headlong from heaven to hell, and again from hell advance to heaven. The emperor from henceforth is nothing but a bare title without body or show."[87]

(7) But no sooner was Antichrist come to his full growth (whereby he plainly revealed and discovered himself) but straightaway, he began to be acknowledged, which is the second part of his revelation, whereof also there are degrees. For first he was acknowledged particularly by various learned and godly men in the time of Gregory VII, and in every age since until the time of Luther.

As for example, the bishops of Germany affirmed Gregory VII to be Antichrist: *Antichristū esse praedicāt*. "Under the name and title of Christ," they say, "he contrives the business of Antichrist: he sits in Babylon in the temple of God: he extols himself above all that is worshiped, as if he were a God, he boasts that he cannot err."[88]

---

[87] Lib. 5 annual. Boior
[88] Aventin, Lib. 5 annual. Boior

And afterward Aventin – either in his own name or in the person of Sigebert – speaking of the times of Gregory VII: "Almost all men," (says he) "that were good, open-hearted, just, ingenuous, and single-hearted, have left in writing, that the Empire of Antichrist did then begin, because they saw those things which our Savior Christ so many years before had prophesied unto us, to happen in that time."

The Bishop of Florence, in the time of Paschal II, preached that Antichrist had come, meaning the pope.

Honorius Augustodunensis applied the prophecies in Revelation concerning Antichrist, to the pope and church of Rome (*Dialogue of Free Will and Predestination*). Bernard of Clairvaux in his time acknowledged a general apostasy, and complained of the state of the church as Antichristian. Johannes Sarisburiensis taught that the pope is Antichrist, and the city of Rome the whore of Babylon. About the same time, Petrus Blesensis wrote that Rome is that very Babylon whereof John speaks in Revelation. Gerhardus and Dulcinus Nauarrensis preached that the pope is Antichrist, and that the clergy and prelates of Rome were the very whore of Babylon prefigured in Revelation. In the time of Alexander III, the Waldenses taught that the pope is Antichrist, and Rome is Babylon.

Joachim the abbot, being demanded of Richard the first king of England, now going towards the holy land, concerning Antichrist, answered thus; Antichrist is already born in the city of Rome, and is advanced in the See Apostolic. And in certain German verses also published at Frankfurt, he affirms that the pope and his priests are antichrists.

Archbishop Eberhard: "Hildebrand," (says he) "about 170 years ago did first, under the show of religion, lay the foundation of Antichrist's kingdom. And straightways after, those priests of Babylon," (says he) "covet to reign alone, they cannot endure an equal. Neither will they cease until they have trodden all under their feet, and do sit in the temple of God, and be extolled about all that is worshiped. Their hunger after wealth, and thirst for honor, is insatiable etc. he that is the servant of servants desires to be the lord of lords, as if he were a god." And again, "He wastes and spoils, he deceives and kills, I mean that man of perdition whom they call Antichrist, in whose forehead a name of blasphemy is written, I am God, I cannot err, he sits in the temple of God, he rules far and wide."

Robert Grosthead, the worthy Bishop of Lincoln, on his deathbed complaining of the pope, and bewailing the loss of souls which happened through the avarice of the popes court, with sighs he said: "Christ came into the world to gain souls, therefore if any fear not to destroy souls, is not he worthily to be called Antichrist?"

William of Saint-Amour, a master of Paris and chief ruler of that university, called the monks and priests the subjects of Antichrist. One Lawrence, also an Englishman and master of Paris, proved the pope to be Antichrist, and the synagogue of Rome to be the great Babylon. About the same time, Maenardus Tyrolius in a public edict calls the popes *effeminate Antichrists*. And again, if they are not Antichrists, I pray you, what are they?

Michael of Cesena, principal of the greyfriars, wrote against the pride, tyranny and primacy of the pope, accusing him to be Antichrist, and the church of Rome the whore of Babylon drunken with the blood of saints. Hayabalus, a friar in the time of Clement VI, preached (and that, as he said, by commandment from God) that the church of Rome is the whore of Babylon, and that the pope with his Cardinals is the very Antichrist. William of Ockham, as Aventin calls him, wrote a book against Charles and Clement VI, wherein he calls the pope Antichrist. Bridget of Sweden, whom the papists worship as a canonized saint, called the pope a murderer of souls, more cruel than Judas, more unjust than Pilate, worse than Lucifer himself. She prophesied that the See of Rome shall be thrown down into the deep like a millstone (according to the prophecy of John in Revelation 18:21). About the same year, Matthias Parifiensis, a Bohemian, writing a book of Antichrist, proved that he had already come, and noted him to be the pope.

Franciscus Petrarch, in many places of his writings, calls the court of Rome the whore of Babylon, the mother of the fornications and abominations of the earth.

Urbanus VI and Clement VII two popes at once, call one the other Antichrist, as Bernard before had called Anacletus, against whom Innocent II was chosen as Antipope. "That beast," says he, "in Revelation, to whom is given a mouth speaking blasphemies, and to war with the saints (meaning Antichrist), occupies the chair of Peter, as a lion ready for the prey."

But most effectually does our godly and learned countryman John Wycliff discover the enormities and heresies of the pope whom he pronounced to be Antichrist (Article 30).

His judgment as in other things, so also in this, that worthy martyr of Christ John Hus followed, who affirms in his book *De Ecclesia*, that he was troubled because he preached Christ, and discovered Antichrist. That the censures of the Romish church were Antichristian, and proceeding from Antichrist: and (as Gerson and the Parisians object against him, Article 16) that in those times and many ages before, there had been no true pope, nor true Roman church: but the popes were Antichrists and the church of Rome the synagogue of Satan. Whose judgment many in Bohemia followed. Sir John Oldcastle, Baron Cobham, that famous and noble martyr of Christ, professed to King Henry V that by the Scriptures, he knew the pope to be the great Antichrist, the son of perdition, etc. Girolamo Savanarola taught that the pope is Antichrist, because he did attribute more to his own indulgences and pardons than to Christ's merits.

About the year of our Lord 1517, Luther began to preach against the pope's indulgences, and afterwards against other errors and abominations of the pope and church of Rome, discovering more plainly than any had done before him, that Rome is Babylon, and the pope is Antichrist. Since his times, this truth has been almost generally acknowledged by the true and reformed churches of Christ.

Seeing therefore we have proven that Antichrist was to sit in Rome professing herself the church of God, and that after the taking away of the Roman Emperor whom he was to succeed in the government of Rome, and there to be revealed both by his own showing himself in his colors, and also by the acknowledgement of others: it cannot be avoided but that the pope is Antichrist. For he and none but he sits, that is, reigns in Rome, professing herself the church of God, and that after the taking away of the Roman Emperor, (not only by the removing of the imperial seat, but also by the dissolution of the Empire in the West) whom he succeeds in the government of Rome, where he has been revealed not only by his own showing himself in his colors, but also by the acknowledgement of others.

(8) Unto the former place of the Epistle to the Thessalonians, we will add two other places out of Revelation, from whence both the place and time of Antichrist may be jointly gathered. The former place is in Revelation 13, where two beasts are described, signifying two estates of the Roman government as they are opposed unto Christ: the former representing the persecuting emperors, and the latter, Antichrist. Of the former he says thus: "I saw a beast arising out of the sea (that is, of many and various peoples which it had vanquished)." Now the description of this beast contains in it the resemblances of those four kingdoms which are described in Daniel, the Roman Empire far surpassing them all.

The first of the beasts in Daniel, signifying the kingdom of the Babylonians, is compared to a lion; the second resembling the kingdom of the Medes and Persians, to a bear; the third representing the monarchy of the Macedonians, to a leopard; the fourth figuring the kingdom of the Seleucids and Lagidae, to a beast with ten horns, resembling so many of their kings, who should tyrannize over Jewry. The Empire of Rome therefore, as if it were compounded of them all, is resembled to a beast having ten horns with so many diadems upon them, both in respect of the ten persecuting emperors, answering the ten Seleucids and Lagidae, as also in regard of the ten kingdoms or provinces into which the Roman Empire in those times was divided, being also like a leopard, having the feet or paws as it were of a bear, and the ravening mouth of a lion. And besides all this, it is said to have seven heads, which afterwards (chapter 17) are expounded to be seven hills, and also seven heads of government etc. and to this beast was given authority or power, over every tribe, language and nation etc., – all of which are proper to the Empire of Rome. The former beast therefore signifies the Roman state, especially as it was under the persecuting Emperors, as Bellarmine confesses.

The second beast, described in verse 11 and so forward to the end of the chapter, is (as Bellarmine says all men do confess) Antichrist: who also is, by the confession of the said Bellarmine, one of the heads of the former beast. By the description of this beast (that we may now note that which serves for the present purpose, reserving the residue until their due time and place) it is apparent, that there is one and the same principal seat of both the beasts, that in that seat the second beast succeeds the former, practicing all the power or authority of the former beast and that before him, that is to say, even at Rome: and that his chief endeavors tend to magnify the beast, that is the Roman state; as in making men to worship it, in causing men to make an image of and to the beast, whereunto he gives spirit and speech, and enforcing men to worship the same: finally in compelling men to take upon them the mark of the beast, his name, and number of his name.

All this, as they argue Antichrist to be a Roman, succeeding the emperors in the government of Rome, so also they fitly and properly agree to the pope, who succeeds the emperors in the government of Rome, where he usurps all and more than all the power of the emperors, challenging a more universal and sovereign – or rather, divine – authority than belonged to them, whose main endeavors are to advance the Roman state, which he calls *the Apostolic See*, and which he makes all men to worship, causing them also to make an image of the empire (which was the head that had received the deadly wound) to and in behoof of the Roman state. This image, I say, is partly in the emperor of Almain, resembling the title ornaments and show of the former emperors, and partly in his own courts not only in Rome, but in all other countries representing the former imperial authority and tyranny both in Rome itself, and in the provinces thereunto belonging.

This image – both in the empire and popish courts – he animates and authorizes. For as there is no question to be made hereof in respect of his courts, so is it as true in respect of the empire, if it is true that which they themselves profess, namely: that which the emperor has, he has it wholly from them; that the empire in the west was renewed by the pope, who translated the title of the Emperor of Rome from the emperor of the east, first to the French, and after to the Germans; that the pope caused this new emperor to be made; that he crowned and authorized him; that he appointed seven Electors in Germany, reserving the confirmation of the election and coronation of the emperor to himself – of which points we shall hereafter speak more at large.

Further, he causes all men to worship the image by him erected, and compels all men to receive the mark of the beast, as also the name of the beast (which can be no other but either Roman or Latin), and the number of his name, and to live in subjection to the See of Rome, and to profess themselves to be Romans and Latins in respect of their religion, as hereafter shall be shown.

(9) The same is proved out of Revelation 17, where there are seven heads reckoned, that is, seven kinds of principal rulers as it were heads of government, whereby Rome has been governed, everyone succeeding another – the sixth head being the emperors, and the seventh Antichrist which is the pope. For Antichrist is one of the seven heads of the beast which has seven heads and ten horns. And this beast signifies the Roman state,

therefore Antichrist is a head of the Roman state. All of this, Bellarmine – after a sort – confesses.[89]

Now it is most certain that Antichrist is none of the first five. heads, for they were past in the apostles' time: neither is he the sixth head which was of the emperors, that then was; for that was to be done out of the way, as the papists themselves do teach, before the revelation of Antichrist.

It remains therefore that the seventh head which is the pope is Antichrist. The eighth head, which also is one of the seven, is the empire renewed by the pope, and is said to be the beast, which was and is not though it be, whereon the whore of Babylon sits.

If it be objected that the seventh head whereby Antichrist is signified was to continue but a short time, as it is said in verse 10, and that this therefore cannot agree to the pope, who has reigned already in Rome many hundreds of years. I answer that this is spoken on purpose, to arm the faithful with patience, who otherwise would think the reign of Antichrist very long, and our Savior Christ also to be slow in coming.[90] Whereas in truth neither is our Savior Christ slow in coming as Peter shows, neither is the kingdom of Antichrist long.

But in respect of God with whom a thousand years are as one day, and in comparison of the eternal kingdom of Christ (with whom the faithful are to reign after they have suffered under Antichrist), it is to be accounted very short. And surely if the whole time from the ascension of our Savior until his return unto judgment is noted in the Scriptures to be very short, and that to this end that we should not think it long, then is the reign of Antichrist (which is but part of this time) much more short. The Holy Spirit in the beginning of the Revelation signifies that the time of fulfilling the prophecies therein mentioned was at hand. And our Savior Christ promised by the apostle that after a very little while he would come, and in the last chapter of Revelation, he says, "Yea, I come quickly." And John likewise in

---

[89] Lib 3., *De Pont*, R.c. 15
[90] 2 Peter 3

his epistle notes that the whole time of Antichrist was but a part of the last hour.

(10) And further whereas the papists object, in respect of the time, that Antichrist is not yet come, because the Roman Empire is not yet dissolved, and consequently that the pope is not Antichrist: it may notwithstanding evidently be shown out of the same chapter of Revelation compared with the event, both that the empire is dissolved, and that Antichrist is already come. For the empire is then known to be dissolved when it is divided among ten who shall have received power as kings, as John notes, the fathers teach, and the papists themselves confess.

But it is most certain that the old empire of Rome is divided among ten kings at the least, who before the dissolution did not have sovereign authority, and that the empire which now is, being but a title, and containing no such kingdoms, is not capable of such a partition. And that Antichrist also has come, it is as evident. For those ten horns which in the apostles' time had not received the kingdom nor sovereign authority, but were governors of the provinces by deputation from the emperor, were after the dissolution of the empire to receive power as kings with the beast; or, as the papists read, after the beast, that is Antichrist. If therefore the governors of the kingdoms into which the Roman Empire was divided, have received power as kings, then it is certain that Antichrist has already come.

For either after him, or at least with him, they were to receive their sovereignty. It is as certain therefore that Antichrist has come, as it is sure that the governors of the provinces which once belonged to the empire are sovereign princes and not lieutenants under the emperor. And that this Antichrist which has already come is the pope, it is plain enough by the same chapter.

- For whosoever succeeds the emperors (who were the sixth head) in the government of Rome, as the seventh head of the Roman state, he is Antichrist.
- But the pope, as the seventh head of the Roman state succeeds the emperors (who were the sixth head) in the government of Rome.
- Therefore he is Antichrist.

If you say that the seventh head was not come in the apostles' time (verse 10) and yet there were bishops of Rome then, I answer that the bishops of Rome, in the first three hundred years, were mean men in respect of their outward estate, and nothing less than heads of the Roman state. And that howsoever afterwards they obtained great authority, and more and more aspired unto the sovereignty. Notwithstanding, until the sixth head was taken out of the way, the seventh was not revealed. But after the sixth head was gone, the seventh succeeded in the government of Rome. Insomuch that now for a long time the city of Rome has so wholly belonged to the pope, as that the emperor has no manner of right therein.

To conclude therefore: if Antichrist was to sit in Rome (professing herself the church of God), and that after the taking away of the Roman Emperor whom he was to succeed in the government of Rome, as has been proven, then it follows necessarily – seeing as these notes agree to the popes of Rome and to none but them – that therefore the pope is Antichrist.

Chapter 4
Of the conditions of Antichrist, and his opposition unto Christ.

(1) Now if to those former notes of place and time, we shall add the rest, and find them all properly to fit the popes of Rome, then may it not be doubted, but that the pope is Antichrist. In the next place therefore let us consider his condition and qualities, in respect whereof he is called the man of sin.

For firstly, Antichrist, in respect of his opposition to Christ, is ἀντικείμενος an adversary, in respect of his pride and ambition, ὑπεραιρόμενος lifted up above all that is called God, etc.[91] From these two notes, therefore we may argue thus:

- He that is such an adversary as the Scriptures describe opposed unto Christ in emulation of like honor, he is Antichrist.
- The pope is such an adversary as the Scriptures describe opposed unto Christ in emulation of like honor.
- Therefore the pope is Antichrist.

The truth of the proposition is testified by the Apostle, implied in the name αντιχριστος which signifies *hostem et aemulum Christi*, and confessed by the adversaries. The assumption Bellarmine would disprove by this slender argument, because the pope actually professes himself the servant of Christ. For even as he professes himself to be Christ's servant, so he terms himself; *the servant of servants*, (which is Ham's title) when as in truth he would be esteemed *lord of lords*. But this is so far from disproving the assumption, as that the pope could not be such an adversary as is described in the Scriptures, and consequently not Antichrist, unless he professed himself

---

[91] 2 Thessalonians 2:4

to be the servant of Christ. Let us therefore consider what manner of enemy Antichrist is according to the Scriptures:

[1] First, he is an apostate or revolter.

[2] He is a disguised enemy or hypocrite; that is, one that is fallen indeed from God and his truth as it were a star from heaven, yet retains the name and profession of Christ; under which name and profession he oppugns Christ and his truth, even as a rebellious subject, when he presumes without commission to levy a power of men against his sovereignty, that he may deceive the rest of the subjects, abuses the name and authority of his prince to color his rebellious practices.

And that this is the property of Antichrist, Hilary has well observed: "It is the property of Antichrist's name, to be contrary to Christ."[92] This is now practiced under the opinion of counterfeit piety: this, under a show of preaching the gospel, is preached, that our Lord Jesus Christ may be denied while he is thought to be preached. Augustine says, "We have found many antichrists who confess Christ with their mouth."[93]

(2) First I say he is an apostate, yea the head of that Apostasy or falling away from the truth, mentioned in 2 Thessalonians 2, insomuch as some of the learned as Chrysostom, Augustine, Theodoret, Theophylact, Oecumenius by that apostasy understand Antichrist himself. Yea Bellarmine himself affirms that by apostasy in that place Antichrist himself may be most fitly understood.[94] But the papists, which falsely hold that the visible church of Christ cannot err, and much less fall away, expound this apostasy or defection, to be a revolt or falling away from the Roman Empire.

Neither do we deny that there has also been a defection from the Roman Empire, yet we deny that it is understood in this place. Ambrose says: "Then shall dissolution draw near because many falling by error shall revolt from

---

[92] *Ad Auxentius*
[93] Tract. 3 in Ioan. Epistol.
[94] Lib 3., *de pont. R.*, chap. 2.

the true religion." "He calls him a revolter," says Augustine, "namely from the Lord God." Cyril: "Now is the apostasy, for men are revolted from the true faith."[95] Chrysostom and Oecumenius: "The apostasy he calls Antichrist himself, because he shall cause many to revolt from Christ." Or else he calls apostasy "the departure from God and the thing itself." The same has Theophylact in effect. And likewise, Theodoret on this place. "The defection," (says he) "he calls Antichrist, himself giving him a name from the thing itself." For his endeavor is to withdraw men from the truth, and to cause them to revolt. Primasius by apostasy understands the forsaking of the truth, and Lyra, the departure from the catholic faith.

But to omit human testimonies, the Holy Spirit who is the best expounder of himself, shows what kind of defection he speaks of. For afterwards in the same chapter,[96] he notes this apostasy to be of those, who because they have not loved nor believed the truth that they might be saved (but have taken pleasure in unrighteousness) are therefore given over by the just judgment of God to believe the lies of Antichrist to their damnation. But more plainly, the same apostle speaking of that apostasy which in these later times was to accompany the revelation of Antichrist: he says (1 Timothy 4: 1-2): "The Spirit speaketh evidently that in the latter times some shall make an apostasy from the faith, attending to erroneous spirits and doctrines of devils, speaking lies in hypocrisy, having their own conscience seared."

(3) Now the papists are as ready to object this apostasy to us, as we are to them. How then shall we discern whether we or they have made this revolt? The apostle in the same place sets down two of those doctrines of devils, as certain notes whereby those which make this apostasy may be discerned. "Forbidding," (says he) "to marry, and commanding to abstain from meats, which God has created to be received with thanksgiving."[97] The former,

---

[95] Catech. 11
[96] 2 Thessalonians 2:10-12
[97] 1 Timothy 4:13

Jerome also has noted to be a mark of Antichrist:[98] *Nota est Antichristi prohibere nuptias*. But these notes agree not unto us, who neither forbid marriage, nor command abstinence from any meats for religion's sake. As for the papists (especially since the times of Gregory VII, they forbid marriage to some men at all times, and certain meats to all men at sometimes and that for religion sake: esteeming of marriage in their clergy worse than adultery or Sodomy; and eating of flesh in Lent, or other forbidden times, as a mortal sin. And as touching the falling away of the church; certain it is, that although neither the invisible church in general, nor any one sound member thereof can fall away from faith either totally or finally: yet not only the members of visible churches, but also the churches themselves consisting of hypocrites, as of the greater part, may fall away.

As the church of England which was in King Edward's days revolted in Queen Mary's time from Christ to Antichrist, so has the church of Rome (which once was famous for her faith)[99] as may appear not only by those notes set down by the apostle in 1 Timothy 4:3, and some others which hereafter shall be noted: but also in those innumerable particulars both in doctrine and manners wherein they have revolted from the purity of the primitive church. And of this catholic apostasy, the pope is head.[100]

(4) Secondly, Antichrist is not an open and outward, but a covert and disguised enemy, oppugning Christ and his church not by open violence, but with all deceivableness of unrighteousness.[101] For he is not so foolish as to profess himself to be Antichrist. Neither could that be which the apostle testifies (as Radulphus Flaviacensis says)[102] that Antichrist should attain unto ecclesiastical honors, and in the temple of God that is the society of the faithful, should take the chair of honor, unless having first pretended a kind

---

[98] In Daniel 11
[99] Romans 1
[100] See Book 2 Chapter 2
[101] 2 Thessalonians 2:10
[102] In Levit. Lib.18 cap.1, apud *Magdeburg. Centur.* 10

of conformity with the faithful he should deceive those of whom he is to be ordained.

Therefore Antichristianism is called *the mystery of iniquity*:[103] whereupon the gloss says, "The impiety of Antichrist is mystical, that is, cloaked under the name of godliness." And, as in the pope's miter was wont, so also in the whore of Babylon's forehead is written a mystery.[104] And Antichrist himself is deciphered as a hypocrite, sitting in the temple of God, professing himself and his followers to be the only true church of God,[105] using the two Testaments, pretending himself, as Jerome says,[106] to be the prince of the covenant, and consequently head of the church; deceiving unsound Christians with a glorious profession of religion (signified by the golden cup)[107] and with a show of counterfeit holiness (otherwise he could never so effectually deceive many Christians, as that the elect should be in any danger to be seduced)[108] speaking lies in hypocrisy,[109] oppugning Christ and his truth under the outward show and profession of Christian religion, having two horns like the lamb,[110] counterfeiting in some things the humility and meekness of Christ, and yet challenging that double power both spiritual and temporal which belongs to Christ the lamb, as our chief priest and king.

And not only that, but speaking also like the dragon, which is to be understood partly of his blasphemous speeches which he does utter, partly of the doctrines of devils which he does teach, partly of those hellish curses which he thunders against the true professors of the faith, partly of those great promises, which like the prince of the world he makes to those that will adore him.

---

[103] 2 Thessalonians 2:7
[104] Revelation 17
[105] 2 Thessalonians 2:4, Augustine, Primasius & gloss. In Revelation 13
[106] In Daniel 11
[107] Revelation 17
[108] Matthew 24:24
[109] 1 Timothy 4:2
[110] Revelation 13:11

These things need no application for those to whom the disguising and more then pharisaical hypocrisy of the pope and papists is known. For must not his holiness be called *sanctissimus*, most holy, when he is most wicked? does not he call himself *servus servorum*, the servant of servants, when in truth he makes himself the King of Kings, and Lord of Lords? And as Faber has observed,[111] the pope in word says that he is the servant of servants, but indeed he permits himself to be adored, which the angel in Revelation refused – from which fact of the pope, as if it were a rule of justice, Antoninus concludes that there is no less honor due to the pope than to the angels.[112] "Whereupon," (says he) "he receives from the faithful adorations, prostration or falling down before him, and the kisses of his feet; which the angel permitted not to be done unto him by John the Evangelist."

Neither was Bernard's complaint either unjust or untrue, *Heuheu, Domine Deus* etc. "Alas Lord God, that they be first in thy persecution, which seem to love the primacy in thy church, and to bear rule."[113] And elsewhere: "A silly contagion," (says he) "spreads itself nowadays through the whole body of the church, etc. All are lovers, and all enemies, all friends, and all adversaries; all domestic or of the household, and none peaceable: all neighbors, and yet all seek their own: they are ministers of Christ, and they serve Antichrist."[114]

And such was the complaint of several bishops in their epistle to pope Nicolas recorded in Aventin:[115] "You bear the person of a bishop," (say they) "but you play the tyrant: under the habit or attire of a pastor, we feel a wolf. The lying title calls you *father*, you in your deeds boast yourself to be another Jupiter. While you are the "servant of servants," you strive to be the lord of lords," etc.

---

[111] Praefat. instit.
[112] Sum. part. 3
[113] Revelation 22, sermon in convers. Pauli.
[114] In Cant. Serm. 23
[115] An. Do. 862. Annal. Boior. lib.4

He counterfeits the Lamb, in calling himself *the vicar of Christ*, and exercising the very same office which Christ himself had while he was upon the earth. And because, by *horn*, in the Scriptures often is meant power: he may be said to have two horns like the Lamb, while he challenges that twofold power which is peculiar to Christ the Lamb as our King and Priest, and usurps both the swords, I mean both spiritual and temporal. He speaks like the dragon, in teaching those doctrines of devils, mentioned in 1 Timothy 4:3 (forbidding to marry and commanding abstinence from meats), in belching forth most horrible blasphemies (whereof we will remember some in the next chapter), in his devilish curses against the saints, and Satanic promises of the world and kingdoms thereof to them that will adore him.[116]

Ecce in potestate nostra est imperium, vt demus illud cui volumus, says Adrian the pope: "Behold the Empire is in our power, that we may give it to whom we will."[117] And whereas Jerome writing of those words in 1 Timothy 4: "They speak in hypocrisy," (says he) "who, being not continent, would seem to be so chaste, as that they condemn marriage, and so abstemious as that they judge those who use the creature sparingly; whereas themselves are given over to belly cheer." What could have been spoken more fitly to show forth the hypocrisy of the pope and papists?!

For do they not – while they condemn and contemn marriage under the show of vowed chastity practice all uncleanness, and while they condemn all moderate eating of flesh, do not they under a color of fasting – feast and feed themselves with the choicest dainties? Do not many of them under the pretense of voluntary poverty gather infinite riches? And does not all their religion stand *in opere operate*, in the bare performance of the outward work, that is to say, in hypocrisy?

Neither are we to omit an hypocritical policy which of late they have used. For when they could not prevail with their sophistry, that is to say,

---

[116] Luke 4:6
[117] Aventin, Annal. Boior. lib.6

with their books of controversies, they hoped to prevail among the simple with their hypocrisy, that is to say, with their books of devotion. Wherein there is a notable show of counterfeit devotion, zeal and holiness, to blear the eyes of the simple and unstayed. But it were to be wished, that as they are, so they were esteemed to be no better than baits of Antichrist, serving to allure men under show of devotion, unto idolatry and apostasy from God: especially if we consider that the principal of these books were set forth by parsons and other Jesuits, who are plainly discovered even by some of their own side, to be mere Machiavellians and wicked atheists.

(5) Thus you see what manner of adversary Antichrist is. Now we must show in particular wherein he is opposed to Jesus Christ. He is opposed unto him as he is Christ, and as he is Jesus: as he is Christ, that is, as he was anointed of God to be our Prophet, our King, and our Priest; in which respect especially he is called Antichrist. He is also opposed unto him as he is Jesus, that is to say, as he is our Savior. So that Antichrist opposes himself both to the offices of Christ signified in the name Christ, and also to the benefits signified in the name Jesus. Now these things also most fitly agree to the pope: who opposes himself to Christ in all these respects, not indeed *aperto Marte* as an open and professed enemy, (for so it becomes not Antichrist, who was to be an hypocrite sitting in the Church of God etc.), but covertly and cunningly.

For we must remember that Antichristianism is the mystery of iniquity, wherein Christ was in word and show to be professed, but indeed and truth, denied. First, them to Christ our prophet he is opposed, partly as he oppugns the prophecy of Christ, and partly as himself is a false prophet. He oppugns the prophecy of Christ: firstly, in denying Christ to be our only prophet (whose voice in the canonical Scriptures concerning matters necessarily to be believed unto salvation, we ought only to hear) whiles he and his followers do teach that the scriptures are not perfect, and that besides the apocryphal writings (which they have matched with the canonical) their own traditions also are necessary, and of equal authority with the Scriptures. Secondly, by withholding from the people the Scriptures (which contain the whole doctrine of Christ our prophet) in a strange language, and also by reading and preaching unto them their own fancies and inventions, out of the legends and lives of saints, and festivals etc. instead of the sincere truth of God. And by these two practices, the pope, while he leaves to Christ the name and title of being our prophet, he takes the thing to himself.

Again, he is opposed to Christ our prophet as himself is the false prophet spoken of in Revelation, teaching Antichristian errors and doctrines of devils. For so many errors, as are taught and held by the pope and church of Rome, are so many oppositions between him and Christ our prophet. Of the errors of the Romish church, there are many centuries or hundreds, and several of them are fundamental. In respect whereof we may truly say that the catholic apostasy (for so I call the Romish religion) is the common sewer of many gross heresies.

(6) But it will be said that even though the pope holds to several errors, yet he teaches not those, which the Holy Spirit has noted as the peculiar doctrines of Antichrist. Whereof the author of the *Wardword* reckons up three, and Bellarmine has a fourth. But neither of them durst mention those two doctrines of devils[118] which Paul assigns to that apostasy, whereof Antichrist is the head,

The first doctrine of Antichrist (say they) is, to deny Jesus to be Christ, which they would prove out of 1 John 2:22. and 4:3, and 2 John 7. But the pope (say they) does not deny Jesus to be Christ.[119] To the prosyllogism or proof of the proposition, I answer that these places of the apostle John do not speak properly of the grand Antichrist, who is the head of the Antichristian body, but of certain petty antichrists, or heretics of those times, which

---

[118] 1 Timothy 4:1
[119] Of this, see more in the 2nd Book and 14th Chapter

denied either of the natures of Christ (for he speaks of such as were then already come into the world), and therefore from thence it cannot be proved that the great Antichrist shall directly and expressly deny Jesus to be Christ. Notwithstanding, seeing as they are called *antichrists* not only because they belong to the Antichristian body as inferior members thereof, but also as it may be thought, because they did after a sort deny Christ as the great Antichrist also should do, although not after the same manner, I do therefore thus far grant the proposition itself, that Antichrist was in some sort to deny Christ. For John does not deal with the manner of how he does deny Christ.

Neither are we to think that Antichrist will deny him after every manner, but in such sort as shall be most consonant to the whole mystery of iniquity, and suitable to the rest of his lying and deceit.[120] That is to say, in outward show and semblance to profess Christ (as those antichrists did, of whom John speaks) but in deed and in truth to deny him. To come therefore to the assumption: let us consider whether the pope and church of Rome do not in some sort deny Christ, Christ may be denied, either in deeds or words. *Quisquis autem factis negat Christum, is Antichrist us est*, "And whosoever in deeds," (says Augustine) "denies Christ, he is Antichrist. Let us therefore mark," (says he) "who it is that denies, and let us not attend to his tongue but to his works. I regard not what he speaks, but how he lives. Works do speak, and do we require words? He is the more lying Antichrist, who with his mouth professes Jesus to be Christ, and by deeds denies him."[121]

According to the lawyer's rule, it is more to testify a matter by deeds than by words. And Tully says,[122] that where the things themselves bear witness, words are needless. And as Antichrist was thus to deny Christ, both as he is the man of sin, and an adversary oppugning Christ and his church: So does the pope, however he professes Christ in word. For even the devils

---

[120] 2 Thessalonians 2
[121] Tract. 3 in Epist. Ioan.
[122] Contra Salust

themselves have in word confessed Christ, whom notwithstanding by their deeds they deny. If therefore the pope is a man of sin (which we shall prove soon) and an adversary opposed unto Christ, (which now we have in hand to prove) then it cannot be denied but that he indeed denies Christ.

(7) Secondly, Christ may be denied in word and doctrine, and that either indirectly and by consequent, or else directly and expressly. He that denies Christ by consequent, however openly he does confess him, does indeed deny him; as those which deny either of his natures, or any of his offices. For such is the necessary coherence of truth within itself, as nothing can by necessary consequence be deducted from it, which is not also true. And therefore it is impossible that the consequent should be false, the antecedent being true. Whereupon it follows that whosoever denies the consequent, does indeed deny the antecedent. Jesus is Immanuel, and consequently God and Man. He is Christ, and consequently anointed of God to be our king, our priest, and our prophet. He therefore that denies any of these, denies Jesus to be Christ.

And further, is Christ truly God? Then is he also Jehovah, one that is of and from himself, namely as he is God; then is he also the Lord and creator of all things, governing all things with his presence and providence. Is he truly man? Then has he a true body consisting of three dimensions, length, breadth, thickness, circumscribed, visible, confined in one place at once, as being but one body not discontinued. Is he the true Messiah and Mediator between God and man? Then is he the only mediator, for there is but one.[123] Wherefore whosoever says, that Christ is not αὐτόθεος God of himself, he denies him to be God: or prefers any creature before him either in heaven or in earth, he denies him to be the Lord and maker of all; or assigns a vicar unto him to supply his absence on earth, denies his omnipresence.

---

[123] 1 Timothy 2:5, Acts 4:12

Again, whosoever says that Christ's body does not consist of three dimensions, that it is not circumscribed, that it is not visible, that it is not contained in one place as all other bodies, yea as all other finite natures are; he denies Jesus to be truly man, and consequently denies him to be Christ.

Lastly, whoever adjoins other mediators unto Christ and in some respects prefer others above him, denies him to be the only mediator, and therefore denies him to be the true mediator, for there is but one, and consequently denies Jesus to be Christ. And thus as the antichrists whereof John speaks[124] (according to Bellarmine's own exposition)[125] did, and as the grand Antichrist (according to our confession) does deny Christ, not only in deed, but also in word and doctrine, although not openly and expressly yet indirectly, and by consequence, so does the pope and church of Rome, deny Jesus to be Christ. For, what a God and Lord, what a creator and governor of all things the pope and papists make our Savior Christ, you may easily conceive: firstly, when they deny him to be αὐτόθεος God of himself, and consequently Jehovah. For whosoever is Jehovah, he is of, and from himself.

True indeed it is, that Christ is *filius a patre, sed Deus a se, quate nus est Deus*: that is, Son of and from his Father, but God of and from himself, namely as he is God. And if he were not of and from himself, he were not God. And although in the concrete we may and must say with the council of Nice, that Christ is God of God, that is, Christ who is God, is from the father who is God (the word *God* being taken personally) because the person of the Son who is *Deus genitus* God begotten is from the person of the Father who is *Deus gignens* God begetting: yet it is not likewise true in the abstract.

For howsoever the Godhead is communicated from the Father to the Son by eternal generation, and from the Father and the Son to the Holy Spirit by eternal procession, yet the deity of the Son and so of the Holy Spirit, being the self same infinite eternal and indivisible essence of the Father, is from, and of, and by, and for itself. And who does not know that

---

[124] 1 John 2:22
[125] Lib 3. *De Pont. R.* cap. 14

such is the simplicity of the divine nature as that God is the Godhead, and the Godhead is God, and consequently that Christ as he is God is the Godhead, which is of and from itself? And therefore to conclude, Christ is God of God, in respect of his person, and he is also God of himself in respect of his essence which is of itself: he is God of God, the name God being used personally and relatively (for he is God the Son, of God the Father: and God begotten, of God begetting) and he is God of himself, the name God being taken essentially and absolutely, namely as he together with the Father and the Holy Spirit is one and the same eternal Jehovah and only true God. In which respect if the papists deny Christ to be God of himself, as they do when they accuse this our doctrine of heresy, and deny him so to be αὐτόθεος (God of himself) as we affirm, they do also deny him to be God.

Secondly, when as not only in heaven they set above him his mother whom they call *the Queen of Heaven*, desiring her to command him, and to show herself to be a mother (as though Christ were as they paint him a baby under his mothers government) for so they say, *Iube natū, and iure matris impera, and again monstra te esse matrē etc.* but also on earth, when every shaveling priest can by breathing out a few words out of his unclean mouth, create his maker (for so they teach, *Sacerdos est creator creatoris sui*, that is, the priest is maker of his maker. And again, *Qui creauit vos, dedit vobis creare se*, He which made you, gave you power to make him),[126] and when he has so done, offer him up to his Father. Wherein every priest among them, being the sacrificer, is after a sort preferred above Christ, who is the sacrifice.

Thirdly, when as they appoint unto Christ a vicar to supply his absence,[127] unto whom they assign all power which is in heaven and earth, yea infinite power, which they say is translated from Christ unto him, what do they else but make Christ a titular king, and with the Epicureans an idle god, who has as it were resigned all his right and authority to the pope.

---

[126] Stella clericor. Serm. discip. Serm. [241] apud Iuellum.
[127] See Chapter 5

What a man they make our Savior Christ who does not know, when they hold, and with fire and faggot persecute those that will not hold the same, that his body is multipresent, that is, present in many or rather infinite places at once, and that discontinued. For they say that it, being in heaven, is also present really and corporally upon the earth, wheresoever their mass is celebrated or their host reserved, howsoever it is not in the space between heaven and earth, nor in those places where the host is not – which is to assign many or rather innumerable bodies to our Savior Christ. And further, that his very body, which they say is really present in the mass, is void of quantity and quality, neither circumscribed, nor visible, nor any way sensible, and consequently, nobody – which in effect is as much as to deny that Christ is come in the flesh, which is the doctrine of that Antichrist whereof John speaks.[128]

And here by the way note the absurdity of papists, who circumscribe the deity of the Father whiles they resemble the same by pictures or images, and deny the humanity of the Son to be circumscribed – and consequently against all reason make the deity finite, and the humanity infinite. The office of Christ is his mediation. Now what a mediator they make him you may easily judge, when they join infinite others with him. For the apostle says that there is but one mediator between God and man, and this one alone our Savior Christ is, or else he is none at all.[129]

(8) Again, Christ may be denied directly and expressly – and that may be done either secretly and in private, or else openlie and in public profession. After the latter sort, Antichrist was not to deny our Savior Christ because he was to be a hypocrite and a disguised enemy – as has been proven. Neither was it necessary that he should deny Christ expressly and directly, and yet this also may be proved of several popes. Who howsoever they professed publicly that Jesus is Christ (which is all that our adversaries

---

[128] 1 John 4:3, 2 John 7
[129] 1 Timothy 2:5

allege in this case, and yet that all is nothing, for the devils themselves have publicly professed Jesus to be Christ) yet privately and among their favorites, they have denied Christ, and not that only, but have shown themselves also to have been mere atheists, and devils incarnate.

For to omit John XXII who denied the immortality of the soul (and of some is called John XXIII; of others XXIV) were not Alexander VI and Sixtus IV, Julius II, and Paulus III, besides several others, very atheists? Were not more than twenty of them known necromancers and sorcerers? Not to speak of them which were not known, which renouncing Christ our Savior, betook themselves to the devil. As namely Sylvester II, Benedict IX, Gregory V, and Gregory VII who also in a rage cast the Eucharist – that is according to their opinion the very body of Christ into the fire – because it did not answer to his questions when he consulted therewith. And what may we think of Clement VII,, who, when he was at death's door, said he should now be certified of three things whereof he had doubted all his life, namely: whether there be a God, whether the soul be immortal, and whether there be a life after this life? Or of Julius III who, being forbidden by the physicians the use of pork, commanded his pork to be set before him, *Al dispette di Dio*, in spite of God?

As for Pope Leo X, he did plainly enough deny Christ when, more than once, he called the gospel *the fable of Christ*. For when he had received an incredible sum of money for indulgences, he said to Bembus, *O quantum nobis profuit illa de Christo fabula!* "O how much that fable of Christ has profited us!"[130] And another time when Bembus alleged for his comfort a testimony out of the gospel, he answered: *Quid mihi narras fabulamillā de Christo?* "What do you tell me of that fable of Christ?" If therefore this be a property of Antichrist to deny Christ, then it cannot be avoided but that according to our adversaries own grounds, the pope who so many ways denies Christ, is Antichrist.

---

[130] Ex. Sibrand. Lull. de pap. Rom. l.10 c.18

And so much of his opposition to the prophecy of Christ. For of the other three doctrines which the papists assign to Antichrist, we are to entreat when we come to answer the objections of the papists.[131]

(9) To the priesthood of Christ our only priest and mediator, who according to the Scriptures, with the oblation of himself once made, has perfectly redeemed us,[132] are opposed:

[1] Their priesthood, whereby Christ is daily offered and his sacrifice repeated in their abominable sacrifice of the mass propitiatory, as they say both for the quick and the dead.

[2] Their own satisfactions as prices of sin opposed to the satisfaction of Christ.

[3] Their adjoining unto Christ other intercessors and mediators, by whose not only intercession they hope to be heard, but also merits, hope to be saved.

Of Gregory they say thus in their prayers,

Hic nos saluet à peccatis,
vt in coelo cum beatis
possimus quiescere.

That is:

"Let him save us from our sins,
that in heaven we may rest with the blessed."

Of Thomas Becket the archbishop of Canterbury, because he died in the pope's quarrel, which like a rebel he maintained against his sovereign king, Henry II, they say full devoutly,

---

[131] See Book 2 Chapter 14
[132] Hebrews 10:12, 14

Tu per Thomae sanguinem, quem pro te impendit,
Fac nos Christ scandere quo Thomas ascendit.

That is:

"By the blood of Thomas, which he for thee did spend,
Make us Christ to come whither Thomas did ascend."

Of Peter and Paul, *Concede vt amborum meritis aeternitatis gloriam consequamur*:[133] "Grant that by the mercies of them both we may obtain eternal glory." To Mary the blessed virgin whom they idolatrously call *Our Lady* and *the Queen of Heaven*, they pray thus: *O unica spes miserorum, libera nos ab omni malo*:[134] "O thou that art the only hope of them that are in misery, deliver us from all evil." And elsewhere they call her, *Desperatorum spem unicam, peccatorum salvatricem*:[135] "The only hope of them which are in despair, and the Savior of sinners." Again, *Mediatrix Dei et hominum, salus et spes in the sperantium*: "O thou the mediatrix between God and men, the salvation and hope of them that hope in thee."

And somewhere it is said:

O regina poli, mater gratissima proli
Spernere me noli, me commendo tibi soli.

"O Queen of heaven, mother most dear to thy son, do not thou despise me, unto thee alone I commend me."

---

[133] Ex. Rom. Breuiar.
[134] Ex/ compassionit. Marie.
[135] Innoc. In orat. De 300. Dier. indulgent. In orat. De 5. [...]

And again:

Cum nulla spes sit altera
nisi tu virgo puerpera
patris parens and filia
cui me reconcilia.

"Seeing there is no other hope, besides thee O virgin mother, the mother and daughter of thy father, to whom I pray thee reconcile me."

And to conclude (for innumerable such speeches might be produced,) they say:

O foelix puerpera
nostra pians scelera
iure matris impera
redemptori.

"O happy mother which does purge away our sins, by thy motherly authority command our redeemer."

So that sometimes they do join unto our Savior Christ other mediators not only of intercession, but also of redemption (which indeed is presupposed in the former) sometimes also they exclude our Savior Christ, when as they say that Mary purges away the sins of all the faithful, and that she and no other is the only hope of them that are in misery and despair.

And not to speak of their blasphemous psalter, wherein they turn that which is spoken in the Psalms either of God or Christ, to the virgin Mary, some of them say, that whereas the kingdom of Christ consists in two things, justice and mercy; Christ reserves justice unto himself, and mercy he has given up to his mother. And therefore one says, *A foro iustitiae Dei appellundum est ad forum misericordiae matris eius*: "From the court of God's justice, we must appeal to the court of his mother's mercy."

(10) As touching the kingdom of Christ, what does not the pope oppugn in it? The realm and kingdom of Christ is his church which he rules by his Spirit inwardly, and outwardly by his word, which is both his scepter and his law, and also by such officers and ministers as he has ordained both in the church and commonwealth. The church and people of God, this son of perdition seeks to destroy.

First by killing the bodies of the true servants of Christ that refuse his mark, in respect whereof he may most worthily be called αβαδδων or *abaddon* that is, a destroyer,[136] and his church the whore of Babylon, which is drunk with the blood of saints and of the martyrs of Jesus, as shall be shown in Book 2 Chapter 7. And as he kills the bodies of those that will not receive his mark,[137] so he murders the souls of them that submit themselves unto him, poisoning them with his damnable errors and making them drunk with the wine of his fornications, after which they shall drink of the cup of God's wrath.

Now in making havoc of men's souls, he takes such liberty unto him, as that if he should draw with him innumerable souls into hell, yet no man may say unto him *Domine cur ita facis?* Sir, why do you so? And in the canon *Si Papa* (Dist. 40),[138] it is said, If the pope do carry with him innumerable people's by troupes into hell, no man in this world may presume to reprove his fault, because he is to judge all, and to be judged of none, unless he be found to err from the faith, which the pope as he is pope cannot do. Hereunto Bellarmine answers that the words of this canon are not the words of any pope, but of Boniface the Archbishop of Mainz.[139] Yea, but say I, the

---

[136] Revelation 9
[137] Revelation 14:9
[138] Gloss. Iur. Can.
[139] Lib. 3. *De Pont. Rom.* cap. 21

pope has so approved this speech being delivered by another, as that he has canonized it, and appointed it for one of the canons of his law, which is more than if it had been spoken by himself. But Bellarmine replies: "If this sentence of Boniface is not true, why do you object to it; if it is true, why do you not receive it?" I answer, because it being not only false, but blasphemous also and Antichristian, is notwithstanding by the pope authorized for a canon in his law.

Moreover, one of the chief works of God's Spirit, the Spirit of adoption, which is special faith, apprehending the righteousness of Christ to our justification, he labors to extinguish in the hearts of men, calling it presumption: acknowledging no other faith but such as is common to the devils (which consists only of knowledge and assent),[140] and yet not requiring that in the lay people whom under the name of implicit faith, he nuzzles in palpable ignorance, and leads them being blind, as Elisha did the Aramites, even whether it pleases him.[141] The pure wheat of God's word he suppresses and keeps from the people in an unknown tongue, and seeds them with the mast of their legends and festivals and lies (I should have said *lives*) of saints.

The laws of Christ he partly dispenses with, and partly abrogates, making them of none effect by his own constitutions and traditions. In the church, instead of the offices and functions ordained by Christ, he has created a new priesthood, erected an hierarchy, consecrated orders and religions of his own. In the commonwealth, he absolves the people from their obedience to their princes if they shall displease him. And it is a principle among them, that it is lawful for him to depose emperors and kings, and to absolve their sworn subjects from fidelity and allegiance towards them.

And thus you see how the pope opposes himself to the prophecy, priesthood and kingdom of Christ. Whereunto I might add how he is

---

[140] James 2
[141] 2 Kings 6

opposed to these offices of Christ, not only in these respects already mentioned, but as an *aemulus*, as an anti-prophet, an anti-priest, and a counter-king seeking in his Antichristian pride to match our Savior Christ in all those offices – but hereof I shall have occasion to speak in the next chapter.

Now to the benefits of Christ he is opposite, as he is an enemy to the grace of god: as he takes away Christian liberty, and takes upon him to make new laws, to bind the conscience: as he abridges the merits of Christ, and ascribes the merit of salvation not only to our own works prescribed of God, but also to such as have been in superstition, will-worship, and idolatry, devised by themselves, as he teaches men to seek salvation elsewhere then in Christ – all of which oppositions of the pope to Christ, whosoever shall duly consider, he will not seek further for Antichrist.

Chapter 5

Of the pride and ambition of Antichrist, advancing himself above all that is called God, etc.

(1) But Antichrist is not only *hostis*, an enemy to Christ, but also (as our adversaries confess), *aemulus Christi*, that is, such an adversary as is opposed unto Christ in emulation of like honor, as the word *Antichrist* does also signify. It remains therefore that we should speak of the pride and ambition of Antichrist, whereby he seeking to match Christ our Savior, advances himself as the apostle speaks, "above all that is called God, or that is worshiped, insomuch that he sitteth in the temple of God, as God, showing himself that he is God,"[142] or as the papists themselves read, "as though he were God."[143]

Where (for avoiding error) we are to understand the pride of Antichrist to be described such as is incident to a wretched man, a man of sin, a son of perdition. And the greatest pride that is incident not only to any man, but to any creature, be it the devil himself (whose Satanic pride Antichrist was to imitate and not to exceed) is this, to seek to be as God.[144]

When therefore it is said that Antichrist "advanceth himself above all that is called God, or that is worshiped," it is not meant that he shall seek to advance himself, above God or the deity itself. For God being infinite in goodness, excellency and power, there cannot be conceived a better, a superior, a greater. And therefore we cannot imagine how Antichrist should advance himself above God. And it is evident that the height of Antichrist's pride here spoken of, is noted in these words, "Insomuch as he shall sit in the temple of God, as God." By "all therefore that is called God," we are to

---

[142] 2 Thessalonians 2:4
[143] Vulgat edit. Rhem.
[144] Isaiah 14

understand all those to whom the name of God is communicated: not essence, for that cannot be communicated to any that is not God.

Now the name of God is communicated to angels in heaven (Psalm 8:5 with Hebrews 2:7, and Psalm 97:7 with Hebrews 1:6) and to princes and magistrates on earth (Exodus 22:28, Psalm 82:1, 6). And whereas it is said "that he shall advance himself above all that is worshiped," we are to understand by the word σεβασμα not God himself, but anything that is worshiped as God, or wherein God is worshiped. So Wisdom 15:17 *images*, and Acts 17:23, *altars* among the heathen are called σεβάσματα. Such in the church of Rome, are saints, images, the cross and relics of saints, the eucharist, etc.

The meaning then of the apostle is this: that Antichrist – being a wicked and wretched man – shall advance himself above all that is called God, as angels and kings, or that which is worshiped, as saints and images and altars, the cross and eucharist itself, insomuch that he shall sit in the temple of God as God, that is, he shall rule and reign in the church of God, challenging a sovereign, universal and divine authority over all those that profess the name of Christ, as if he were a god upon earth, showing himself whether by words or by deeds that he is God, or which is all one, behaving himself *tanquam sit Deus*, as though he were God.

The like things were foretold of Antiochus Epiphanes, who is thought to have been a type of Antichrist (Daniel 11:36). But (to come to the application of this prophecy) if Antiochus were comparable to the pope in advancing himself above all that is called God – or if I shall not prove out of their own (I mean popish) writings, that he has lifted up himself in such manner as is scarcely credible to be incident unto a mortal man – then let not the pope be deemed Antichrist, but rather look for some other, who shall go beyond him in Antichristian insolence and Satanic pride.

(2) From this place therefore of the apostle, I argue thus:

- Whosoever advances himself above all that is called God or that is worshiped, insomuch that he sits in the temple of God, as God, taking upon him as though he were a God, he according to the testimony of the apostle, is antichrist, that is, *Aemulus Christi*, such an enemy as in a kind of emulation seeks to match Christ and to be equal to him.
- But the pope of Rome (as shall be proven) advances himself above all that is called God, or that is worshiped, insomuch that he sits in the temple of God as God, taking upon him as though he were a God upon earth.
- Therefore according to this testimony of the apostle the pope is Antichrist.

And first that the pope advances himself above all that is called God, it is plain, because he lifts up himself not only over kings and emperors on earth, but also above the angels in heaven. Of his lifting up himself above kings and emperors, is the testimony before alleged in 2 Thessalonians 2:4 especially to be understood. For he speaks of such an advancement whereby Antichrist should be revealed, as was to be hindered for a time by the Roman Empire. Let us then consider how he advances himself above kings and emperors who are called God's.

The pope, if you will believe him and his followers, is the king of kings and lord of lords,[145] by whom princes reign,[146] and from whom the right of kings depends.[147] For you must know that as they full solemnly dispute, the empire or temporal rule,[148] as well as the priesthood or ecclesiastical

---

[145] Paulus 4. ad ducem Floret. in bulla. Rod. Cupers. meritò rex regū & do|minus dominan|tium censetur Papa, re{que} ipsa existit. pag. 43. num. 39. c. solitas, extr. de maior. & obed. &c. per venerabilē opt. qui filij sunt legitimi. Antonius de Rosellis.
[146] Lib. Carem.
[147] Clem. 5. in cōcil. Vienn.
[148] R. Cupers. pag. 251. nū. 62.

dominion is translated unto the successors of Peter; that the right of rule and direct dominion of the empire and kingdoms belongs to the pope,[149] howbeit he commits the exercise thereof to emperors and kings: that emperors, kings, and all princes receive their right of governing their kingdoms from the pope,[150] and that by him they are confirmed, and by him deposed: that to him emperors and kings as being but his vassals are bound to swear allegiance and fidelity;[151] that he so far surpasses the emperor as the sun excels the moon,[152] that is, according to their astronomy, 750 times, or rather as the creator is superior to the creature.[153] Therefore kings and emperors when they come into the presence of his holiness, must, after obeisance done in three several distances, fall down before him and kiss his foot,[154] even as Mantuan says of him:

Ense potens gemino, cuius vestigia adorant
Caesar, et aurato vestitimurice reges.

And if they be in presence when he takes horse,[155] the emperor or chiefest prince that is present must hold his right stirrup, and when he is mounted, must hold the bridle, and play the lackey for a certain space, and likewise when he alights, must hold the right stirrup; which if he happen to mistake as being not used to service, he must look for a check, as we read of Adrian IV, who bitterly checked Frederick the Emperor for holding the stirrup on the wrong side.[156] Or if it be his pleasure to be carried aloft on

---

[149] Idem pag. 52. num. 28. & p. 1. 251. n. 63. & 64.
[150] Idem pag. 28 num. 7.
[151] c. tibi domino. dist. 63. &c. 1. de iuretur.
[152] c. solitae de maior. & obed.
[153] Gloss. ibid. Sta[...]st. Orichovius quantum Deus praestat sacerdoti, tantū sacerdos praestat regi. qui re|gé anteponit sacerdoti, is anteponit creaturā creatori. Apud Iuellum.
[154] Lib. [...] erem. 1. sect. 5. cap. 3. & lib. 3. sect. 1. cap. 3.
[155] Lib. 1. c[...]erē. sect. 2. c. 3.
[156] Helmoldus Chron. Slauor: l. 1. c. 81. & Bal: de vit. pont.

men's shoulders, the emperor, kings, and princes that are present, must put under their shoulder and help to carry his holiness for a space, and whiles he is on foot the emperor or chiefest prince must bear up his train.[157] If the emperor is at the pope's feast, his duty is before dinner to hold the pope water to wash his hands, and to bring in the first mess. For indeed *Imperator est minister Papae*: the emperor is the pope's minister.[158]

(3) These are but matters of ceremony. But as he vaunts that the whole right of kings depends on him, so he challenges authority and power to translate kingdoms, to create and depose kings, to translate the empire from nation to nation, and to give the same to whom it pleases him. "The emperor," (says he) "is emperor by us."[159] Whence has he the empire but from us? Behold the empire is in our power to give it to whom we well. And accordingly he has deposed several kings and emperors, and created others, as I shall not need to prove, for both they and their followers boast thereof.[160]

And if you desire some other examples of their insolent and Antichristian behavior towards emperors and kings, did not Gregory VII make Henry the Emperor – who came in all humility to submit himself unto him with his wife and child – dance attendance at his gate barefoot and bare-headed by the space of three days, before he would grant them any access unto him?

When the Emperor Frederick Barbarossa was excommunicated by the pope, and his son taken prisoner in Venice, he came to Pope Alexander III, into the Church of Saint Mark there, to the end that he might be absolved,

---

[157] lib. caerem. 1. sect. 2. & 5. de processione pontificus & Caesaris per vrbem. Lib. 1. c. 8. caerem.

[158] Lib. caerem. 1. sect. 3. Antonin. sinn. part. 3. tit, 22. cap. 5. §. 13. E. venerabilem de elect

[159] Hardian, apud. Aventin, lib. 6

[160] Bellarmine, *De Pont. Rom.*, lib.3 cap.16

and his son restored.[161] Where, before all the people, the pope having commanded the Emperor to prostrate himself upon the ground and so to ask pardon, he sets his foot in the neck of the emperor, saying, "It is written, *Super aspidem et basiliscum ambulabis, et conculcabis Leonem et Draconem*: You shall walk upon the asp and cockatrice, and shall tread upon the lion and the dragon," to which indignity – when the emperor, being not well able to brook made answer, "Not to you but to Peter," – the holy father, treading on the emperor's neck, replied, *Et mihi et Petro*: "Both to me and to Peter."

And when Henry VI came to be crowned emperor, and to that end knelt before Celestine III sitting in his pontifical chair, did not he after he had set the imperial diadem on his head, and as some say with his feet, kick it off with his foot again? What should I tell you of Innocent II? How he caused his own with the emperor's picture to be set up in the Lateran Palace, himself sitting in his pontifical throne, and the emperor kneeling before him and holding up his hands as unto God, with these verses subscribed,

Rex venit ante sores, iurans prids vrbis honores,
Post homo sit Papae, sumit quo dante coronam,

That is: "The king of the Romans comes before the gates, swearing first to the honors and privileges of the city, afterward he becomes the pope's man, of whose gift he receives the imperial crown."

(4) And thus has the pope lifted up himself above all that is called *God* upon earth, that is to say, kings and emperors: let us now consider whether he exalts himself above those which are called gods in heaven, that is to say, the angels.

First, in general it is avouched by himself and his approved writers, that the power of the pope is greater than all other created power. *Potestas*

---

[161] Naucler. generat. 40.

Papaemaior est omni alia potestate creata:[162] That unto him is given all power above all powers as well of heaven as of the earth.[163] *Qui totum dicit nihil excludit*, "He that says all excludes nothing:" that to the vicar of the creator, that is the pope, every creature is subject:[164] and more particularly, that he has *vicariatum Christi*,[165] Christ's vicarship, not only about things in heaven, in earth, in hell, but also above the angels both good and bad: *Pontificem Romanū habere imperium in angelos ac daemonas*: That the pope has rule over the angels and devils.[166] That he has power to command the angels, for so they say: *Papa Angelis habet imperare*,[167] and *Papa angelis praecipit*.[168]

And according to these testimonies which avouch his right, this is the pope's practice. For not only does he challenge for greater honor and reverence to be done to himself then is due to the angels (for he accepts adorations and fallings down before him, which the angels refuse because they are our fellow servants), but also he takes upon him to command the holy angels at his pleasure to remove souls departed out of purgatory into heaven.

Clement VI, in his bull concerning those who should come to Rome to celebrate the Jubilee, commanded the angels of heaven that if any of them should die in that journey, to bring their souls – being wholly freed from Purgatory – into the glory of Paradise. His words were these: *Prorsus mandamus angelis paradisi, quatenus animam à purgatorio penitus absolutam, in paradisi gloriam introducant.*

(5) It remains that I should show how the pope advances himself above the σεβάσματα, that is the things wherein God is worshiped, or which are

---

[162] Antonin. sum. pact. 3. lit. 22. c. 5.
[163] Concil. Lateranēs. sub Leo. 10. sess. 10.
[164] Innocent. Papa. extr. de constit. R. Cupers. pag. 28. num. 5.
[165] Felinus apud Iuellū.
[166] Nicolaus Egmūdanus apud Bal. de vit. pōl.
[167] Gregor. Haimburg. in appellat. Sigism. apud Iuell.
[168] Camotensis

worshiped as God in the church of Rome, as namely the saints, the cross, the altar, and their god of bread.[169]

As for the saints they are subject to the pope *quoad canonizationem*, standing at the courtesy and free disposition of the pope whether to be deified that is as they speak to be canonized, or to be deposed. For such is his authority (if you will believe him) in canonizing saints, that he can canonize whom he will, yea, of a damned person cast into hell he can make a saint in heaven, and contrariwise he can un-saint those who before were canonized.

The cross – which they say is to be worshiped with divine worship – is notwithstanding made an ensign of the pope's authority, and is borne before him as the mace before the magistrate, or the sword before the prince, and when their procession is at an end it is laid under his feet. And that he may be known – even literally so – to sit in the material temple as if he were a god, it is to be noted that his seat in the church is above the altar.

But their chief σεβασμα is their god of bread, which, because they imagine it to be Christ himself, it is worshiped among them as their maker and redeemer, notwithstanding in the pope's processions and journeys it is made an attendant on his holiness. For I shall not need to tell you now which you heard before, how Pope Hildebrand, when it did not answer his demands as being not used to speak, did cast it into the fire. It is worthy to be remembered which is reported by Johannes Monlucius,[170] the Bishop of Valence, who was the French king's ambassador at Rome, and testified by others, that when the pope is to travel abroad, three or four days before, he sent the eucharist (that is their christ; their maker) on horseback accompanied with muleteers and horse-keepers, and courtesans and cooks with sumpter horses and all the baggage of his court. Afterwards, the pope – who professes himself his vicar – followed, attended with cardinals, primates,

---

[169] Antonin part 3., tit. 22, cap.5. S. 5; Troilus Maluit, in tract. De canonis. Sanct. 3. dub.; Antoninus part 3., tit. 22, cap.5. S. 6; Traianum Gregorius per orationem sua a poena inferni quae infinita est absoluit.

[170] Lib de religione ad Reginam matr[...], Fulmen bruit. Pag. 12 & 13

bishops, and potentates. And when he came near to the place where he traveled, their christ was brought to meet him on the way, so that it may be carried before him into the town.

But with what difference of honor is he and his attendant carried in such solemn processions? The pope either rides upon a goodly white horse under a stately canopy, or else is carried aloft upon noble men's shoulders in a chair of gold, while the christ of the papists – the pope's attendant – is carried upon a simple hackney in comparison, with no such magnificence, and yet that hackney is the pope;s vicar appointed in his steed to carry the monstrance. In a word, he is *supremū numen in terris*: the chief or supreme σεβασμα that is to be worshiped on earth.[171]

(6) But let us come to the height of Antichrist's pride. For it is not sufficient for the pope to be lifted up above all that is called God, or that is worshiped, unless he take upon him as if he were God, and seek to match himself with Christ, as the name *Antichrist* imports:[172] that unto him the height of Antichrist's pride may also be applied, which is described in these words, "insomuch that he sitteth in the temple of God as God, behaving himself as if he were God," or (which is all one) "showing himself that he is God."

For of his followers and flatterers he is said to be all and above all, the cause of causes, and the first cause.[173] *Bald. in c. ecclesia vt lite pendente*, that he is *numen quoddam, visibilem quendam Deum praese serens*, a certain divine majesty showing himself to be a certain visible god: agreeable to the prophecy in 2 Thessalonians 2:4, αποδεικνυντα εαυτον, that is as Beza translates, *praese ferens, hebr. moreh i. facrens se apparere*, of some he is called

---

[171] Stapleton in epist. dedicat. ante princip. doctrin.
[172] In c. ecclesia, vt lite pendente, & in Concil. Lateran. sub Iu[...]o. Bald. in l. barbar. de off. praet.
[173] Gomesius de regul. cancell.

terrenus Deus or *Deus in terris*: a god upon earth.[174] In the Lateran Council it was said to him, and he heard it willingly, *Tu es alter Deus in terris*: "You are another God upon earth,"[175] in honor of that hellhound Sixtus IV, it was written and presented to his view, that he is worthily believed to be a god upon earth,

Orac'lo vocis mundi moderaris habenas,
Et merito in terris crederis esse Deus.

"By the oracle of your voice you govern the world,
and worthily are you believed to be a God upon earth."

The canonists call him "Our Lord God the pope." For so it is written not only in several old editions, but also in that new edition which by the authority of Pope Gregory XIII was corrected and published, *Credere dominum Deum nostrum Papam, conditorem dictae decretalis and istius, no sic potuisse statuere prout statuit, haereticum censeatur*: to believe that our Lord God the pope the author of this, and the aforesaid decretal, could not decree as he has decreed, it ought to be judged heretical.

And as they willingly hear themselves called God (and not only themselves hear or read it, but by their authority appoint the same to be published unto the world) so they are content to be worshiped and adored as God. Neither was the complaint of Frederick II untrue: *Pontifices Romanos affectare dominationem and diuinitatem, atque vt ab hominibus haud aliter, imó, magis quàm Deus timeantur*:[176] "That the popes of Rome affect lordship, and divinity, and that they may be feared of men no otherwise, yea more than

---

[174] Decius c. 1. de constitutionit. Cardill. pro concil trident. Bald. Cod. sentent. rescindendi. 1. vit. & de electione. Felin. c. ego. N de iure|ius.
[175] Christoph. Marcellan [concil] Lateran. sess 4. In arca triumph. Impress. Lugduni, anno. 1555
[176] Epist ad Othon. Bauar. duc. apud Aventin. lib. 7,

God." Franciscus Zabarella, a Cardinal of Rome, says: "The popes have been made to believe (such is their pride) that they can do all things that they list, even unlawful things, and that they are *plusquam Deus*, more than God."[177]

These are more than sufficient to prove that the pope takes upon him as if he were a God, although he should not in word affirm any such thing of himself. But so shameless is this Antichrist, that he affirms the like things of himself,[178] as namely: that those things which he does, are done by a divine power: and the reason is given by his lawyers, because the pope canonically elected, is a God upon earth.

Whereupon Innocent IIII uses these words, *vt nostrum prodeat de Dei vultu iudicium:*[179] that "our judgment may proceed from the face of God." That Peter and consequently his successor the pope (for to that purpose it is alleged) is assumed into the fellowship of the undivided unity. And in one place he not only affirms,[180] but by testimony also confirms that he is God.[181] *Satis euidenter* (says he)[182] *ostēditur, a seeulari potestate nec ligat prorsus, nec solvi posse pontificē, quē constat a pio principe Constantino Deū appellatū: nec posse Deū ab hominibus iudicari manifestū est.* Where the pope proves he cannot be judged by any secular power, by this reason:

- God cannot be judged of men.
- The pope is God.
- Therefore the pope may not be judged of men.

This assumption, he approves of by the forged testimony of Constantine. And therefore not unworthily by a worthy bishop in Aventin,

---

[177] Apud. Iuellum.
[178] Gregor. 9. de translat. episc. c. quanto. & canter corporalia
[179] vt eccles. benefie. c. ut nostrum. Capistran. fol. 23.
[180] Bonifac. in 8. de elect.
[181] C. Fundamenta in sexto.
[182] Distinct. 96. c. satis cuidenter.

the pope is said to be Antichrist, in whose forehead this name of blasphemy is written: *Deus sum, errare non possum.* "I am God, I cannot err."[183]

(7) But as I said, the name *Antichrist* signifies such a one as seeks to match Christ. Let us therefore further consider how this agrees to the pope. For if the pope does seek to match himself with Christ, then by this argument alone if there were no more, he may be certainly convinced to be Antichrist. In Christ we consider his natures and his offices, As touching his nature, the pope – if you will believe their blasphemies – *aeque ac Christus Deus est, ens secundae intentionis compositum ex Deo et homine*:[184] as well as Christ, he is God, a being of the second intention compounded of God and man. And as Christ in respect of the one nature is greater than man, and in regard of the other less than God, so they say of the pope, *Est quasi deus in terris, major homine, and minor Deo, plenitudinem obtinens potestatis*:[185] "He is as it were a god upon earth, greater than a man, and less than God, having the fullness of power."

That he is a man I shall not need to prove, even if some of his followers cannot well tell what to make of him. They say he is the wonderment of the world, neither God nor man, but a neuter between both.[186] That he would be supposed and acknowledged as a God, besides all the allegations in the former section, it appears also by the divine properties which are attributed to the pope. His holiness (that is to say) the pope (for his holiness is himself) is *Deus vindictae*,[187] the God of revenge, true without error, yea without possibility of erring, for he cannot err, whose will must stand for reason as if it were the rule of justice.[188]

---

[183] Lib. 7. Eberhard, [etc.]
[184] Extrau. in Ioan. 22.
[185] Ioan. a Capistr de Papae & ecclesiae authoritate.
[186] Nec deus es, nec homo: quasi neuter es inter virumque.
[187] Ps. 94. 1. Rod. Cupers de ecclesia pag. 61. num. 52.
[188] Sub finem tit de censib. exact. & procur in Clement. ad verbum volumus & Abb. Panorm. de constitut. de translat. episc. c quanto in gloss.

For even as some of his friends say he often beats upon that of the satire,[189] *Sic volo sic iubeo, sit pro ratione voluntas*: "So I will, so I command, my will must stand for reason." And therefore it were no better than sacrilege to call in question any of his doings.[190] For power, whether you understand *potestatem*, or *potentiam*, that is authority or might, he would seem to be infinite in respect of both, for infinite power is given unto him.[191]

And if unto Christ was given all power in heaven and in earth, then the pope who is his vicar has the same power.[192] He indeed is the cause of causes, of whose power none must inquire, seeing of the first cause there is no cause:[193] yea to doubt of his power, is no better than sacrilege.[194] *Excepto peccato potest quasi omnia facere quae potest Deus*:[195] "Sin excepted, the pope may do all things as it were which God may do." He can change the nature of things, yea, of nothing he can make something, and of injustice righteousness, for he has the fullness of power.[196]

(8) If you respect his office he has the same which Christ had while he was on the earth, howbeit there are great odds in their outward estates.[197] For it is not sit that the pope should resemble Christ who now is glorified in heaven, as he was contemned, but as the pastor of the whole world supernal and heavenly, and as he shall come to be our judge, to whom it is certain that all men of necessity must obey.[198] For it is evident that the work of redemption being accomplished, the power of Christ was extended as well in

---

[189] Gerochus apud Aventin. lib. 5.
[190] Dist. 40. non nos in gloss.
[191] Lib. caerem. 1. sect. 7.
[192] Cupers de eccl. pag 50. num. 45. 46. De maior. & obed. c. vnam sanctam in gloss.
[193] Bald. c. ecclesia. vt lite. pendente.
[194] In L. sacrilegij. c. de crim. sacril.
[195] Panormit. ex Hostiensi. extr. de translat. praelat. c. quanto. & de electi. c. licet.
[196] De translat. episc. c. quãto in gloss.
[197] Bellarm. *De Pont. Rom.* l. 5. c. 4.
[198] R. Cupers de eccl: pag. 50. num. 45. 46. Bellarm. de concil, l. 2. c. 17. & de pot. Rom. lib. 2. c. 31. Ioan. de turrecre. sum. de eccl. lib. 2. c. 27. & cap. 80. R. Cupers. pag. 34. num. 1. Bonifac. 8. c. quoniã de immunit. in 6. Panormit

heaven as in earth (Matthew 28): "All power is given unto me in heaven and in earth," which power is translated unto his vicar, etc., in respect of his office therefore, he is the foundation, the head, the husband, the Lord of the universal church, in unction Christ, and is therefore to be called *Christus Domini*: "the Lord's Christ."[199]

Now if it be objected that Christ alone is the head of the catholic church[200] and so of the rest,[201] answer is made, that Christ and the pope in the church are *vnū & idem caput*, one and the same head, and do make one and the same consistory,[202] for it were a monstrous thing that the church should have two heads.[203] And to the same purpose says a cardinal of Rome, "The judgment of the pope is reputed the judgment of God, and his sentence, and his consistory, the consistory of God" – and therefore Christ and the pope are not properly two heads, but one, as Boniface VIII declared in *extrav. c. vnam sanctam*.[204]

But to speak more particularly of his offices. For prophecy, he is the universal or ecumenical bishop, and pastor of pastors, the ordinary or bishop of the whole world: who is come a light into the world, but men have loved darkness more than light, who has the supreme authority of interpreting the scriptures, who is the supreme judge in controversies of religion, having an heavenly arbitration, and as it were a divine and infallible judgment, who is above general councils, for although in a general council the universal church is represented, in so much that nothing is greater than the council, *Tamen Papa eidem omnimoda supereminet authoritate*: "Notwithstanding the pope surpasses the same in all manner authority," whose judgment is to be preferred before the judgment of the whole world, insomuch that if the

---

[199] R. Cupers de eccl
[200] Ephesians 1:21-22, 4:15, 5:23, Colossians 1:28
[201] Ephesians 5:24, John 3:29, 2 Corinthians 11:2, 1 Corinthians 3:11-12
[202] R. Cupers. de eccl. pag. 128. num. 36.
[203] Idem pag. 30. num. 8.
[204] Several footnotes are hard to make out in this place, and I have thus not included them.

whole world should determine against the pope, we must stand to his sentence, for so they say, *Papae sententia totius orbis pleouo [sic.] prefertur.* And again, *Si totus mundus sentiret* (or as the gloss reads: *sententiaret*) *contra Papam, videtur quod sententiae Papae standum esset, vt 24. q. 1. haec est fides, haec gloss.* Who is of greater authority than all the saints, and in respect thereof is of great perfection then the whole body of the church besides?

But it is not sufficient for this Antichrist to prefer himself above the whole church which is the body of Christ, unless also he sought in respect of the prophetic office to match himself with Christ the head of the church – yea, and in some respects to overmatch him.

(9) He seeks to match himself with Christ:

[1] In taking upon him to make new articles of faith, and to propound doctrines not contained in the Scriptures as necessary unto salvation.

[2] In making five sacraments more than Christ appointed, (some whereof he prefers above baptism) and those two which Christ has ordained he has so altered and changed as that the one is scarcely, the other not at all the same. And whereas Christ ordained the sacrament of his body and blood in two kinds, they notwithstanding his institution will have it administered to the people but in one kind. For so it is professed in the Council of Constance, that although Christ administered this venerable sacrament unto his disciples under both kinds of bread and wine, and although in the primitive church this sacrament was received of the faithful in both kinds, notwithstanding this custom of receiving the bread only was upon good reason brought in, for the avoiding of some dangers and scandals.

[3] In making their own devices, decretals and traditions of equal authority with the word of God. Innocentius III commanded that the words of the canon of the mass should be held equal to the words of the gospel. Pope Agatho decreed that all the constitutions of the Apostolic See are to be received, as authorized by the divine voice of Peter himself. And in the same distinction, this is the title or argument of one chapter, *Inter canonic as*

Scripturas, decretales epistolae connumerantur, that is, "Among the canonical Scriptures, the decretal epistles are numbered." Which in the chapter itself is absurdly proved out of Augustine misalledged. And as touching traditions (whereby are meant all points of popery, which as themselves confess are not contained in the written word) the holy Council of Trent has ordained that they are to be received, and honored *Pari pietatis affectu ac reverentia*: with as great affection of piety and reverence, as the written word of God. This decree, when a certain bishop disliked it, Cervini the pope's legate (who afterwards was pope, called Marcellus II) caused him to be expelled out of the council.[205] And lastly, lest he should seem in anything to be inferior to Christ our prophet, he confirms his doctrines by miracles as they call them.

(10) And thus the pope matches himself with Christ our prophet: let us now consider how he advances himself above him – which he manifestly does in preferring his own and the church's authority above the scriptures. And if the church is above the Scriptures, then much more is he. For he not only *virtualiter est tota ecclesia,* that is, virtually the whole church, but also his power alone exceeds the power of all the whole church besides.[206] Now that the authority of the church and much more of the pope who is superior to the church, is above the Scripture, it is both generally affirmed and by some particulars confirmed, Cardinal Cusanus entitles his book, *De authoritate ecclesia and concilij supra and contra scripturā: Of the authority of the Church and council above and against the Scripture.*

Sylvester Prierias, master of the pope's palace, says: "Indulgences are warranted unto us, not by the authority of the Scripture, but by the authority of the Church and pope of Rome, which is greater."[207] Boniface the Archbishop of Mainz says: "That all men so revere the Apostolic See of Rome, that they rather desire the ancient institution of Christian religion

---

[205] Iacobus Nachiantes Clodiae follae episcopus. Bal. in vita Marcelli secundi.

[206] Hervaeus de potest. Tap. e. & R. Cupers. Petrus de palude, de potest. Papae […]

[207] Contra Lutheri conclusiones de potestate Papae.

from the pope, than from the holy Scriptures." This saying the pope has so approved, that he has caused it to be inserted into the canon law.[208] The particulars which prove the pope to advance himself above the Scriptures are these:

[1] Because he has, as they say, authority to add to the canonical Scriptures, other books that are not in the canon. And that those which are in the canon, have their canonical authority from him. In the 19th Distinction *cap. Si Romanorum*, Pope Nicolas not only matches their decretal epistles with the holy Scriptures, but also affirms that the Scriptures are therefore to be received, because the pope has judged them canonical. Another says, "Whosoever rests not on the doctrine of the Roman church and Bishop of Rome as the infallible rule of God, *à qua sacra scriptura robur trabis & authoritatem*, from which the sacred Scripture draws strength and authority, he is a heretic."[209] Eckius says, *Scriptura nisi ecclesiae authoritate non est authentica*: "The Scripture is not authentic but by the authority of the church." For I will not tell you how some of them have not been ashamed to say that the Scripture without the authority of the church, is of itself no better worth than Aesop's fables.[210] Pighius says, "The authority of the church is above the Scriptures, because the authority of the church has given the Scriptures canonical authority."

[2] Secondly, whereas the Scriptures are not the words and syllables, but the true sense and meaning thereof. They teach that the Scriptures are to be understood according to the interpretation of the pope and church of Rome, and that sense which the pope assigns to the Scriptures, must be taken for the undoubted word of God.[211]

"The pope, (says one) "has authority so to expound the Scriptures, that it is not lawful to hold or think the contrary." A cardinal of Rome says, "If any

---

[208] Dist. 40. c. si Papa.
[209] Sylvester Prierias Contra Lutherum
[210] Vid. Chemnitz. Exam. part. 1 pag.47
[211] Heruaus de potestate Papa

man have the interpretation of the church of Rome concerning any place of Scripture, although he neither know nor understand whether and how it agrees with the words of the Scripture, notwithstanding he has *ipsimum verbum Dei*, the very word of God."[212] And if the sense which they give is different, according to the variety of their practice and diversity of times, we must acknowledge that the Scripture is to follow the church and not the church to follow the Scriptures. Whereupon Cardinal Cusanus, "It is no marvel," (says he) "though the practice of the church expound the Scriptures at one time one way and at another time another way. For the understanding or sense of the Scripture runs with the practice. And that sense so agreeing with the practice is the quickening Spirit. And therefore the Scriptures follow the church, but contrariwise the church follows not the Scriptures."[213]

And this is that which one who was no small fool in Rome avouched, "The pope says he may change the holy gospel, and may give to the gospel according to place and time another sense."[214] And to the same purpose was the speech of that blasphemous cardinal, that if any man did not believe that Christ is very God and man, and the pope thought the same, he should not be condemned. To conclude therefore with Cardinal Cusanus,[215] "This is the judgment," (says he) "of all them that think rightly, that found the authority and understanding of the Scriptures in the allowance of the church, and not contrariwise lay the foundation of the church in the authority of the Scriptures."

(11) [3] Thirdly, the pope challenges authority above the Scriptures, when he takes upon him to dispense with the word and law of God. For

---

[212] Cardinal. Hosius de expresso Dei verbo.
[213] Nicol. Cusanus ad Bohem. epist. 7.
[214] Henricus Doctor magister sacri palatij Romae ad legatos Bohemicos sub Felice Papa. 1447.
[215] Cardinal. s. Angeli ad cosdens legatos Bohemicos. Ad Bohemos epist. 2.

whosoever takes upon him to dispense with the law of another challenges greater authority than the others, and it is a rule among themselves, *In praecepto superioris, non debet dispensare inferior*: the inferior may not dispense with the commandment of the superior.[216]

That the pope does dispense with the laws of God it is evident. For scarcely is there any sin forbidden there, where with he does not sometimes dispense, nay, whereof he will not, if it be for his advantage, make a meritorious work. Incest is an horrible sin, forbidden by the law of God and by the law of nature. And yet there is no incest, excepting that which is committed between the parents and the children, which he has not authority indeed to dispense with: for as they say, he may dispense against the law of nature. The pope dispensed with Henry VIII to marry his sister-in-law, and with Philip the late king of Spain, to marry his own niece.[217] Pope Martin V dispensed with a certain brother that married his own sister. And Clement VII licensed Petrus Alvaradus the Spaniard for a sum of money, to marry two sisters at once, etc.[218]

Disobedience to parents, perjury that is breaking of lawful oaths, rebellion against lawful princes, murdering of a sacred prince, are condemned by the law of God as heinous offenses. But if children shall cast of their parents to enter into a Sodomitic cloister, if the pope shall absolve the subjects from their oaths and forbid them to obey their princes, if he shall excommunicate a lawful prince, or suborn a wicked traitor, to murder his sovereign: then disobedience to parents, perjury and rebellion in subjects, murdering of sacred princes, is not only a warrantable but also a meritorious act. For as you have heard, *Papa ex iniustitia potest facere iustitiam*: "The pope, of sin, can make righteousness." And that the pope may thus dispense with the word of God, his canonists and divines do variously dispute. One says,

---

[216] Antonin. Part 3. tit. 22 cap.6 S.2
[217] 25 q.6 authoritatem in gloss.
[218] Antonin. Part 3. tit. 1 cap.11 S. quod Papa. sum. Angel. Dict. Papa.

Potestas in divinas leges ordinary in Romano pontifice residet:[219] "Power over the laws of God remains ordinarily in the pope of Rome." Others say, *Papa potest dispensare contra ius divinum. Privilegium contra ius divinum concedi potest:*[220] "The pope may dispense, or grant a privilege against the law of God;" that is, as another says: "he may dispense against the law of God in particular, but not in general."[221] *Papa potest dispensare contra Apostolum*: "The pope may dispense against the apostle." The pope may dispense against the New Testament upon a great cause.[222] The pope may dispense against the epistles of Paul. And to put this matter out of doubt which is so doubtfullie handled by some popish writers, this question in *Summa Angelica* is determined and decided, out of various authors approved in the church of Rome, that as in the precepts of the second table the pope cannot dispense universally (for that were not to dispense with them, but wholly to abrogate the laws themselves) but in particular cases *vbi ratio legis desicit*: where the reason of the law fails, so he may dispense with all the precepts of the Old and New Testament.

But how shall we know where the reason of the law fails? This may partly be known by those examples in the Scripture where God himself dispensed with his laws. But where there is no example of God's dispensation in the like case, then it appertains to the pope alone to declare *when* and *in what particular case* the reason of the law fails. "And I firmly believe," (says the author of that book) "that if any man, craving a dispensation in any case against the law of God, interpose not importunity of reward or suit, but simply put himself into the hands of the pope by declaring his case, that God will not suffer his vicar to err in dispensing."

So that whereas the laws and commandments of God are to be understood with this exception only *Nisi Deus ipse aliter voluerit*, unless God

---

[219] Michael Medina, Chri|stian. paraenes. lib. 7. c. 17. Gratian. part. 1. pag. 76
[220] 16. q. 1. de decimi in gloss. Dist. 34. c. Lector. 15 q. 6. authoritatem.
[221] Abb. Panorm. extr. de diuortus. cap. fin.
[222] Felin. de constitut. cap statuta canonum.

himself otherwise appoint, because he alone may dispense with his own laws: notwithstanding by the popish divinity they are to be understood with this exception: unless the pope otherwise appoints – that is: we are bound to keep every commandment of God, unless the pope interpose his authority between God and us (as the tribunes of the commonality among the Romans were wont to intercede against other magistrates) and exempt us from the obedience thereof.

(12) And as the pope may dispense with all the laws of God, so in the last place, he may and does take away some, and abrogate others. *Papa potest tollere ius diuinum ex parte non in totum:*[223] the pope may take away the law of God in part, but not in whole.

Thus he takes away the second commandment out of the decalogue, because with it his idolatry cannot stand, and to make up the full number of ten he divides the last commandment into two, against all reason and authority of antiquity. But that commandment concerning images and diverse others the pope also abrogates by his countermands. God forbids us either to worship or to serve any but himself (Matthew 4:10, 1 Samuel 7:3, Exodus 20:3).

The pope commands us to worship angels and saints, yea and the relics of saints. God forbids the making and worshiping of images, the pope commands the contrary. God condemns stews; the pope allows them – yea, one of them built a famous stews.[224] God condemns concupiscence as a sin; the pope allows it for no sin. God commands all the faithful to drink from the cup in the Lord's supper; the pope forbids the same. God commands every soul to be subject to the higher powers; the pope exempts his clergy *a iugo seculari*: from the secular yoke. God commands all to marry, who have not the gift of continence; the pope forbids all his clergy, though never so incontinent, to Mary.

---

[223] Felinus de maior. & obed. cap. fin.
[224] Six. 4. Concil. Trid. Sess. 5

Besides, it is evident that the pope's laws in the church of Rome are in greater estimation than the laws of God, the obedience of them being more straightly urged, and the disobedience thereof more severely punished, than of God's laws. As for example, it is more safe for a man in the church of Rome to be a mere atheist and a worshiper of no God, than not to be a worshiper of their god of bread, though otherwise a good Christian; better for a priest to be a Sodomite than to marry; better to be a drunkard and whoremonger than to eat flesh in Lent; better with the begging friars to set forth a new gospel (which they called the gospel of the Holy Spirit and the eternal gospel, wherein they taught that Christ is not God, and that his gospel is not the true gospel, and no more to be compared with their gospel than the nutshell is to be compared with the kernel)[225] than for that learned man William of Saint-Amour to write against them and their gospel, for him the pope disgraced and deposed from all his dignities when he would not suffer them to be disgraced: him he sent into exile, when he retained them in his high favor. Yet because he would rather *be* Antichrist than *seem* so, he caused the friars' gospel, when it was complained of, to be burnt, yet secretly; that his friars might not be disgraced nor scandalized. Better for private men to read any books of ribaldry or any villainy whatsoever, then to read any part of the Scriptures in their own tongue.

To these, many other particulars might be added wherein the pope advances his own laws above the commandments of God, and his own authority above the authority of the Scriptures. Let us therefore humbly conclude according to the popish humility, that as the pope is above the Church, so the Church is above the scriptures. *Humiliter confitemur* (says a papist) *ecclesiae authoritatem esse supra Euangelium*: "We humbly confess that the authority of the church is above the gospel."[226]

---

[225] Matthew Paris, 1254; Bal. in lib. de vitis pontif. in append; John Foxe
[226] Ioan. Maria verractus apud Iuellum.

(13) To his prophetic office let us add his priesthood. For the pope forsooth is *Pontifex Optimus Maximus* (an epithet which the Heathen give to their chief god Jupiter) he is that great priest according to the order of Melchizedek,[227] whose foot must be reverently kissed of his cardinals when he rides into any city in his *Pontificalibus*,[228] and the bishop of the city beginning this anthem, *Ecce sacerdos Magnus*: "Behold the great priest."[229] He is the prince of priests, and head of the Christian religion. He is that priest of priests, who remits both fault and punishment both to quick and dead, whereas Christ remits only to the living: and (as they say) forgives the fault but not the punishment, neither does this indulgent father grants pardon alone for sins past, but also for offenses to come.

(14) But I hasten to his kingly office. For he indeed is the king of kings and lord of lords,[230] the lion of the tribe of Judah,[231] to whom all power is given in heaven and in earth, yea and under the earth.[232] For as he has a triple crown, so he has a triple empire, in heaven and in earth, and (where Christ has none) in purgatory. His power is greater than all other created power, extending itself in some sort unto things celestial, terrestrial and infernal, so that of his power that may be verified which is said in the Psalm of Christ, and that aptly because he is Christ's vicar: "Thou hast put all things under his feet." *The beasts of the field*, that is, men living on the earth; *the fishes of the sea*, that is to say: the souls in purgatory: *the fowls of heaven*, that is to say: the angels and the souls of the blessed.

Another wrote and taught that the pope is the Lord of things in heaven, on the earth, and under the earth.[233] In heaven, for as you have heard he has

---

[227] Amicii epistol. dedi. ad Gregor. 13.
[228] Lib. carem. sect. 12. c. 5.
[229] c. fundmenta. de elect. in 6.
[230] Paul. 4 ad ducem Florentin. in bulla.
[231] Stenchus. & Sim. Begnius in orat. in concil. Lateran. sess. 6.
[232] Lib. 1. carem. sect. 7. Pius 5. in bull. ad re|gem & reginā matrē Galliae. Antonin. in sum. part. 3. tit. 22. ca. 5. §. 1. & 5. & 6. Psalm 8, Hebrews 2:8.
[233] Nicol. Egmundanus apud [Balauin].

power over the angels and saints, and souls departed. *Papa angelis praecipit, & potestatem habet in mortuos:*[234] "The pope commands the angels, and has power over the dead." In earth, for he is, *Totius orbis Dominus:*[235] "the lord of the whole earth," having *caelestis & terrestris potestatis Monarchiam:*[236] "the monarchy of the heavenly and earthly power," obtaining the kingdom of the whole world,[237] unto whom indeed belongs that prophecy, *Dominabitur à mari ad mare and à flumine us{que} adterminos orbis:*[238] "He shall rule from sea to sea, and from the river unto the ends of the world." His power reaches over all the faithful principally, and secondarily also over the infidels: for under his feet, that is, under his jurisdiction are put *the beasts of the field*, that is the Pagans; *oxen*, that is Jews and heretics; and *sheep*, that is Christians, and it extends itself unto all the parts of the world, not only known but also unknown, insomuch that the parts of the new found world are at his disposition to distribute and bestow.[239]

And that the Pagans are subject to the pope it appears, because the pope rules the world instead of Christ. But Christ has full jurisdiction over every creature. Seeing therefore that the pope is Christ's vicar, no man may lawfully withdraw himself from his obedience, even as none may lawfully withdraw himself from the obedience of God. *Anton. part. 3. tit. 22. §. 8.* The deacon who invested the pope was wont to use these words: "I invest you into the papacy, *Vt praesis vrbi & orbi*: That you may rule both the city and the world." And likewise the Cardinal Bishop that anointed him, used this form of words: *Egoto inungo in pontificem vrbis and orbis.* Now this empire or

---

[234] Camotensis
[235] Epist. ded. Amicij ad Gregor. 15. praefix. Capistr.
[236] De Maior c. vnam sanctam.
[237] Extra de statu regular. [periculum] in gloss.
[238] Lib 1. caerem. sect. 7. & capistran. fol. 57.
[239] Capistran. 2.2. fol. 24. Antonin. part. 3. tit. 22. §. 8. Alexander distributed the new-found world, between the kings of Spain and Portugal. Lib. 1. caerem. sect. 1. c. 4. Cardin. Episcopus. Hostiensis

monarchy which the pope has over the whole world is twofold,[240] for he has the two swords, as it is stoutly proven out of the gospel, where one of Christ's disciples says, *Ecce duo gladij,* "Behold two swords:" civil and ecclesiastical.[241] For as Pope Nicholas says, *Christus beato aeternae vitae clauigero terreni simul and coelestis imperij iura commisit:*[242] "Christ has given to blessed Peter the key bearer of eternal life (and so to the pope) the right both of the earthly and heavenly empire."[243]

Civil, as has been shown over all kings and rulers, in respect whereof he writes himself "king of kings," for all secular power is immediately given to the pope: and he is above kings even in temporal matters, yea he alone is the true lord of temporal things. Wherefore Pope Boniface VIII, sent unto Philip the French king and told him that he was lord both in spiritual and also in temporal matters, throughout the world. "And therefore that the king should hold his kingdom at his hand, and honor and worship him, *Vt dominum regni sui*: as the lord of his realm, (Stenchus), for otherwise to think and hold, (he said) it was heresy.[244]

And as touching the Roman Empire, the government thereof belongs to the pope, being God's vicar on earth, as unto him by whom kings do reign. And surely whosoever denies the temporal sword to be in the power of Peter, does full ill attend to the word of the Lord, saying unto him, "Put up thy sword into the sheath."[245] And did not the Lord, I beseech you (as some

---

[240] Capistran. 2.2. fol. 24. Antonin. part. 3. tit. 22. §. 8. Alexander distributed the new-found world, between the kings of Spain and Portugal. Lib. 1. caerem. sect. 1. c. 4. Cupers, *De Eccles.* Pag. 337

[241] Capistran. 2.2. fol. 24. Antonin. part. 3. tit. 22. §. 8. Alexander distributed the new-found world, between the kings of Spain and Portugal. Lib. 1. caerem. sect. 1. c. 4. Boniface 8. de maior. c. vnam sanctam.

[242] Capistran. 2.2. fol. 24. Antonin. part. 3. tit. 22. §. 8. Alexander distributed the new-found world, between the kings of Spain and Portugal. Lib. 1. caerem. sect. 1. c. 4. Dist. 22.c.1. omnes

[243] Ioan de Parisijs de potestat. Pap. cap. 20. Ioan. Maior. 4. sent. q. 2. dist. 20.

[244] Martinus Polonus. & in epist. ad eundē, [scire] te volumus, quòd in spiritualibus & temporalibus nobis subes. Nicol. Gillius. annatium gallic, scriptor

[245] Caeremon. lib. 1. cap. 2.

of the pope's favorites full solemnly dispute),[246] command Peter in Luke 5:4 to launch into the deep, that he might signify the height of power in Peter?[247] And again, why did the Lord send Peter only to the sea to fish with an angle or hook, but that he would insinuate that he intended to set Peter over the whole surging sea of this tempestuous world? And why does he command him to fish with an iron hook, but that he was disposed to commit unto him the sword both of the spiritual and temporal empire?

Hereunto we may add that worthy dispute of Antoninus Archbishop of Florence, *part. 3. tit. 22. cap. 5. §. 17*, that the pope – being the vicar of Jesus Christ in the whole world – has, instead of the living God, the universal jurisdiction both of spiritual and temporal things.[248] But the immediate administration of temporal things he receives not unless in the regions of the Western Empire by reason of the grant made to the church by Constantine. Now, that he uses not the temporal administration in other countries, but only in the parts of Italy etc. this is not for want of authority, but that he would nourish in his sons the bond of peace and unity. For since the empire was divided, and in several parts differently and tyrannically usurped, the church – to avoid the scandal of the Jews – has made herself tributary with Peter, etc.

And as touching those who say the pope has dominion over the whole world, not in temporal matters but in spiritual ones only, they are like the counselors of the king of Syria, who said in 1 Kings 20: "their gods are gods of the mountains and not of the valleys." For so they say the popes are gods of the mountains, that is of spiritual goods, but they are not gods of the valleys, because they have not the dominion of temporal goods. And in the

---

[246] De maior. & obed. cap. vnam sanctam.
[247] Ioan. Capistr. de Pap. & ec|cl. author. 1. 2. sol. 21. & 122. duc in [altum] designaret altitudinem potestatis &c. s. 15.
[248] Ioan. Capistr. de Pap. & ec|cl. author. 1. 2. sol. 21. & 122. duc in [altum] designaret altitudinem potestatis &c. s. 15.

same place he adds that "from the sentence of all kings and princes, men may appeal to the pope."

As touching his ecclesiastical authority which (as some say)[249] is the foundation of the church, he is superior and greater than all the residue of the universal church, and this is proved by seven arguments: [1] because he is the pastor of the universal church,[250] [2] because he is the head of the universal church, [3] because he is that prelate which has authority over the whole church, [4] because he is the prince of the universal church, [5] because he has supreme power in the church, [6] because he alone has fullness of power in the church, and [7] because he is Christ's vicar general in the whole universal church.

For in the Apostolic See, the Lord has placed the princehood of the whole church,[251] and therefore worthily is he called *Ecclesiae princeps ac rex regū torra*: "the prince of the church and king of the kings of the earth;"[252] yea *Princeps optimus maximus*:[253] "of whom the salvation of the church universal after God depends."[254] He is the head, the root, the monarch, the fountain of ecclesiastical power, having the same consistory with God, and judgment seat with Christ. For so they write: *Idem tribunal Christi & Papa in terris: Inter Papam and Deum vnum & idem sit tribunal, vnumque & idem consistorium*:[255] "He makes laws which bind the conscience and that with guilt of mortal sin" – he is the living law,[256] yea he has all laws in the closet of his breast, and he can dispose above law and retains the fullness of power so as he needs no

---

[249] Th. Aquin. in 2. sent. in fine. Antonin. part. 3 tit. 22. cap. 6. §. 6.
[250] de turrecrem. in summ. de eccles. lib. 2. cap. 80.
[251] Dist. II. c. nolite errare.
[252] I. de turrecrem lib. 3. summ. cap. 9.
[253] Amicij epist. dedic. ad Gregor. 13. praefix. Capistr.
[254] Dist. 40. c. si Papa, et R. Cis. pers pag. 29. Ioan. Andreas in c. quanto de translat. Panorm. c licet. de elect.
[255] I. de turrecrem. summ. lib. 2. cap. 8. & R. Cupers. pag. 29. n. 16. & 42. n. 14.
[256] R. Cupers. pag. 62. n. 66. de constitut. c. licet in sexto. R. Cupers. pag. 29. n. 1.

addition,[257] he alone has the fullness of power, as being the prince of the church's laws.

And even as the first mover governs the church triumphant, so does the pope rule the church militant.[258] For seeing in the church triumphant there is one sovereign prince to whose obedience that whole church is most perfectly subject, that is to say, God: it follows necessarily that one sovereign prince rules over the whole church militant, that is to say the pope, whose commandments all are bound to obey.[259] And thus much of the pope's power, in heaven and in earth, in respect whereof it is said that the jurisdiction and care of the whole world is committed to the pope, not only as by the name of the world is imported the earth, but also as by the name of the world is imported heaven, because he has received jurisdiction over heaven and earth.[260]

(16) There remains the third part of his kingdom which he has in purgatory. For as one of their approved authors says, *Purgatorium est peculium Papae*:[261] "Purgatory is the pope's peculiar," where, as also in hell, he has so great authority, as that by his indulgences, he is able to deliver thence so many souls as it pleases him, and to place them in heaven and in the seats of the blessed.[262] Insomuch as this is become a problem in the church of Rome, whether the pope may empty all purgatory wholly and at once, and by Antoninus the Archbishop of Florence it receives this determination under a threefold distinction, namely: that in respect of his absolute jurisdiction the pope may be communicating his indulgences absolve all that are in purgatory from that pain, and so make a jail delivery.[263]

---

[257] I de turrecrem. l. 3. c 64.
[258] R. Cupers. de eccl. pag 166 n. 28.
[259] Clement. lib. 5. de haereticis. c. ad nostrum in gloss.
[260] Antonin. sum part. 3. tit. [22]. §. 1.
[261] Angelus Parisiensis.
[262] Fulm brut. ex. bulla Clement. 6.
[263] Antonin. part. 3. tit. [22] cap. 5. §. 6. & 7.

For seeing Gregory the Pope by his prayer absolved Trajan from the pain of hell which is infinite, therefore much more may the pope by communication of indulgences absolve all that are in purgatory from that punishment which is but finite. And forasmuch as Christ may take away all pain, therefore the pope also – who is his vicar – may. This the pope may do in respect of his absolute power. But if you regard the orderly execution thereof, in that respect the pope may not nor ought so to do. Neither indeed is he pleased to let out any from the pains of purgatory unless he be well pleased for his indulgences and pardons. Howbeit I must needs confess, it was a cheap year of souls when Leo X sent Torelius about with his pardons, offering to everyone for the payment of ten shillings (but not a penny under) to set at liberty the soul of any one which they should name in purgatory And lastly if you respect God's acceptation, that is, whether God would take it well that the pope should release all that be in purgatory at once, or not, Antoninus answered, "He cannot tell." And to conclude this kingly office of the pope with that venerable acclamation of the reverend fathers in the council of Lateran, "You are all and above all, to you all power is given in heaven and in earth." And again, "In the pope is all power above all powers in heaven and in earth."[264]

And thus it appears evidently that the pope is Antichrist, not only because he is an adversary opposed unto Christ, as was proved in the former chapter, but also because he is *aemulus* and as it were a counter-christ, who seeking to match our Savior Christ, "advanceth himself above all that is called God, or that is worshiped, insomuch that he sitteth in the temple of God as God," showing and demeaning himself as though he were a god upon earth.

---

[264] Sess. 10. in orat. Steph. Patracensis.

Chapter 6
Of other vices or sins of Antichrist.

(1) Now are we to entreat of other vices and sins of Antichrist. For albeit by the application of the two former notes concerning the opposition of Antichrist unto Christ, and his incredible ambition in advancing himself above all that is called God, it plainly appears that the pope of Rome merits to be called by that peculiar title of *Antichrist*, the man of sin, because those two notes wherein the apostle insists as sufficient proofs thereof, do most properly agree unto him.[265]

Notwithstanding, many other notorious sins of the popes may be produced for the further evidence of this truth, of which sins some are common to very many of them, and some are common to them all. For howsoever the crimes and enormities of such deep dissemblers, as these Antichristian popes have been, were many times either not commonly known to the world, or being known were not communicated to posterity, the writers of those times being for the most part the servile flatterers of Antichrist: yet notwithstanding many of them were known, and of those which were known many are recorded to have been guilty of fearful crimes, besides those which either were not known or not recorded.

For to begin with their horrible impiety towards God, have not many of these most holy fathers betrayed themselves to be very atheists and scorners of religion? Such were those which before I named:[266] John XXIV, Alexander VI, Sixtus IV, Paulus III, Julius II, Julius III, Leo X, and besides them, John XII a.k.a. XIII who used to blaspheme God, and at his dice to call upon the devil, and in his feasts to drink unto him.[267] Many of them also (as commonly those which renounce God betake themselves to the devil)

---
[265] 2 Thessalonians 2:3-4
[266] See Chapter 4 Section 8
[267] Luitprandus lib. 6. Fascic, temp.

have been known sorcerers and necromancers, besides those which were not known. It is recorded even by popish authors of Sylvester II that he did homage to the devil, and that by the devil he was placed in the papacy, to which end he had be, taken himself both in body and soul to the devil.[268] Such a one was Gregory VII, as Cardinal Benno testifies, and such also were all the popes from Sylvester II to Gregory VII.

But among them, Benedict VIII a.k.a. IX, who before his papacy was called *Theophylact*, is most worthy to be remembered. For he was wont in woods and mountains to sacrifice to the devil, and by magical art to allure women unto him. He kept a sparrow which brought him news from all coasts. And when he had sold the papacy to Gregory VI for 1,500 pounds and thought by sorcery to recover it again as he first had gotten it, and to that end consulted with the devil, he had his neck wrung in sunder; his successor Gregory VI, being a sorcerer as well as he, and now as it may seem in greater favor with the devil then he. And to these three which I have named some twenty more may be added. But now I come to speak of their sins against the second table.

(2) For many of them have been murderers and otherwise barbarously cruel. As for example Gregory VII, who poisoned six popes to make himself a way to the papacy, and sought to murder Henry the Emperor as he was at his prayers in the church.[269] Innocent IV sought to poison Conrade the Emperor. Clement VI caused the Emperor Louis of Bavaria to be poisoned. King John was poisoned by a monk when the pope had given a sentence that he should be deposed, and so was Henry of Luxembourg even in the eucharist, and that as some report by the appointment of the pope.

By the pope was William Parry suborned to murder our gracious Queen Elizabeth; so was the Jacobine that murdered Henry III, King of France. In the church at Florence a massacre was intended, and Giuliano de' Medici

---

[268] Fascic. tempo. Stella. Platina. &c.
[269] Bal. ex Mario Mat. Paris. in Henr. 3.

murdered by the appointment of Sixtus IV, the elevation of the sacrament being made the sign or watchword when this murder should begin.[270]

Alexander VI, for 200,000 crowns, poisoned the great Turk's brother who was at Rome. He also, or as some say, his son, appointed his servants to minister poison to certain cardinals and senators whom he had invited, but the servers, mistaking the cups and giving him from the same, dispatched of him together with the rest. Paul III poisoned his mother and his nephew, that to him might descend the whole inheritance of the Farnesian family.[271] He poisoned his sister whom he used as his harlot, because she fancied others more than himself: and that he might more freely abuse his own daughter Constantia, he poisoned Bosius Sfortia her husband. He poisoned one bishop and two cardinals because they inclined to the gospel. I might be long in this argument, but these may serve for a taste.

But if besides these you desire to hear some other examples of their cruelty, you may remember how Stephen VI caused the body of Formosus the pope to be taken out of the grave, and having cut of two of his fingers and cast them into the Tiber, he buried the body among the laity: which body eight years after Sergius III caused again to be taken out of the grave, and having cut of the other three fingers, he cast them and the body itself into the said river, and condemned him and all his acts, which other popes notwithstanding as Romanus I, Theodorus II, and John X ratified and approved. Likewise Boniface VIII caused the body of Hermannus of Ferrara, who before had been canonized for a saint, after 30 years to be plucked out of his grave, and to be burnt. Urbanus VI cast seven cardinals into prison because they favored Clement VII and in spite of him put five of them into sacks and drowned them. And this is some part of their behavior among themselves. For of their cruelty toward the saints and martyrs of Jesus, who is able sufficiently to entreat?

---

[270] Volaterran. geograph. lib. 5. & Politianus de coniuratione Pactiana.
[271] Bal. *De Rom. Pont. actis.*

(3) To their cruelty, I will add their perfidious treachery and traitorous practices, especially towards the emperors and princes of Christendom. For firstly, the emperors of Greece, by the pope's rebellious opposition against their sovereign lords in the ungodly defense of images, were bereaved of their dominions in the West, by which means the empire – being rent asunder and weakened – way was made for the Turk. And however at first they seemed to honor their newly erected emperors in the West whom they created for their own defense, yet afterward they never ceased until they had gotten superiority over them. And ever since it has been their practice to strengthen and advance themselves and their own See by weakening and dejecting the emperor and all other Christian princes. And this they had effected by several devilish policies. As first they have used to pick quarrels against them, and upon any pretext or color of a just quarrel to excommunicate them and to absolve their subjects from their obedience. And if by these means they would not be brought into subjection, then to depose them if they could, and to set up others against them. And if other means failed, to raise up wars against them, and to send forth Crusades into all Christendom with large indulgences and promises of heaven to all that would fight their battles. And besides this, they have also forbidden all other Christians to use any traffic with them and their subjects: and not only that, but they have exposed the princes themselves, sometimes their subjects also, to the violence of murderers, and their countries and kingdoms as a prey to spoilers, warranting any to bereave the prince or the subject of their lives, and to take their kingdom as a prey.

Thus besides many others was Emperor Henry IV used by Gregory VII and Paschal II, who not only excommunicated the worthy emperor, absolved his subjects from obedience, but also both under hand suborned such as should murder him, and openly set up against him in the empire, first Rodolphus the duke of Sweden, and then his own son: and in the end the good emperor being deposed, imprisoned, and dead in prison, his body might not for five years be vouchsafed Christian burial. Thus was Otto IV used by Innocentius III, and Louis IV by John XXII, Benedict XII, and Clement VI, by whose means also he was poisoned. Thus several kings of France, besides him that now is, have been entreated.

But especially Louis XII, a good king, by Julius II, a notable Antichrist. For he not only excommunicated Lewis, and interdicted his land, but also stirred up all Christians against him, promising great indulgence and pardon of all sins, to everyone that should by any means whatsoever kill any Frenchman. In his own person also he went to war against him, and as he being armed brought forth his army on the bridge over Tiber, he cast his keys into the river, and drew his sword, using this speech in the hearing of many thousands: "Seeing as Peter's keys do naught avail us, I will therefore use Paul's sword."

And to conclude, thus also have our kings been dealt with, as king John, and Henry VIII and our gracious Queen Elizabeth, whom (to omit the other) the popes have excommunicated, absolved her subjects from obedience, as much as in them lies deposed her from her crown, exposed her to the violence of her secret and open enemies, raised rebellions against her, suborned cutthroats to murder her, sent forces into Ireland to win that kingdom from her, stirred up the Spaniard and aided him against her, and lastly by an Antichristian devotion, given her realm of Ireland to the Spaniard. But whom Antichrist cursed, Christ blessed, insomuch that, having through the Lord's goodness outlived eight popes since she came to the crown, in the end after a long and happy reign she died in peace. Another practice of Antichrist has been this: to bereave the right owners of their crowns and kingdoms, and to set up others which had no right, that they being advanced by his means, should be obliged as vassals and feed men unto his See.

And to this end, when contentions have risen between Christian princes, he has not only nourished the same, but also taken part with the one against the other; that the one being by his means vanquished and overcome, the other may acknowledge the pope for his good lord. To this end was the title of the Roman Empire translated from the Greeks to the French in Charlemagne, and from the French to the Germans in Otto, whom the pope caused to swear homage and fealty to him. To this end, Pepin was crowned King of France, and Childeric deposed and shorn a monk. But I shall not need to insist in the enumeration of examples, for scarcely is there any kingdom in Europe, if any at all, which the pope has not in former times by these and other means made subject and tributary to his See, using the kings as his vassals and making them swear homage unto him.[272]

A third stratagem which the popes have used to weaken the emperors and princes of Christendom, and strengthen themselves, has been this: to persuade them to go with their forces and chief of their strength into Palestine for the recovery of the Holy Land from the Turks and Saracens; that in their absence he might work his will in any part of Europe, not fearing their strength if they should return, being weakened by those wars; but rather hoping they should not return to make resistance. And to this purpose consider only the dealing of Alexander III and Gregory IX with the emperors Frederick I and II.

For Alexander III – fearing the power of Frederick Barbarossa – by Hartmannus the Bishop of Brixia, persuaded him to go with his army into Palestine for the recovery of the Holy Land. In the meantime, the pope sent a picture of the emperor to the sultan, persuading him that he would apprehend him by some secret ambush, which happened accordingly. The emperor, having been released by the sultan, after his return came to Venice, where the pope as you heard before trod on his neck, etc.

The other Frederick was first excommunicated by Gregory IX because he did not go to Palestine according to his appointment, at the length to satisfy the pope's pleasure.[273] He took his voyage, and having recovered

---

[272] Vide Fulm. brutum pag. 74.
[273] Bal. ex Mario & Matth. Paris.

Jerusalem and other places from the sultan, and made truce with him for ten years, he sent these glad tidings to the pope, who having received the letters, caused the messengers to be slain, and gave out that the Emperor was dead. For the pope having a month's mind[274] to the kingdoms of Sicily and Puglia, whereof Frederick was the true heir, desired according to Saul's old policy against David, to have him dispatched by the infidels, and to that end was so earnest to have him gone. For in his absence, he seized on those kingdoms, and wrote to the sultan that he should in no case restore Jerusalem unto the emperor. And when the emperor returned, the pope excommunicated him again, because he had made truce with the sultan, and would not absolve him until he had paid for his absolution on 100,000 ounces of gold.

(4) But now the filthy lechery of these hollow fathers, who would seem so chaste as to condemn marriage in their clergy, offers itself to be spoken of. For although it be a rule among them, *Si non caste, tamen caute*: "If not chastely, yet carefully," and one of their popes professes:[275] *Honestius esse pluribus occulte implicari: quàm aperte in hominum vultu and conscientia cum vna ligari*: that "it is more honest to have to do with many women in secret, then openly in the face and notice of men to be tied to one, whether in marriage or otherwise" – and therefore in all likelihood, a small part of their uncleanness (which they sought by all means to conceal) is known to the world.

Yet notwithstanding, very many of them have been detected and known to be most filthy fornicators and adulterers, besides John VIII or rather Joan who was a harlot in man's apparel, and was delivered of a child in open procession. In this bed-role of whoremongers and adulterers (besides those which I either know not or do not remember) are numbered, by several authors, these which follow: Sergius III, who by the notable strumpet Marozia begot John XII, Zando, who in fornication begat John XI, and

---

[274] A requiem mass observed a month after a person has died.
[275] Nicol. I

spent his time among harlots – both these Johns being as bad or worse than their fathers. John XIII also was so given to whoredom as that he is said to have turned the palace of Lateran into a stew. And being at length taken in adultery, he was wounded to death by the husband of the adulteress. Such were John XIV, XIX, XXI, and XXIV. Likewise Benedict VI and IX, who by sorcery allured women unto him, and made them follow him up and down like Cades.

In like manner, Benedict XII, who kept many strumpets, and among others the sister of Francis Petrarch, whom by great rewards he had purchased of her brother Gerhard. Such were Christopher I and Callixtus III Gregory VI, and Gregory VII called Hildebrand, who as also Victor III were very inward with Maude the countess. Innocent IV had many bastards, and so had Innocent VIII, who also used to paint his face. Nicolas III by his concubine begat a child which in nails and hair was like a bear, which some impute to the pictures of bears which he, being of the ursine family, had caused to be made in his house. And therefore Martin IV, who kept the same concubine, fearing the like mischance, caused the pictures of the bears to be taken away. Boniface VIII kept many harlots, and had several "nephews" by them – for so they call their bastards. Clement V was a common whoremonger and patron of harlots, and so were Clement VI, Clement VII, Clement VIII, who was even worse than such, and Clement VIII that now is, has been no better than he should be. And such were Pius IV who died between two harlots, and Sixtus V of late memory, etc.

(5) These are ordinary matters in the Romish votaries, among whom those popes may be counted for men of the chaster sort, who have offended only by fornication and adultery. But, as very many of their votaries, so also several of the popes have fearfully sinned against nature by incest and sodomy.

Neither are we to marvel thereat, seeing they do not only embrace the means of lust, as idleness, fullness of bread, and abundance of worldly delights and carnal pleasures, but also reject the remedy appointed of God, which is marriage; but especially because they being idolaters are by the just judgment of God given over to their lusts and to a reprobate sense, insomuch that they commit abominations against nature. It is recorded of John XIII and XXIII a.k.a. XXIV that, besides all other their whoredoms and adulteries, the one committed incest with Stephana, his father's concubine; and the other with his brother's wife. Alexander VI – not contented with several other strumpets which he kept, by whom he had six bastards – committed incest with his own daughter Lucretia. He also gave leave to Cardinal Mendoza to abuse his own bastard son in incestuous sodomy and sodomite incest. Paul III committed incest with two of his nieces, prostituted one of his sisters to Alexander VI, to get a cardinalship, and poisoned another because she affected some other of her lovers more then himself, neither did he abstain from his own daughter Constantia. Of Pius V, it is said that he kept incestuous company with his own sister.

Sixtus IV was not only a filthy whoremonger and sodomite himself, but also – to incite and encourage others to the same filthiness – he built a famous stew, not only of women, but also of males also. And he gave license to the Cardinal of St. Lucy and to all his family; that they might in the three hot months of the year freely use sodomy. Julius II abused unto Sodomy, besides others, two young noblemen of France, whom Anne the Queen had sent to Rome and committed to a cardinal to be informed. Julius III made his "Ganymede," a cardinal, and neither did he as some write abstain from committing sodomy with the cardinals themselves. His Legate at Venice (a fit cover for such a pot) Johannes a Casa. Archbishop of Beneventum, set forth a book in Italian meter in commendation of this sin, for which the Lord destroyed Sodom and Gomorrhe with fire and brimstone from heaven. Such sinners against nature were, as authors testify, Benedict I, Clement VII, John XIII, XIV, and XXIV, Leo X, and Paul III, whose bastard son Petrus Aloysius, I cannot pass over with silence.

For he, treading in his father's steps, and being greatly loved and advanced by him, besides incest with his sister Constantia, and rapes with other women, and buggery with several men, he forced a sodomite rape upon Cosmus Cherius a worthy bishop, using the help of his men to hold him by violence, while he committed that outrageous act. But it is shameful to speak that which they are not ashamed to do.

(6) And yet this is not all that is to be alleged against the popes, that several of them have been atheists, many of them sorcerers, murderers, traitors, adulterers, and sodomites. For many of them have been most foul monsters (as some of their own writers call them) compounded of these and other horrible crimes. Such, besides others, were Sixtus IV, John XXIV, Alexander VI, Clement VII, and Paul III, etc. Neither may it be objected that, although several popes have been men of sin, yet many of them have been holy men and saints of God, and consequently not Antichrists. For however all the Roman bishops of the first 600 years are revered as saints and so called of popish writers, as Saint Sylvester, Saint Leo, Saint Gregory etc. a very few only excepted, yet a very few of them which have lived this thousand years are even by popish flatterers esteemed saints, and those few which are, are honored among them not for any true holiness, but either for the Antichristian advancing of their See, or for some supposed miracles which were no better than the lying signs and wonders of Antichrist.[276]

But so far indeed these apostatic popes have been from being saints in the sight of God, that all of them have deserved to be called men of sin, sons of perdition, outlaws, although some of them were not so wicked as the rest. Men of sin, because besides those peculiar sins wherewithal every of them were severally infected, the whole order or succession of them has been guilty of many other crimes also, as common to them all, several whereof the Holy Spirit has set down as notes of Antichrist. As namely those which I

---

[276] Onuphr. Pontif. Romani. Chronologia praefixa chatechismo Canisij.

have already proven to be in the pope, heresy, opposition or enmity to Christ, apostasy, hypocrisy, and Satanic pride.

For if the pope is a heretic or false prophet teaching the doctrines of devils, if a notorious hypocrite, if an apostate, yea the head of the catholic apostasy, if an adversary opposed unto Christ, though a covert and disguised enemy, if the king of pride advancing himself most insolently above all that is called God, as we have proven him to be, then we need not doubt, but that in respect of these sins though he had no more, he deserves to be called the man of sin.

(7) But unto these, diverse others may be added, as first and principally the idolatry, superstitious and counterfeit religions of the pope and church of Rome. For the whore of Babylon, whereby is signified the Antichristian state, is described in the scriptures not only as a spiritual adulteress, but also as the mother of all fornications and abominations in the earth, which with the golden cup of her fornications, that is idolatries and superstitions, has made drunk the kings and inhabitants of the earth.[277] Now the idolatry of the pope and church of Rome is manifold and grievous.

[1] As first, to the bread in the sacrament, which being a small creature they worship as their maker and redeemer, neither do they think that they can worship it enough, and therefore in the worship thereof the chief part of their solemn service consists.

[2] Secondly to the cross and crucifix, and images of the trinity, all which as they teach are to be worshiped with divine worship, and are so worshiped among them.

[3] Thirdly, to the blessed virgin Mary, who has been worshiped among them as much or rather more than God. Her, they call their *lady* and *goddess*, and *queen of heaven*. In her they repose their trust and affiance, to her they fly in their necessity, of her they crave all good things, and from her they expect

---

[277] Revelation 17

remission of sins and eternal salvation, in honor of her they have devised and used various services, as offices, litanies, rosaries, psalters etc. full of blasphemous idolatries.

[4] Fourthly to saints departed, who have succeeded the tutelary gods of the heathenish Romans, there being almost no country, city, parish, trade or profession which had not their several saints to patronize them, no disease nor other calamity in themselves or their cattle for which they had not their peculiar saints, as it were *Auerruncos deos*: to turn away those evils from them. In the merits of saints they trust for remission of sin and for eternal life. Them they adore, to them they pray, and not only them do they worship, but also their images also and relics – wherein the papists are more gross idolaters than the very heathen.

For the Gentiles did not worship the images themselves, but the persons represented by them; but the papists hold that the very same worship is due to the image which belongs to the person whom it resembles. To these notorious idolatries, we may add their various counterfeit religions and orders devised or authorized by the pope,[278] which are so many by-paths misleading men out of the only true way which leads unto heaven, and besides them innumerable traditions, superstitions, trumperies, and fooleries.[279]

Upon all which notwithstanding the fond people of all nations, in these parts of the world, have so strangely doted, as that they may most truly be said to have been besotted and made drunk with the wine of the whore of Babylon's fornications, that is to say, with the idolatries and superstitions of the Church of Rome.

(8) Upon their spiritual adultery, that is to say, their manifold and gross idolatry, has followed their carnal adultery and uncleanness. For seeing by

---

[278] Papa solus nouas religiones creat, & approbat.
[279] Antonin. part. 3. tit. 22. cap. 5. §. 21.

their idolatry they had dishonored God, as the Gentiles did, therefore the Lord has given over them also to their hearts' lusts unto uncleanness.

Neither have they only been guilty of uncleanness in themselves, but also the causes thereof in others; while they extenuate the sin of fornication as though it were but a venial sin, and reckon adultery among the less and lighter offenses: whiles they dispense with these sins and give men leave to committee them without controlment, or else assign unto them ridiculous punishments: but especially whiles they forbid marriage unto all their clergy, and maintain open stews. For in forbidding marriage they open a gap to all uncleanness.

Tolle de ecclesia (says Bernard) *honorabile coniugium and thorum immaculatum, nonne reples eam concubinarijs, incestuosis, seminifluis, mollibus, masculorū concubitoribus, and omni deni{que} genere immundorum?* "Take out of the church honorable marriage and the bed undefiled, and do you not fill it with keepers of concubines, incestuous fellows, Gomorrahans and Sodomites, and in a word with all kinds of unclean persons?"

For proof hereof, read but the acts of English votaries, who yet may not be compared with those of hotter countries, remember the survey taken here in England before the dissolution of abbeys, wherein our irreligious houses were found to be little better than stews of both sorts; not to speak of their secular priests who were known for the most part to have been the town-bulls were they dwelt.[280]

Neither will I tell you of the innumerable murders of infants, besides those which died in their mothers' wombs to prevent their parents shame. As for common stews, they are maintained not only in other popish countries and cities, but even in Rome itself, and not only maintained by the pope, but maintainers also of the pope, to whom they pay as if he were their baud a yearly pension, which amounts sometimes to 30,000, sometimes to 40,000 ducats. It is said of Paul III that in his tables he had the names of 45,000

---

[280] Vid. praefat. I. Bale ad lectore libri sui de actis Pontif.

courtesans who paid a monthly tribute unto him. Which, besides his patronizing of filthiness, argues his coveting of filthy lucre, of which we are also briefly to speak. For of him in respect of these two vices, filthiness and covetousness, it was said in old time,

Eius auaritiae totus non sufficit orbis:
Eius luxuriae meretrix non sufficit omnis.[281]

"Neither does the whole world suffice his covetousness,
nor all harlots his lechery."

(9) Of the insatiable avarice of the pope and court of Rome many instances might be given. For they have found out innumerable ways and means to scrape together incredible sums of money out of all countries, without measure or modesty, without shame or show of honesty. But it shall be sufficient by application of Peter's prophecy concerning false teachers in these latter times,[282] to show, that through covetousness they have with feigned words and doctrines of their own coining made merchandise of all those that would hearken unto them.

As for example, they have feigned that Peter was ordained of Christ the monarch of the whole church, that to him was committed the right both of the spiritual and temporal monarchy; that in this monarchy the pope succeeds Peter as Christ's vicar general, as the universal bishop, as the lord of the whole earth. They have feigned a *Donation of Constantine* wherein he should not only give the city of Rome to the pope, but also resign unto him the whole empire of the West. Upon these grounds they have obtained both of princes and prelates, which their greedy covetousness armed with such authority shamed not to demand. England, France, Germany and other

---

[281] Mat. Paris in identic. 3
[282] 2 Peter 2:3

countries have been exceedingly; or, as some speak, miserably impoverished by the intolerable exactions of the pope and his court.[283]

For firstly, the first fruits he claimed of all spiritual promotions, which in these parts of Europe subject to that See, did amount unto 2,460,843 florens.[284] The first fruits of the spiritual livings in France, and the charges of obtaining the same livings, have been observed in three years, to amount unto 946,666 French crowns.[285] By the same title he took upon him to bestow or rather to sell openly and without shame the livings of the church: and not only when they were void, but also before hand, and that to various men. Insomuch that sometimes ten, sometimes twelve have purchased advowsons or reversions of the same preferments against the next avoidance.[286] But which of all them, when the living fell, was to have the benefit of the pope's grant, that was to be decided at Rome: whither they were to their great charge, but to the enriching of the Romish harpies, to repair. This gainful trade may well be called making merchandise of men: for together with the benefices the poor people were bought and sold. In respect here of Blondus says that "all Europe almost sends tributes to Rome, greater or at least equal to the revenues of the old times," *Dum singulae ciuitates à Romano pontifice boneficia sacerdotalia accipiunt*, while the spiritual promotions in every city are received from the pope.[287]

Moreover his yearly perquisites of elections, preventions, dispensations, licenses and many such like merchandises the titles whereof, with their taxes or prices, are set down in the book called *Taxae cancellariae Apostolicae*, are thought to surmount 900,000 florens – not to speak of his smoke-farthings and Peter-pence, which nevertheless did arise to no small sum. But besides his ordinary taxations, his extraordinary exactions were intolerable. For he

---

[283] Ludouic. 9. [obstit] an. 1228. tit. de [tallij]
[284] Jewel. ex lega|tione Hadrian. 6. excus. Wittembergae. 153
[285] Fulm. brut. ex postulatis senatus Paris. Ludovico [...]
[286] Ibid. art. [62]
[287] Rom. instaur. Lib. 3

has not been ashamed to demand the tenths of all spiritual livings, in some whole realms, for many years together: yea sometimes the third part of their living that were resident, and the half of theirs that were non residents, and that for several years – and sometimes also all the money and goods of them that deceased.[288] Out of France alone in the time of Pope Martin V, the pope and court of Rome received nine million. In England, the pope's prayer was almost as great as the revenues of the crown, as Bonner testifies.

(10) But his most odious merchandise is his setting to sale all manner of sin, which is called *Taxa poenitentiaria apostolica*, whereby is promised impunity to everyone who having committed any sin, be it never so grievous, pays according to the rate for his absolution: as namely for adultery, incest, sodomy, the abomination not to be spoken of committed with beasts, willful murder, parricide, perjury, and such like. Hereof a notable canonist writes thus:

Curia vult marcas, bursas exhaurit and arcas:
Si bursae pareas, fuge Papas and Patrlarchas:
Si de deris in arcas, and eis impleboris areas,
Culpa solueris qua{que} ligatus eris.

But with what difference I pray you were these crimes rated? Indeed he that would be absolved from adultery or incest, it must cost him four turons; if from both together, it must stand him in six turons. And what if a priest busy the body of a party excommunicated in Christian burial, or if he chance upon ignorance to say mass in a place interdicted? Either of these faults must cost him six turons and two ducats. And here it is to be noted that the pope in a covetous policy forbids many things which God does not forbid, namely

---

[288] Mat. Westmonast. an. 1301. Mat. Paris. an. 1246. Sylu. lotorum commun. In preafat. in lib. Steph. Gardiner. de vera obedient. Vid: Muscull loc. comm. de Eccl. ministr. tit. Nundinatio Rom. pontif. & Fulm. brut. pag. 62. Ioan Monachus.

to this end that the straiter his prohibitions are, the more often he may have occasion to dispense there with. As for example, he forbids marriage in kinsfolk unto the seventh degree, but for money he will dispense therewith in all degrees of kindred, excepting that which is between the parent and the child.

(11) They have with feigned words through covetousness persuaded the world, that the pope has all laws in the closet of his breast, that he is the supreme judge in all causes and controversies, that to him lies appeal from all judges whatsoever, and that immediately.[289] By which channels have flowed abundance of riches into the sea of the pope's treasury. And fitly is it compared to the sea whereunto all rivers flow, and yet does not overflow.[290]

"It is lawful," says one of their own lawyers, "to appeal from any to the pope immediately. This," (says he) "they have provided that they might draw controversies unto their court, and so might satisfy their own avarice, which notwithstanding they shall never do, noting that it is insatiable."[291]

And hereunto appertains that acclamation of one of their own chronographers, for having shown that scarcely there was any spiritual promotion which was not become litigious, and the cause brought to Rome, but not with empty hand:[292] "Rejoice," says he, "Our mother Rome, for the floodgates of the treasures in the earth are opened, that unto you may flower rivers, and heaps of money in great abundance. Rejoice over the iniquity of the sons of men, because in recompense of so great evils, there is a price or reward given unto you. Be glad for your helper, Discord, which has burst out of the bottomless pit of hell, that unto you, many rewards of money might be gathered in heaps. You have that which you always thirsted after. Sing a song, for by the wickedness of men, and not by your religion, you

---

[289] Antonin. sum part. 3. tit. 22. cap. 5. §. 17.
[290] Theodoric. Niem. tract. 6. c. 37.
[291] Petr. Ferrariens. inform. sent. indefin. §. sed ad quēcunque
[292] Abbas vrsperg. pag. 321.

have vanquished the world. Unto you does not the devotion of men or pure conscience draw them, but the committing of manifold crimes, and the decision of controversies procured by money."

Furthermore with feigned words they have taught that there is a purgatory, wherein the souls of many of the elect are tormented for a time, that out of this purgatory the souls may be delivered by the prayers of the living; especially, by the satisfactory prayers of those whom they call religious, by masses and trentals of masses, by the works of supererogation and merits of others applied unto them. By this conceit, which was the foundation of religious houses, the pope's clergy had gotten the chiefest possessions of all Europe into their hands.

"Monasteries," (says one of their own writers) "were founded in times past, for devotion, though nowadays for rapine and covetousness: insomuch that they have at this day destroyed the world, and brought to nothing the state of the empire and of all lay men. Wherefore all such places, as are or shall be made, may worthily be called nets framed to catch lay men's goods."[293] In this small land of ours the revenues of the irreligious houses, which were dissolved, did arise according to the old rents (which are scarce the tenth part of the true value) to the sum of a hundred thirty four thousand six hundred and three pounds, two shillings fourpence halfpenny.

Neither are the pope's own revenues arising from these grounds to be omitted. For purgatory indeed is his peculiar, and the merits of saints and works of supererogation which are the treasure of the church, are in his disposition. So that by his applying thereof to whom he pleases, he can either shorten their time in purgatory, or wholly set them at liberty by his indulgences and pardons accordingly as he is paid for the same.

And yet there are many more devices and feigned words, whereby the pope makes merchandise of men for the enriching of himself and his clergy. As by his jubilees, and canonization of saints, by his promising of remission

---

[293] Petr. Ferrariens. in form. libell. quo agitur ex substit. §. ex suo corpore

of sins and eternal life to those that will fight his battles or execute his wicked designs: by his doctrines of merits and works of supererogation, of invocation of saints, of adoration of images and relics, of pilgrimages, and in a word by all the doctrines almost of popery, I mean those, which be peculiar to the pope and church of Rome, which are feigned words doused in devilish policy to maintain their insatiable lust, ambition and covetousness.

By all this which has been said it plainly appears that the pope most worthily deserves to be called the man of sin – especially if you consider that in respect of several of the aforesaid sins, he is such a sinner as Jeroboam was, who caused all Israel to sin. For he is not only an apostate, but also the head of the catholic apostasy: not only an heretic, but the false prophet and broacher of popish heresies: not only an idolator and adulterer, but also the cause and author of these abominations in all the Christian world, making all sorts of men drunk with the wine of his fornications.

(12) It remains therefore that we should consider whether the other two titles of Antichrist do belong to the pope, namely that he is *the son of perdition*, and *the outlaw* or *lawless person*.

As touching the former, there is no question to be made but that if he be the man of sin as has been proved, he is also the child of perdition, in that sense that Judas is so called in John 17:12. And that he deserves most justly to be called the *outlaw* or *lawless person* it is most evident. Not only because he is a transgressor of the law (for seeing every sin is ἀνομία: a transgression of the law, therefore he that is the man of sin, must needs be ο ανομος *the outlaw*) but also because he professes himself to be the son of Belial, that is to say a man without yoke, who takes himself to be bound to no law, but challenges authority to break all laws or at least to dispense with them.

For firstly, as touching the laws and authority of men, *Papa solutus est omni lege humana*, that is: the pope is not bound to any human law. *Legi non subiacet vlli*, he is subject to no law.[294] And according to the fullness of power he may, as himself professes, *de iure supraius dispensare*, dispense with the law above law: yea he may do all things, *supraius, contraius, and extraius*, above law, against law, and without law. And therefore of all others most worthily called *the outlaw*. And as for human authority, he is to judge all, but to be judged by none. *Nec totus Clerus, nec totus mundus potest Papam iudicare aut deponere*: "Not the whole clergy, nor the whole world may judge the pope or depose him."[295]

Neither does he indeed subject himself to the law of God. For he does not only take upon him to dispense with the word and law of God, as you heard before, but also thinks he may lawfully break the laws of God. He has been made to believe that he may do all things, even unlawful things, and that he is more than God, as Zabarella says. And therefore some of them, when they have been admonished of their wicked practices, have tended to answer, "Am not I pope?"[296] – thereby signifying that being pope he might do what he wishes.

Neither is he indeed subject to any other law but to his own will or rather lust. *In ijs quae vult, est es proratione voluntas*: In those things which he will, his will is unto him for reason. *Legi non subtacet vlli: Iudiciumque est pro lege suum*, He is subject to no law: and his judgment is instead of law.[297] So that of him is verified that prophecy concerning Antiochus the type of Antichrist, that he would do what he wished, and that his will should be to him for a law. To this purpose his followers say, that he is *lex vivens*, a living law, and has all laws in the closet of his breast, that he can of wrong make

---

[294] Casus Papales apud Hostiensem &c. Innocent. 3. extr. de concess. praebend. c. pro. posuit. Bald. in c. [com]. super de causi proprict. & possess.

[295] Petr. de palude, de potestate Papae art. 4.

[296] Joan 13

[297] Extr. de transat. episc. c. quanto in gloss. inter casus papales. Dan. 11. 16. R. Cupers de ecclesia pag. 29 num. 1. & 62. vum. 66. de constitutionib. c. licet. in sexto. Hostiens. Francisc de Ripa. R. Cupers. pag. 68. num. 32. & Dist. 40. non nos in gloss. Extra de concess. praebend. c. proposuit in gloss dist. 40. non nos in gloss. Ioan. de Parisiis c. 20. Concil. com. l. in purgatione Sixti. Dist. 40. Non os in gloss.

right, of injustice righteousness, that to him all things are lawful. That the pope's power is absolute, and extends as far as he wishes: that he may not be accused of simony, nor murder, nor adultery, nor any other crime, excepting heresy which they say elsewhere is not incident unto him.

Nay, his actions may not be inquired into, neither may any man say unto him, "Sir, why do you thus?" Yea, it were no better then sacrilege to call in question the pope's fact, and to judge of his actions *est ponere os in caelum*: it is to set a man's face against heaven. To accuse him is to commit the sin against the Holy Spirit, which shall never be forgiven neither in this world nor in the world to come.

But what if it is apparent that he has committed adultery or murder, or that himself is a wicked man, as indeed many of them have been monsters of men? Indeed, the actions of the pope must be interpreted in the good part. For if a priest when he is seen to be over-familiar with a woman must be thought to bless her, much more is it to be presumed on the pope's behalf. Or if they are so black as that they will admit no other color, then the facts of the pope must be excused, such as the murders of Samson, the thefts of the Hebrews, and the adultery of Jacob.[298] And to the same purpose says another: "Every fact of the most holy father must be interpreted in the good parte, and if it be theft or anything that is in itself evil, we must interpret it to be done by divine instinct."[299]

And as touching his person, the pope, be he never so wicked, is always presumed to be good. *Quis enim sanctū dubitet esse quem apex tantae dignitatis attollit? In quo sidesint bona acquisita per meritum, sufficiunt quae à loci praedecessore praestantur.*[300] "For who would doubt that he is holy," (says the pope of himself) "whom the height of such great honor advances? In whom if good things gotten by his own merit be lacking, those suffice which are performed by the predecessor in the same place" – meaning Peter. And

---

[298] Dist. 40. Non nos in gloss.
[299] Ioan. de Parisus de potest. reg. & papali
[300] Dist. 40. Non nos. Papa semper praesumitur bonus ibid. in gloss.

again, "There is a certain spirituality according to state, when a man is in the most holy and most spiritual state, and in this state is the pope alone. And therefore everyone must call him most holy father."[301]

Seeing as therefore the pope is the man of sin, and a most notorious transgressor of God's laws; seeing as he holds himself bound to no law but esteems his own lust for a law; seeing as his transgressions of the law must not be called into question, but either must be commended as virtuous actions, or, excused as done by divine instinct;

>seeing as himself though never so wicked must be deemed
>most holy in that he is pope – it cannot be denied,
>but that above all men he most deserves
>to be called ο ανομος, *the outlaw*, or
>*lawless person.*

---

[301] De maior. & obedient. c. vnā sanctā in gloss.

Chapter 7

Of the miracles, or rather lying signs and wonders of Antichrist.

(1) And thus much may suffice to have spoken of the qualities and conditions of Antichrist: now we have to entreat of his actions and effects. And first of his miracles as he calls them, or rather, as the Holy Spirit terms them: *lying signs and wonders*. In speaking whereof I will not stick to use Bellarmine's own grounds.[302] For whereas there are three things (as he says) mentioned in the Scriptures concerning the miracles of Antichrist, it shall appear by the help of God, that all which the Scriptures have foretold concerning this matter, do most fitly agree to the pope and church of Rome.

The first is that Antichrist and his followers should do many signs and wonders which they call miracles. For so says our Savior Christ in Matthew 24:24 (which prophecy, the papists themselves understand of Antichrist and his adherents): "They shall work great signs and wonders, insomuch that the very elect, if it were possible, should be seduced." "He says, they shall work great signs, and not he," (says Bellarmine) "because not only Antichrist but his ministers also shall work signs." And the apostle, speaking of Antichrist, says that his coming shall be according to the efficacy of Satan in all power in lying signs and wonders.[303] And likewise John in Revelation 13:13 affirms that Antichrist works great signs in the sight of men.

And that this note agrees to the pope and church of Rome, it is most evident. For they abound with innumerable signs and wonders which they call miracles. Insomuch that there is among them almost no saint or author of any sect, who is not renowned for many fair miracles; no temple or monastery of note, no image or relics of saints unto which the people went on pilgrimage, which was not famous for miracles; no doctrine which cannot be proved out of Scripture, that is to say, no point of popery which

---

[302] Lib. 3 de pont. Rom. cap. 15
[303] 2 Thessalonians 2:9

they have not commended to the people and authorized by such signs and wonders as they call miracles. And in regard to these miracles (which they esteem as a note of the true church) they contemn and despise all other churches, which do not vaunt of miracles as they do.

(2) And yet notwithstanding, all their miracles are worth nothing. First, because they serve to confirm untruths as shall be shown, and therefore are not to be regarded. Secondly, because the vain brag of manifold miracles among those that profess the name of Christ in these later times (wherein miracles need not for the confirmation of God's truth, which heretofore has been sufficiently confirmed) is so far from being a note of the true church, as that rather it is a plain sign of false teachers, and an evident mark of the Synagogue of Antichrist. For their own devices indeed and doctrines of men do still need signs and wonders to confirm them. But the truth of the gospel which we profess has been sufficiently confirmed by the miracles of our Savior Christ, and of his apostles and disciples. Whosoever therefore will not believe this doctrine, thus confirmed, neither will he believe though one should rise from the dead to preach unto him.

Again, miracles are granted not for the believers, but for thē that live in infidelity.[304] And as Augustine says, *Quisquis adhuc prodigia, vt credat, inquirit, magnum est ipse prodigium, qui mundo credeme non credit*:[305] "Whosoever yet seeks after wonders that he may believe, is himself a great wonder, who when the world believes, does not believe." And therefore in another place he says, *Contra istos mirabiliarios cautum me fecit Deus meus*, etc.:[306] "Against these miracle-mongers my God has made me wary," saying, "There shall arise in the last days false prophets working signs and wonders, that they might bring into error, if it were possible, the very elect."

---

[304] Tharasius in cōcil. Nicen. 2
[305] *City of God*, Book 22 Chapter 8
[306] Tract. 13 in Ioan

Likewise Chrysostom, or whosoever was the author of those learned *Homilies Upon Matthew* in the 49th homily (where he proves that the true church of Christ cannot now be known or discerned by signs or other means, but only by the Scriptures) he says, that now the working of signs and wonders is altogether taken away (namely among the true professors) and the working of counterfeit miracles is more found among false Christians. And that Peter in the history of Clement, declares that unto Antichrist shall be granted the power of working full, that is to say, profitable signs, So that now we cannot know the ministers of Christ by this that they work profitable signs, but because they work no signs at all. And the papists themselves confess, yea Bellarmine would seem to set it down as one of his grounds, that to Antichrist and his followers shall be granted the power of working many and great signs and wonders. And therefore, unless the pope and his followers did vaunt of their miracles, we should lack one good argument to prove the pope Antichrist.

And thus it appears that the first point concerning the miracles of Antichrist does fit the pope, and so fit him, as that from hence he may be proved Antichrist. For unto whomsoever in these latter times this properly and only belongs, to boast of their miracles, they are Antichrist and the synagogue of Antichrist.

For the Scriptures have foretold that by Antichrist and his adherents many signs and wonders should be wrought in these latter times. But to the pope and church of Rome in these latter times this properly and only belongs to vaunt of their manifold and great miracles. For the Jews want them: the Turks disclaim them, professing that their religion must be propagated not by miracles but by force and arms. All other Christians which already believe the truth, seek not signs which they know among true believers to be superfluous, and in others to be badges of Antichrist; therefore the pope is Antichrist and the Church of Rome the Synagogue of Antichrist.

(3) The second thing which the Scripture notes is what manner of miracles they are which Antichrist was to work. This the apostle (says Bellarmine) declares in one word, when he calls them *lying wonders*, or as the words are, σημειοις και τερασιν ψευδους *signs and wonders of lying*, that is: most lying signs and wonders.[307] Now they are called *lying wonders* either in respect of the end, which is to seduce men by confirming untruths; or in regard of their substance, which is counterfeit.

And thus Chrysostom expounds the words of the apostle:[308] "And he says *lying wonders*, that is either false and counterfeit, or else leading into falsehood." Augustine likewise recites these two expositions, that they are called lying signs and wonders, "because he shall deceive the senses of mortal men by counterfeit shows and appearances, that he may seem to do that which he does not: or else because howsoever they shall be true wonders, they shall draw unto lies such as shall believe that they could not be done but by the power of God, not knowing the power of the devil," etc.[309]

First I say they are called lying signs in respect of the end, which is to seduce men (Matthew 24:24), to make them believe lies and to deceive them (2 Thessalonians 2:10-11, Revelation 13:14). For this is the end whereunto the signs and wonders not only of Antichrist, but of all false prophets, are referred to in Deuteronomy 13:1-2. Out of which places of Scripture, we are to observe that the Lord many times suffers false prophets and antichrists to work strange signs and wonders for the trial of the faithful, and seduce those that will not believe the truth that they might be saved.

"If there arise among you," (says the Lord) "a prophet or dreamer of dreams, and give thee a sign and wonder, and the sign and wonder which he has told thee, come to pass, saying, let us go after other gods which thou hast not known, and let us serve them: thou shalt not hearken unto the words of

---

[307] 2 Thessalonians 2:9
[308] On 2 Thessalonians 2
[309] Augustine, *City Of God*, 20.19

the prophet, or unto that dreamer of dreams. For the Lord your God proves you, to know whether you love the Lord your God with all your soul, and with all your heart, etc."

Our Savior Christ also has forewarned us, that in these latter times there shall arise false christs and false prophets which shall show great signs and wonders, so that if it were possible they should deceive even the very elect. In like sort, the apostle in 2 Thessalonians 2 notes that the coming of Antichrist shall be according to the efficacy of Satan "in all power and lying signs and wonders, and in all deceivableness of unrighteousness in them that perish," etc., "on whom God shall send the efficacy of deceit that they may believe lies." Likewise, John the divine prophecies of Antichrist, that he should do great wonders, whereby he should deceive them that dwell on the earth.[310]

Hereby therefore it is evident, that false prophets and Antichrists many times have power to work great signs and wonders, not only in show and appearance, but in deed and in truth. Whereby they – endeavoring to deceive all and to make them believe lies – are permitted both in the justice of God to seduce the wicked, and in his mercy to try the faithful. And therefore signs and wonders as they have not always been signs and tokens of true teachers and professors of the truth, but only then when they have been wrought for the confirmation of the truth.[311] So in these later times, the same being wrought for confirmation of untruths are undoubted signs of the synagogue of Antichrist.

(4) Let us then consider whether such signs and wonders are wrought in the church of Rome. It is recorded of Gregory VII, who was the first of the popes which was openly acknowledged to be Antichrist, that as he was a notable sorcerer, so he wrought many signs and wonders, and among the

---

[310] Revelation 13:13-14
[311] Miracles are divine testimonies whereby the Lord bears witness to his truth. Hebrews 2:4

rest, he used to shake fire out of his sleeves. And of his votaries, after he had forbidden marriage in the clergy, Aventin writes that "upon that occasion many false prophets did as it were cast mists, and by fables and miracles did turn away the people of Christ from the truth."[312] And again, "false prophets did then arise, false apostles, false priests, who by counterfeit religion deceived the people, wrought great signs and wonders, and began to sit in the temple of God, and to be advanced above all that is worshiped. And while they endeavor to establish their own power and dominion they have extinguished Christian charity and simplicity."[313]

And since those times the church of Rome has much boasted of her manifold miracles, which have been partly devised and partly wrought for the confirmation of such Antichristian doctrines and idolatrous superstitions as cannot be confirmed by the Scriptures, as namely the absurd doctrine of transubstantiation, and adoration of the breaden god, the heathen doctrine of purgatory, and superstitious prayer for the dead, the idolatrous invocation and worshiping of saints, the more-than-heathen adoration of images and rotten relics: the Antichristian advancing of the pope above all that is called God or worshiped: and such like doctrines of devils and lies of Antichrist, for the confirmation whereof the miracles of the apostate church of Rome have been invented.

But however many miracles they produce for the countenancing of such untruths, these are so many arguments to prove their church Antichristian, and their pope Antichrist. Because as Antichrist and his followers were in these latter times to abound with signs and wonders, but always such as serve to lead men into error, so neither Turks nor Jews, nor any other churches of Christians, but only the pope and church of Rome, do vaunt of miracles, and yet all their miracles are such as serve to deceive men, and to make them believe untruths. And therefore, although they were in respect of their substance neither counterfeit nor fabulous (as indeed the most of the miracles

---

[312] Annal. Boior. Lib. 4
[313] Lib. 5

in the church of Rome are), yet were they to be esteemed as notes and signs of false prophets and antichrists, because their end is to seduce men, and confirm lies.

(5) Secondly, they are called lying signs in respect of the substance, being (as Augustine speaks) *vel figmenta mendacium hominū, vel portenta fallaciū spirituū*:[314] "either fictions of lying men, or wonders of deceitful spirits." And such are the miracles whereby the aforesaid points of popery are warranted and confirmed. And of them there are three degrees. For many of them were such fabulous fictions, ridiculous fables, incredible lies, (whereof their legends and festivals are full), as none would ever believe, were they not intoxicated, and made drunk with the whore of Babylon's cup of fornications, and also given over of God to believe lies.

And these loud lies and more-than-poetical fictions were in such request in the church of Rome, that the records of them (I mean their legends and festivals and such like fabulous treatises) were both publicly and privately read in the vulgar tongue, when the holy Scriptures were kept from the people in an unknown language.

The first degree then is of such miracles as never were indeed, nor yet in appearance, but in the opinion only of men besotted and given over to believe incredible untruths. The second is of such as were fantastical and in appearance only, as being crafty conveyances of deceitful men, or juggling tricks of legerdemain – as for example, the nodding or moving, the smiling or frowning, the sweating or speaking of images, the apparitions of souls deceased, the manifold cures supposed to be wrought by saints departed or their images and and such like.

For of these two sorts there be innumerable wonders recorded, in their legends and festivals and lives of saints, which are either altogether fabulous, as being reports of things which never were not so much as in appearance,

---

[314] De Unitat. Eccl. 16

or if any such things have been done in the sight of men, they have been either praestigiatory conveyances of wicked men, or mere illusions of the devil. The third degree is of such as were lying miracles in respect of the form (as Bellarmine speaks) although true in respect of the matter. For however they were things truly done, yet they surpassed not the whole strength of nature: whereas true miracles are supernatural, neither can be wrought by any natural causes whether known or unknown, but only by the omnipotent power of God. And such lying signs are the principal miracles of the apostate church of Rome.

Neither is the pope and all his adherents able to produce any one true miracle wrought by the finger of God for the confirmation of those doctrines which are peculiar to that church, that is, to speak more plainly, for the proof of any point of popery. But all their miracles as they are lying signs and wonders in respect of their ende, so also in regard of their substance, being either merely fabulous and therefore such things as never were not so much as in show and appearance, or merely fantastical, that is such things as were in show only and not in truth, or merely natural and therefore but counterfeit miracles effected by the power of the devil.

(6) Some of their own writers confess that sometimes there is great deceiving of the people in feigned miracles by the priests and their adherents for temporal gain.[315] And another says, "In the sacrament, flesh appears: sometimes by the conveyance of men, sometimes by the operation of the devil."[316]

I once did see an image of Saint Nicolas as it was said, when it with many others was burnt in the marketplace at Chester by the appointment of my father then bishop there, which was made with such a device that if one standing behind did pull a certain string which was in the back part thereof, it would move the hand as if it blessed the people. But that it may appear

---

[315] Nicol. Lyran. In Daniel. 14 [sic]
[316] Alexander de Hales

that in the Church of Rome were lying miracles, and that the popish people were given over to believe lies, I will for a taste recite a few examples out of their own records.

Their *Golden Legend* (so called because as gold excels all other metals, so that book excels all other books)[317] – in the invention of the body of St. Fermin the martyr – reports that after the sun had miraculously sent his beams through a stone wall upon the grave, and thereupon they had dug there to find the body, there issued thence such a sweet smell as they thought that they had been in paradise.

This odor spread itself not only through the city of Amiens where the body lay, but also unto several other cities. The sweetness whereof as it moved the people of various cities to bring their oblations to this glorious saint: so it cured some a far off (as the lord of Beaugency) from their diseases. But when this body was taken up and carried in the city of Amiens, strange wonders were wrought. For then (that I may use the words of the English legend) "the elements moved them by the miracle of this saint." The snow – that was at that time great on the earth – was turned into powder and dust by the heat that was then, and the ice that hung on the trees became flowers and leaves, and the meadows about Amiens flowered and became green. And the sun – which by its nature should go low that day – ascended as high as it is on St. John's Day at noon in the summer. And as men bare the body of this saint, the trees inclined and worshiped the body, and all manner sick men of what malady they had, they received health in the invention of the blessed body of St. Fermin, etc.

In *The Legend of St. Patrick the Irish Saint,* by whose prayer indeed all venomous beasts were banished out of Ireland (for you may not think it was so before), we read – and reading, smile – that once upon a time, when a sheep was stolen, he admonished all the people that whosoever had stolen it should within seven days restore it to the owner. The seven days being

---

[317] Namely: in lying

expired, the sheep was not restored. Then (says the legend), Patrick commanded by the virtue of God that the sheep should bleat and cry in the belly of him that had eaten it. And so it happened that in the presence of all the people the sheep cried and bleated in the belly of him that had stolen it.

(7) In *The Legend of the Annunciation of Our Lady*, we are told of a noble knight who betook himself unto an abbey, and because he was unlearned, there was a master assigned unto him. But either he was so dull or the inventor of the tale so doltish, that in a long time he could learn no more but these two words: *Ave Maria*. These words, as he always had in his mouth while he was alive, so they grew out of his mouth when he was dead. For these words (says the legend) he had so sore imprinted in his heart that he always had them in his mouth, wherever he was.

At last he died, and was buried in the churchyard of the brethren. It happened after that upon his grave there grew a right fair fleur-de-lis, and in every flower was written in letters of gold: *Ave Maria*. Of which miracle all the brethren were marveled, and they did open the sepulcher, and found that the root of this fleur-de-lis came out of the mouth of the said knight, and they soon understood that our Lord would have him honored for the great devotion he had to say these words: *Ave Maria*.

Likewise in *The Book of the Conformities of St. Francis*, which book I could wish were more common, that popery might appear unto all in her colors, there is a miracle recorded for the proof of transubstantiation; that on a time friar Francis – saying mass – did find a spider in the chalice, which he would not cast out but drunk it up with the blood. Afterwards, rubbing his thigh, and scratching where it itched, the spider came whole out of his thigh without any harm to either.

But if the bread and wine after consecration be turned into the very body and blood of Christ, then more marvelous and I am sure more true is the story of Victor the Pope, and William Archbishop of York,[318] and Henry the emperor of Luxembourg, all of whom were poisoned, the two first with that which was in the chalice, and the emperor with the host which a monk had poisoned. And to these, many more worthy miracles of the Church of Rome may be added. But you will say that however, there are many miracles wherein the Church of Rome glories, yet notwithstanding, those special miracles which are assigned to Antichrist in the Scriptures have not been wrought by the pope or any of his followers.

(8) This is indeed the third thing which Bellarmine observes: that whereas there are three examples of Antichrist's miracles specified in the Scriptures: yet none of them have been wrought either by the pope or any other in the church of Rome.

But I answer, that of these three miracles one agrees not to Antichrist, as shall be shown hereafter, and the other two agree to the pope. For however Bellarmine and other papists from these grounds do argue that the pope is not Antichrist, yet from thence may the contrary be gathered.[319] The former of these miracles is that Antichrist or at least his ministers shall make fire come down from heaven. The second, that he shall cause the image of the beast to speak.[320]

These two miracles Bellarmine understands literally, and from thence argues thus:

- Antichrist or his ministers, shall make fire come down from heaven, and shall cause the image of the beast to speak.
- But neither the pope of Rome at any time, nor any of his followers have caused fire to come down from heaven, nor yet made the image of the beast to speak.

---

[318] In the year 1154
[319] The author of *The Wardword*
[320] Revelation 13:13

- Therefore the pope is not Antichrist.

The argument is grounded on Revelation 13:13, understood literally. For such is the absurd perverseness of the papists, that in other parts of Scripture which are simple and plain they do hunt after mystical and allegorical senses, but in this Book of the Revelation which is most mystical and allegorical, without all reason they insist on the literal sense.

As for example in that thirteenth chapter, where the Holy Spirit speaks of the mark of the beast, which the followers of Antichrist should receive on their foreheads and on their right hands, they grossly understand this of a real and visible mark wherewithal men of all sorts should suffer themselves to be branded as the slaves or cattle of Antichrist.

Where the Holy Spirit speaks of the image of the beast, which Antichrist puts life into and causes to speak, they understand it of a material image animated and made to speak. Where the Holy Spirit speaks of fire to come down from heaven, they understand it of material fire brought down from heaven – which course, whosoever follows in expounding the prophecies in the Revelation, must never look to see them verified in the event.

This I speak, not that literally they do not agree to the pope, but because (the mystical sense being the more likely to be true) our adversary grounds his argument wholly upon the literal interpretation. But I will make it plain that both these miracles agree to the pope not only in the mystical sense, but also in the literal. And to that purpose let us consider these miracles severally.

(9) And first as touching that of fire, which Antichrist shall cause to descend from heaven, if it be literally understood, you shall perceive that it agrees to the pope, because in several popish miracles there has been (as they say) fire brought down from heaven.

But seeing the place is rather to be understood mystically and allegorically, as well as other prophecies of the Revelation, we are not therefore by the coming down of fire to understand literally a real descending of material fire, but that which mystically in the Scriptures is meant by the coming down of fire from heaven.

You are therefore to be informed that descending of fire from heaven, in the Scriptures signifies three things:

[1] God's approval of the religion and sacrifices of his servants.

[2] His sending down of the graces of his Spirit upon his children.

[3] His vengeance executed from heaven upon his enemies.

For the first, it is clear that the Lord informer times used to testify his approbation of the religion and sacrifices of his servants, by sending fire from heaven to consume their sacrifice: in which respect he is said to answer them by fire from heaven, as in Leviticus 9:24, 1 Chronicles 21:26, 2 Chronicles 7:1 – whereunto some add Genesis 4:4, and Jude 13 & 19. When therefore the people of Israel halted between Jehovah and Baal, Elijah – to prove that Jehovah whom he worshiped was the true God, and his worship the true religion – by prayer miraculously caused fire to come down from heaven to consume the sacrifice (1 Kings 18:38).

Whosoever therefore does by such signs and wonders confirm that doctrine and religion which he professes, as though God answered him by fire from heaven, he may be said to cause fire to descend from heaven, in the sight and opinion of men; who think such miracles to be wrought by the finger of God, according to this example of Elijah, that is, so to have confirmed his religion in the opinion of men, as if he had with Elijah fetched fire from heaven.

If therefore the pope of Rome or his ministers have, by as strange signs and wonders in the opinion of men, confirmed their religion – as though God from heaven approved thereof, as he was wont to signify his approbation in answering by fire from heaven – then they may be said to have made fire to come down from heaven, although they never had caused material fire to descend.

But if besides many other strange signs and wonders which they call miracles, they have confirmed their superstitious religion and Antichristian doctrines by bringing fire from heaven, then can it not be denied but that this place does most fully and properly agree unto them. But you must remember how Saint John says "in the sight of men," not that they have done so indeed, but only that they have made men believe so.

(10) As for example, to prove that their sacrament of the altar after the words of consecration is the very body of Christ, and to be worshiped no otherwise then Christ himself, we have a narration in their festival which was wont solemnly to be read in the church on Corpus Christi day – the words whereof I will recite unto you.

"Also we find," (say they) "that in Devonshire beside Exbridge was a woman lay sick and was nigh dead, and sent after a holy person about midnight to have her rights. Then this man – in all haste that he could muster – arose and went to the church, and took God's body in a box of ivory, and put it into his bosom, and went forth towards this woman. And as he went through a forest in a fair meadow that was next his way, it happened that the box of his bosom [fell] into the ground: and he went forth and knew it not and came to this woman and heard her confession. And then he asked her if she would be houseled [that is, would receive the eucharist], and she said, "Yes, Sir." Then he put his hand in his bosom and sought the box. And when he could not find it, he was full sorry and sad. And said, "Dame, I will go after God's body and come soon again to you," and so went forth sore weeping for his simpleness.

And so as he came to a willow tree he made thereof a rod, and stripped himself naked, and beat himself that the blood ran down by his sides, and said thus to himself: "Ah you simple man! Why have you lost your Lord God, your maker, your former and creator?" And when he had thus beat himself, he did on his clothes and went on forth.

And then he was aware of a pillar of fire that lasted from earth to heaven, and he was all astonished thereof, yet he blessed himself and went towards it. And there lay the sacrament fallen out of the box into the grass, and the pillar shone as bright as any sun, and it lasted from God's body to heaven.

And all the beasts of the forest were coming about God's body, and stood in compass round about it, and all knelt on four knees, save one black horse that kneeled but on that one knee. And that black horse was a fiend of hell, who had turned himself into that shape that men might steal him, as diverse had done and were hanged for him, etc."

If any man objects that all this narration is a foolish fiction, I answer that this was as verily believed as it was solemnly read. And therefore to countenance their abominable idol of the mass, they have – in the sight, that is, in the judgment, opinion, and belief of men – caused fire to come down from heaven that it might point out the body, and from it reach to heaven.

(11) To win credit to such saints as they have canonized, and consequently to cause men the more devoutly to pray unto them, to adore their images and relics, to go on pilgrimage to them, they have coined in the life or legend almost of every saint, strange and incredible miracles. And this is the ordinary conclusion of many legends.

Then let us pray to this worthy saint, or glorious martyr, that he will pray to God for us, that by his merits we may have pardon and forgiveness of our sins, or something to the like effect. We read of several of their saints, who when they have been beheaded, have carried their heads in their hands – some one mile; some two miles.[321] And it is a wonder that, hasting from so sharp a banquet, they did not leave their heads behind them for haste. Among many other miracles they tell us of fire also which they have caused to come down from heaven in the sight, that is judgment and opinion, of men besotted and given over to believe their monstrous untruths. In the life

---

[321] Saint Iustinian the monk. Saint Osisha. Saint Fulcien and Saint Victorice.

of Protus and Hyacinth, they make fire to come down from heaven to kill Melancy, the false accuser of Eugene. They have brought down a pillar of fire reaching from heaven unto the earth where the body of Saint Edward the martyr lay. Upon the head of Saint Martin, as he was saying mass, they have fetched down a tongue of fire from heaven to make him equal as they say to the apostles. In the fable of Saint George, they make fire to come down from heaven to burn the idols with their temple and priests.

In the life of Barbara, we read that when her own father being her persecutor had drawn his sword to slay her, she was miraculously taken up in a stone and carried into a mountain; where two shepherds were feeding their sheep. And when one of them had betrayed her to her father, and she in her charity had cursed him, soon his sheep became locusts and he consumed into a stone. Then her father, having apprehended her, delivered her to the judge, who put her to death, whereupon they brought down fire from heaven to consume her father.

Their doctrine of purgatory and prayer for the dead, is confirmed by many wonders and strange apparitions of souls departed, begging masses for their deliverance out of purgatory. And in like manner it is reported that when Birstan the Bishop of Winchester staying all night in the churchyard, as his manner was, said over his psalms for the souls departed, coming to these words *requiescant in pace* – let them rest in peace, he heard the voice of an infinite number out of the graves crying, Amen. But to this purpose also in their legend they have made fire to descend from heaven.

When they tell us of a certain bishop, who, appearing in the clouds of heaven to another here upon earth, did let some fire drop upon him to give him a taste of the torments in purgatory. Besides these examples, many others might be found if they were worth seeking in their fabulous writings, as also in some other of their stories which testify that several times in the church of Rome, fire has been brought down from heaven.[322]

---

[322] Ioan. Linturius in appead. ad fascic. tempor.

But these which I have recited may suffice, in seeking and setting down whereof I should have thought my time and pains not well bestowed (such are the ridiculous fooleries of popery, wherewith the churches in the time of darkness have been pestered) saving that I considered that the more incredible the report is of popish miracles, the more evidently it is proved, both that the pope is Antichrist, and the papists the followers of Antichrist, upon whom God has sent strong illusions that they might believe lies.

In the first sense therefore, the prophecy of Revelation 13 fits the pope and church of Rome, who by great signs and wonders do so confirm their Antichristian errors and superstitions in the sight, that is, in the judgment, opinion, and belief of men besotted and made drunk with the whore of Babylon's cup of fornications, as though God did seem to approve thereof in answering by fire from heaven. And this interpretation seems to be confirmed by the words, for it is not directly said that Antichrist should cause fire to come down from heaven, but only thus: that he does great signs, insomuch that fire descends from heaven in the sight of men. That is, insomuch that in the judgment of men God seems to answer him by fire from heaven, and to bear witness to his doctrines by miracles wrought by the finger of God.

(12) But the descent of fire signifies also the bestowing of the grace of God's Spirit which is called *fire* in Matthew 3:11 and Acts 2:3. In this sense, the pope may be said to make fire come down from heaven, but we must add before men, that is in their opinion and conceit. For he indeed, as the church of Rome believes, gives not only the graces of the Spirit to men, but also the power of sanctification both to men and also to some creatures of his own, as to his *Agnus Dei*, and his holy water sprinkle, etc. And in this sense does Primasius expound this place.

Thirdly, the coming down of fire signifies the wrathful vengeance of God executed upon his enemies, which often in the Scriptures is called *fire*, to wit, *the fire of God's wrath*.[323] As Elijah therefore brought fire from heaven to consume the two Captains and their fifties: so Antichrist, according to this interpretation, shall with a divine revenge, as it were with fire from heaven, take vengeance upon his adversaries, but here also we must add before men, who shall think that those against whom Antichrist shall send the thunderbolt of his wrath, are punished with a divine revenge, and as it were with fire from heaven. This also is verified of the pope of Rome, who with a divine revenge (as he indeed is *Deus vindictae*: The God of revenge) pursues his enemies, but especially with *the thunderbolt of excommunication* as they themselves do call it.[324] Which as it is terribly sent from this Jupiter of Rome, so is it fearfully executed with putting out and casting down of lights from above, as if the fire of God's wrath were at their command, or as if with Gregory VII they could shake it out of their sleeves.[325] And well may this be reckoned among the wonders of Antichrist.

For it were more than a wonder, that kings and emperors should by excommunications from the pope be either so daunted in themselves or abandoned of their subjects as some have been, but that the popes have professed and their followers have believed, that God himself does whatsoever is done by the pope, who being canonically elected is a God upon earth, and has the same consistory and judgment seat with God himself, whose vicar he would seem to be; and consequently that those kings and emperors were deposed of God, who were excommunicated by the pope: whereas other princes and people that are not made drunk with the cup of their fornications have esteemed their bulls of excommunication as Bullas that is bubbles, and the fire of vengeance which they cause to descend in the sight of men, as painted fire, or as the thunder and lightning of Salmoneus, who (as the poet describes him not unlike to the pope)[326]

---

[323] Revelation 20:9
[324] R. Cupers. de eccl. pag. 61. num. 52.
[325] Gregor. 7. in epist. ad German. apud Aventin. lib. 5.
[326] Aeneid. 6.

Flammas Iouis and sonitus imitatur Olympi: "imitates the lightnings of Jupiter, and the thunder of heaven."

But howsoever it is, whether this descending of fire from heaven is to be understood literally or mystically, the prophecy of the Holy Spirit concerning this first miracle of Antichrist is verified of the pope and church of Rome, who have caused fire to come down from heaven according to the literal sense. And according to the allegorical interpretation, they have so confirmed their doctrines by signs and wonders, as if God had answered them by fire from heaven. And secondly they have taken upon them to bring down the fire of God's Spirit, and to bestow his grace as it pleases them. And lastly, they have according to the example of Elijah with a divine revenge and as it were with fire from heaven, taken vengeance of their enemies; not to speak of his punishing with fire all those that will not adore him.

(13) And thus much may suffice to have spoken of the first miracle.

- The second miracle (says Bellarmine) is that Antichrist or his ministers shall make the image of the beast to speak.
- But never did the pope, nor any minister of his, make an image to speak.
- Therefore, says he, the pope is not Antichrist.

But I answer that this prophecy – even according to the popish interpretation agrees to the pope and his followers, among whom it has been an usual practice to put life as it were into images in the sight and opinion of simple men, making them to sweat, to smile, to frown, to nod, to beck and many times to speak, which might happen without a miracle, for the devils sometimes did speak in the images of the heathen – notwithstanding, we are not after a popish, that is to say, a gross manner, but after a prophetic and spiritual manner to understand this mystical prophecy of the Holy Spirit concerning the image of the beast.

For if we understand the beast itself mystically, as needs we must, or else we shall make but a beastly interpretation of it. So we are in like sort to expound the image of the beast with the life and speech thereof. The beast itself signifies the Roman state especially under the heathen emperors, as has been shown. The image therefore of the beast must signify a state which has some resemblance thereof, or at least the name and title of the Roman Empire (as images bear the name of that which they resemble), and is indeed but an image thereof.

Thus, besides the pope's courts both in Rome and other countries, is the empire renewed in the West, which besides the name and some titles and ornaments has little or nothing of the old empire. For the old empire consisted in the government of Rome and the provinces thereunto belonging, none of which the emperor has as a sovereign prince by right of the empire, and therefore is said to be the beast which was and is not though it be,[327] being indeed, as it is here called, but an image of the former beast. The life of this empire is the imperial dignity, and the speech are his edicts.

Whosoever therefore caused this empire, which in the west had lain void for 325 years, to be renewed; whosoever at the first created this emperor, and since has taken order for the election of the emperor, and confirms the election; he may be said to have caused the image of the beast to be made, and to have put life into it, and to have procured authority unto it, whereby it speaks.

(14) Now to whom all this is to be applied, let Bellarmine himself be the judge. For he, in his books *De translatione imperij Romani*, by many testimonies labors to prove, first, that the empire of Rome was translated, but he might better have said renewed, in the West, and as it were revived by

---

[327] Revelation 17

the authority of the pope, and that Charles the Great in whom this empire was renewed, received the same by no other title but by the authority of the pope. And that is the sum of his first book. Secondly, that the empire of Rome was translated from the family of Charles the Great, and from the French nation to the family of Otto, and the nation of the Saxons and Germans, and that Otto was advanced to the empire by the pope, which is the scope of the second book.

Thirdly, that the seven electors of the empire were ordained and appointed by the pope, which is the argument of his third book. And in his first book[328] he sets down the state of that controversy thus:

"The question is," (says he) "Who is the author of this translation [or rather, *renovation*]? For the emperor of the east continued after until the year 1452. and before this time had by the pope's means lost his right in Italy and Rome, and therefore nothing was translated but the name and title) and who it was that gave the name dignity and power of the Roman emperor, and Caesar Augustus in the west, to Charles the Great and his successors. We answer," (says he) "that which the consent of all nations proclaims: that Pope Leo III was either the only or the chief and principal author of this translation, and that the Dutch nation is to acknowledge the receipt of the empire from the pope."

Unto the testimony of Bellarmine and of all those authors whom he cites, we will add the profession of the popes themselves. Innocent III said that the seven electors had their authority, *ab Apostolica sede, quae Romanū imperiū in persona magnifici Caroli à Graecis trāstulit in Germanos:*[329] "From the Apostolic See, which translated the Roman Empire in the person of Charles the Great from the Greek to the Germans." "Upon which translation," says Bellarmine, "the Roman commonwealth returned again to the same state

---

[328] Chapter 4
[329] Decret. Gregorian. de electione. c. venerabilem

wherein Constantine the Great established it, and wherein it remained from Valentinian the elder unto Augustulus."[330]

Likewise Adrian IV. "The Roman Empire," says he, "was translated from the Greeks to the Alemains, that the king of the Alemains should not be called emperor before he was crowned by the pope. Before his consecration he is king, after he is emperor. *Vnde igitur habet imperiũ nisi à nobis?* From whence then has he the Empire but from us? By the election of his princes he has the name of a king: by our consecration he has the name of emperor, Augustus, and Caesar. *Ergo per nos imperat.* Therefore he is emperor by us. Call to mind antiquities. Zacharias advanced Charles and gave him a great name that he should be emperor etc. *Imperator quod habet, totum habet à nobis.* Whatsoever the emperor has, that he has wholly from us. As Zacharias translated the empire from the Greeks to the Germans, so we can translate it from the Germans to the Greek. *Ecce in potestia nostra est, vt demus illud cui volumus.* Behold it is in our power to give it to whom we will. For therefore are we appointed of God over nations and kingdoms, to destroy and pluck up, to build and to plant."[331]

In the *Clementine Homilies*,[332] it is professed that the pope has translated the Empire from the Greeks to the Germans: that he has given power and authority to certain of their princes to elect a king to be emperor: that the king thus chosen receives from the pope the approbation of his person unto the Empire, as also his anointing, consecration, and imperial crown: and that in respect hereof, the emperors are to submit themselves unto the pope, and to bind themselves unto him by an oath of fealty and obedience. And elsewhere in their law it is said, *Imperator tenet imperium a Papa, vnde tenetur praestare iuramentum homagij scil. quod vasallus praestare solet domino suo.* "The emperor holds his empire from the pope," whereupon he is bound to

---

[330] De trãslat. imper. li. 1. cap. 4.
[331] Ad archiep. Treuir. Moguntin. & Agrippin. apud Auentin. lib. 6.
[332] Cap. Romani de iureiuran do.

perform the oath of homage, to wit, which the vassal uses to perform unto his lord.

(15) Thus therefore this argument is returned upon the adversary:

- Whosoever causes the image of the beast to be made, puts life into it and causes it to speak, he is undoubtedly Antichrist.
- But the pope of Rome has caused the image of the beast to be made, puts life into it, and causes it to speak.
- Therefore he is Antichrist.

The assumption is proved, because the image of the beast is the empire renewed in the west: the life is the imperial dignity, and the speech are the edicts thereof. This image the pope causes to be made, this he puts life into, this he has made to speak. For first he renewed the empire in the west, after it had laid void by the space of 325 years, when he anointed and crowned Charles the Great emperor of the west, and so caused him to be acknowledged, after he translated the empire to the Germans, among whom he has appointed seven electors as it were to renew this image, but so as himself puts life thereinto, by approving the person and ratifying the election, and makes him to speak by anointing him emperor and giving unto him the name and title of Augustus and Caesar. These things I shall not need further to prove, because they are matters whereof the pope and papists do greatly boast. And therefore from their own profession we may conclude that the pope is Antichrist.

Chapter 8
Of the name and mark which Antichrist shall impose upon men of all sorts, with some other effects.

(1) The second effect of Antichrist is noted in Revelation 13:16-18. "And he made all both small and great, rich and poor, free and bond, to receive a mark in their right hand or in their foreheads. And that no man might buy or sell, save he that had the mark, or the name of the beast or the number of his name. Here is wisdom: let him that has understanding count the number of the beast: for it is the number of a man: and his number is six hundred sixty and six."

Of which prophecy Bellarmine says thus:[333] *Fatentur omnes pertinere omnino ad Antichristum verba illa Ioannis Revelation 13*, etc.: "All men confess that those words of John in Revelation 13 do undoubtedly belong to Antichrist." From this ground therefore we may reason thus:

- Whosoever enforces all sorts of men according to this prophecy to take upon them the name of the beast, or the mark or number of his name, he is Antichrist.
- But the pope of Rome enforces all sorts of men according to this prophecy to take upon them the name of the beast, or the mark and number of his name.
- Therefore he is Antichrist.

For the clearing of this argument, two things are to be considered: firstly, what this name, number, and mark is; secondly, whether the pope imposes the same upon all sorts of men. The number is expressed in the text to be 666. And it is plainly said to be the number of the name. That we may not think it to be the number of the time when Antichrist should appear, as

---

[333] Lib. 3. de pontis. Rom. c. 10

some have imagined. Neither can it in any good sense be said that Antichrist enforces men to take upon them the number of that time.

And it is called the number of the name, because in the letters of the name this number is contained. For it is the manner of the Hebrews and Greeks to use their letters for notes of number, according to their order in the alphabet etc. it is also called the number of a man, because (as it may seem) the name of the beast, containing this number, is also the name of a man. And this I take to be the most simple interpretation.

(2) What the name is whereof the Holy Spirit here speaks, it may easily be gathered out of the text. For:

[1] The Holy Spirit does not speak of Antichrist's name properly, but of the name of the beast which Antichrist should cause all sorts of men to take upon them. If therefore we know what the beast is, it will not be hard to tell what the name is. The beast – whose name *Antichrist* shall compel men to take upon them – is the former beast described in the beginning of the chapter. For so it is said, that Antichrist the second beast, "exerciseth the authority of the former beast, that he causeth men to worship the first beast whose deadly wound was healed: that he causeth an image to be made to the beast, that he giveth spirit to the image of the beast, that he suffereth none to buy or sell which have not the name of the beast: which cannot be understood but of the former beast."

Now that beast described in the former part of the chapter is without doubt the Roman or Latin state, as has been proved heretofore and the papists sometimes confess; the name whereof without question is Roman or Latin. If therefore the name Roman or Latin in the learned tongues contain the number 666, then the name of the beast which Antichrist causes men to take upon them, is Roman or Latin. But in what language are we to account the number of the beast's name? Surely either in Greek which is most likely, because the Revelation was written in Greek or in Hebrew, because the

Revelation (as some think) was given in Hebrew to John, being a Hebrew-born. Or else we may take the beast's name according to his own language set down in Hebrew characters, because the Latins do not use their letters as the Hebrews and Greeks do in numeration. For seeing as we know what the beast itself is, we might well take that name which fits this number any of these ways.

Irenaeus (whose master Polycarp had been John's disciple) reports that those who had seen John face-to-face did teach that the number of the name of the beast according to the computation of the Greeks by the letters which be in it, shall contain 666. He therefore sets down three names in Greek letters containing that number: in two whereof there is no show of reason that either of them should be this name, seeing neither of them (I mean Ευανθας and Τειταν) is the name of the beast.

The third name, is Λατεῖνος, whereof he writes thus: *Sed & Λατεῖνος nomen sexcentorum sexaginta sex numerum; and valde verisimile est. Quoniam verissunum regnum hoc habet vocabulum, Latini enim sunt qui nunc regnant*: "But the name *Lateinos* also contains the number 666, and it is verse likely, because the most true kingdom has this name. For they are Latins which now reign." Which in effect is as much as if he had said that the name Latin is very likely, because it has the number 666, and is the name of the beast which figures *verissimum regnum* the most true kingdom, that is the Latin or Roman state. The name of the beast therefore in Greek, containing the number, is Λατεινος, that is to say: *Latin*.

(3) In Hebrew the beast's name comprehending that number is רומיית, that is *Roman*. For the beast's name being a collective noun or name, may indifferently, according to the manner of the Hebrews, be uttered either in the masculine or feminine gender. And the feminine termination does better fit the prophecy, not only because it renders the just number, but also because the beast as it is subject to Antichrist being the adulterous Roman state, is elsewhere in the feminine called *the whore of Babylon* and *the mother*

George Downame

of fornications. The most usual name of the beast in it own language, that is, the Latin tongue, is *Romanus*, which in Hebrew characters is, as Master Fox supposes, רמענוש, to the knowledge whereof as himself reports he attained by earnest prayer.

And that the name *Latin* or *Roman* in the learned tongues is the name whereof the Holy Spirit speaks, it appears because everything here spoken of the name, agrees fitly and properly thereunto. For firstly, it is the name of the beast. Secondly, it contains the number 666, as may appear by this supposition:

Λ	30	ר	200	ר	200
α	1	ו	6	מ	40
τ	300	מ	40	ע	70
ε	5	י	10	נ	50
ĩ	10	י	10	ו	6
v	50	ת	400	ש	300
o	70				
ς	200				
	666		666		666

Thirdly, it is such a name as he, to whom all other notes of Antichrist do agree (I mean the pope) enforces men to take upon them, as shall be shown. Fourthly, because the name *Latinus* or *Romanus* is also the name of a man. For *Latinus* was one of the ancient kings of Italy, and Romanus was one of the popes. Wherefore I do not doubt to conclude that the name is *Roman* or *Latin* in the learned tongues. For howsoever many others' names may be produced which comprehend the number 666, yet either they are not the name of the beast, or are such names as Antichrist was not to impose upon men. But of this, more hereafter.[334]

(4) Now let us see what that mark is whereof the Holy Spirit speaks. *Character* is as it were a cognizance and a note of difference whereby men of any profession, or religion, are known and distinguished from others. And it is partly inward and partly outward. The inward is that which is imprinted in the soul; the outward is that which is either expressed or received outwardly, as namely in the forehead, or in the right hand.

In the forehead that is by outward profession, and in the right hand that is by operation, as the ordinary gloss expounds. As for example, the character or mark of a Christian or servant of Christ is subjection unto Christ and acknowledgement of him to be our head and Savior. This inwardly is the grace of a true faith wrought in the soul by the finger of God's Spirit, whereby we believe in Christ our Savior. For those that truly believe are sealed or signed to salvation.[335] That which outwardly is expressed, is either by concession of the mouth, or operation of the hands. In respect whereof, profession of the Christian faith may truly be said to be the outward mark of a Christian, as also *determinat us modus us viuēdi*, etc. (as the Schoolmen speak) the certain manner of living according to the law and religion of Christ.

So that he who believes with his heart and confesses with his mouth that Jesus is Christ, and also frames his life according to the law and doctrine of Christ, he may be said to have the mark of God (Revelation 9:4), both in the heart by believing, and in the forehead by profession, and in the right hand by operation. See Roman 10:9-10 and 2 Timothy 2:19. And furthermore, the outward marks received to testify our subjection unto Christ and our communion with him, as also to distinguish us from men of other religions, are the sacraments of Christ, as baptism and the Lord's supper. And thus you

---

[334] Book 2 Chapter 10
[335] Ephesians 1:13

see the mark of a Christian which is but one in substance, namely the true acknowledgement of Christ, is thus variously expressed and testified.

(5) The like may be said of the mark of the beast, which is also called *the mark of his name*.[336] The beast as we have proved is the Roman state, the name is Roman or Latin. The mark therefore of the beast is that whereby they of the Romish or Latin religion whom we call papists, are distinguished from others, that is their subjection unto the pope as their head and acknowledgement of the See of Rome. This inwardly in the soul is their implicit faith: whereby every papist is bound hand over head to believe whatsoever the pope or Church of Rome believes, and rather because they are to be persuaded that neither of both can err. That which outwardly is expressed is either by confession of the mouth or operation of the hands.

So that the profession of the Romish religion and certain manner of living according to the laws and customs of the pope and church of Rome may also be said to be the mark of Antichristians, even as the observation of the heathen rites is called (2 Maccabees 4:10) *the character of the Greeks*.

Whosoever therefore in heart believes whatsoever the pope and church of Rome do or shall believe, and outwardly professes the Romish religion and frames his life according to the laws and customs of the church of Rome, as for example to fall down before images, to adore the eucharist, to frequent the mass etc., he may be truly said to have the mark of the beast. Moreover, the outward marks received to testify their communion with the church of Rome, are certain sacraments of their holy mother church, which as they say do *imprimere charactere indelebilem*, imprint a character that cannot be done away, and therefore are not to be iterated, as namely their sacraments of confirmation and orders.

In the former whereof (which they prefer before baptism) all young ones are anointed in the forehead with oil, which they call *chrisma salutis*, the

---

[336] Revelation 14:11

chrism of salvation, and without which they will have none to be accounted Christians. *Nunquā erit Christianus* (say they in their law) *nisi confirmatione episcopali fuerit Chrismatus.*[337] In the latter, those of their clergy besides their shaving on their heads, are anointed also on their heads, as bishops, or on their hands as priests. Thus you see also how the characteristic note or mark of Antichristians which is one in substance, namely subjection to the pope and acknowledgment of the See of Rome, is variously expressed and testified.

Whosoever therefore since the revelation of Antichrist is a Roman or Latin in respect of his religion, acknowledging the pope's supremacy, and professing himself a member of the church of Rome, that is to say, in one word every resolved papist, has the mark of the beast, his name and number of his name.

(6) Now it remains that, by application of this prophecy to the pope, I should show that he causes all both small and great, rich and poor, free and bond, that he should give them a mark in their right hand or in their foreheads: And that no man might buy or sell, save he that had the mark, or the name of the beast, or the number of his name. Whereby this much is meant: that Antichrist by his usurped dominion and tyranny should make all sorts of men subject unto him, and to testify their subjection both by words and deed: and that he should suffer none to live among them or to enjoy the benefits of human society, but such as acknowledge the See of Rome, profess themselves members of the Roman church, and use the Latin religion and service. All which does fully and only agree to the pope of Rome. For he, by his devilish policy usurped authority, lying wonders and all deceitfulness of unrighteousness, had not only brought all men both high and low into subjection, but also persuaded them that upon necessity of salvation, and pain of damnation, they were to subject themselves unto him, and both by word and deed to testify their subjection.

---

[337] De consecrat. dist. 5. c. vt iciuni.

Hereunto belongs that oracle (for so sometimes they call their their decrees) of Boniface VIII *Subessa* (says he) *Romano pontifici, omni humana creaturae declaramus, dicimus, definimus & pronunciamus omnino esse de necessitate salutis*:[338] "To every human creature, we declare, affirm, define, and pronounce, that to be subject to the pope of Rome it is a matter altogether necessary to salvation." Whereupon the gloss says, *Quic quid saluatur est sub Romano pontifice*: "Whatsoever is saved, is subject to the pope." The same is concluded by Thomas Aquinas, and others, that to be subject to the pope is of the necessity of salvation.[339]

Stephen V a.k.a. VI decreed that such canons as were concluded upon and given out by the See of Rome, are of necessity unto salvation to be observed. Calixtus II straitly forbade any to dissent from the church of Rome: "For as the Son came to do the will of his Father, so Christians must do the will of their mother the church of Rome. For to gainsay the church of Rome is heresy.[340] Those who deny the pope to have both powers, deny the gospel: and those who deny the pope to have the primacy of the universal church,[341] their error is equal to the error of the Greek, who deny the Holy Spirit to proceed both from the Father and the Son.[342] If therefore you will not be a heretic, this must be thy faith: that as there is one God immutable, so there is one vicar general of God upon earth (namely the vicar of Rome) whose ship is stable.[343] For seeing as in the triumphant church there is one supreme prince to whose obedience all that church is most perfectly subject – to wit, God[344] – it follows necessarily that one supreme prince is president over the whole militant church, to wit, the pope, whose precepts all are

---

[338] Extr. de Maior. & obed. c. vnā sanctam.
[339] Lib. de error. Graecor. c. 72. Antonin. sum. 3. part. tit. 22. c. 6. §. 5. An. 884
[340] Ex. 1. Bal. act. pontif. Rom. Capistran fol. 26.
[341] Cupers. pag. 46. in summar. num. 9.
[342] Cupers. pag. 56. num. 21.
[343] Capistran. fol. 32
[344] Clementin. lib. 5. de hareticis, cap. ad nostrum in Gloss.

bound to obey. And this privilege Christ has given to the church of Rome, that all must be obedient unto it, as unto Christ."[345]

Therefore he sustains the sentence of condemnation [upon whosoever rejects obedience to the pope],[346] as if he contemned God's omnipotence.[347] And to conclude as I began with another oracle or canon of their law, *Peccatum igitur paganitatis incurrit, quisquis dum Christianum se esse asserit, sedi apostolica obedire contemnit:*[348] "He incurs therefore the sin of Paganism, whosoever professing himself to be a Christian, renounces obedience to the Apostolic See."

(7) And as he has made all to subject themselves unto him, all I mean whose names are not written in the book of the lamb, (for this is the universality that the papists brag of) so he has caused all both small and great, rich and poor etc. to testify their subjection, as namely by pinning their faith on his sleeve, and binding themselves to believe as he believes: by professing his Antichristian faith and religion of popery; by observing his popish that is to shy superstitious and idolatrous rites and customs, as frequenting masses, adoring images and relics, worshiping the cross and eucharist, praying to saints, yea to sticks and stones, going on pilgrimage, praying in Latin and that on beads, etc. by taking his mark both on the forehead in the sacrament of confirmation, and on the hand in the sacrament of orders, but especially by taking an oath of fidelity and obedience unto him. For therein especially they receive his mark both in the forehead by solemn profession, and in the right hand which they lay on the book. This oath not only graduates, priests, and bishops, but kings and emperors were compelled to take it.[349]

---

[345] Anton. part. 3. tit. 22. cap. 6. §. 5.
[346] This section is unclear in the original.
[347] Ibid. cap. 5. §. 17. ex Gloss. ordin. Papae applicata.
[348] Dist. 81. c. si qui sunt.
[349] Vid. Meditat. 1. Foxij in 14. cap. Apoc. Decret. Gregor. libro 2. tit. 24. de iureiur. c. Ego N. Clementin. lib. 2. de iureiur. c. Romani.

And whereas it is said that Antichrist should take order that none might buy or sell, unless he have the mark, or the name of the beast or the number of his name: that speech does so fit the popes of Rome as that it might seem rather to be a narration of that which they have done, than a prophecy of that which they were to do. For Martin V in his bull annexed to the council of Constance gave straight charge to all governors, that they should not suffer any Christians (such as John Wycliffe, John Hus and Jerome of Prague who in that bull are condemned for heretics) who acknowledge not the See of Rome, nor embrace the doctrines and traditions of holy mother church, not believing as the church of Rome believes, nor living in the communion of that church, that is to say, which have not the mark, nor the name of the beast, nor number of his name, they should not suffer them I say, *domicilia tenere, larem fouere, contractus inire, negotiationes and mercaturas quaslibet exercere, aut humanit at is solatia cum Christi fidelibus habere*. To keep neither house nor hearth, to make contracts, to exercise any traffic or merchandise, or to have any comforts of human society with other Christians.

In like sort Paulus III when Henry VIII of famous memory had shaken off his yoke, and renounced his mark, he forbade all men to use any traffic or merchandise, or to make any contracts or covenants with him and his subjects: he deposed as much as in him lay, by his bull of excommunication, the king, disabled his posterity, absolved his subjects from obedience, exposed his subjects and their goods to violence and spoil, according to the inscription in his coin, *Gens and regnum quod non seruierit mihi exterminabitur*, The nation or kingdom which serves not me, shall be rooted out.

The like thunderbolt, Pius V sent out against our Sovereign Lady of blessed memory Queen Elizabeth: and Sixtus V against Henry the King of Navarre (now King of France) and Henry prince of Condee. And hereunto serve their bloody inquisitors at this day, who are to suffer none to live, or to have the benefit of human society, who are but suspected of schism or heresy. And who is a heretic? That does not believe as the pope and church of Rome believes, though he believes according to the Scriptures. And who is a schismatic? He that does not acknowledge the pope to be the head of the church.[350]

Seeing therefore the pope of Rome causes all sorts of men to take upon them the mark of the beast, and suffers none to buy or sell that have not the mark or name of the beast or number of his name, it cannot be avoided but that he is Antichrist.

(8) And these were the principal effects of Antichrist noted in the Scriptures, whereunto some others may be added out of Revelation 13, which have in part been touched heretofore: as firstly, that he exercises all the power of the former beast. Secondly, that he causes men to worship the former beast. Thirdly, that he forces men upon pain of death to worship the image of the beast. All of which, as well as the former, agree to the pope.

For as touching the first, who does not know that the pope has swayed the Roman state for many hundred years? Exercising a more sovereign and absolute authority over men of all sorts, then ever the heathenish emperors did. For he indeed has the authority of the king of kings over his subjects; he is *perpetuus dictator*, whom the princes of the world adore and worship.[351]

He is as Boniface VIII in the great jubilee year of 1300 (having shown himself the one day in his pontifical vestments, and the second in the imperial robes) proclaimed of himself: "I am pope and emperor, I have both the heavenly and the earthly empire, and as they speak in their law, the monarchy of both powers; he has the princehood of the whole world, as we have heard before." And where does he exercise this authority? In the sight of the beast, that is, at Rome, which is his papal seat, and in the government whereof he succeeded the emperors.

---

[350] Antonin. part. 3. tit. 22. c. 5. §. 11.
[351] Bald. in c. ecclesia, vt lit. pendent. Bloud. Rom. instaur. lib. 3.

(9) And that the pope makes the inhabitants of the earth to worship the former beast, it is as evident; seeing his main policies and chief endeavors serve to magnify the Roman state. To this end, besides many other policies in part observed before, do his jubilees tend, wherein he uses to promise plenary remission of all sins to all that either come on pilgrimage to Rome, or miscarry in their journey. As also the incredible indulgences and pardons which he grants to those which shall come as pilgrims to Rome, to visit the holy places there, especially the seven churches which are privileged above the rest. To which purpose there is reported in an old English book[352] (and the report no doubt was currant in times of popery) the whole pardon of Rome granted by several popes, a part whereof I will briefly recite for their behoove, to whom the absurdities of popery are not known.

The seven privileged churches, whereof not only that author speaks, but ⟨◊⟩ also of late has written a whole book,[353] are: [1] the church of Saint Peter in the Vatican, [2] the church of Saint Paul without the walls, [3] the church of Saint Laurence without the walls, [4] the church of holy cross in Jerusalem, [5] the church of Saint Mary Major, [6] the church of Saint Sebastian without the city, and [7] the church of Saint John Lateran.

To all them that daily go to the church of Saint Peter, Sylvester granted the third part of all their sins released, and 2800 years pardon. And the merits of as many *lentons* or *quarins*. Now a *quarin*, says my author, is to go woolward and barefoot for seven years, and to fast from bread and water on the Fridays,[354] to come under no covered place unless he is to hear mass in the church door or porch, or drink out of no other vessel but in the same that he made his vow in. He that does all these points seven years together, does, and wins a *quarin*, that is to say, a *Lenton*.

Besides, there is an image of our Lord about the church door, having between his feet one of the pence that God was sold for; as often as you look

---

[352] Arnaldus Londinens.
[353] De 7. Urbis ecclesys.
[354] Part of this sentence is unclear and omitted.

upon that penny you have 1,400 years of pardon. In that church are eleven altars, of which seven are especially privileged with grace and pardon. At the first altar is the visage of our Lord; whoever looks on that, has 700 years of pardon, etc. Before the quire door stand two crosses; whoever kisses the crosses has 500 years pardon. From the annunciation to the assumption of Our Lady, hangs a cloth of Our Lady's own making before the quire, and as many times as a man beholds it, he has 400 years of pardon, etc.

(10) They that visit the church of Saint Paul without the walls have 48,000 years of pardon. In the same manner on Childermass Day 4,.000 years of pardon. In the same manner on the vias of Saint Martin when the church was hallowed: 14,000 years of pardon, and as many *quarins*, and the third part of all sins released. Those that visit the church of Saint Laurence, at the high altar have 18,000 years of pardon and as many *quarins*. And whoever goes thither every Wednesday, he delivers a soul out of purgatory, and quits himself of all sins. In the church *Sancta Crucis*, that is, of the holy cross,is given 100,000 years of pardon and as many *quarins*, and every Sunday a soul out of Purgatory, and the third part of all sins released.

To those who visit the church of St. Mary Major, it is granted at the high altar 14,000 years of pardon, and as many *quarins*; and at the altar on the right hand, 19,000 years of pardon. And Pope Nicolas IV and S. Gregory each of them granted thereto 10,000 years of pardon. And from the ascension of our Lord unto Christmas, you have there 14,000 years of pardon, and as many *quarins*, and the third part of all sins released. To them that visit the church of St. Sebastian is granted forgiveness of sins and all penance. At the high altar is given 2,800 years of pardon, and at the first altar in the church, 2,400.

There is a vault where lie buried 49 popes that were martyrs: whoso comes first into that place delivers eight souls out of Purgatory of such as he most desires, and as much pardon thereto, that all the world cannot number nor reckon. And every Sunday you deliver there a soul out of purgatory. In that vault stands a pit in which Peter and Paul were hid 250 years, he that put his head into that pit and takes it out again, is clean of all sins. To that place, five popes each of them granted a thousand years of pardon, and as many *quarins*. And so the grace that is at St. Sebastians is grounded that it cannot be taken away.

To those that visit the church of St. John Lateran, Pope Sylvester gave as many years of pardon, as it rained drops of water the day that he hallowed the same church. And that time it rained so sore, that no man had seen a greater rain before that day. And when he had granted this, he doubted whether he had so much power. Then a voice came from heaven, and said, "Pope Sylvester, you have power enough to give that pardon." And God granted this much thereto, that if a man had made a vow to Jerusalem, and lacked good to do his pilgrimage, if he went from St. Peter's Church to St. John Lateran's, he shall be absolved from that promise. And any time that a man comes to Saint John Lateran's, he is quit of all sins, and of all penance, with that that he be penitent for his sins. Blessed is the mother that bears the child that hears mass on Saturdays at Saint John Lateran's. For he delivered all them that he desired out of Purgatory to the number of 77 souls.

An item on the tower of the church stands as a double cross, that was made of the sword wherewith John was beheaded, and every time a man beholds that cross he has 14,000 years pardon. At the high altar a man may have remission of all sins, and of all penance, and innumerable pardon more than he needs for himself. There is a grave wherein John laid himself, he that put therein his head he has 100,000 years of pardon, and as many *karins*.

These indulgences with many such like (which for brevity's sake I omit) my author says are written in a marble stone before the choir door etc. Besides these seven, there are many inferior churches whereunto great indulgences have been granted by the popes. There are named in the aforesaid book, twenty-six churches, wherein is granted to those who visit any of them 1,000 years pardon, and in some 3000, in others 5,000 some, wherein promise is made of release from a third part of sins, and in some from all sins. Here is a church of Saint Gregory, in which whosoever is buried, he shall never be damned. "Thus," (says my author) "may a man have at Rome great pardon and soul health. Blessed be the people and in good time born that receives these graces and well keeps them," etc.

(11) Hereby it appears that the pope causes the inhabitants of the earth to worship the beast with seven heads, that is, seven hills: that with the city of Rome (which we have proved to be the whore of Babylon) the inhabitants of the earth have committed spiritual fornication, and that with the cup of her fornications they have been infatuated and made drunk. And that the pope has caused men upon pain of death to worship the image of the beast which he has animated and put life into, it is easy to prove, whether you understand it literally or mystically.

For literally, as they have put life and motion into images and made them to speak in the sight of men; so have they suffered none to live that would not participate with them in their idolatry which they call worshiping of images. Mystically, the image signifies either the pope's court, or empire renewed, or both: the one resembling the authority and power, the other bearing the name and representing the dignity of the old empire. Of the pope's court at Rome, and of his legates and officers abroad there is no question to be made, but that none are suffered to live which worship not them. And it is true also of the empire.

But by worshiping the image of the beast, we do not understand obedience to the emperor in his lawful decrees: but the obedience performed unto him as he is an image of the persecuting emperors, inspired by the pope, and serving as his minister to establish and propagate the Romish religion. In this sense as he who obeys him worships the image of the beast, and is in the same predicament with those that receive the mark of the beast (Revelation 14:9), so he that obeys him not is put to death; and dying in this quarrel is in the same happy state with those which refuse to receive the mark of the beast.[355]

---

[355] Revelation 14:13, 15:2

Chapter 9

Of those things which Antichrist was and is to suffer.

(1) We have heard what Antichrist was to do to others: now let us consider what the Holy Spirit foretells shall be done unto him. There is mention made in Revelation 17:12 of the ten horns, that is the rulers of the ten provinces subject to the empire in the West, who although in the apostle's time had not received kingdom or sovereign authority, but were deputies only under the emperor, yet after the decay of the empire in the west, they together with Antichrist divide the Roman empire among them, reigning by sovereign authority, he in Rome and part of Italy, they in the other provinces.

Of these ten horns it is said that they for a time should give their power and strength to the beast, meaning Antichrist, and that in his quarrel they shall fight against Christ the lamb in his members. But the blood of martyrs being the seed of the Church, and the truth prevailing when it is most oppugned, Christ by the constancy of his martyrs and preaching of his word overcomes. For though in respect of the manner of his resistance he seems a meek lamb: yet he shall be sure to overcome, because he is the King of kings and Lord of lords; being able by weak and foolish things (as they are esteemed in the world) to overcome the wise and strong.

And however those few in comparison that stood with him were condemned for heretics and schismatics, yet they are called *chosen* and *faithful servants of the Lord*. Whereas contrariwise the general multitudes (whereof the catholic apostasy consists) are the slaves of Antichrist, and subject to the whore of Babylon. For the waters whereon she sits are peoples and multitudes, nations and tongues. But when as our Savior Christ shall discover Antichrist, and by the ministry of the word, as it were the breath of his mouth, waste and consume him: then shall the ten kings, which before had joined with him, set themselves against him, and those which before had committed fornication with the whore of Babylon, shall hate her and make her desolate and naked, and shall eat her flesh and shall burn her with fire. And that this decay of the Antichristian state does follow upon the preaching of the gospel, it appears in Revelation 14:6-8, where it is said that upon the preaching of the everlasting Gospel, an angel says, "It is fallen, it is fallen, Babylon that great city: for she gave to all nations to drink the wine of the wrath of her fornication."

For until this time that Christ discovers Antichrist and in some measure consumes him with the spirit of his mouth, the ten kings are given over by God to support with one consent the beast and purple harlot; whom, after Antichrist is discovered, they shall hate and oppugn.

(2) But let us come to the application. For even as from this place I proved before that Antichrist is already come, so may I now from hence conclude that the pope is that Antichrist.

That Antichrist has come, it is as certain as that the provinces of the Empire are not ruled by deputies of the emperor, but by sovereign princes, who have together with Antichrist divided the empire among them. And that the pope is that Antichrist it is as certain. For he it is, who, as well as the kings, has risen by the decay of the empire in the west: he it is, and no other, to whom these kings have with one consent given their strength and power, submitting themselves unto him as his vassals, swearing to maintain and support him, fighting his battles and drawing their sword at his beck.

And being made drunk with the cup of his fornications they fought against the lamb, and persecuted those servants of Christ whom Antichrist condemns as heretics and schismatics: who notwithstanding are in truth the called, chosen, and faithful; though few and despised in the world. When as contrariwise the universality of people whereon the whore of Babylon sits, and whereof the adulterous church of Rome consists, are but the branded slaves of Antichrist. But however these kings, while they were besotted and given over by God in his just judgment that they should submit themselves to the Antichrist of Rome, did seek by all means to support him.

Yet when Christ had discovered him to be Antichrist, and by the preaching of his word as it were the spirit of his mouth began to waste and consume him, and more and more since the times of Luther to abate the opinion which men had conceived of him; then these princes – not all, but some of them – began to revolt from Antichrist, and to hate the Antichristian whore of Babylon the city and church of Rome, and as much as in them lies have left her desolate and naked; and the rest in God's good time shall accomplish his will.[356]

For this prophecy concerning that which Antichrist was to suffer, is as yet fulfilled but in part. And still there remains to be fulfilled the final destruction of Rome the seat of Antichrist, before the end of the world, foretold in Revelation 18, and the final overthrow of Antichrist at the glorious appearing of Christ at his second coming, prophesied in 2 Thessalonians 2:8 and Revelation 19:20.

Seeing therefore Antichrist – the great enemy of Christ and his church – is to be overthrown by these three means, by the powerful ministry of the word, by the puissant strength and power of Christian princes, by the glorious coming of Christ to judgment; all faithful ministers are to be stirred up seriously and earnestly to oppose themselves against Antichrist, that by their ministry as it were the spirit of Christ's mouth, he may be more and more wasted and consumed.

All true Christian princes are to be excited not only to hate the whore of Babylon, but also according to the prophecy of the Holy Spirit to make her desolate and naked, to eat her flesh and burn her with fire, and to do to her children as she has done to the servants of Christ.[357]

And finally all sound Christians are to be exhorted, earnestly and continually to pray that the Lord Jesus would not only consume Antichrist,

---

[356] See Chapter 2, Section 11.
[357] Revelation 18:6

giving success to the ministry of his servants: but also that he would hasten his second coming and destroy him at his glorious appearing.[358] Even so Lord Jesus, come quickly. And thus have I shown that the prophecies of the Holy Spirit in the Scriptures concerning Antichrist do most fitly and properly agree to the pope of Rome, whereupon I do necessarily conclude that therefore the pope of Rome is the grand Antichrist described in the Scriptures.

FINIS.

---

[358] Revelation 22:17, 20

Book 2

The second book, maintaining that the pope is Antichrist.

Chapter 1

We answer Bellarmine's first argument concerning the name Antichrist.

Having in the former book sufficiently proved by evident demonstration out of the word of God that the pope of Rome is Antichrist, it remains that we should maintain this our assertion against the arguments of the papists.

For as the force and evidence of our proofs may persuade us to embrace this truth; so the weakness and sophistry, which appears in the objections of our adversaries may confirm us in this persuasion. And rather if we consider either the weight of this controversy itself, or their will and skill to maintain their part; or lastly the advantage which they seem to have in this controversy.

For first the controversy itself is of such consequence, as that if our assertion be true, then is all popery overthrown, and all controversies between us and them easily decided, then are all papists limbs of Antichrist, and all their doctrines peculiar to them, errors of Antichrist. And if you respect their will, you need not doubt, but that they, being wholly devoted unto the pope, have done their best endeavor to free their head and Lord from all imputation of Antichristianism. And for their skill, they being men of great learning and much reading, you may be well assured that they have scarcely omitted anything, which may be said in so weighty a cause. And questionless, they have no small advantage in this controversy being to prove the negative part.

For whereas we cannot prove the affirmative but by the concurrence of those manifold properties and marks which the Holy Spirit has assigned unto Antichrist: they on the other side have liberty to disprove the same, and to prove the negative, if they can but show plainly and evidently, that any one several and essential mark, ascribed unto Antichrist in the Scriptures, does not agree to their lord god the pope.

For if the Scriptures foretell us as touching the place, that Antichrist shall have his seat in Babylon, that is, Rome, which being situated on seven hills, had in the apostle's time under the emperor, and since under the pope, dominion over the kings of the earth, and that in Rome, professing herself the Church of God, because it is said, that Antichrist shall sit in the Temple of God: as concerning the time, that he should sit in Rome, after the removing and taking away of the Emperors, whom he was to succeed in the government of Rome, as has been shown out of these places: 2 Thessalonians 2:7-8, Revelation 13 and 17; and in respect of his conditions and qualities, that he should be for opposition an adversary, although a disguised enemy: for pride and ambition, advancing himself above all that is called God. For his other vices, a man of sin in general, and more specially an horrible idolator, in regard to his effects, that he and his followers should be workers of signs and wonders, in the sight of men, that he should compel all sorts of men to receive the mark or name of the beast, or number of his name. And lastly, for that which he was to suffer, that Christ shall consume him with the breath of his mouth, that is, the ministry of the gospel; and that thereupon the ten horns which first assisted him, shall afterwards assault him.

It follows therefore, that unto such as we affirm to be Antichrist, all these notes are to be applied (as we have applied them all to the pope of Rome), whereas contrariwise the denial of any one essential property, is an argument sufficient to prove the negative.

As for example, if any man will take upon him to prove that the Turk is Antichrist, because some of the marks seem to fit him, he shall never be able to prove it, because all the properties do not agree unto him. For neither has he his seat in Rome, neither does he sit in the Church of God, neither is he a covert and disguised, but an open and professed enemy: neither may he be matched with the true Antichrist, either in advancing himself above all that is called God, or in idolatry, or in lying signs and wonders, etc. And from any of these we may reason thus:

- Antichrist was to have his seat in Rome, which is mystical Babylon.
- The Turk does not have his seat there.
- Therefore he is not Antichrist.

Antichrist sits in the church of God; the Turk does not, etc., wherefore it would be much easier to prove the negative, if it were true, than the affirmative. If therefore the papists, having bent all their forces and employed the uttermost of their skill to prove that which were most easy to prove, if it were true, shall notwithstanding be found unable to produce any one sound and sufficient argument, to clear their pope from Antichristianism, then do we not have we just cause to confirm ourselves in that truth, which before has been demonstrated, namely: that the pope is Antichrist?

(2) Let us therefore consider their arguments, and conceits whereupon their arguments are grounded: not as they are propounded by the elder papists, which lived in the days of our forefathers (for their conceits concerning Antichrist were mere dotages), but as they are delivered by the refiners of popery the Jesuits, and namely by Bellarmine, whose books are as it were a shot whereunto many of them, as it seems, have contributed.

Bellarmine therefore in his third book *De Pontifice Romano*, reduces all his arguments to nine heads: [1] concerning the name Antichrist; [2] concerning his person, whether he be but one man, or a state and succession of men; [3] concerning the time of his coming, and death; [4] of his proper name; [5] of his nation and followers; [6] of his seat; [7] of his doctrine and manners; [8] of his miracles; [9] of his reign and battles. From all these, he hopes (although in vain) to prove that the pope is not Antichrist.

(3) And first from the name he argues thus:

- Antichrist is *hostis & aemulus Christi*, that is, such an enemy as is opposed unto Christ in emulation of like honor.
- The pope is not an enemy, nor opposed unto Christ in emulation of like honor.
- Therefore the pope is not Antichrist.

The proposition which we not only grant, but also take to be the ground of some of our proofs, that he labors to prove, and in that proof spends almost the whole first chapter. But the assumption, wherein is all the controversy between us and them, that in a manner he takes for granted – in both playing the part of a right sophister.[359]

For which of our writers ever denied, that ἀντίχριστος signifies *hostem et aemulum Christi*? Although Musculus[360] also says that Antichrist is he who, being an enemy unto Christ, professes himself to be his vicar, and says that the word may signify so much, yet he denies not the former signification, but retains the same with this addition: that Antichrist is such as one as challenges unto himself the office and authority of Christ himself, and being indeed an enemy, and a counter-Christ, professes himself to be the Vicar or Vicegerent of Christ upon earth.

And this may be proved by the meaning of the name. For ἀντί in composition, commonly signifies three things; opposition, equality, substitution. Opposition, as in the word αντιχεμεινοσ; equality, as αντιθεος, αντιχειρ; substitution, as αντίπαλος; Proconsul, ανθύπατος, Propraetor or Legatus Praetoris; αντιπρότης, the putting of one case for another: and in this sense the sacraments of the New Testament, substituted and ordained instead of the old, are called the ἀντίτυπα of them.[361] And all these significations sometimes are incident to one and the same word. As αντιαρχηγός signifies sometimes, *contrariae partis ducem*: the chieftain of the

---

[359] Wolfgang Musculus, *Common Places*, chapter on the power of the magistrates.
[360] See Book 1 Chapter 4 Section 1
[361] 1 Peter 3:21

contrary part; sometimes *propraetorem*, that is, one who in the province has the same authority which the Praetor has in the city: sometimes also him *qui est vice praetoris*, as the lieutenant or deputy. In like sort, all these significations may be applied to the word ἀντίχριστος, and it in them all most fitly agrees to the pope who, being indeed an enemy unto Christ, and challenging unto himself the office and authority of Christ, as if he were a counter-Christ, does also profess himself to be the Vicar of Christ.

(4) "Yea," but says Bellarmine, "*Antichrist* cannot by any means signify *the vicar of Christ*: firstly because ἀντί properly signifies *opposition*." I answer that ἀντί simply signifies for; and in composition, as many times it signifies against, so sometimes also equal or like, and sometimes for or instead, as Greek writers and lexicographers do teach, etc.

Secondly, "We must," (he says) "understand the word as it is used in the Scriptures." But in the Scriptures it is used to signify an enemy of Christ, which we do confess: albeit his proofs are ridiculous, alleging 2 Thessalonians 2 and Matthew 24, where the word ἀντίχριστος is not once used. Notwithstanding we accept his ground: that we are so to understand the word *Antichrist* as it is used in the Scriptures. Now it is used in the epistles of John only, and there ascribed not to open and professed enemies, but to such as being enemies, notwithstanding professed the name of Christ, as the heretics of those times.

Thirdly, "all those authors," (says he) "which have written of Antichrist, have under that name understood a notable false Christ, who shall affirm himself to be Christ." If they mean that Antichrist shall be such a false christ, as shall plainly and directly affirm himself to be Christ the only Messiah, that affirmation agrees not with that Antichrist whom the Scriptures describe. If they hold that although in words he professes himself a follower and servant of Christ, and yet indeed obtrudes himself upon the church, as if he were Christ, taking upon him the titles, attributes, offices and authority of Christ, which in effect is as much as if he should say; "I am Christ" (Christ being a name of office) we also confess so much, and also profess that the name Antichrist in this signification, most fitly agrees unto the pope.

Fourthly, he alleges Henry Stephen, but neither he nor any approved author denies that *Antichristus* may signify he who, being an enemy of Christ, professes himself to be his vicar.

And therefore all these four arguments are frivolous: for although Antichrist do signify an enemy to Christ, yet that does not hinder but that it may signify him which is the vicar of Christ: [1] Because he who in *profession* is the vicar of Christ, may in *deed* be the enemy of Christ. [2] because the composition of the word imports so much. [3] Because the beast which figures Antichrist is said to have two horns like the Lamb: for *horn* in the Scripture signifies *power*, and the two horns his twofold sovereign power. Whosoever therefore challenges this twofold power, as the Vicegerent of Christ he has two horns like the lamb: and the same person, as he is the Vicar of Christ in profession, so is he also that Antichrist, which is resembled by the two-horned beast. The Scriptures therefore describe Antichrist, both as an enemy of Christ, and as the vicar of Christ – an enemy indeed, and vicar in profession.

(5) And so much of his proposition, which we hold to be most true, that *Antichrist* according to the signification of the word is *hostis & aemulus Christi*, but also we add that the word may signify also such an adversary as obtrudes himself unto the Church, as a *Prochristus*, that is, as a vicar of Christ.

Let us therefore come to his assumption, and consider how he proves that the pope is not *hostis & aemulus Christi*, an enemy, and one that seeks to match himself with Christ. Indeed, because the pope confesses himself to be the servant of Christ, and subject unto him in all things, neither does he by any means say that he is Christ, nor make himself equal unto him. As if he should say, he that professes himself to be the servant of Christ, is not an enemy of Christ, and he that does not call himself Christ, nor make himself equal unto him, he is not *aemulus Christi*.

As touching the former, I answer, that unless the pope did confess himself to be the servant of Christ, he could not be such an adversary as Antichrist is described to be in the Scriptures, that is, a covert and disguised enemy, who under the name and profession of Christ, oppugns Christ and his truth. And although he professes himself to be the servant of Christ, does it therefore follow, that he is not an enemy to Christ? Surely no more than it follows that he is *Servus servorum Dei* indeed, because he calls himself so.

Deceivers – such as Antichrist is – pretend good names. False prophets, such as Antichrist is, are wolves in sheepskins; neither are any enemies so pernicious or dangerous, as those which make semblance of friendship. And that the pope is *aemulus Christi*, that is, an adversary opposed to Christ in emulation of like honor, we have proved heretofore at large, showing how in many things he matches himself with Christ, and in some things advances himself above him.

So that the former part of his speech does not prove his assumption, as being inconsequential; the latter needs proof, as being untrue. And yet this is all that he brings to prove that the pope is not *hostis & aemulus Christi*. But the untruth of this assumption, we have heretofore demonstrated at large, when we concluded thus:

- He that is such an adversary as is described in the Scriptures, opposed unto Christ in emulation of like honor, he is Antichrist as the papists confess.
- But the pope is such an adversary as is described in the Scriptures, opposed unto Christ in emulation of like honor, as we then proved at large.
- Therefore the pope is Antichrist.
-

Chapter 2

We maintain that Antichrist is not one definite and singular person.

(1) The second argument which Bellarmine uses to prove that the pope is not Antichrist, is drawn from the person of Antichrist, namely: that Antichrist is one certain man, whereas the popes have been many. His reason is thus framed:

- Antichrist is but one singular person.
- The pope (meaning the order or succession of popes) is not one singular person.
- Therefore the pope is not Antichrist.

To the proposition I answer, that as the pope is one, so is Antichrist. The pope is one person not in number and nature, as one certain and singular man, but one at once by law and institution, though successively as many as have enjoyed the papacy.

For even as the papists, when they say that the pope has been the head of the church and vicar of Christ these 1500 years, do not mean any one pope, but the order and succession, so we when we say that the pope has been Antichrist almost these thousand years, we mean not any one pope only, but the whole row or rabble of them since the year 607.[362]

And thus Antichrist, that is, the head of the Antichristian body, which was revealed after the taking away of the Roman Empire, and is to continue after a sort, until the end of the world, is one person: one, I say, at once ordinarily, but continued in a succession of many.

---

[362] See Book 1 Chapter 1 Section 4

The proposition thus denied by us, Bellarmine labors to confirm by authority of the Scriptures and testimonies of the fathers. Out of the Scriptures, he produces five testimonies.

[1] The first is John 5:43: "I am come in my Father's name, and you receive me not: if another shall come in his own name, him will you receive." In these words, Bellarmine understands Christ to speak of Antichrist, as of one singular person: And that he would prove by testimonies of the fathers, and four reasons. But Bellarmine and the rest of the papists, which make this collection out of this place, either ignorantly mistake, or willfully deprave this text.

{1} For first, whereas our Savior Christ speaks indefinitely, of any false teacher which should come unto them in his own name, that is, not sent of God, they expound him, as if he had spoken definitely of one singular Antichrist.

{2} Secondly, whereas Christ speaks not only indefinitely, but also conditionally, If another come, they expound him, as if in a simple and proper axiom or proposition he had prophesied of the coming of Antichrist: as if he had said, that other counterfeit messiah, that is to say, that singular Antichrist, shall come in his own name, and him you will receive. And thirdly, whereas Christ speaks of those Jews to whom he speaks, they understand him to speak of those which shall be in the end of the world.

But let us consider his proofs. The fathers, says he, do testify that these words are spoken, *de uno Antichristo*: of one Antichrist.

{1} First I answer, that although several of the fathers expound these words of Antichrist, yet none of them has that word *Uno*, one: and therefore the Jesuits collection is absurd. The fathers understand this place of Antichrist, therefore Antichrist is one singular person. For the fathers also understand that place in Matthew 24:24 of Antichrist, where our Savior Christ speaks in the plural number, of false christs and false prophets which should arise, and confer that place with this. And therefore they may seem to understand this speech of our Savior, as if he had said: "If another comes in his own name (as many indeed shall come) such will you receive." And sure it is, that the Jews have received more than one of such as have come in their own name.

{2} And secondly I answer, that the fathers had no reason to restrain these words unto Antichrist alone, as though Christ had prophesied of the Jews receiving of Antichrist for their messiah, seeing his speech is neither simple nor definite, but conditional and indefinite. Whereby our Savior Christ would show the untoward disposition of the Jews, who as they rejected him who was sent of God, so they would be ready to receive any other that should come in his own name, not sent of God. And so Nonnus, in his paraphrase upon this place, expounds these words: "But if any other come," etc.

(iii) And lastly, if these answers will not suffice, let the adversary conclude his argument drawn from the authority of the fathers in a syllogism, and when he has so done, let him prove the proposition, which must be this:

- Whatever those fathers write concerning Antichrist is true.
- (And then the assumption, which is to this effect): but this, those fathers write that Christ speaks those words, *de uno Antichristo*, of one singular Antichrist.
- And then (which will never be) I will yield to the conclusion.

(2) But omitting his testimonies, let us come to those arguments which he draws out of the text, to prove that Christ in these words speaks of one singular Antichrist. "First," says he, "Christ opposes unto himself another man, that is, person to person, as appears by these words, {*I*}, {*another*}, etc." His reason is thus to be framed:

- Where these two words, {*I*} and {*another*}, are opposed one to the other, we are to understand that as {*I*} signifies one singular person, so also {*another*}.
- But in this place, {*I*} and {*another*} are opposed.
- Therefore, etc.

I answer: where the other is taken definitely for that other, as ὁ ἄλλος is used John 18:16. and 20:2-4 there the proposition may be true. But where it is used indefinitely, as ἄλλος, *another*, in this place, it is most false: for in such speeches, to a certain and definite person, is opposed an indefinite and uncertain. As for example Job. 31:8: "What I sow, let another reap," meaning *any other*; 1 Corinthians 3:10: "I have laid the foundation and another buildeth thereon, but let everyone take heed how he buildeth thereon." Such examples are ordinary. As if I should say, this argument I call a childish reason, another would call it a dotage, and so I let it pass.

His second reason is this:

- Whom the Jews shall receive for their Messias, he is but one particular man.
- Antichrist shall be received of the Jews for their messiah, as Christ here says.
- Therefore Antichrist is but one singular man.

Answer: Christ does not here foretell that Antichrist shall be received of the Jews for their messiah. For first, his speech is conditional, therefore not a prophecy. Neither does he foretell what they were to do, but shows them what in respect of their present disposition they were ready to do, if any false teacher should obtrude himself unto them. Secondly, it is indefinite, and therefore not to be restrained to a certain person. Thirdly, he does not say that they shall receive another for their messiah coming in his own name, but only that they shall receive him. Fourthly, those Jews to whom and of whom our Savior speaks, were not to be alive at the coming of the great Antichrist, according to the opinion of the papists themselves, therefore our Savior speaks not of the Jews receiving of Antichrist, and much less of Antichrist as one particular person.

Thirdly (says he):

- All false prophets come in the name of another, not in their own name.
- But Christ here speaks of one that should come in his own name.
- Therefore he speaks not of false prophets.

He might as well have concluded against the Scriptures, that Antichrist is not a false prophet.

- "For false prophets," says Bellarmine, "come not in their own name."
- Antichrist comes in his own name.
- Therefore, if Bellarmine's argument is good, Antichrist is not a false prophet.

But I answer that Antichrist and all other false prophets may be said to come both in their own name, and also in the name of God. In their own name because they are not sent of God, in which sense our Savior Christ here speaks, "I am come," says he, "in my Father's name, sent from the bosom of my father who has sealed and sent me to this work of mediation, and you receive me not: If another shall come in his own name, not sent from God," or as Lyra expounds those words, *in nomine suo*, in his own name, that is, not having the aforesaid testimonies from God, whereby to warrant his calling from him, "such will you receive." They are said also to come in the name of God and of Christ, because they pretend (although falsely) a calling and commission from God. Jeremiah 14:14-15, Matthew 24:5.

For whereas Bellarmine expounds these words thus, in his own name, that is, shall not acknowledge any God, but advance himself above all that is called God, and assigns such a coming to the expected messiah of the Jews, it is absurd. For the Jews expect a messiah to be sent to them from God. And therefore if any shall take upon him to be their messiah, and be received of them, he will without doubt profess himself to be sent of God. And such a one may be said to come in his own name, because he is not sent of God, and in God's name, because he pretends a calling and commission from him.

Fourthly (says he):

- If Christ had spoken of false prophets, whereof many were to come, he would not have said, "if another come," but "many come."
- But the second is false.
- Therefore the first.

I answer: if Christ had spoken simply and definitely, one other shall come, there had been some show of reason in the argumentation of the adversary. But seeing he does not so speak as Bellarmine dreams, but conditionally and indefinitely, "if another shall come," there is not so much as any show of reason in this argument.

(3) The second place which Bellarmine produces is 2 Thessalonians 2:3, where the apostle entreating of Antichrist, speaks of one certain and particular person, as appears by the Greek article, ο ανθρωπος της αμαρτιας

ο υιος της απωλειας, the *man of sin, the son of perdition, the outlaw*. His reason is thus to be framed:

- Unto whatsoever the Greek article is prefixed, it is signified to be one certain and singular thing or person.
- Unto the Antichrist that man of sin, the son of perdition, the outlaw, the Greek article is prefixed.
- Therefore the Antichrist is but one certain and singular person.

The proposition he proves by the authority of Epiphanius, who says that the Greek articles restrain the signification to one certain thing, so that ανθρωπος signifies man in general, but ο ανθρωπος one singular man. And therefore Bellarmine marvels greatly that none of us who would seem to have skill in the tongues has observed so much.[363] But it were more to be marveled that Bellarmine should in this weighty cause affirm that which he knows to be false, but that he has Epiphanius upon whom to the father this untruth; and yet Epiphanius does not say that the addition of the article does always restrain the meaning to one certain and singular thing, but that it signifies the discretion or difference of the name. Howbeit that is not perpetual, for many times the article is added for ornament only and fullness of speech, when as in respect of the sense περισσός, it is redundant or superfluous.

And here there are more examples than there are leaves even in the New Testament. And therefore both in the same and like sentences the article sometimes is used, sometimes omitted without any alteration of the sense. As Luke 4:4: ουκ επ αρτω μονω ζησεται ο ανθρωπος. But in Matthew 4:4, where the same speech is recorded: ουκ επ αρτω μονω ζησεται ανθρωπος. And again where the article is used for difference's sake, it does not always point out one certain and singular thing, but only when it is used

---

[363] Haeresi 9. [quae] est Samaritanorum.

διακριτικός, for a demonstrative particle, as John 1:29: ιδε ο αμνος του θεου "Behold the Lamb of God." John 4:29 μητι ουτος εστιν ο χριστος: "Is not this that Christ?" For more usually it is used διακριτικός, that is, for difference, when it serves not to signify one special, but to distinguish the whole kind. In which sense ο ανθρωπος και ο υπερανθρωπος, is all one, as philosophers say, as Mark 2:27: "The Sabbath was made δια τον ανθρωπον, for the man, not the man for the Sabbath;" John 2:25: "He needed not that any should bear witness περι του ανθρωπου, of the man (meaning any man) for himself knew what was, εν τω ανθρωπω, in the man."

So Numbers 19:11 (which is the law that Epiphanius wrongly alleges): Ὁ ἁπτόμενος τοῦ τεθνηκότος πάσης ψυχῆς ἀνθρώπου ἀκάθαρτος ἔσται ἑπτὰ ἡμέρας: "he that toucheth" (that is, whosoever toucheth) "the dead body (that is, any dead body) of any man, he shall be unclean seven days." Whereas Epiphanius therefore alleges it thus: "If any man touch the dead, he remains unclean until the evening, and he shall be washed with water, and shall be cleansed" – and from the force of the article (which is not in the text as he alleges it, if there be not a fault in the print) proves that by the dead is to be meant not any dead man, but only Christ: it is evident that his memory failed him.

For the law which pronounces a man unclean until the evening for touching a dead body is understood of the dead bodies of beasts, but that which speaks of the dead body of a man, pronounced him unclean for seven days, and is (as even now you heard) understood of the dead body of any man whatsoever.[364] And the reason for this law is, first because a dead man is a spectacle both of our sin, and of God's curse for the same: and secondly, because the Lord would, by the detestation of the bodily death, teach the Israelites to abhor the spiritual death of the soul in sin. And therefore Epiphanius not unworthily reproves the hypocrisy of the Samaritans, who

---

[364] Leviticus 11

under pretense of this law, abhorred the dead bodies of men, when as themselves were dead in sin.

So when we say, the pope, the emperor, the king, the priest, the minister, the eye, the hand, we mean not one particular, but the whole kind, as 1 Peter 2:17 τον βασιλεα τιματε, "Honor the king:" not this king only, but any whosoever is king; 1 Timothy 3:2: δει ουν τον επισκοπον ανεπιληπτον ειναι, "it behooves therefore the bishop (not this or that bishop, but everyone that has that calling) to be without reproof." Matthew 6:22: ο λυχνος του σωματος εστιν ο οφθαλμος: "The light of the body is the eye." See 1 Corinthians 12:15-16, Matthew 12:34, etc. So when we say, *the good man* or *the wicked man*, we mean either generally all, or indefinitely any that be such, Matthew 12:35: ο αγαθος ανθρωπος εκ του αγαθου θησαυρου της καρδιας εκβαλλει τα αγαθα και ο πονηρος ανθρωπος, etc. "The good man out of the good treasure of the heart, bringeth forth the good things; and the evil man," etc.

(4) Sometimes again the article is used εμφατικός, to signify that which is most notable in that kind, and therefore most worthily (or as we say κατ' εξοχήν) deserves that name. And of this use is Epiphanius' rule to be understood: "Where the article is added unto some definite and notable thing, there is always confirmation by the article, namely, that the word is not to be understood indefinitely or indifferently of any; but without the article it is to be taken of any one indefinitely."

This latter part of the rule, if it is true, proves that the speech of our Savior, John 5, εαν αλλος ελθη, "if any other come" is indefinite. But neither does the article used εμφατικός, always point out a certain and singular thing, though sometimes it does. As ὁ θεός in a Christian's mouth signifies the true God only, as Epiphanius says. So when we say *the apostle*, meaning Paul; *the poet*, meaning among the Greeks, Homer, and among the Latins, Virgil; *the orator*, Demosthenes or Tully; *the wise man*, Solomon.

But when we say, ο βασιλιάς (which is another of Epiphanius' examples) and mean thereby not indifferently any king but by an emphasis that prince to whom we are subject, we do not always nor for the most part understand one certain king, but all or any to whom the sovereignty of our country appertains, whether he be king or queen. As when we say, "the king supreme governor of the church," no time prescribes against the king, the king's highway, the prince's laws, etc.

In like manner, when we say, ο ανθρωπος (which is Epiphanius' third example) or as the apostle more distinctly speaks, ο ανθρωπος του θεου, *the man of God*.[365] For although by this emphasis not any man is meant but the minister of God, yet it signifies not one certain minister, but any one of that function called thereunto of God. And in this sense, is the pope called *the Antichrist*: and the Antichrist in the same sense is called *the man of sin, the son of perdition, the outlaw*.

But this proves not, that therefore the Antichrist is but one certain and singular man. For even as the devil, το ακαθαρτον πνευμα, the unclean spirit,[366] although there be many wicked ones is called, ο πονηρός, the evil, and yet there be many devils, and as the bishop of Rome since the time of Boniface III, is called *the pope* (whereas before, the name *pope* was attributed to other bishops) and yet there have been many popes. So although all heretics deserve to be called *antichrists*; all profane men, *men of sin*; all reprobates, *sons of perdition*; all sons of Belial, ανομοι, or *outlaws* – yet notwithstanding the pope of Rome since the time of Boniface III deserves to be called κατ' εξοχήν *the Antichrist, the man of sin, the son of perdition, the outlaw*. This, as it does not prove that the pope signifies but one singular person, so neither does it evince that the Antichrist signifies one certain man.[367] For look what they can say, of the Antichrist in this case; the same may be said of the pope.

---

[365] 2 Timothy 3:17
[366] Luke 11:24
[367] See Book 1 Chapter 6

(5) The third place is like the second, and therefore a short answer may serve. 1 John 2:18 reads: ηκουσατε οτι ο αντιχριστος ερχεται και νυν αντιχριστοι πολλοι γεγονασιν: "You have heard that the Antichrist comes, and even now there are many antichrists," where the article is prefixed before *Antichrist* so properly called; but the name of Antichrist generally taken is uttered without an article, which most plainly shows that Antichrist – properly taken – is but one man, but generally taken it signifies all heretics. As if he had said:

- ο αντιχριστος signifies but one certain man, because the article is prefixed.
- The Antichrist so properly called is ο αντιχριστος.
- Therefore the Antichrist so properly called, is but one certain man.

The prosyllogism or proof of the proposition I have already proven to be most false, when as I shown that whereas there are four uses of the article at the least, Bellarmine's observation holds only in one, and that the least usual, namely: when the article is used for a demonstrative particle. And that the article added to a word does not always signify one certain and singular thing, I will show by some other examples, which will sit nearer the papists.

In 2 Thessalonians 2:7 ο κατεχων, "he that hindereth," is expounded by the fathers, and acknowledged by the papists, to signify the emperor of Rome, not any one particular, but the state and succession of emperors. Again, Matthew 16:18, where there is not only the article, but also the pronounce demonstrative, επι ταυτη τη πετρα, "upon this rock," the papists would have understood by that rock, which Peter confessed, which is Christ, or faith in him; not only Peter himself, but also (although most falsely) the whole succession of popes.

And therefore by their own doctrine, the article does not always, no not when it is joined with a demonstrative particle, signify one certain and particular thing or person. Thirdly, in the place before alleged, ο ανθρωπος της αμαρτιας, *the man of sin, the son of perdition*,[368] is understood by some to signify not only the head of the Antichristian body, but the whole multitude of those who join with Antichrist.

Augustine recites this opinion, and is so far from disliking it, that Bellarmine alleges it as Augustine's. Neither are we to think this interpretation to be dissonant from the manner of speech used in the Scriptures: seeing η γυνη, the woman in Revelation 12:6 signifies the church of Christ; and πορνης, the harlot and η γυνη, the woman in Revelation 17:1 & 18, the city and church of Antichrist. And that I may come to the proposition itself, and omit other examples, αντιχριστος sometimes signifies the Antichristian body or company of Antichristian heretics.

(6) For better proof whereof let us consider the acceptance of the word: ο αντιχριστος, *the Antichrist* in the place alleged,[369] and elsewhere in the epistles of John, in which only it is used, and not elsewhere in the Scriptures. In the place which Bellarmine cites the apostle seems to reason thus:

- When the Antichrist is come, it is the last hour.
- Now antichrists are come.
- Therefore now is the last hour.

Where either *the Antichrist* and *Antichrists* signify the same, or else there be four terms in the apostle's argument, which Bellarmine dares not avouch: And afterwards in verse 22, he plainly shows that everyone that denies Jesus to be the Christ (as many antichrists or heretics did, of which he spoke in verse 18) is ο αντιχριστος the Antichrist.

---

[368] 2 Thessalonians 2:3
[369] 1 John 2:18

In chapter 4 of the same epistle,³⁷⁰ he bids them try the spirits, that is, their teachers, because many false prophets were come into the world, and gives them this note whereby to try them: "Every spirit," (says he), "which confesseth Jesus Christ to be come in the flesh, is of God, and every spirit which does not confess that Jesus Christ is come in the flesh is not of God. And this is the spirit of the Antichrist, which you heard was to come, and even now already is in the world." Likewise in the second epistle: "Many deceivers are come into the world which do not confess that Jesus Christ is come in the flesh, this is the deceiver and the Antichrist."³⁷¹

By these testimonies it is evident that ο αντιχριστος does not only signify the head of the Antichristian body (which is not one singular man, but is continued in a succession of many) but also sometimes any heretic that oppugns the natures or offices of Christ: and sometimes the whole body or company of heretics opposed unto Christ. For John plainly affirms that those many heretics and deceivers of his time, are the Antichrist.³⁷² And whereas Paul prophecies of Antichrist that he should come into the world, and should be destroyed at the second coming of Christ, John affirms that Antichrist, of whom they had heard that he should come, was then already come into the world.

From which places I argue thus:

- If ο αντιχριστος the Antichrist in the epistles of John, and ο ανθρωπος της αμαρτιας, the man of sin, ο ανομος, the outlaw, in the Epistle of Paul to the Thessalonians do signify one certain and singular man – as the papists affirm – then it will follow necessarily, that one and the same man, who was come into the world in Saint John's time, shall be in the world at the second coming of Christ. For John says that the Antichrist was come in

---

[370] 1 John 4:3-4
[371] 2 John 7
[372] 1 John 2:22

- his time, and Paul says that the outlaw shall be consumed with the spirit of Christ's mouth, and destroyed at his glorious appearing.
- But the latter is incredible, for since the time of John, 1500 years have expired already.
- And therefore the former (which is the assertion of the papists) is absurd.

ο αντιχριστος therefore signifies sometimes the whole body of heretics from the ascension of Christ, until his second coming: sometimes any heretics which are limbs of that body: sometimes the grand antichrist, who is the head of that body, and is called κατ' εξοχήν the Antichrist. Wherefore in respect of those heretics and limbs of Antichrist in the apostle's times, Antichrist is then said to have entered, and as it were, to have set his foot into the world.

And accordingly, the apostle Paul says, that even in his time the mystery of iniquity – that is, Antichristianism – was working (namely by those which belonged to the body of Antichrist) although covertly and underhand, until the head of that body was revealed as he was, after the empire in the West was dissolved, and the emperor which hindered was done out of the way; according to the prophecy of the apostle (2 Thessalonians 2:7-8). And thus you see what a slender argument this is taken from the article, although it be used as one of the principal demonstrations generally of all the papists, that write of this argument, but more especially of Bellarmine, who thinking it too good to go for one argument, has divided it into two.

(7) His fourth testimony is taken out of Daniel 7:11-12, where Antichrist is called a king, and not a kingdom, who of the ten kings which he shall find in the world, shall take away three, and shall make the other seven subject to himself.

But I answer that Daniel speaks not of Antichrist at all, but of Antiochus Epiphanes, and therefore this allegation is impertinent. For the learned of our times have made it evident, that the four kingdoms whereof Daniel speaks, were ended before the incarnation of Christ, and that the fourth kingdom which many have taken to be the monarchy of the Romans, was the kingdom of the Seleucids and Lagidae in Syria and Egypt, so far forth as the people of Jewry was subject thereunto, and is therefore described as the most terrible of all the four, because it was most troublesome to the Jews. And that the ten horns were ten kings of Syria and Egypt, which successively tyrannized over the people of the Jews; Antiochus Epiphanes being the tenth and the last of those kings which tyrannized over Jewry.

But because in outrageous cruelty and cursed hostility – not only against the people, but also against the religion of the Jews – he surpassed all that went before him; of him therefore Daniel speaks so plainly and distinctly, that he has seemed to some rather to write an history of him, then a prophecy; as shall hereafter more fully be shown, when as we shall also manifestly declare that this which Bellarmine adds concerning Antichrist's killing of three kings,[373] and subduing of the other seven, is but a dream, which is indeed so far from all probability of truth, as that it cannot be verified of that party whom Daniel describes.

Daniel describes him as the tenth; Bellarmine makes him the eleventh, as if it were a beast of eleven horns. Daniel speaks of ten kings, which successively ruled over the Jews; Bellarmine makes him speak of ten, who together with the eleventh, should be at one time in the world. Of those ten Daniel says, that three were plucked up before the tenth, and as it may seem by his means, but of the other six, either all or the most were dead before he was borne: Bellarmine makes him to kill three and subdue the other seven, which indeed lived not in his time, as shall be shown hereafter out of the eleventh of Daniel, where the succession of these ten kings, and the affairs of

---

[373] Chapter 16

the tenth – who can be no other but Antiochus Epiphanes – are particularly and fully described.

This argument, drawn from the misconstruing of Daniel, Bellarmine although he knew it to be nothing worth, yet he was content to make a flourish with it, because he had some of the fathers to father it upon. Afterwards he comes nearer to the purpose, and says, that Calvin – as some of the fathers before him, to wit, Cyprian and Jerome – affirms, and so does Bellarmine himself elsewhere, that Daniel speaks of Antiochus Epiphanes, who was a type of Antichrist. Therefore leaving his former hold, he reasons thus:

- Such as is the type or figure, such is the thing figured.
- Antiochus the type was but one singular person.
- Therefore Antichrist that is figured is but one.

The proposition is to be understood of the proportion and likeness only in those things, in respect whereof the type is a figure, and not generally in all things. As for example, the high-priest was a type or figure of Christ, but therefore it does not follow that there was but one high-priest, because Christ is one. The papists hold that Melchizedek, who was but one, was a type of their mass-priests, which are many. Joshua, David, and Solomon, were types of Christ, but therefore not like unto him in all things. So Antiochus may not unfitly be said to have been a type of Antichrist, because as Pharaoh was a type of other tyrants which oppressed the Church of God; so he in falsehood deceit, pride, idolatry, cruelty, and persecuting of the Church of God, resembled Antichrist the man of sin, which is an enemy, and is listed up about all that is called God, or that is worshiped.

In which respects Antiochus was so fit a type of Antichrist, that Rabbi Levi Gershon – alleged by Bellarmine in the end of chapter 12 – applies whatsoever is spoken of him in Daniel 7 and 11 to the pope of Rome. If therefore you understand the proposition generally, it is false: if particularly, the whole argumentation is fallacious.

(8) His fifth testimony is Revelation 13 and 17. For these places are to be understood of Antichrist, as Irenaeus teaches, and as it is plain by the likeness of the words in Daniel and John, etc. His reason is thus framed:

- If Daniel spoke of one king, then also John.
- But the former is true.
- Therefore the latter.

The proposition, wherein there is indeed no coherence, he proves by the similitude of their words: First, because both make mention of ten kings who shall be in the earth when Antichrist shall come. It is true that both make mention of ten horns, but with such difference as that otherwise there is no likeness. Antiochus in Daniel, by whom Bellarmine would have us to understand Antichrist, is the last of the ten, and not one besides the ten; otherwise the fourth beast, were a beast of eleven horns: Antichrist is one besides the ten horns in the Revelation, and of Bellarmine sometimes is called the eleventh. Bellarmine's Antichrist in Daniel is the little horn signifying indeed but one man, but the true Antichrist in the Revelation is called not an horn, but the beast, whereby not one man, but a state is signified.

The ten horns in Daniel are so many kings which succeed one another, in the kingdom usurped over the Jews, before the coming of the Messiah; the ten horns in the Revelation are so many rulers over diverse kingdoms, which receive their kingdom together, not only after the incarnation of Christ, but also after the dissolution of the Roman Empire. So that in truth nothing is here alike, save that in both there is mention of ten horns.

"Secondly," says Bellarmine, "both of them foretell that the kingdom of Antichrist shall continue for three and a half years." But I answer that neither of both assign that time to Antichrist. For first Daniel assigns a time, and times, and parcel of time, that is, three years and ten days, to the persecution under Antiochus, whereby the public worship of God was for that time interrupted, namely: from the 15th day of the month Kislev in the 145th year of the kingdom of the Seleucids (1 Maccabees 1:57); unto the 25th of the month of Kislev in the year 148 (1 Maccabees 4:52).[374] But of this more hereafter. Neither does John anywhere assign three years and an half to the reign of Antichrist: but to the beast with seven heads and ten horns, which signifies the Roman state either generally as it is opposed unto Christ, or particularly as it was governed by the sixth head, that is, the emperors, he assigns forty two months, which are not literally to be understood.[375] Now Antichrist is not the beast with seven heads, but one head of the seven, and is described under the second beast as our adversaries also confess, which in plain terms is called *another beast*.[376] For how can he be that beast, if he is another? And of this also, I shall have better occasion to speak more fully hereafter.

Lastly, he flies to the authority of the fathers as his last refuge; but neither do these fathers expressly say that Antichrist shall be but one man; neither if they did, can any sound argument be drawn from their testimonies, unless Bellarmine were able to prove that whatsoever these fathers have written concerning Antichrist is true.[377]

And again, several of the fathers – as Irenaeus, Origen, Chrysostom, Jerome, Rufinus, Primasius, Augustine, expounding that place: Matthew 24:24, which speaks of more than one, as spoken of Antichrist – they could not understand Antichrist to be but one. Yea but the fathers say, that

---

[374] See Chapter 16
[375] Revelation 11:2, 7 & 13:1, 5
[376] Revelation 13:11
[377] See Chapter 8

Antichrist shall be a most choice instrument of the Devil, that in him shall dwell all the fullness of devilish malice bodily, even as in the man Christ dwells the fullness of the divinity corporally. But although this allegation were true (as I will not thereof dispute), yet is it impertinent, for the pope (meaning the whole succession of Antichristian popes) may be a notable instrument of the devil, etc. and yet hereof it does not follow that there has been only one pope. As touching the other assertion of Antichrist's reign three years and a half, we are hereafter to entreat.

(9) Now that Antichrist is not one singular man, but a whole state and succession of men, it may appear by these arguments.

First by conference of 2 Thessalonians 2 with the epistles of John, for John plainly says that ο αντιχριστος, *the Antichrist*, of whom they had heard that he should come, was in his time.[378] And of whom had they heard it, but of Paul in 2 Thessalonians 2, where in like sort, the apostle says, that even in his time the mystery of iniquity – that is: Antichristianism – was working: noting that Antichrist in some of his members was already come, although he were not revealed, until that which hindered was taken out of the way?

Now as Paul and John do both testify, that the Antichrist was in their time; so Paul also shows that Antichrist shall remain unto the second coming of Christ (2 Thessalonians 2:8), for although he should be wasted and consumed before by the spirit of Christ's mouth (that is, the ministry of the word) yet he should not be utterly destroyed until the second coming of Christ. From hence therefore we reason thus:

- If Antichrist were in the apostles' time, and was to remain until the second coming of Christ, then Antichrist is not one singular man, but a succession of men; unless they will say, that one and the same man may live upon the earth from the apostles' time

---

[378] 1 John 4:3, 2 John 7, 1 John 2:18

until the coming of Christ, of which time there are already above 1500 years expired.
- But Antichrist was in the apostles' times, and is to continue until the second coming of Christ, as the two apostles Paul and John do plainly testify.
- Therefore Antichrist is not one singular man.

(10) Of this syllogism, Bellarmine cannot deny either the proposition, or the assumption. Only he distinguishes the former part of the assumption, namely: that Antichrist in the apostles' time had come indeed, but not in his own person, but only in his forerunners.

And this he would prove; first, by a similitude, which he might have known from Plato to be a most slippery argument:

"As Christ came in the beginning of the world not in his own person, but in his forerunners the patriarchs and prophets; so Antichrist came in the apostles' time not in his own person, but in his forerunners, the heretics and persecutors of the church."

In which similitude there is no proportion, unless that which is in question is taken for granted, namely; that Antichrist is but one particular person, as Christ is. For if Antichrist be a succession of heretics, then might he be said to come in the first of the rank; although the chief of that order, which principally is called Antichrist, was not yet come.

And secondly, the protasis or proposition of this similitude is untrue. For although Christ might be said to be come from the beginning in respect both of the truth of the promise, and also of the efficacy of his merits, which is extended to all the faithful from the beginning: yet we never read, neither can it truly be said that he came in the patriarchs and prophets: especially seeing the Holy Spirit makes a kind of opposition between God's sending of them, and the coming of Christ, who was not sent before the fullness of time came.³⁷⁹ Neither are the prophets or patriarchs anywhere called *the forerunners of Christ*, for forerunners go a little before, as John the Baptist did, who therefore is worthily called προδρομος, *the forerunner*. If any man objects that as Christ spake in the prophets,³⁸⁰ so Antichrist in the heretics, I answer, that this latter is true not of Antichrist, but of the devil, who is a lying spirit in the mouths of all false prophets.

Thirdly, the reddition [elucidation] is contradictory to that which the apostle John delivers. For he says plainly that the Antichrist with the article prefixed, and that Antichrist whom they heard was to come, was already entered into the world (1 John 4:3, 2 John 7), and thence proves that therefore it is the last hour, because Antichrist was to come in the last hour (1 John 2:18). So that in this similitude nothing is sound, no proportion in the whole, no truth in the parts.

(11) Wherefore by a new supply of arguments, he labors to make good this exposition. And as touching the place in Paul, he argues first from the authority of the fathers and interpreters, whereof some understand by *the mystery of iniquity*, the persecution under Nero; others the heretics of those times which secretly seduced many. The former had no reason to call the open persecution of Nero a *mystery*, who also although he were an enemy, yet belonged not to the body of Antichrist, who is a disguised enemy and a pretended Christian. The latter exposition we do embrace.

For we hold Antichrist to be the whole body of heretics in the last age of the world, who under the name and profession of Christ advance themselves against Christ, first secretly, as in the apostles' times; afterwards more openly, when that which hindered, was taken out of the way. Of this body as every member severally and all jointly is Antichrist (and therefore John calls the heretics of his time Antichrists, and of them all says that they are the

---

³⁷⁹ Hebrews 2:1, Matthew 22:37, Galatians 4:4
³⁸⁰ 1 Peter 3:19

Antichrist:) so especially the head of this body, which we have proved to be the Papacy, is κατ' εξοχήν called *Antichrist*.

Wherefore although Antichrist was after a sort come, and the mystery of iniquity wrought in the Apostles time, yet Antichrist was not revealed until the head of this body appeared, that is, until the pope became Antichrist, who since the year of the Lord 606 has shown himself in his colors: first by usurping supreme authority over the universal church, and afterwards by claiming sovereignty over kings and emperors, as we have heretofore shown.

Seeing therefore the heretics of whom the fathers speak did belong to the body of Antichrist, it cannot be denied but that Antichrist, when they were in the world, was come in some of his members, and had as it were set his foot into the church.

(12) Secondly, from our own confession he would seem to drive us to great absurdity. For (says he) if Antichrist had come in the apostles' times, and if Antichrist has his seat in Rome, then it will follow that Peter and Paul were the true antichrists, and Nero or Simon Magus the true Christ. For there were no other bishops of Rome then, but Peter and Paul, with whom Nero and Simon Magus contended. I answer that it cannot be proved out of the Scripture, or by any sound argument that Peter and Paul were bishops of Rome: and although they were, it would not follow upon our assertion that therefore they were Antichrists, and much less that Nero or Simon Magus was Christ.

For when we say that Antichrist had come in the apostles' time, we speak of the body of Antichrist with John. Whon we say that Antichrist has his seat in Rome, we speak of the head of this body, who especially is called Antichrist: whom we do with Paul acknowledge not to have been revealed, until that which hindered was taken out of the way, that is, until the Roman Empire in the West was dissolved; but afterwards by degrees he was advanced in the papacy, "above all that is called God; sitting in the temple of

God, as if he were God," that is, ruling and reigning in the Church, as if he were a god upon earth.

And surely if the head of the Antichristian body was to be revealed not long after the dissolution of the Roman Empire in the West, and was about the same time with the rulers of the provinces to attain unto his kingdom, as has been shown; and lastly, if he shall continue in the world after he is revealed, until the second coming of Christ, then it follows necessarily that even this head of the Antichristian body, cannot be anyone singular man, but is continued by a succession of many from the time of his revelation until the end of the world: of which time there is almost a thousand years expired.

But both in this argument, and in the former, Bellarmine sophistically begs the question. For in his arguments there is no consequence unless this be taken for granted:

- Antichrist is but one man.
- Antichrist came, in the heretics in the apostles' time.
- Therefore he came not in his own person.

This is a good argument, if Antichrist were but one man, which is the question. If Antichrist were in the apostles' time, and if Antichrist must sit at Rome, then he that was then bishop of Rome was Antichrist; a good argument if Antichrist were but one man, which is the question.

(13) Now whereas John says that Antichrist in his time was come, Bellarmine feigns him to speak of Antichrist, as he says, "Our Savior spake of Elijah in Matthew 17:11: "Elijah indeed shall come (namely in his own person) but I say unto you, Elijah is already come *in suo simili*, in his like, that is, John the Baptist." So John speaks of Antichrist, that he had indeed to come in his own person, but now he had come in his type."

You see to what silly shifts this worthy champion of the pope is driven! For first he fathers upon Christ that Jewish fable, which with the Jews the papists hold against Christ himself. For whereas Malachi had prophesied of the coming of Elijah before the day of the Lord[381] – meaning the first coming of Christ – our Savior Christ plainly avouches in Matthew 11:14 that John the Baptist was that Elijah, who according to the prophecy of Malachi was to come.[382]

Now John the Baptist was called Elijah because he came in the spirit and power of Elijah, to turn the hearts of the fathers, etc., as the angel also applies that prophecy in Luke 1:17. But suppose that Christ had spoken of Elijah according to Bellarmine's conceit; yet how does it follow that therefore John speaks of Antichrist after the same manner? No more than it follows, that David should long after his death be sent again to govern the people of God: because it was prophesied by Ezekiel, that the Lord would raise up a pastor for his people, even David his servant, etc.[383]

But as by the name of *David* in Ezekiel is meant not David himself, but Christ, of whom David was a type: so by the name of *Elijah* in Malachi, is not meant Elijah himself, but John the Baptist, who resembled Elijah in spirit and power in reforming the church of God.

(14) Our second argument is this:

- That which in the prophecies of the Scriptures – especially in Daniel 7 & 11 and Revelation 13 & 17 – is described under the name and figure of a beast, is not one singular thing or person, but a whole state or succession.
- Antichrist is described in Revelation 13 under the name and figure of a beast.

---

[381] Malachi 4:5
[382] Malachi 4:6, Luke 1:17
[383] Ezekiel 34:23-24 & 37:35, Jeremiah 30:9

- Therefore Antichrist is not one singular person, but a whole state and succession.

The proposition is proved by induction of particular examples. As in the Daniel 7, by the lion, is figured the kingdom of the Assyrians and Babylonians; by the bear, the Medes and Persians; by the leopard, the Greeks and Macedonians; by the beast with ten horns, the Seleucids and Lagidae, and so chapter 8. In Revelation 13, there are two beasts described, the former signifying the state of the Roman Emperors; the second signifying the state of Antichrist.

Bellarmine answers that Daniel, as sometimes by the beasts he signifies whole kingdoms, so sometimes also particular persons. As in Chapter 8, by the ram, he understands Darius the last king of the Persians; by the goat, Alexander the Great. In which answer, the upright dealing of Bellarmine with the Scriptures appears. For in Daniel 8:20, where that vision is expounded, the angel's words are these: "The ram which thou sawest, having two horns are מַלְכֵי the kings of the Medes and Persians." And the goat is the King of Javan or Greece (meaning as before *the kings* or *kingly estate*, as appears plainly by the words that follow, and not as Bellarmine says, *Alexander*) and the great horn between his eyes is the first king, namely Alexander, which being broken, four other stand up in their stead.[384]

As Daniel therefore by several beasts means not so many particular men, but whole states and orders of men; and as John in Revelation 13 by the former beasts does not mean any one emperor, but the whole state and succession of emperors at the least;[385] so the Holy Spirit in the same chapter by the second beast describing Antichrist, means not any one particular person, but the whole state and succession of Antichristian popes, to whom (as heretofore has been shown) that description wholly agrees.

---

[384] Daniel 8:20
[385] Revelation 13:11

And whereas Bellarmine adds that Paul when he entreats of Antichrist, speaks not of any one of the four beasts in Daniel, but of the little horn mentioned in Daniel 7:8, I answer that the apostle speaks neither of the one nor of the other; and therefore the former part of Bellarmine's speech is vain, for no man says so; and the latter is false. For the little horn is not Antichrist, but Antiochus Epiphanes, who lived over 200 years before the incarnation of Christ, who although he were but one man, might – not unfitly – be called a type of Antichrist, who is a state or succession of men.

(15) Our third argument is taken from that apostasy, which the apostle foretells in 2 Thessalonians 2. For where he speaks of a defection (whereof Antichrist is the head) without addition,[386] we understand a general defection of the visible church, which as it began to work in the apostles' time; so was it to increase until the revelation of Antichrist, and to continue more or less until his destruction.[387] This apostasy – because it cannot be the work of one man, or of a few years – evidently proves that Antichrist is not one singular man, but rather a state and succession of men.

To this, Bellarmine, for want of one good answer, makes many. "First," (says he) "by that apostasy we may, very well (nay he says *rectissime*) understand Antichrist himself, as several of the fathers teach" – and what will he infer thereupon? that therefore Antichrist is but one man? Nay rather, the contrary is to be inferred. For if *apostasy* be put by a metonymy of the adjunct for the subject, or rather of the effect for the cause, that is, for the parties which do revolt: then it follows that *Antichrist* (who according to this interpretation is signified by apostasy) does not signify one man, but the whole body and company of those that do revolt, that is, the whole body and kingdom of Antichrist, which we have proved to be the apostate Church of Rome.

---

[386] 2 Thessalonians 2:3
[387] 2 Thessalonians 2:7

And so Augustine, whom Bellarmine alleges in the very same place which he cites, reading in the concrete, *nisi venerit refuga primum*:[388] "Unless the apostate first come," and expounding what is meant by *the temple* – not the temple at Jerusalem, but rather the Church of God, because the apostle would not call the temple of the devil, the temple of God – propounds the opinion of some which he does not dislike, *Vnde nonnulli non ipsum principem*, etc., whereupon some understand in this place not the prince himself, but his whole body as it were, that is, the company of men pertaining unto him together with their prince, to be Antichrist. And they think that it might more rightly be said in Latin as it is in the Greek, that he sits (*non in templo Dei, sed in templum Dei*) not *in* the temple of God, but *as* the temple of God, as though he were the temple of God which is the church – where as has been shown, notably sits the pope and Church of Rome.

And here we are by the way to note, whereas Bellarmine says that Antichrist shall be such a notable apostate that he may be called *the apostasy* itself, that seeing as none can be an apostate which has not been a Christian, then by this assertion therefore of Bellarmine, Antichrist shall not be a Jew, but a backsliding and revolted Christian.

(16) "Secondly," (he says) "by *apostasy*, we may understand a revolt from the Roman empire, as many of the Latin fathers do expound." To omit the dissension of the fathers, which proves that their exposition can be no good rule of interpreting the Scriptures, we do confess that before the manifest revelation of Antichrist, there was to go, not only a defection from the faith, but also a revolt from the Roman Empire. But as the revolting from earthly kingdoms is never in the Scriptures termed *apostasy*, so is it not here signified; but as the word elsewhere is used, and by the most and best writers here is expounded, αποστασια, signifies a falling away from God, a

---

[388] Augustine, *City of God*, Book 20 Chapter 19

defection or departure from the true faith, as heretofore I have shown. Augustine says, *quem refugam vocat, vtique a domino Deo*:[389] "whom he calls a renegade, namely, from the Lord God."

Neither can it be denied but that this apostasy is that which afterward the apostle calls *the mystery of iniquity*, which was working in and by the heretics of those times, whom also Bellarmine calls the forerunners of Antichrist, because they perverted the faith.

And therefore the defection caused by Antichrist is an apostasy from the faith, according to the prophecies of the apostle, that in these latter times several should make an apostasy from the faith, and should turn away their hearing from the truth, and shall be turned unto fables.[390]

(17) Thirdly, although we should grant (says he) that by *apostasy* is to be understood a defection or revolt from the true faith and religion of Christ, yet it is not necessary that it should be an apostasy of many years. For it may be that the Apostle speaks of one great apostasy which shall be only in that most short time of Antichrist's reign, that is, of three years and a half.

But this bare guess of Bellarmine ought not to be of so great weight with us, as the plain speech of the apostle compared with the event. And therefore it is but vain to tell us what might be, seeing we have seen the contrary to be, which the apostle foretold should be. For as the apostle told us that there should be an apostasy; so he says, that the mystery of iniquity whereby many were seduced, did work already even in his time, and insinuates that it should work until the full revelation of Antichrist.

And the event has shown how by degrees this apostasy has been wrought even from the primitive church, until it came to that height wherein it continued until Antichrist began to be acknowledged. And surely as this general apostasy could not grow at once, but by degrees: so can it not

---

[389] Augustine, *City of God*, Book 20 Chapter 19 Section 2
[390] 1 Timothy 4:1, 2 Timothy 4:4

be abolished at once, but by degrees; and therefore was not like to be an apostasy of three years and a half only.

Neither is it credible that by one man the greatest part – not only of Christians, but also of the Jews – should be seduced in three and a half years, seeing as Christ in the like space of time could not, as he was a man and minister of the circumcision, convert many of the Jews, notwithstanding that his doctrine was more effectual, and his miracles more admirable than those of Antichrist can be.

Yea the apostles and some others of the disciples, who for such a long time scarcely went out of Jewry, were able to prevail but with a few of the Jews in comparison with those which rejected their doctrine. And shall we think that Antichrist, who (as the papists hold) shall be but one man, shall in three and a half years, seduce the remnant of the Jews, and all the visible church of God dispersed into so many parts of the world?

And whereas he alleges Augustine as a favorer of this guess, therein he abuses the authority of that learned father, to seduce the ignorant, who only delivers the judgment of others concerning the mystery of iniquity, and that to this effect:[391] that the mystery of iniquity works in evil men in the church and counterfeit Christians, when as they revolt from the truth, and that unto this mystery belongs the revolting of those of whom John says: "They went out from us, but were not of us," etc.[392] And that this mystery should still work, that is, that unsound men in the church should more and more revolt until they make a sufficient number for Antichrist. But there is never a word of this defection caused either by one man, or in so short a time, but rather the contrary, as has been shown.

(18) Fourthly, he answers that although it should be granted that this apostasy is of many ages (which he says cannot well be denied, seeing as the

---

[391] Augustine, *City of God*, Book 20 Chapter 19
[392] 1 John 2:19

apostle says it began to work in his time) yet it is not necessary that it should appertain to one body under one head, neither that it appertains to the kingdom of Antichrist, but rather is a disposition thereunto, happening in several dominions upon sundry occasions, etc. But this fourth answer is overthrown by the first: wherein this apostasy was made so proper to Antichrist, as that by it Bellarmine thought we might most fitly understand Antichrist himself, or rather as we showed, the whole body and kingdom of Antichrist.

And further, we have shown heretofore that the whole body of apostates and heretics professing the name of Christ, is Antichrist, and after a more special manner the head of this body and apostasy. And therefore it follows that all of this apostasy – professing the name of Christ – belongs to this body and kingdom of Antichrist.

And whereas he says that this apostasy is only a *disposition* to the kingdom of Antichrist, etc., I answer that all the degrees of this apostasy going before the revelation of Antichrist, were a disposition not to the being, but to the revealing of Antichrist. For in the apostasy, Antichrist was as John plainly shows, neither could he be *revealed* unless first he *was*. Whereupon Theodoret says, *Defectionem appellate Antichristi praesentiam*: he calls apostasy the presence or coming of Antichrist. But is it not very likely, do you think, that there has been a disposition or preparation already of more than 1500 years in most parts of the world, for the reign of one man three and a half years?

(19) Fifthly and lastly, "although we should grant," (says he) "that a general apostasy from the faith, having now continued many years, is the kingdom of Antichrist: yet it would not follow that therefore the pope is Antichrist. For it is not yet decided who has made this defection: they or we. And it is easier to prove that they have made this defection, for they have revolted from that Church and religion whereof their forefathers were, which we have not done," etc.

In the four former answers, Bellarmine turned back upon us, hoping thereby to repel the force of our argument. But those being spent, in this he turns his back upon us and betakes himself to his feet, and leaving the defense of the question in hand, runs to his chief hold.

For whereas we prove that Antichrist is not one man – contrary to their assertion, by this argument among others, because that general apostasy of the visible Church continuing for many ages, whereof Antichrist is the head, cannot be the work of one man or of a few years – Bellarmine answers thus in effect, that although your argument be very good to prove that Antichrist is not one man; yet notwithstanding here of it follows not, that the pope is Antichrist.

Why, never any of us used this argument: Antichrist is not one man, therefore the pope is Antichrist. But in this assertion of ours, we answer your chief demonstration whereby you would prove that the pope is not Antichrist, and where in especially you please yourselves, reasoning as has been hard, after this manner: Antichrist is but one man, therefore the pope is not Antichrist. And after you have proven this by many worshipful demonstrations, and stoutly denied our contrary arguments, now in the end you make this coward's brag. Although this should be granted which you say to prove that Antichrist is not one man, yet it does not follow that the pope is Antichrist.

(20) But let us pursue the Jesuit in his flight. "Although this should be granted," says he, etc., "yet it follows not that therefore the pope is Antichrist. For the question yet is, who has made this apostasy, we or you."

Well then, let us join in this issue. If the apostasy be on our side, let us be thought to belong to Antichrist; if this apostasy be in the Church of Rome, whereof the pope is head; then let it be acknowledged, that the pope is the head of this apostasy, and consequently Antichrist.

"But you," (says the Jesuit) "have revolted from the Church and religion of your forefathers, that is, from the Church of Rome and Latin religion. And therefore when you read, *unless there come a revolt*, etc., it is a wonder that you do not apply that prophecy to yourselves."

The apostasy whereof the apostle speaks, is not a separation from the Church of Rome that now is, nor a forsaking of Romish or popish religion, but a revolting from God; a departure from the true faith and religion of Christ unto Antichristianism and idolatry. We, in forsaking the church of Rome, have come out of Babylon according to God's commandment,[393] and in revolting from the pope, have returned to God. And therefore this apostasy does not touch us. But you – say I to the papists – have revolted from the true faith and religion of Christ unto Antichristianism and idolatry, as besides the infinite particulars wherein your apostasy consists, may briefly appear by these notes.

First, the apostle, speaking of the same apostasy in another place, has these words. "The Spirit speaketh plainly, that in the latter times some shall make an apostasy from the faith, attending to erroneous spirits and doctrines of devils, speaking lies in hypocrisy and having their own conscience seared."[394] Now who these are that make this apostasy, the apostle further describes by specifying two of those doctrines of devils, as certain notes whereby to know them. "Forbidding to marry, and commanding to abstain from meats, which God has created to be received with thanksgiving," etc. But as I have shown heretofore these notes touch not us, and properly agree to the papists, therefore this apostasy is among them.[395]

Secondly, this apostasy is among those who are fallen from the true religion and worship of God, into idolatry and superstition:

---

[393] Revelation 18:4
[394] 1 Timothy 4:1
[395] Book 1 Chapter 4.3

- For the apostate church is the idolatrous church signified by the whore of Babylon, the mother of fornications.
- But the Church of Rome is strangely addicted to idolatry and superstition, and for the same deserves to be called *the whore of Babylon*; whereas we through the mercy of God are free from idolatry.
- And therefore the apostasy is with them and not with us.

For the apostasy is of them that are made drunk with the cup of the whore of Babylon's fornications, as the papists are, and we are not, who have come out of Babylon.

Thirdly, the apostasy is of those that receive the name and mark of the beast as the papists do, and not of those that refuse it as we do.

The fourth note or touchstone as it were, to try who have made this apostasy, is the word of God: for that is the true faith and the true religion which is contained and prescribed in the written word of God.

Now our desire is that the Scriptures may be acknowledged the only rule of faith and manners. Unto the Scriptures we appeal in all controversies, and desire to be judged by them; unto the reading of the Scriptures we exhort our people, that they may be further edified and confirmed in that truth which we do teach and profess.

The papists contrariwise – not daring to stand to the Scriptures – fly to their unwritten verities, traditions, decretals, doctrines and authorities of men both besides and against the Scriptures: and in a word, that the prophecy of the apostle foretelling this apostasy, might be verified in them, they have asserted their hearing from the truth, and are converted unto fables.[396]

They cannot abide to hear that the Scripture should be the only rule of faith and manners. They cannot endure to see any of their people to read the

---

[396] 2 Timothy 4:4

Scriptures, and therefore desire to keep it from them in an unknown language. The foundation of their truth is the authority of their church, and in the church, of their pope, who, they say, cannot err. But if the pope teaches doctrines of devils, and speaks lies in hypocrisy (as the apostle has prophesied especially of them) then is there in that Church little soundness of truth, that is built upon so unsound a foundation. Thus therefore I reason:

- The head of the general apostasy is Antichrist.
- The pope is the head of the general or catholic apostasy.
- Therefore he is Antichrist.

(21) To the three former arguments, a fourth may be added. The seven heads of that beast which signifies the Roman state, are not so many persons, but so many heads or states of government, whereby the commonwealth of the Romans, has been at different times governed.

The sixth head was the state of emperors; the seventh, Antichrist, as the papists confess; the eighth (which also is one of the seven), the state of emperors renewed. Whereby it evidently appears, not only that Antichrist is not one man, but also that the pope (who is the seventh head) is Antichrist.

Chapter 3

Concerning the time of Antichrist's coming.

(1) To withdraw our minds from beholding Antichrist in the See of Rome, and to make us look for the expected messiah of the Jews that never shall come, the papists labor by might and main to persuade us that Antichrist is not yet come. For even as the learned of the Jews, when Christ was among them, contrary to their one persuasion, for worldly respects refused the true Messiah, and made the people expect another which never shall be; so the learned among the papists having Antichrist among them, for worldly respects cannot endure that he should be acknowledged; but teach the people that he is not yet come, and describe unto them such an Antichrist as themselves may well know shall never come, as by the grace of God shall appear in the particulars.

Now as touching the time of Antichrist's coming, Bellarmine first recites several "false and erroneous opinions," as he calls them, and afterward sets down six solemn demonstrations to prove that he has not yet come. In the former, he spends a good long chapter, reckoning up several opinions both of the fathers in former ages, and also of "heretics," as he calls them; in latter times, mingling the truth with errors, that the credit of both might be alike.

As touching the fathers, because he takes it for granted (which is the thing in question) that Antichrist is not to come before the end of the world, which we deny according to the Scriptures:[397] he would make their opinion concerning the approaching of Antichrist, which they held according to the prophecies of the Scripture compared with the event, of no better credit then their conceit of Christ's approaching unto judgment, grounded not so much upon the Scriptures, as upon their own conjecture.

---

[397] 1 John 2:18, 2 John 7, 2 Thessalonians 2:7

For to omit their conjectures concerning Christ's coming confuted by experience, what can Bellarmine answer to the sound argument either of Jerome or Gregory, concerning the coming of Antichrist, confirmed by experience, alleged by Bellarmine himself?

Jerome,[398] applying the prophecy of Paul in 2 Thessalonians 2:6-8 that Antichrist should appear when he that hinders (meaning the Roman Emperor) was taken out of the way, to his time, wherein not only the imperial seat had been removed from Rome (which was the first degree of taking out of the way that which hindered) but also Rome itself in distress, being taken of the Goths, and the Empire in decay: *Quitenebat* (says he) *de medio fit, and non intelligimus Antichristum appropinquare?* "He which did hold, is taken out of the way; and do we not understand that Antichrist does approach?" And likewise Gregory, *Omnia quae praedicta sunt, fiunt: Rex superbia prope est*: "All things which were foretold do come to pass; the king of pride is at hand."[399] These arguments, alleged also by us, Bellarmine – because he could not answer – he thought to discredit by reckoning them among erroneous conceits.

(2) But let us come to his heretics, who "although they all agree in this, that Antichrist is come, and that it is the pope; yet," says Bellarmine, "they are divided into six opinions." The first opinion – namely of the Samosatenians in Hungary and Transylvania – is not worth mentioning, being of such heretics as deny the Trinity, and also the divinity of Christ, with whom, though we have as little to do as the papists, saving that some of our men have soundly confuted their heresies, while the papists held their peace; yet he numbers our opinion with theirs, as Christ was numbered among the wicked; that by this mixture of truth with falsehood, he might discredit the truth.

---

[398] Epist.ad Geront. De Monogamia
[399] Lib. 4 epi. 38

As for the rest, it is easy to show that all Protestants almost that have written in this argument, and namely those whom Bellarmine alleges, do agree in the substance concerning the coming of Antichrist. And that there is no such difference among them, as Bellarmine would bear us in hand. For concerning this matter, this is the received opinion of our churches.

When – with John in his epistles – we speak of *antichrist* meaning the whole body of heretics and antichrists, we hold with John that even in the apostles' times, Antichrist had as it were set his foot in the Church, and that from that time the mystery of iniquity, that is, Antichristianism, did more and more work, until the head of this body the man of sin was revealed. This – with Paul – we hold to have been done, after that which hindered was removed out of the way.

But when we speak of the head of this body, who κατ' εξοχήν is called *the Antichrist*, figured by the second beast in Revelation 13. of whom also the Apostle entreats in 2 Thessalonians 2, the constant opinion of the learned is this: that of the revealing or manifest appearing of Antichrist, there were two principal degrees.[400] The first was about the year 607, when Boniface III obtained supremacy over the universal church. The second after the year 1000, when he claimed and usurped both swords, that is, a sovereign and universal authority, not only ecclesiastical over the clergy, but also temporal over kings and emperors. They had long aspired to this second sovereignty, but never attained it until the time of Gregory VII.

We hold then that Antichrist was come and shown himself in Boniface III, and that after this his birth as it were, he grew by degrees, until he came to his full growth in Gregory VII, in whose time and in all ages since, the pope has been by some acknowledged to be that Antichrist.

(3) Now as touching his coming or birth, which is the chief matter in question, all agree. Illyricus and the other writers of *The Centuries*, as

---

[400] See Book 1 Chapter 3

Bellarmine confesses, hold that about the year 606, Antichrist was born when Phocas granted to the Bishop of Rome that he should be called the head of the whole Church. Of the same judgment is Chytraeus. For although he confesses that the smoke of false doctrine ascending out of the bottomless pit began sooner to obscure and darken the truth,[401] yet he says that in the year 607, Boniface III was by Phocas ordained *the angel of the bottomless pit*, meaning thereby Antichrist, when he received from him the title of *ecumenical bishop*. Luther – perceiving that the papacy consists of the two swords – taught that there is a twofold coming of Antichrist: the first with the spiritual sword after the year 600, when Phocas gave him the Antichristian title; the latter, with the temporal sword, after the year 1000.[402]

Bullinger does not say, as Bellarmine falsely charges him, that Antichrist first appeared in the year 763, for he above all others most plainly and distinctly has delivered that truth which we do hold.[403] *Pontifex Romanus* (says he) *initium quidem dominij jecit sub Phocá: sub regibus Francorum fundauit regnum: ampliauit autem sub. Henricis et Fridericis: confirmauit demum sub sequentibus aliquot regibus: regnat nostro seculo ac praecedentibus aliquot*: "The pope of Rome laid the beginning of his dominion under Phocas; under the French Kings he founded his kingdom; under the Henrys and Fredericks he enlarged it; under some other kings which followed he confirmed it: he reigns in our and some former ages."

Musculus, whom he names in the sixth place, does not say that Antichrist came about the year 1200, but by the tyranny of the popes, and usurped dominion over the church, by their shameless simony, by their excessive riot, and devilish pride, by their abominable lusts and uncleanness, he concludes that the church of Rome is Babylon, and the seat of Antichrist, and adds that Bernard was of the same mind, who seems to have signified that Antichrist was then come, and that only it remained that the man of sin

---

[401] In Revelation 9
[402] De supput. annorum Mundi.
[403] Revelation 13

should be revealed (that is, acknowledged and detected, as Musculus understands him). "This discovery of Antichrist," says he, "has followed in our age." And thus you see a notable consent of all our writers whom he alleges in the main point, concerning the time of the coming of Antichrist.

(4) Now let us see what he objects against this received truth. Concerning the time of his coming with the spiritual sword, he objects that Phocas did not give the title of universal to the pope, but called him the head of the churches, as Justinian before him had done, and also the council of Chalcedon. And therefore no reason why the coming of Antichrist should be placed in the time of Phocas.

As touching the title, good authors affirm that he received from Phocas both the title of the head of the church, and also of universal or ecumenical Bishop. And no doubt he sought for, and by suite obtained that which John of Constantinople had before claimed. Neither is there any great difference between these two titles, as they are now given to the pope, save that to be the head of the universal church is the more Antichristian style.

And although titles of honor and preeminence were sometimes given to the church of Rome, as the chief or head of the churches, the mystery of iniquity working before the revelation thereof in the papacy; yet before this grant of Phocas, which was obtained with much ado and contention, the church of Rome had the preeminence and superiority over all other churches excepting that of Constantinople, not in respect of authority and jurisdiction (which after this grant, it more and more practiced) but in respect of order and dignity: and that for this cause especially, because Rome whereof he was bishop, was the chief city, as it is specified in the council of Chalcedon and in the council of Constantinople.

And for the same cause was the patriarch of Constantinople sometimes matched with him, sometimes preferred above him; because Constantinople (which they called *new Rome*) became the imperial seat.[404] Yea and the bishops of Ravenna, because their city was the chief in the exarchate of Ravenna, whereunto Rome was for a time subject, strove with the Bishop of Rome in the time of the exarchs for superiority.

Seeing therefore that now the pope of Rome had with great contention and ambition obtained the supremacy and sovereignty over the universal church; and now entitled himself the head of the universal church (a title peculiar unto Christ) the head I say, not only in respect of excellency and dignity, as a chief member of the church (as he had been in former times by some acknowledged, because he was the bishop of the chief city; but also in respect of authority and jurisdiction, as being the prince and supreme governor of the church universal, we do therefore worthily call this sovereign dominion challenged over the universal church, the first revelation or open coming of Antichrist.

(5) Concerning the coming of Antichrist with the temporal sword after the year 1000, he objects that from the year 700, the pope had received temporal dominion, and that about the year 715, he excommunicated the Greek emperor. etc.

But Bellarmine knows well enough that we speak not so much of the pope's temporal dominion over those parts which they call the patrimony of Saint Peter; but of that which they call and challenge to themselves, *Utriusque potestatis temporalis and spiritualis Monarchiam*: the monarchy of both powers, temporal and spiritual.

I answer therefore, that the pope indeed had a temporal dominion before, but not general, and that he had long endeavored to get the superiority over the emperors, but never so fully attained unto it, as in the times of Gregory VII, and afterwards.

---

[404] Tempore Mauritii.

For Gregory VII, as Aventin says, *Primus imperium pontificium condidit*, etc:[405] "first founded the Papal Empire, which his successors," says he, reckoning unto his own times, "for these 450 years, in spite of the world, and notwithstanding the emperors, have so held, that they have brought all in heaven and hell into subjection. From this time forward, the emperor is nothing but a bare title, without substance," etc.

And thus have I answered whatsoever is in his third chapter, pertinent to the matter in hand, omitting (as my manner is) his other wranglings, as being either altogether impertinent, or merely personal.

---

[405] Annal. [Boem.] lib.5

Chapter 4

Maintaining – against Bellarmine's first demonstration – that Antichrist has already come.

(1) To prove that Antichrist has not yet come, and consequently that the pope is not Antichrist, he brings six slender conjectures from six signs, which, as shall be shown, are neither proper nor necessary. And these, by a strange kind of logic, he indeed calls six demonstrations. For so have I read of some troubled with melancholy, who have thought every straw or small reed in their hands, to have been so many spears.

"We must know," (says he) "that the Holy Spirit in the Scriptures has given us six certain signs of the coming of Antichrist. Whereof two go before, namely: the preaching of the Gospel throughout the whole world: and the desolation of the Roman Empire. Two accompany Antichrist, to wit, the preaching of Enoch and Elijah, and the most grievous persecution of the church, insomuch that the public service of God must wholly cease. Two come after, namely the ruin of Antichrist after three years and a half: and the end of the world. Of which signs, none," (says he) "is yet fulfilled."

We hold the contrary, namely: that all those signs, which the Holy Spirit has given concerning the coming of Antichrist are fulfilled; and that those which are not yet fulfilled, are none of those signs which the Holy Spirit has assigned. For I will not stand now to tell you how fitly he makes the death of Antichrist, and the end of the world, which according to Bellarmine's conceit, follows after his death, to be two signs of his coming.

(2) The first sign which goes before the coming of Antichrist, is the preaching of the gospel throughout the world. From whence he reasons thus:

- If the gospel has not as yet been preached throughout the world, then is not Antichrist as yet come.
- But the gospel has not as yet been preached throughout the world.
- Therefore Antichrist has not yet come.

But in this argument nothing is sound: no necessity of consequence in the proposition, nor truth in the assumption. The proposition, notwithstanding he would prove, because our Savior Christ makes this universal preaching of the gospel a fore-runner of Antichrist in Matthew 24:14: "This gospel of the kingdom shall be preached in all the world, for a testimony to all nations."

But our Savior Christ does not say that the gospel shall be preached throughout the world before *the coming of Antichrist*, but before *the end*, as it follows in the very same verse: "and then the end shall come." Whereby we are to understand either the destruction of Jerusalem, which is most likely, or the end and consummation of the world, as Bellarmine expounds it.

And therefore unless he take it for granted, that the coming of Antichrist shall not be before the very end of the world, which we do constantly deny, as being the matter in question between us, there is not so much as any show of reason in this allegation, being understood according to his own exposition, which also is false.

Neither is it the purpose of our Savior Christ to signify unto his disciples the time of Antichrist's coming, but by way of answer to the question propounded by his disciples in verse 3, to show them when Jerusalem should be destroyed, as also to give them some signs of his coming, and of the end of the world.

But because the former part of this chapter is variously abused by the papists in this matter concerning Antichrist, I think it needful by way of a short analysis to give you the true meaning thereof; that by one labor all their cavils may be refuted.

(3) Whereas therefore our Savior Christ had foretold his disciples the utter desolation of Jerusalem, and destruction of the temple: they being persuaded that the temple and city of Jerusalem should not have an end before the end of the world, demand therefore of our Savior Christ when should be the end of both. "Tell us (they say in verse 3) "when these things shall be: that is, when the temple shall be destroyed, and what shall be the sign of thy coming, and of the end of the world?" This question, having two parts, receives an answer to both.

To the former, concerning the destruction of Jerusalem, from verse 4-23. To the latter, concerning the coming of Christ, and the end of the world, from thence to verse 42. As touching the former, our savior prophecies firstly of the calamities and troubles which should go before the destruction of Jerusalem unto verse 15, and secondly of the destruction itself, and the grievousness thereof unto verse 23.

The troubles and calamities which were the forerunners of the destruction of Jerusalem, were either temporal or spiritual. The temporal: either public and common, or peculiar to the disciples of Christ among the Jews. The public, wars, and rumors of wars, famine, pestilence, earthquakes, which were but the beginning, ωδινων, of sorrows in the land of Jewry, being about to be delivered of her inhabitants (verses 6-8). The peculiar troubles to the Christians, persecution and hatred for Christ's sake; and the effects thereof in the unsound, falling away, and betraying and hating one another (verses 9-10). The spiritual, in the teachers spirits of error and heresy (verses 5 & 11). In the hearers, seduction by false prophets and falling away (verses 11-12).

Now unto this prophecy are admixed both admonitions and consolations. *Admonitions*: that they should take heed of false prophets (verse 4), and that they should not be troubled or dismayed with rumors of wars (verse 6). *Consolations* grounded upon a twofold promise, first of salvation to those, who, notwithstanding these temptations, shall persevere to the end (verse 13). Secondly, of the success of their ministry, that before the desolation of Jerusalem, the gospel should be preached throughout the world for a testimony to all nations (verse 14). And therefore that they should not fear, lest together with Jerusalem, his church should be overthrown. For before the destruction of Jerusalem he would by their preaching to all nations, both Jews and Gentiles, plant his church in many nations of the world.

And for as much as the temple and city of Jerusalem were types and figures of the church of Christ which were to be abolished when the church of Christ should be established, therefore he adds that upon the planting of his church by their ministry should the end and destruction of Jerusalem come. And these were the calamities which went before the destruction of Jerusalem.

The destruction itself is described partly by the efficient, foretold by Daniel 9:27, that is to say, the Roman armies besieging Jerusalem in Luke 21:20, which because they were idolaters are called abominable, and because of the desolation which they were to bring upon Jerusalem are called desolators,[406] and by a metonymy in Matthew 24:15, *the abomination of desolation*, and by a synecdoche in Daniel 9:27, *abominable wings* (that is armies) *bringing desolation*: partly by the grievousness of the destruction verse 21. To this prophecy also he mixes counsel and consolation. *Counsel*, that they which shall be in Jewry provide for themselves by flight (verse 16-18), in respect whereof he both pities the women and such as give suck, and bids them pray that their flight be not in winter, nor on the sabbath day (verse 19-20). His consolation is that for the elect's sake, the time of the siege shall be shortened, for otherwise none of the Jews could escape, as Chrysostom also expounds (verse 22). This exposition is plainly confirmed by conference

---

[406] Sic Augustine. ad Hesychiū et Chrysost. homil. 49. in Mat. oper. imperfect.

of this chapter of Matthew with Luke 21, where the same question being propounded in verse 7 concerning the end of Jerusalem alone, receives an answer peculiar to the destruction of Jerusalem, unto verse 25.

And whereas in Matthew 24:15, Christ uses these words, "when you shall see the abomination of desolation which in Daniel is called the abominable wings bringing desolation, standing in the holy place," this in Luke is thus expounded:[407] "When you see Jerusalem besieged with armies (which Daniel foretold should bring desolation upon it) then understand that the desolation thereof is near," and therefore he advises them which shall be in Jewry to fly so soon as Jerusalem shall be besieged, etc. Because there shall be great affliction in those days, namely in Jewry and Jerusalem, as Luke restrains it:[408] "For there shall be great distress in the land, and wrath in this people, and they shall fall on the edge of the sword, and shall be carried away captive into all nations, and Jerusalem shall be trodden under foot of the Gentiles until the times of the Gentiles be fulfilled, and then shall be the end of the world,"[409] the signs whereof he adds in the next words.[410]

(4) By this analysis of the text and conference with Luke, it evidently appears that all these predictions from verse 6 to 21 in Matthew and in Luke 21:7-29 concern the destruction of Jerusalem, which happened within forty years after this prophecy was delivered.

Neither may we think that our savior Christ would intermingle the prophecies concerning the destruction of Jerusalem and the end of the world, thereby to nourish the aforesaid error of his disciples, who imagined that the end of Jerusalem should not be before the end of the world, as appears by their question.

---

[407] Luke 22:20
[408] εν τω λαω τουτω
[409] Luke 21:23-24
[410] Luke 21:25

For even afterward in verse 34, where seems the greatest mixture, our Savior Christ speaks distinctly. For whereas our Savior had spoken first of the end of Jerusalem, and then of the end of the world severally, and had given signs of both, whereby they might know the approaching of either, as by the budding of the fig tree they gather summer to be near, he defines the time of the one, and the other he leaves indefinite: 'Verily I say unto you, this generation shall not pass, until all those things," says he, pointing as it seems towards Jerusalem as he sat in the Mount of Olives, "be fulfilled."

And as touching the end of the world, he notes both the certainty thereof, and the uncertainty of the time. Of the former he says: "Heaven and earth shall pass away," (and that with a noise, as Peter says)[411] "but my words shall not pass away, howbeit of that day and hour (namely, wherein the Son of man shall come, and wherein the heavens shall pass away) none knoweth, no not the angels of heaven, but the Father only."

Whatsoever the papists therefore allege out of the former part of the chapter as favoring any of their fancies concerning Antichrist, as namely the preaching of the gospel before the coming of Antichrist, the abomination of desolation, and the most grievous tribulation in the time of Antichrist, etc., may easily be answered.

(5) But if these prophecies are compared with the history and event, we shall find this truth to be more evident, seeing that all these predictions had their complement at or before the destruction of Jerusalem. For (to omit the rest) the apostle testifies in Colossians 1:6, 23, Romans 1:8 and 10:18 that the gospel was in his time preached in all the world; and therefore before the desolation of Jerusalem, which happened about two years after his death.[412]

From whence also evidently appears how false Bellarmine's assumption is, as being contradictory both to the prophecy of Christ in this place, as also

---

[411] 2 Peter 3:10
[412] Eusebius. Lib. 3

to the testimony of the apostle testifying the fulfilling thereof in his time, according to the commission given to the apostles, that they should go into all the world and teach all nations (Matthew 28:19, Mark 16:15), which was accordingly performed (Mark 16:20). And thus Chrysostom also expounds this place,[413] that before the end, that is, the destruction of Jerusalem, the gospel was to be preached throughout the world, and proves by the same testimonies of Paul, that this prophecy was fulfilled before the taking of Jerusalem.

But if it seem incredible unto any that the gospel should be preached throughout the world in so short a time: he must consider firstly that by *the whole world* is not to be understood every small corner and unknown part of the world: but by a synecdoche, the greatest part of the world then known and inhabited, as in Luke 2:1. And by *all nations*, not all and every nation, but *all sorts*, that is, both Jews and Gentiles. For both here and elsewhere there seems to be an opposition made between the whole world and the land of Jewry: between all nations and the Jews. For whereas before the church was contained in Jewry, and the word preached to the Jews, our Savior shows that before the desolation of Jerusalem, the gospel should be preached commonly in all parts of the world, and not only in Jewry; and indifferently to all other nations, and not peculiarly to the Jews. Secondly, he is to consider, both the multitude of the preachers and dispersers of the gospel, and also the infinite power of God's Spirit, and miraculous efficacy of his word preached in that it could in so short a time spread itself so far as it did. Thirdly a distinction is to be made between preaching the gospel and receiving it. For it was preached in all the world, but not received everywhere.

And that our Savior signifies where he says that it should be preached in all the world for a testimony to all nations, to leave those which embrace it not, without excuse. If then the preaching of the gospel throughout the

---

[413] Homil. in Matthew 24

world be not made by Christ our Savior a sign of Antichrist's coming, and yet notwithstanding it be most true, that according to the prophecy of Christ, the gospel was preached in all the world before the desolation of Jerusalem, what show of reason is there in this demonstration? And this is all that I think worth answering in his fourth chapter.

(6) For to what purpose should I tell you of his argument, which notwithstanding he says it was now no time to prove, to wit, that before the coming of Antichrist the gospel should be preached throughout the world, because the cruel persecution of Antichrist should hinder all public exercises of true religion: and therefore was to be preached generally throughout the world either before the time of Antichrist, or not at all? This, we shall in part find time to answer in his fourth demonstration.

In the meantime, we answer firstly that the grievous tribulation, before which our Savior says the gospel was to be preached in all the world, is not the persecution under Antichrist, but the affliction of the Jews at and before the destruction of Jerusalem by the Romans, as I have manifestly proved. And secondly, that if the general preaching of the gospel were made a sign of Antichrist's coming, as it is not, but of the end; yet is it not necessary that it should be preached generally throughout the world at one time, for it might suffice that in one age it were preached to one nation; and in another age, to another people.

And therefore although during the persecution of Antichrist, the gospel was not preached generally and at once to all nations, yet in that time it might be preached to some nations, where it had not formerly been preached, and therefore might be preached to all nations before the destruction of Antichrist, though it were not before his coming. Or to what end should I spend any time in answering the testimonies of the fathers, who supposed that the gospel should be preached in all the world before the coming of Antichrist, seeing according to the meaning of our Savior Christ, it was to be preached in all the world, before the destruction of Jerusalem? Or what account should we make of his objections, wherein he alleges that the gospel has not as yet been preached throughout the world, seeing our Savior who cannot he has prophesied, and the apostle by the same spirit of truth has testified, that before the destruction of Jerusalem, the gospel of the kingdom was preached in all the world.

And therefore the papists in this point, while they study to contradict us, are not afraid to give the lie to our Savior Christ. Neither are his cavillations, whereby he endeavors to avoid and elude those testimonies of Scripture, which do testify that the gospel was in the apostles' times preached in all the world, worth the mentioning. For whereas Paul says, "No doubt their sound went out through all the earth, and their words into the ends of the world,"[414] Bellarmine cavils that the apostle used the past tense instead of the future, as if he had said, "no doubt their sound *shall* go through all the earth." But (say I) the apostle proves that the Jews had heard the gospel, because the sound of the preachers thereof were gone through all the earth, and therefore they from whom the gospel proceeded to other nations, could not be ignorant thereof. And again, whereas the same apostle says that the gospel in his time was in all the world, and adds that it did bring forth fruit even as it did among the Colossians.[415] Bellarmine answers that the apostle would not say that it was actually, but virtually, as they say, in all the world. But how could it bring forth fruit, unless it were actually?

And besides, the apostle in the same chapter says that the gospel had been preached to every creature under heaven, which is a more large speech than this prophecy of our Savior in Matthew 24:14. To conclude, if by the end in that place is to be understood the end of the world, as Bellarmine will need to have it contrary to the text, yet the gospel before the and might be preached throughout the world, and yet not before the coming of Antichrist. If by *the end* is to be understood *the end of Jerusalem*, as I have manifestly

---

[414] Romans 10:18
[415] Colossians 1:6

proven, then according to our Savior's prophecy, the gospel was preached in all the world, in the apostles' times. But that the general preaching of the gospel should be a sign of Antichrist's coming, the Scripture has never a word.

Chapter 5

Maintaining – against Bellarmine's second demonstration – that Antichrist has already come.

(1) The second sign going before Antichrist is, as Bellarmine says, the utter desolation of the Roman Empire. From whence this demonstration is raised:

- If the Roman Empire is not yet utterly destroyed, then Antichrist has not yet come, because the utter desolation of the Romaine Empire is a certain sign going before his coming.
- But the Roman Empire is not yet utterly destroyed.
- Therefore Antichrist has not yet come.

We confess that before Antichrist could be revealed by exercising a sovereign dominion in Rome, it was necessary that the emperor, so far forth as he hindered this revelation of Antichrist, should be taken out of the way. But that there should be such an utter desolation of the empire, as that there should not remain so much as the name of the Emperor or king of the Romans, that we do utterly deny.

He that hindered was taken out of the way, partly when the imperial seat was removed from Rome to Constantinople, and that to this end (as they have set down in the donation of Constantine) that the city of Rome might be left to the pope, but especially when as after the division of the Empire into two parts, the Empire in the West (which properly was the Empire of Rome) was dissolved, and lay void for many years. All this was accomplished before Boniface III attained the Antichristian title.

Neither does the reviving of the western empire in Charlemagne after it had been void for 325 years hinder the revelation or dominion of Antichrist, but rather proves that Antichrist had then come. For this new empire erected by the pope's means is the image of the beast (that is, of the old empire) which Antichrist the second beast causes to be made, and puts life thereinto. It is the beast whereon the whore of Babylon sits, and therefore is so far from hindering Antichrist, that it supports him.[416]

This beast, which was an imperial state, but is not indeed, though in title it is, as being but an image of the old empire, is said to be the eighth head of the beast, and yet one of the seven; whereas Antichrist by the confession of papists is the seventh.[417] Wherefore although the old empire in the West (which hindered) was done out of the way, and indeed dissolved before the revelation of Antichrist; yet even with and under Antichrist, there was to be an imperial state in name and title, which is the beast whereon the whore of Babylon sits, as I have heretofore proved.[418]

(2) But let us come to his arguments. The first whereof is this. If before Antichrist's coming, the Roman Empire is to be divided into ten kings, whereof none shall be called king of the Romans; then is not Antichrist yet come, for yet there is a king of the Romans: but the first is true, therefore the last. The proposition he takes for granted, although it cannot be denied but that upon the desolation of the empire in the West, it was divided among ten kings at the least; who although they had the provinces of the Empire, yet none of them was called the king of the Romans. The proposition therefore is false, and the reason may be returned upon our adversary. For seeing these ten kings had not received their kingly power in the Apostles time, but were to receive it either after the beast (which is Antichrist,) as some read; or with the beast as others: it is evident therefore, that when the ten rulers of the provinces had received authority as kings, then Antichrist was come.[419] But many hundred years since, the rulers of the provinces

---

[416] Revelation 13
[417] Revelation 17
[418] Book 1 Chapter 3 Section 3
[419] Revelation 17:12 [...] μετα του θηριου

ceased to be deputies under the Emperor, and obtained power as sovereign kings, dividing among them the western Empire, therefore many hundred years since Antichrist had come.

The assumption he proves out of Daniel chapter 2, where (says he) is described the succession of the chief kingdoms unto the end of the world by a certain image, the golden head whereof signifies the kingdom of the Assyrians; the breast of silver, the kingdom of the Persians; the belly of brass, the kingdom of the Grecians; the legs of iron, the kingdom of the Romans divided into two parts, etc. And in chapter 7, the same kingdoms are signified: the last which has ten horns being the kingdom of the Romans. "Now," (says he)[420] "as the two legs have ten toes which are not legs, and as the ten horns are not the beast, so the Roman Empire shall be divided into ten kings, whereof none is the king of the Romans."

Answer: [1] This argumentation of Bellarmine implies a contradiction. For if there be in Daniel described a succession of kingdoms which shall continue to the end of the world, whereof the Roman is the last: then the Roman Empire shall not utterly be destroyed before the coming of Antichtist, which goes before the end of the world. But however the common opinion has been, that the fourth kingdom mentioned in those chapters is the Roman Empire; yet by the learned, especially of these latter times, it has been most clearly proved, that by it is understood that kingdom of the Seleucids and Lagidae, which tyrannized over the people of Jewry. For the Seleucids who were kings of Syria, and the Lagidae who were kings of Egypt, were the two legs of the image, and were also the fourth beast:[421] the ten kings of these two kingdoms, which successively usurped dominion over the Jews, were the ten horns of the beast; which being most true as hereafter also shall be shown, it appears evidently, that this whole argumentation is impertinent.

---

[420] Subtiliss.
[421] Chapter 16

But suppose that Daniel had spoken in those places of the Roman Empire, yet that which Bellarmine would infer thereof, would not follow. For by the beast is signified the kingdom itself, and by the horns the several kings, who although they are not the kingdom itself signified by the beast, no more than the horns are the beast, yet are they so many kings of that kingdom, which is signified by the beast. As for example: Seleucus, Antiochus, and the rest of the ten kings signified by the ten horns, and as Bellarmine speaks, by the ten toes, though they were not the kingdom of Syria and Egypt itself; yet were they kings of that kingdom, and therefore this argument of Bellarmine is very frivolous.

(3) [2] His second proof is out of Revelation 17, where John describes a beast with seven heads and ten horns, upon which beast, a certain woman sits, which he expounds to be the great city sitting on seven hills, that is to say, Rome. "The seven heads as they signify seven hills, so also seven kings, by which number," (says he) "all the Roman emperors are understood. The ten horns are ten kings, which shall reign together." And lest we should think that these shall be Roman kings, he adds: "These kings shall hate the harlot, and make her desolate, because they shall so divide the Roman Empire among them, that they shall utterly destroy it."

Here Bellarmine, as you see, confesses that Rome is the whore of Babylon, and consequently the seat of Antichrist, and not Rome under the old emperors, but Rome after the dissolution of the empire. And that the ten horns are so many kings, among whom the Roman Empire should be divided, and that these ten kings were to receive their kingdom together; and consequently that these are not the same ten horns whereof Daniel speaks, which reigned successively in Daniel 11. And whereas Bellarmine says, the seven heads signify all the emperors, it is untrue. For the Holy Spirit names seven, because they were seven indeed, and therefore numbers them:

"Five are fallen, the sixth is, and the seventh is not yet come." But all this is besides the present purpose.

How then does he prove, that before Antichrist comes, the Roman Empire shall be so utterly destroyed, as that not the name of a Roman emperor or king of the Romans should remain? Because the empire shall be divided among ten kings, which are not Roman kings. But that proves not that the name shall not remain: for he that is none of those ten kings, may have the name of the emperor or king of the Romans, as namely the beast which was, and is not, though it be, which is the eighth head, and is one of the seven, that is to say, the emperor erected by the pope.

And why may none of these be called the king of the Romans? First indeed, because they shall hate Rome, and make her desolate. As though he that has the title of *the King of the Romans*, may not hate Rome notwithstanding that title, as indeed some of the emperors have done. Secondly, because they shall so divide among them the Roman Empire, as that they shall utterly destroy it. Where you see by a circular disputation, the question brought to prove his argument, and yet experience shows, that although the empire is dissolved, and also divided among the beast (that is Antichrist) and ten kings, there does notwithstanding remain the name and title of the emperor or king of the Romans.

And so much now shall suffice to have spoken of that place, from whence I have heretofore proven both that Antichrist has already come, and that the pope is Antichrist.

(4) [3] His third proof is out of 2 Thessalonians 2: "And now what hindereth you know, that he may be revealed in due time, only he which holdeth must hold, until he be done out of the way, and then that wicked man shall be revealed." That this is to be understood of the Roman Empire, he not only affirms, but also confirms by the testimonies of several of the fathers, which we are so far from denying, that from hence, as one special argument, we prove the pope to be Antichrist.

But neither the apostle nor any of the fathers (excepting Lactantius, whose prophecy in this point the papists themselves do think to be erroneous) does say, that the Empire of Rome shall so utterly be abolished as that not so much as the name of the *Emperor* or *King of the Romans* shall remain; which Bellarmine should have proven. For otherwise that the empire was indeed dissolved before the revelation of Antichrist, the Holy Spirit prophesied, the event has proved, and we do willingly confess: *Quo tenebat, de medio fit,* (says Jerome in his time)[422] *and non intelligimus Antichristum appropinquare?* He which held, is taken away, and do we not understand that Antichrist is at hand?

"Yea but," (says Bellarmine) "the Roman Empire is not yet utterly destroyed, and therefore Antichrist is not yet come." Neither is it necessary: it is sufficient, that he which hindered the revelation of Antichrist, was done out of the way, which was done first by removing the imperial seat from Rome, which was to be the seat of Antichrist, as has been proven. Secondly, by the dissolution of the empire in the West.

As for the empire renewed by the pope, that does not hinder Antichrist, but rather furthers him, as has been shown; and therefore there is no necessity that it should be taken away. Neither is there now an emperor of the Romans indeed, but only in title, without the thing itself, as enjoying neither the city of Rome itself, nor yet the provinces. And therefore either unskillfully or sophistically are these emperors, who have no imperial authority either in the city or the provinces, compared with those ancient emperors, who although they had the empire, lacked Rome itself.

(5) And hereby appears the error of our adversaries, who think that Antichrist comes not before the utter desolation of the Roman Empire, whereas neither of the apostles Paul or John do say so, but rather the contrary, as has been shown. For to omit the rest before alleged, John says,

---

[422] Ad Gerontia, De Monogamia.

Revelation 13. That one head of the beast, meaning the state of the emperors, had indeed received a deadly wound, both in respect of Rome the head city, and of the emperors in the West, but was cured, therefore not utterly destroyed: and cured by the pope, both in respect of the city, and in regard of the Emperor. And therefore the pope is Antichrist, as some of our writers infer, because this wound was to be cured by the second beast, which figures Antichrist.

And Ambrose says upon 2 Thessalonians 2 that Antichrist shall restore liberty to the Romans, but in his own name. Bellarmine answers that he reads nowhere in John that the beast, which signifies the Roman Empire, was to be cured by Antichrist. Yea, but this he might have read: that the second beast, which is Antichrist, causes the image of the beast (that is, the new empire) to be made, and puts life unto it. For by this renewing of the empire, Bellarmine elsewhere professeses that the Roman Empire was restored to the same estate, wherein it was before Augustulus.[423]

But what has Bellarmine read in John? Indeed, that one of the heads of the beast should die, and shortly after rise again by the help of the devil; which the ancient expound of Antichrist, who shall feign himself to be dead, and by devilish art rise again, that so by resembling the true death and resurrection of Christ, he might seduce many. First, it is evident that the former beast does not figure Antichrist, but the Roman state, and that under the Roman emperors especially.

Secondly, it is not said that one of the heads did feign itself dead, and by the help of the devil did rise again (which needed not, if the death were counterfeit) but that one of the heads had received a deadly wound, and was cured again. The head was the state of the emperors, to wit, the sixth head, which received a deadly wound in Augustulus, after whom the empire in the West lay void for 325 years. But this head was cured after a sort in Charlemagne and his successors, in whom there was an image of the former

---

[423] De translat. imperij. lib. 1. c. 4.

Emperors erected by the pope. And therefore this state of emperors renewed in Charlemagne and his successors, is said to be the eighth head of the beast, and yet is one of the seven.

So that the sixth head which before was wounded to death, was cured, and after a sort repaired in them. This in substance is confessed by Bellarmine himself in this chapter where, understanding by the two legs of the image in Daniel, the Western and Eastern Empire, he says, That the Western, which was the one leg, failed, namely, in Augustulus, and was after erected in Charlemagne, and that (as elsewhere he boasts) by the pope.

Now whereas Bellarmine labors to prove that this head which was wounded to death and revived again, is not Charles the Great, he shows himself ridiculous in fighting with his own shadow. For by *the head* is not meant any one man, but the state and succession of emperors, which was interrupted and cut off in Augustulus, and renewed in Charles the Great, and his successors. And that which is added concerning the universality either of worship, or of rule, is not spoken of the head which was revived, but of the beast, which was to have one of his seven heads wounded to death and cured again.[424]

---

[424] Revelation 13:7-8

Chapter 6

Answering his third demonstration, concerning Enoch and Elijah.

(1) Now we are to come to those signs, which in Bellarmine's conceit are to accompany Antichrist, the former whereof is the coming of Enoch and Elijah in the flesh, to oppose themselves against Antichrist, and to convert the Jews. From whence Bellarmine reasons thus:

- If Enoch and Elijah have not yet come again in the flesh, then Antichrist has not yet come.
- But Enoch and Elijah have not yet come again in the flesh.
- Therefore Antichrist has not yet come.

To the proposition I answer; first, that if Enoch and Elijah were to come in their own persons before the second coming of Christ, as some of the Ancient have thought, and that to oppose themselves against Antichrist, as the papists dream: yet it does not that therefore Antichrist should not be come before their coming. It is sufficient that they come before his overthrow, and the second coming of Christ. And therefore if they were indeed to come, their coming might yet be expected, notwithstanding the truth of our assertion that Antichrist has already come. But if Enoch and Elijah are not to come again in their own persons before the end of the world, to fight against Antichrist, what force of argument is there in this worthy demonstration?

This therefore Bellarmine makes the question, which he goes about to prove. First, by testimonies of Scripture. Secondly, by consent of the fathers. Thirdly, by reason.

(2) "There are four Scriptures," (says Bellarmine) "to prove that Enoch and Elijah in their own persons shall come against Antichrist." Howbeit this is a manifest untruth; for no place of Scripture speaks of Enoch's return.

The first is Malachi 4:5: "Behold I will send unto you Elijah the Prophet, before the great and fearful day of the LORD come, and he shall turn the hearts of the fathers unto the children, and the hearts of the children unto their fathers." This place makes no mention of Enoch, but only of Elijah, and by *Elijah* is meant not Elijah the Tishbite, but John the Baptist: who (as the angel applying to him this prophecy says) should go before the Lord Jesus "in the spirit and power of Elijah, that he may turn the hearts of the fathers unto the children," etc.[425] And our savior Christ most plainly affirms, that John the Baptist "is that Elijah who was to come, and if you will receive," (says he) that is, "if you will give credit to my speech, this is that Elijah who was to come,"[426] and adds: "He that has ears to hear, let him hear."

This shows that the papists neither have hearts to believe Christ, nor ears to hear him: but have open both hearts to receive and ears to hear the fables of the Jews: who as they yet look for their messiah, so they look also for Elijah to be his forerunner. For as Jerome wrote upon this place of Malachi: "The Jews and Judaizing heretics think that before their messiah, Elijah shall come, and restore all things. Hence it is, that unto Christ this question is propounded in the gospel, *what is that which the Pharisees say, that Elijah shall come?* To whom he answered: *Elijah indeed shall come: and if you will believe, he is already come* – by *Elijah* meaning John." And therefore in Jerome's judgment it is but the opinion of a Judaizing heretic to expect the coming again of Elijah in his own person.

"Yea but," (says Bellarmine) "this place cannot be understood of John the Baptist, but of Elijah only. For Malachi speaks of the second coming of Christ which shall be unto judgment: For so he says, before the great and

---

[425] Luke 1:17
[426] Matthew 11:14

terrible day of the Lord come; for his first coming is not called great and terrible, but the acceptable time and day of salvation. Whereupon it is also added, least when I come, I strike the earth with a curse. But Christ in his first coming came not to judge, but to be judged."

(3) Answer: Bellarmine must give us leave to believe the Angel of God, and our Savior Christ, rather than himself, who is not afraid, as it seems, to give the lie to the Spirit of God speaking in both.[427] Neither can he prove that Malachi speaks of the second coming of Christ: for therein the papists err worse then the Jews.

For both the text itself, and also the application thereof by the angel and our Savior Christ, do prove that Elijah was to come before the first coming of Christ, which is great to the godly, and terrible to the wicked. And therefore in the beginning of the third chapter, the prophet speaking most plainly of the first coming of Christ, before which the Lord promises to send his messenger, that is, John the Baptist, to prepare the way before him,[428] signifies, that this coming is great and fearful (verse 2): "But who may abide the day of his coming? and who shall endure when he appeareth? for he is like a purging fire, and like fuller's soap, and he shall sit down to try and fine the silver."

Of the same coming he speaks in the beginning of the fourth chapter: "Behold the day comes that shall burn as an oven," etc. showing how terrible it shall be to the wicked. "But unto you that fear my name," (says the Lord in verse 2) "shall the sun of righteousness arise, and health shall be under his wings," etc.

And before this great day comes, he promises them to send them Elijah, that is, John the Baptist, to whom our Savior applies the prophecy of Malachi in 3:1 and 4:5. In like sort, John the Baptist himself describes the first coming of Christ as terrible in respect of the wicked. "Now," (says he) "is the axe laid

---

[427] Luke 1:17, Matthew 11:14, Matthew 17
[428] Matthew 11:10, Mark 1:2

to the root of the trees," etc. (Matthew 3:10; and 3:11-12): "He that comes after me is mightier than I: he will baptize you with the Holy Spirit and with fire, which has his fan in his hand, (using the like similitude that Malachi did) and will purge his floor, and gather his wheat into his garner, but will burn up the Chaff with unquenchable fire." Simeon also says of our Savior, that he was appointed both for the fall of the wicked, and rising of the godly.[429] And elsewhere he is called a stumbling stone, and a rock of offense,[430] upon which stone, whosoever falls, he shall be broken in pieces; but on whomsoever it shall fall, it shall all to grind him.[431]

If notwithstanding all this which has been alleged, any man shall think the first coming of the Lord, not so fitly to be called *terrible*; I further answer, that the Hebrew word *norah*, signifies also *reverend*, *to be feared*, or *had in reverence*, as in Genesis 28:17, Deuteronomy 28:17 & 7:21, and so is translated by Tremellius and Junius in this place of Malachi. And thus both that word, and others of the same root are used in the signification of reverence, or filial fear.

And whereas it is added, that Elijah should be sent to convert the people, "lest when I come," (says the Lord) "I should strike the earth with a curse," the meaning is, that the Lord would send his messenger to prepare the way before him, that some of the people at the least, might be ready to receive our Savior Christ, least if all should reject him, he should be provoked to strike the land: for at his second coming, he shall without peradventure strike the earth. And in this exposition of Malachi besides others, Arias Montanus[432] the most learned writer among the papists, does wholly agree with us; expounding this prophecy of John the Baptist, whom he calls another Elijah, and of the first coming of Christ.

---

[429] Luke 2:34
[430] Romans 9:33
[431] Matthew 21:44
[432] On Malachi

Thus therefore I answer: First that Malachi speaks not of Enoch, but of Elijah only; and secondly, of Elijah's coming, not with Antichrist, but before Christ: thirdly, and that before the first coming of Christ: fourthly and consequently, not of Elijah literally, but of John the Baptist, who came in the spirit and power of Elijah.

(4) The second place is, Ecclesiasticus 48:10 and 44:16. In the former place, it is said of Elijah that he was appointed to reprove in due season, and to pacify the anger of the Lord's judgment proceeding to fury, and to turn the hearts of the fathers unto the children, and to set up the tribes of Jacob. In the latter it is said of Enoch, as Bellarmine reads that he pleased God, and was translated into Paradise, that he might give penance unto the Gentiles.

First I answer to both places, that although this book of the son of Sirach is very commendable; yet it is not of canonical authority, being but a human writing, as appears not only by the former place alleged, but also by that erroneous conceit concerning Samuel, chapter 46:23. Secondly, in neither place is it said that either of them should come to oppose themselves against Antichrist; that from hence their return into the world, should be made a sign of the coming of Antichrist. But as touching the former place, severally I answer with Jansenius, one of the best writers among the papists (however Bellarmine wonders at him that he should consent with us in the truth, being a popish bishop) that although the ancient writers have thought that Elijah was to come again, yet it cannot be evinced out of this place.

For we may say that Ecclesiasticus did write this according to the received opinion of his time, grounded (as they thought) upon the words of Malachi, that Elijah was truly to come in his own person before the messiah when as that was not to be fulfilled in his own person, but in him that was to come in the spirit and power of Elijah. True indeed it is, that not only the author of that book, as it seems, but the Jews in general, understanding the words of Malachi literally, did expect that Elijah in his own person should return before the coming of the messiah. But our Savior Christ reforms this error, applying the prophecy to John the Baptist.

And secondly I answer, that if Bellarmine will argue out of Ecclesiasticus, according to his meaning, he must prove that Elijah was to come in his own person, before the first coming of the messiah, of which Malachi speaks, and before which this author as all the rest of the Jews, do hold that Elijah was to come: And therefore the papists might as well with the Jews, look for their messiah, as for Elijah.

Now as touching the other place, it is a wonder that Bellarmine would allege it for this purpose. But that having nothing to say to the purpose, he is desirous to say something to blear the eyes of the simple. The original text has these words,[433] Ενὼχ εὐηρέστησε Κυρίῳ καὶ μετετέθη, ὑπόδειγμα μετανοίας ταῖς γενεαῖς, that is, Enoch pleased the Lord God, and was translated for an example of repentance to the generations: that is, that the generations present and to come, might be moved by his example, to turn unto the Lord and to walk before him, knowing by his example that there is a reward laid up for those that turn unto the Lord, and walk before him as Enoch did. But will Bellarmine hence conclude that therefore Enoch is to come again in the flesh, to oppose himself to Antichrist?

(5) The third place is, Matthew 17:11: "Elijah indeed shall come, and shall restore all things." "These words," says Bellarmine, "are plainly to be understood, not of John, but of the true Elijah. For John was already come, and had finished his course, and yet the Lord says in the future tense: *Elijah shall come.*" I answer that by the evangelist Mark, who speaks in the present tense: "Elijah indeed coming first restoreth all things," the meaning of our Savior Christ appears to have been this. *Elias quidem venturus fuit primum, & restituturus omnia*: "Elijah indeed was to come first, and was to restore all things, but I tell you that Elijah is already come, and they have done unto

---

[433] Ecclesiasticus 44:16

him what they listed, as it is written of him, meaning John the Baptist." As if he had said: "The prophecy indeed concerning Elijah is true, but I tell you it is already fulfilled." For as he says in another place: "John the Baptist is that Elijah who was to come," then what could be spoken more plainly?

Bellarmine answers that John the Baptist was the promised Elijah, not literally, but allegorically. So we affirm also, and further add, that Elijah was not promised literally. For our Savior Christ plainly affirms that John the Baptist is that Elijah which was promised. And both he and the angel understand that prophecy of Malachi 4:5 not literally of Elijah the Tishbite, but allegorically of John the Baptist, who was, as it were, another Elijah.[434]

"Yea but the disciples," says Bellarmine, "who had seen the transfiguration – when they asked Christ: *What is that which the scribes say, that Elijah must first come?* – speak of the same Elijah, whom they had seen with Christ in the mount: and therefore Christ making answer to them, that Elijah indeed shall come, speaks of the same Elijah."

It does not follow, for the disciples speak according to the erroneous opinion of the scribes, who understanding Malachi literally, thought that Elijah was to come in his own person, and thereupon (as it is thought) inferred, that Christ was not the true Messias, because Elijah came not before him. But Christ answers them according to the true meaning of Malachi, applying his prophecy to John the Baptist, who is figuratively called *Elijah*. Yea but it cannot truly be said that John the Baptist restored all things: for to restore all things, is to call all the Jews and heretics, and perhaps some of the seduced Catholics to the true faith, as Bellarmine objects.

This is indeed the popish conceit: that Enoch and Elijah shall preach against Antichrist 1260 days, at the end whereof, they shall be put to death by Antichrist, and after three and a half days, shall rise again. Within a month after their death, Antichrist shall be destroyed in the Mount of Olives and 45 days after that, Christ shall come to judgment. In the meantime, so

---

[434] Matthew 11:14

effectual shall the preaching of Enoch and Elijah be, that they shall restore all things, that is, they shall call all the Jews and heretics, and perhaps the seduced catholics.

But how does this agree with the prophecies of our Savior Christ, concerning the lack of faith at his coming, and the uncertainty of the time of his appearing? As touching the former he says "The son of man when he comes, shall he find faith upon the earth?"[435] And as touching the other, he has foretold that the end of the world shall be sudden and unlooked for, even as it was in the days of Noah and Lot.[436] But if this conceit of the papists be true, there shall be more true believers at the end of the world than ever had been at one time before; and the day of Christ's coming, after the revelation of Antichrist, but especially after his death, shall be precisely known, and accordingly looked for.

Now whereas he says that John did not restore all things, which (as Christ says) Elijah should do, I answer that Christ speaks according to their understanding, and therefore that John the Baptist did restore all things in that sense that Elijah was, according to their conceit, to restore all things. But by restitution in this place, we are to understand the reformation of the people and church of the Jews (to whom the messenger and forerunner is promised, and not to heretics and seduced catholics) wherein John the Baptist was another Elijah. Neither is this restitution ascribed to the Baptist, as though it had been perfected by him, but because he began that, which Christ was to bring to perfection. So that John the Baptist may truly be said to have made this restitution inchoative.

(6) The fourth place is Revelation 11:3. "I will give to my two witnesses, and they shall prophesy 1260 days." These words he affirms (but without all

---

[435] Luke 18:8
[436] Matthew 24:39, Luke 17:26, 18

reason) are to be understood of Enoch and Elijah, who are not once mentioned in all that chapter.

Neither can those two witnesses signify Enoch and Elijah, because they are to be killed by the beast, and their bodies shall lie dead in the streets of the great city for three and a half days. For Enoch and Elijah were taken up into heaven: where in soul at the least they enjoy the glorious presence of God. For otherwise, their estate were worse than that of the rest of the faithful departed: and so their translation should rather have been a punishment than a blessing or prerogative unto them, without question therefore their souls at the least are in heaven.

But whether they are there in soul alone, or in soul and body, there may be some question: but if they are there in body, it cannot be that their body is mortal (as the papists would have it) and subject to death. For how can corruption inherit incorruption?[437] Or how can it be truly said, that Enoch was translated that he should not see death, if notwithstanding his translation, he shall suffer death?

If therefore their bodies are in heaven, undoubtedly they were in the translation changed, and by that change became immortal, as the bodies of them shall, who shall be alive upon the earth at the second coming of Christ.[438] If their souls alone are in heaven, their bodies being dissolved and returned into dust, then either they must come in their own bodies, or in others. If in others, then must we hold the flitting of souls into different bodies, if in their own, then shall they not only rise before the resurrection,[439] but also after their resurrection, die again. All of these absurdities plainly show, that the popish opinion concerning the coming of Enoch and Elijah is a mere fable, whereby men are kept in security, that they should not with vigilance wait for the coming of Christ, because as yet

---

[437] 1 Corinthians 15:50
[438] 1 Corinthians 15:51, 53
[439] 1 Thessalonians 4

indeed, Enoch and Elijah are not returned. The two witnesses therefore cannot signify Elijah and Enoch.

But if I should add, that Bellarmine cannot prove that this place entreats of Antichrist, but rather of the beast with seven heads arising out of the sea, that is, the Roman state either generally, or especially under the emperors, as may be gathered by comparing Revelation 11:2 & 11:7 with 13:1 & 13:5. I would then know to what purpose he alleges this text to prove, that Enoch and Elijah shall come against Antichrist, if neither the one nor the other are here meant.

(7) Unto these testimonies of Scripture, he adds the consent of the fathers, who hold that Enoch and Elijah shall in their own persons come in the time of Antichrist. And to this purpose he names many, but yet among all the ancient which he cites, only Gregory is alleged to the purpose, who in his *Morals*, expounding the words of Bildad the Shuhite as spoken of Antichrist, testifies that in his time Enoch and Elijah shall come, which is as true, as that Bildad spake of Antichrist.[440]

Of the rest, some speak of the return of Elijah only, and that to convert the Jews (without mention of his resisting Antichrist) being deceived by the corrupt translation of the Septuagint who in Malachi 4:5, read *Elijah the Tishbite*, and thereby gave occasion to the readers to expound those words of Elijah literally: whereas in the Hebrew, and also in other translations we read *Elijah the Prophet*, which may truly be applied to John, who was a prophet; and by the testimony of our savior Christ, more than a prophet.

Others, who besides Elijah mention the coming of another, agree not among themselves. Victorinus,[441] refuting the opinion of some who thought the two witnesses to be Elijah and Elisha, or Elijah and Moses, says, all our ancestors by tradition have delivered that it is Elijah and Jeremiah. Hilary,[442]

---
[440] Lib. 14. c.11
[441] On Revelation 11
[442] in Mat. con. 20.

refelling those which thought the two witnesses to be Elijah and Enoch, or Elijah and Jeremiah, contends that they must be Moses and Elijah. Hippolytus, to Enoch and Elijah, adds John the Divine, who (as he says) shall come with them before the coming of Christ.

All of these opinions of the fathers give us a sufficient proof, into what uncertainties men are carried, when they will be wise above that which is written. For seeing the Holy Spirit has not named these two witnesses, it is hard especially for them, who lived (as themselves thought) before the fulfilling of this prophecy, to define whether by these two witnesses is not meant a sufficient, though a small number of God's witnesses, whom he shall raise to testify his truth even in the hottest persecution of the beast; or if they are two and no more, to determine particularly and by name, who they are.

(8) Unto these testimonies in the last place he adds a reason, to make up this demonstration, which may thus be concluded:

- If Enoch and Elijah were taken up before their death, and yet live in mortal bodies wherein once they shall die; then shall they come in the time of Antichrist to set themselves against him.
- But Enoch and Elijah being taken up before death do yet live in mortal bodies, wherein they are once to die.
- Therefore they shall come in the time of Antichrist to set themselves against him.

The proposition is unnecessary, and the assumption untrue. For though we should grant that they yet live in mortal bodies, and that their death is yet deferred, yet how does this follow: that they live to resist Antichrist and to be slain of him?

"Yea but," says Bellarmine, "there can be no other reason given. Of their translation, there is this reason, that there might be evident examples of reward and happiness laid up both for the upright in Enoch, and for the zealous in Elijah."

Of their yet living in mortal bodies, if they did so according to the opinion of some of the fathers, that reason might be given, which they allege, to wit, to convert the Jews. But the assumption also is false. For it is untrue that they live in mortal bodies, or that they shall ever die. For where, I beseech you, do they live in mortal bodies: in the earthly paradise, or in the heavenly? In the earthly say the papists; but that was defaced either at or before the flood: so that although the place remains, yet no paradise remains, as Bellarmine elsewhere confesses.[443] And if they were living in the earthly paradise, how is it said, they were taken up, as it is plainly said of Elijah, that he was taken up into heaven?[444] Or what privilege or reward have they above others, if all this while they have wanted God's glorious presence which others enjoy, and hereafter are to be slain by Antichrist? Or how was Enoch translated that he should not see death, if notwithstanding his translation, he must die the death?

If in the celestial paradise, that is the third heaven as Paul speaks,[445] it may first be doubted, whether they are there in body, because it may be thought that Christ was the first that in body ascended into heaven: or if their bodies are there, we must hold that in the translation they were changed into immortal and incorruptible bodies, as theirs shall, who shall be found living upon the earth as the second coming of Christ, and shall be wrapped up into the air. For this I say with Paul: that flesh and blood cannot inherit the kingdom of heaven, neither does corruption inherit incorruption.[446]

---

[443] Lib. 1. de Sanctor. beatitud. C. 3
[444] 2 Kings 2:11
[445] 2 Corinthians 12
[446] 1 Corinthians 15:54, 1 Thessalonians 4:17, 1 Corinthians 15:50

(9) But will you see under one view how far this slender conjecture taken from the coming of Enoch and Elijah is from being a demonstrative proof.

First, he cannot prove necessarily that they are still in their bodies. Secondly, if they are in their bodies, he cannot prove that their bodies are mortal. Thirdly, if their bodies are mortal, it is not necessary that they should return into the world and die, because at the end of the world they might be changed with the rest that then shall be living, as some also have thought.[447] Fourthly, if they should return into the world and die, there is no necessity that they should come in the time of Antichrist. Fifthly, if it should be granted that they are to come against Antichrist, yet it would not follow that therefore Antichrist is not yet come: but this only would follow, that Antichrist is not yet destroyed, which we do not deny.

And this was his third demonstration, whereby he proves that Antichrist has not yet come, and consequently that the pope is not Antichrist. To conclude therefore, must this not be a good cause, that by so learned a man is so stoutly proven?

---

[447] Justin, q.85 *Ad Orthodoxos*

Chapter 7

Answering his fourth demonstration, concerning the most grievous persecution under Antichrist.

(1) The second sign accompanying Antichrist, from whence Bellarmine draws his fourth demonstration, is the most grievous and notorious persecution of the church, in so much that the public service of God shall wholly cease. His demonstration is thus to be framed:

- When Antichrist comes, there shall be the most grievous and manifest persecution that ever was, insomuch that the public service of God shall wholly cease.
- But as yet there has been no such persecution, neither has the public service of God wholly ceased.
- Therefore Antichrist has not yet come.

Of his third argument, and consequently of the proposition and assumption, there are three parts, which severally are to be considered, that the persecution under Antichrist is: [1] most grievous, [2] most manifest, and [3] such as shall cause all God's worship to cease. As touching the first, he reasons thus:

- Under Antichrist shall be the most grievous persecution.
- As yet, this most grievous persecution has not been, especially under the pope.
- Therefore Antichrist is not yet come, neither is the pope Antichrist.

The proposition, namely, that the most grievous persecution is under Antichrist, he proves by two testimonies. The first is Matthew 24:21: "And then shall be great tribulation, such as has not been since the beginning of the world, neither shall be." The other is Revelation 20:7: "Then shall Satan be let loose," namely: "after the thousand years are expired."

Answer: We doubt not but that the persecution under Antichrist was to be very grievous, because the Holy Spirit testifies so much in Revelation 17:6, where the whore of Babylon is said to be drunk with the blood of the saints, and with the blood of the martyrs of Jesus. But his proofs are not to the purpose. For the place in Matthew, as heretofore has been shown, and as appears by the text itself, is to be understood of the calamities, which at the destruction of Jerusalem by the Romans, the Jews sustained. "For when you see," (says our savior Christ) "the abomination of desolation spoken of by Daniel the prophet standing in the holy place,"[448] that is, as Luke expounds,[449] "when you see Jerusalem compassed about with armies (which Daniel calls *the abominable wings of desolation*)[450] then let those which are in Jewry fly unto the mountains," etc.

And his reason is, "because then there shall be great affliction, such as has not been from the beginning of the world until now, neither shall be."[451] Which Luke expresses thus: "For there shall be great distress in the land, and wrath εν τω λαω τουτω, in this people, and they shall fall by the edge of the sword, and shall be carried captive into all nations, and Jerusalem shall be trodden underfoot of the Gentiles, until the times of the Gentiles be fulfilled."[452]

(2) As touching the thousand years mentioned in Revelation 20, after which Satan was to be loosed. Although the expiration of them falls in Antichrist's reign, yet we are not to begin his reign there, as appears plainly in Revelation 20:4.

---

[448] Matthew 24:15
[449] Luke 21:20
[450] Daniel 9:27
[451] Matthew 24:21
[452] Luke 21:23-24

Neither is that letting loose of Satan to be understood of the persecution only under Antichrist: for it is manifest by the text, that within those thousand years, many martyrs were put to death by Antichrist for refusing to receive his mark, and that the greatest part lay dead in Antichristian errors and superstition in verses 4 & 5, and by the 8th verse, that Satan was let loose not only to stir up persecution against the faithful, but also and that principally to stir up universal wars between the nations of the world, between Gog and Magog, that is, as some expound, the papists and Mohammedans. Now I would gladly know of Bellarmine when these thousand years began, and when they expired: for hereof there are several opinions, but I will touch the principal:

[1] That these thousand years begin with the incarnation of Christ, and determine accordingly, when as Sylvester II had obtained the papacy by the help of the devil, after whom followed in the Antichristian seat a succession of notable sorcerers.

[2] That the thousand years begin about the 73rd year of Christ, at which time the people of the Jews being destroyed, and the church of Christ of a particular became catholic and dispersed throughout all nations, the devil as it is in the end of chapter 12, seeks by all means to overthrow the seed borne of the Church of the Jews, that is, the Churches of Christ begotten unto God by the ministry of the Apostles and Disciples of Christ. Whereupon it is said in chapter 20 (where the former story, as some think is continued) that the angel binds Satan for a thousand years, which ended in the year 1073, which being expired, the devil is loosed, and Gregory VII a.k.a. Hildebrand (a notable sorcerer and murderer, in whom Antichrist came to his full growth) was installed in the papacy. Augustine began this account much about this time.[453]

[3] That these 1000 years take their beginning from the time of the revelation, which was about A.D. 96, and consequently ended about the year

---

[453] Augustine, *City Of God*, Book 20 Chapter 8

1096, in which year those universal wars were raised for the recovery of Jerusalem and the holy land out of the hand of the Saracens, which the Holy Spirit here seems to speak of between the nations of the earth. In this expedition there met at Jerusalem 600,000 footmen, and 100,000 horsemen out of Christendom, besides eight or nine other expeditions afterwards, for the recovery indeed of the holy land.

[4] Others begin this account at the beginning of Constantine's reign, which happened not long after the year 300 who, being the first Christian Emperor, gave peace to the church of God, and according to this account the thousand years expired about the year 1300, in which year the Turkish Empire began in Ottoman; and pope Boniface VIII most insolently and Antichristianly challenged, especially in that his year of jubilee, a universal dominion over the world, both spiritual and temporal.

All of these opinions being severally probable, it is more than probable that those 1000 years have already expired, and consequently that Antichrist has already come. For as Bellarmine teaches, the devil was to be loosened in the time of Antichrist, and the text plainly shows that before the expiration of the thousand years, and loosing of the devil, many were slain by Antichrist. So that the testimonies which he alleges are against his purpose. For the great tribulation whereof Christ speaks is already past, and the thousand years whereof John speaks, already expired: and therefore if Bellarmine's allegations be to the purpose, then Antichrist is come.

(3) But supposing his proposition to be thus far true, that the persecution of the church under Antichrist, shall be very great and grievous (for that under him shall be the greatest tribulation that ever was or shall be, I dare not avouch, because our Savior has said that the calamities of the Jews at the destruction of Jerusalem, were the greatest that ever were or shall be to the end of the world), let us come to his assumption, and consider whether there has not been great and grievous persecution of the church, under the pope.

Bellarmine confesses that many of our religion have been put to death by them: but he makes it a matter of nothing. First, because this persecution, if it were so to be called, is not comparable with the persecutions under the heathenish emperors, and especially under Diocletian, by whose authority 17,000 Christians were slain in one month. And secondly, because more of them have been slain by Protestants in France and Flanders within 10 or 15 years before Bellarmine read these controversies, which was in the year 1577, than had been burnt of our men by the inquisitors in a hundred years. And thirdly, if there has been any persecution in these latter times, the Catholics have suffered it rather than the Protestants.

To which I answer, that I cannot tell whether the papists in persecuting the faithful have been more cruel and barbarous, or he in cloaking their cruelty, shameless. For to omit the spiritual calamities inflicted by the pope, and fearful havoc of men's souls, wherein he takes such liberty to himself, that if he carry whole troops of souls into hell, no man may say unto him, sir, why do you so? omitting, I say, these spiritual calamities which are most grievous, and in respect whereof the tribulation of Christian people has been more grievous under the pope, then under any heathenish tyrants, and to speak only of outward troubles: why are not the persecutions of the Protestants under the pope, comparable with those in the primitive church?

For durance, they have been longer and more continual; for number, more slain in France alone under the name of Albigensians, Waldensians, and Huguenots, for refusing the mark of the beast, than were slain in any one of the ten persecutions throughout the world: besides infinite more, as Saunders confesses in other countries,[454] on whom the papists have practiced most savage cruelty. The Duke of Alba in the Low Countries alone, caused within a very few years 36,000 to be executed.

"Yea but in Diocletian's time," (says Bellarmine) "there were in one month 17,000 Christians martyred." Yea but in France alone, say I, under

---

[454] Demonstrat. 34

Charles IX, within one month were slaughtered in the massacre at Paris and Lions, and some other places, as some say, 40,000 as others, above thirty thousand, that is to say, twice as many as in Diocletian's month, without all order of law, but with most perfidious treachery, and barbarous cruelty. And this bloody massacre applauded by the pope and his cardinals, was committed within five or six years before Bellarmine read these controversies concerning the pope, that is to say, the year 1572.

And yet this cruel cardinal of the purpled harlot, the church of Rome, which is embrued [stained], and as it were dyed red with the blood of the saints and martyrs of Jesus, is not ashamed to say, that within 10 or 15.years there have been slain more Catholics in France and Flanders, then had been burnt by the Inquisitors these 100 years. As touching the inquisitors, they can kill all whom they find of the religion, and that I am sure they spare not to do. Vergerius, who could well tell, witnesses that within the space of 30. years, there were put to various fearful deaths by the bloody inquisition, a hundred and fifty thousand Christians.[455] But we speak not only of those which have been burnt, or by other more exquisite torments martyred by their means (although the number of them in all countries cannot be reckoned) but we speak also of those that have been in great multitudes, by outrageous massacres, most butcherly murdered.

(4) But what Catholics, I beseech you, have been put to death by Protestants for their religion? Bellarmine answers that many of them have died in the civil wars in France and Flanders. It may be that the Protestants in these civil wars under-taken for their own defense, that they might be free from such outrages, have slain in lawful battle many of the papists, as contrariwise many of themselves have been slain. But what is this to the purpose? Thus many in the armies of Antiochus Epiphanes, the most cruel persecutor of the Church of the Jews, were slain in Jewry in the time of the

---

[455] Bale, *De Act. Pontific.*

Maccabees, as well as they had slain many of the Jews. But I say again, what Catholics (as they call them) have been put to death for religion? As for those few that have been executed among us, what one was put to death, that was not found guilty either of treason or rebellion, or some such capital crime? And yet the papists report, and in books do publish, that I cannot tell how many of them are martyred here in England for their religion. Neither are they ashamed to write, and in Rome to publish that some of them have been put into bears' skins and baited with dogs, which also they have set out in tables.[456]

But compare, I beseech you, with those many that were martyred in Queen Mary's five years, those few that have been executed in Queen Elizabeth's forty five years. Compare the causes, which make persecution in the agents and martyrdom in the patients. What one put to death of those which were burnt in Queen Mary's time for any crime, but only for religion, which they call heresy? what one of the Catholics, as they call them, in Queen Elizabeth's time executed, who was not found guilty of some capital crime? Compare the estate of papists living among Protestants at this day, as in England, with the estate of Protestants living among papists, as in Spain. Is anyone suffered to live among them, that is but once suspected to be of our religion? Is not every such one either privately murdered, or publicly brought to the stake? Among us, who is not suffered to live, although he is known to be of the Romish religion? To live, did I say? Nay, God be merciful unto us that suffer them so to live as they do, to the encouragement and infection of others.

I speak not only of ordinary papists, and those that are at liberty, but of the ringleaders also that are in custody: whose life has been more easy and pleasant, and maintenance more plentiful, then of the most students or ministers among us.[457] Yea but there is cause (will they say) that we should

---

[456] Eccles. Anglic. Trophea [...] Printed at Rome An. 1584. cum priuileg. Gregor. 13
[457] Let the castles of Wisbigh and Fremingham be witness

deal worse with you, then you with us. Nothing less. They object to us only heresy, and that as truly as the Jews did to Paul, which we do truly object unto them, and in regard thereof, might, nay should do to the children of Babylon, as they have done to us.[458]

But besides many gross and capital heresies, which raze the foundation, we truly object unto them, that their religion brings with it, treason against the prince, and rebellion against God. Treason against the prince: not only because of their confederacy with the chief enemies of our state, the pope and Spaniard, in regard whereof those Jesuits and priests, which come among us from overseas, as also those which harbor them, are worthy of death: but also because more generally they holding the pope's supremacy and authority to depose princes, and also, believing that the pope in his definitive sentence cannot err, they cannot but approve the Bull of excommunication, wherein Pius V (as much as was in him) deposed our queen of famous memory, and absolved her subjects from all allegiance to her. Rebellion against God: because it persuades an apostasy and falling away from God, into gross and palpable idolatry. Of which fault whosoever are found guilty, that is, to persuade others to idolatry, by the law of God they ought not be suffered to live, because they have persuaded an apostasy from God (Deuteronomy 13).

All this notwithstanding, we deal too remissly with them, and they deal most barbarously with us. And yet indeed, if there is, or has been, any persecution in the church in these latter times, the catholics are they which suffer it, and not the Protestants. Alas poor wolves, how cruelly they have been handled among the sheep of Christ!

(5) But to proceed: "As the persecution under Antichrist, says Bellarmine, shall be most grievous, so shall it be most manifest." For thus he reasons:

---

[458] Revelation 18:6

- The persecution under Antichrist shall be most manifest.
- This under the pope is not manifest.
- Therefore this is not the persecution of Antichrist.

The proposition is proven, because then all the wicked shall *aperto marte*, oppugn the whole church: and not only those that be infidels and open sinners, but the hypocrites also and false brethren, shall then join themselves to Antichrist, and discovering themselves, openly assault the Church. And is not this well guessed, do you think, contrary to the word of truth, uttered by our Savior Christ?

For whereas our Savior has said, that the good and bad shall grow together like wheat and tares, until the day of the great harvest, Bellarmine tells us that when Antichrist comes, there shall such a separation be made, that there shall not an hypocrite be left in the church, but all the wicked without exception, shall be together in Antichrist's host, and shall openly oppugn the whole church of the saints.[459]

But such separation is not to be looked for, until Christ shall sever the lambs from the goats. And therefore if we must not believe that Antichrist is come, until such a separation be made: assuredly Christ will come upon us to judgment, while we look for Antichrist.

Yea but Augustine says: "Now there be many false brethren in the church," *At tunc erumpent omnes (inquit Augustinus) in apertam persecutionem ex latebris odiorum*:[460] "But then all shall burst forth," says Augustine, "out of their covert hatred, into open persecution." If Augustine had said so, we might well have esteemed his speech to have been but a human conjecture, rather than a prophecy divine. But Bellarmine without all shame falsifies his words. For Augustine in that place speaking of those words in Revelation

---

[459] Omnes prorsus impios simul futuros in exercitu Antichristi
[460] Augustine, *City of God*, Book 20 Chapter 11

20:7, *Soluetur Satanas de custodia sua & exibit ad seducendas nationes*: "Satan shall be let loose out of his ward, and shall go forth to seduce the nations," *Exibit autem dictum est* (says he) *in apertam persecutionem, de latebris erumpet odiorum*: "Now it is said that he shall go forth, viz. into open persecution; he shall break forth of the courts of hatred, speaking of the devil alone, and not of all the wicked."

And thus was his proposition doughtily [determinedly] proven, being nevertheless according to his sense, repugnant to the Scriptures, which describe Antichrist, not as an open enemy, but as a secret; and decipher Antichristianism, not as a professed hostility, but as a mystery of iniquity, as has been shown.

(6) Let us come to his assumption – that this manifest persecution has not been, neither is, as yet – and why? First, because there are now so many false brethren in the church as never were more; speaking of the church of Rome, wherein it is hard indeed to find a true Christian. But shall not Antichrist come while there are false brethren in the church? Or rather shall we not think that the apostasy of false brethren in the church of Rome and pretended Christians, whereof Antichrist is the head, is a good argument of his coming?

Secondly, because no man can tell when this persecution began. That, if it were true, does not disprove the greatness of the persecution, but argue the length. Yea but under Nero, Domitian, and the rest of the persecuting emperors, it was well known when the persecutions began, and when they ended. That happened because there was some intermission of those persecutions, but these persecutions under Antichrist they have no end, nor yet intermission, except it be when they have none to persecute. But how does it appear that none know when these persecutions of Antichrist began? Indeed, because some of us say that Antichrist came in the year 200, others in 606, others in 773, others in 1000, others in 1200.

The vanity of this objection, which now like a double colewort,[461] he sets before us again, as has been shown before. For of these opinions, only two belong to us, and those are not different. For we hold, that as the whole sovereignty and tyranny of the pope consists in his two swords, which he did not attain at once, but by degrees: so we make two degrees of Antichrist's coming: firstly, with the spiritual sword in the year 607, and secondly, with the temporal, after the year 1000, which was more fully obtained than before, in Gregory VII, in whom, as has been said, Antichrist was come to his full growth.

Since that time, he has been more and more revealed, and by some acknowledged. Upon which acknowledgment there has followed separation from him, according to the commandment of God, and refusal of his mark: whereupon persecution has ensued, and never has ceased where any such have been found, where the pope has to do. Neither are we with Bellarmine ignorantly to confound the time of his coming, with the beginning of his persecution. For he did not begin to persecute, until men began to forsake him, and men did not forsake him until he was discovered what he was, and acknowledged; neither was he acknowledged, until he came to his full growth.

(7) And thus the two first parts of this demonstration, concerning the persecution of Antichrist, how great and manifest it should be, are already answered, although in truth not worth the answering. The third part is concerning the public service of God and ceremonies of the church, which (he says) in the time of Antichrist by reason of that grievous persecution shall wholly cease. His reason is thus framed:

---

[461] A *colewort* is an archaic term for *cole*

- When Antichrist is come, the public service of God, and daily sacrifice of Christians (meaning the sacrifice of the Mass) shall cease.
- But as yet the public service of God, and daily sacrifice of Christians, has not ceased.
- Therefore as yet Antichrist is not come.

To the proposition I answer, that Antichrist being a hypocrite and pretended Christian (as has been proven) shall not abolish all worship of God, and much less at his first coming. For Bellarmine makes this interruption of God's service a fruit of his greatest persecution. His persecution (as I said) is a consequence of men's forsaking him; and that of his acknowledgement: and that, of his showing himself in his colors, when he was come to his full growth, whereunto he attained not at the first, but by degrees.

But this proposition is proven, says Bellarmine, out of Daniel 12:11: "From the time when the daily sacrifice shall be taken away, are days 1290." "Where," (says he) "Daniel speaks of the time of Antichrist." For the exposition of this place, we need not with Bellarmine run to the fathers, seeing as by conference thereof with some other places in Daniel, whereunto it has reference, it may most plainly be shown, who it is that takes away this daily sacrifice, and what that sacrifice is.

In Daniel 8:11 and 11:31, it is affirmed that by Antiochus Epiphanes and his armies, the daily worship of God should be taken away. When therefore Daniel asked when there should be an end of these things, the Holy Spirit answered, that from the time that the daily sacrifice was taken away, and the abomination of desolation placed, whereof he had spoken in Daniel 11:31, there would be 1290 days.

For of the restitution of God's service, and delivery of the Jews from the tyranny of Antiochus, there are foretold diverse degrees at diverse times, which agreeably to these prophecies of Daniel, are noted in the histories of

Josephus, and of the Maccabees: for from the interruption of God's service, to the first restitution thereof by Judas Macchabeus, were three years and ten days, namely from the 15th of Kislev, in the 145th year of the Seleucids (1 Maccabees 1:57) unto the 25th of Kislev, in the year 148 (1 Maccabees 4:52), which term Daniel calls in Daniel 7:25 "a time, and times, and parcel of time."[462]

Unto the victory obtained by the Maccabees, whereby the forces of Antiochus were expelled out of Jewry, and thereby the restitution before begun, established, were three years and a half, as Josephus testifies; which Daniel in 12:7 calls "a time and times, and half a time," unto the time that Antiochus being stricken with the hand of God, after his discomfiture and flight from Persepolis, promised to restore the religion of the Jews, and what else they desired, were 1290 days; unto the time of his death: 1335.

And that these are prophecies concerning Antiochus, I will hereafter show more at large.[463] In the mean time to the present objection I answer, that by the daily worship or sacrifice here mentioned, we are to understand, not the sacrifice of Christians to be taken away by Antichrist, but the daily sacrifice of the Jews, which was interrupted and taken away by Antiochus Epiphanes.

It was the custom of the Jews (says Chrysostom) to offer a sacrifice to God every morning and evening, which they called ἐνδελεχισμοῦ, which sacrifice was taken away by Antiochus: and the same is testified by Josephus and the author of the first book of the Maccabees.

(8) To this place of Daniel although nothing at all to his purpose, Bellarmine trusts so much, that upon it as it were his groundwork, he builds three conclusions, as you shall hear after we have also considered his assumption.

---

[462] In memorie hereof the Encaenia, that is, the feast of the dedication, John 10:22. was celebrated on the 25. of Kislev. 1. Macca. 4. 59.

[463] Chapter 16

The assumption he proves by experience; as though it did testify that the public service of God had neither been taken away under the pope; nor had the sacrifice of Christians ceased. But if by *the public service of God*, he means his true worship and service in spirit and truth: assuredly it has been taken away in the papacy, except will-worship, superstition, and Idolatry be the true worship of God. As touching Christian sacrifices; we acknowledge the sacrifice of praise, the sacrifice of a broken and contrite heart, the sacrifice of obedience wherein we offer ourselves, the sacrifice of alms whereby we offer our goods; these sacrifices, no Antichrist can wholly take away.[464] As for the sacrifice of the mass, we hold it to be a monstrous abomination, wherein the holy sacrament of the Lord's supper, is turned into an abominable idol.

Seeing therefore there is no soundness of truth either in the proposition or assumption, must we not think that the question in hand is soundly concluded? And yet upon these grounds, Bellarmine does not only infer the question in hand, but two more also. "From hence," says he, "three things may be gathered.

First, that Antichrist has not yet come, becàuse the daily sacrifice still continues." He might as well have concluded with the Jews that Christ is not yet come, for he was to abolish the daily sacrifice (Daniel 9:27) partly by his own sacrifice, unto which the shadows of the law were to give place; and partly by the overthrow of the temple, in which and not elsewhere it was to be offered.

His second conclusion is that the pope of Rome is not Antichrist, but rather an adversary unto him; seeing he does adore and maintain this sacrifice, which Antichrist is to abolish. Nay, rather by ordaining this propitiatory sacrifice, and erecting a new priesthood to offer the same, the pope shows himself to be Antichrist. For by this priesthood, Christ is denied to be our only priest; by this sacrifice, his sacrifice on the cross is supposed not to be sufficient. In this sacrifice, the humanity of Christ (as has been

---

[464] Hebrews 13:15, Psalm 51:17, Romans 12:1, Hebrews 13:16

shown) is overthrown, and a god of bread set up in his room to be worshiped and adored. In this sacrifice, Christ after a sort is made inferior to every mass-monger, who as they can make their creator by breathing out a few words (*hoc est corpus meum*) so when they have made him in their conceit, they offer him up to God, to be a sacrifice propitiatory both for the quick and the dead.

His third conclusion is that the heretics of this time above all others are forerunners of Antichrist, because they desire nothing more, then the overthrow of this sacrifice of the mass. Nay rather as appears by the former answer, they show themselves the limbs of Antichrist, who overthrowing the sacrament of the Lord's supper (which we have reduced to the first institution) seek to uphold this mass and heap of all abominations and sacrilegious idolatry. And how are all these things proved? Indeed because Daniel has prophesied that Antiochus was to take away for a time the daily sacrifice of the Jews, therefore Antichrist has not yet come, therefore the pope is not Antichrist, therefore those that dislike the mass are forerunners of Antichrist.

And so with these three conclusions, as it were so many ropes of sand, he knits up his fourth demonstration.

Chapter 8

Answering his fifth demonstration, concerning the term of Antichrist's reign, namely: three and a half years.

(1) There remain two demonstrations (as he calls them) proving that Antichrist has not yet come, taken from those signs which follow Antichrist, to wit, the death of Antichrist after three and a half years, and the end of the world. Where Bellarmine teaches us not to look for Antichrist, until he is gone; not to expect his coming, until the world has an end. For if these are signs that Antichrist is not yet come (as Bellarmine makes them) then may we argue now, and so may argue even until the end of the world:

- Until Antichrist is dead and the world has an end, Antichrist does not come.
- But at yet (may we say now, and so may say until the end) Antichrist is not dead.
- Neither as yet has the world an end; therefore as yet Antichrist is not come.

By this argument therefore you see, how fitly these two signs are made the ground of two demonstrations, that Antichrist is not yet come. Now as touching the former, Bellarmine reasons thus.

The fifth demonstration (namely: to prove that Antichrist is not yet come) is taken from the continuance of Antichrist:

- Antichrist shall not reign but three years and a half.
- But the pope has reigned spiritually in the church for over 1500 years, neither can any be assigned that has been taken for Antichrist, who has reigned precisely three years and a half. The pope therefore is not Antichrist.

- Wherefore Antichrist has not yet come.

His reason is thus to be resolved:

- If neither the pope is Antichrist, nor any other, who hitherto has been taken for Antichrist; then Antichrist has not yet come.
- But neither the pope is Antichrist, nor any that hitherto has been taken for Antichrist.
- Therefore as yet, Antichrist has not come.

Where you see by a circular disputation, the Jesuit for lack of better arguments, brings the main question (namely whether the pope be Antichrist) as an argument to prove that Antichrist has not yet come, and consequently that the pope is not Antichrist.

- The pope is not Antichrist. Why? Because Antichrist has not yet come.
- And why has Antichrist not yet come? Because the pope is not Antichrist.

He may as well go on, for there is no end in a circle:

- And why is not the pope Antichrist? Because Antichrist has not yet come.
- And why has Antichrist not yet come? Because the pope is not Antichrist.

And thus Bellarmine, as you see, dances in a round.

(2) But to come to the purpose, how does he prove that neither the pope is Antichrist, nor any other that has been taken for Antichrist? By this syllogism:

- Antichrist shall reign but three years and a half precisely.
- But neither the pope, nor any other that has been taken for Antichrist, has reigned three years and a half precisely.
- Therefore neither the pope is Antichrist, nor any other that as yet has been taken for Antichrist.

The assumption, which he might have proved by a truth, he chooses to prove by a falsehood. For whereas he might have said and that truly, that the pope has reigned spiritually in the church above 900 years, and therefore above three years and a half; he says, he has reigned (meaning an universal reign over the whole church, or else he proves not his assumption) above 1500, which is untrue. For he could not obtain this universal reign, before the year 607. But all the controversy is concerning the proposition. For we do grant that the popes have reigned and tyrannized in the church, almost a thousand years, and therefore, above three years and a half.

Let us therefore consider how he proves that Antichrist shall reign for three and a half years precisely. He proves it by several prophecies of the Scriptures, and guesses of the fathers, which were no prophecies. And first he alleges these places: Daniel 7:25, 12:7, and Revelation 12:14, where we read (says he) that the reign of Antichrist shall continue a time and times and half a time, that is, a year and two years and half a year. And so he says, "John expounds it in Revelation 11 and 13 by 42 months, and 1260 days."

I answer that none of these places defines the time or term of Antichrist's reign. Daniel speaks not of the time of Antichrist's reign, but of that time wherein the Jews were to be afflicted, and the temple and service of God in Jerusalem was to be profaned by Antiochus Epiphanes, which time the angel reckons differently, as was in part shown in the last chapter, and shall hereafter be more fully declared.⁴⁶⁵ For of their deliverance from the tyranny of Antiochus, there are four degrees, obtained at four different times, all which seem to be noted by Daniel.

The first, is the restitution of God's worship and renovation of the temple by Judas Maccabeus. From the profanation therefore, which was on the 15th of Kislev in the year 145 unto this restitution made on the 25th of Kislev in the 148th year, were 3 years and 10 days, which Daniel calls a "time and times and parcel of time," in Daniel 7:25, and as some think, in Daniel 12:7.

The second degree was the victory of the Jews against the forces of Antiochus Epiphanes, whereby they were expelled out of Jewry and the restitution began to be confirmed, which happened after three and a half years, as Josephus notes, who also affirms that for so long Antiochus had caused the daily sacrifice to cease, his words are these: τὸν ναὸν ἐσύλησε καὶ τὸν ἐνδελεχισμὸν τῶν καθ' ἡμέραν ἐναγισμῶν ἔπαυσεν ἐπ' ἔτη τρία καὶ μῆνας ἕξ: "He also spoiled the temple, and put a stop to the constant practice of offering a daily sacrifice of expiation for three years and six months."⁴⁶⁶

The term (as some think) that Daniel in 12:7 calls *a time and times and half a time*. The third degree is the deadly sickness of Antiochus after his flight from Persepolis, at what time he promised all good things to the people of the Jews. From the profanation to this time, Daniel reckons 1290 days until his death which happened 45 days after, to wit, in the beginning of the 149th year, he reckons 1335 days.

Now whereas Bellarmine says that the term of Antichrist's reign shall be three and a half years precisely, and says that this term is expressed in Revelation by *1260 days*, and in Daniel by *1290*, he seemed not to have been well advised: for 1290 are not 1260, nor three and a half years precisely. And

---

⁴⁶⁵ Chapter 16
⁴⁶⁶ Josephus, *Jewish Wars*, Book 1 Chapter 1

therein he contradicts himself, and makes John in the same matter to be repugnant to Daniel.

(3) As touching the places in Revelation, it is hard to prove that the times mentioned in chapters 11-13 are the same (which he must prove, or else by conference of these places he proves nothing), and if they be the same (as indeed they are not) it will be as hard to define where we are to begin the account. But these two things may be affirmed. First, that all these times are not to be understood literally: And secondly, that none of them define the time of Antichrist's reign.

The 42 months in chapters 11 and 13 signify the time of the persecution under the Roman emperors either only or especially: for in Revelation 11:2, it is said that the Gentiles shall tread upon the holy city for 42 months. But Antichrist (as the papists hold) shall be the prince of the Jews and counterfeit Christians. And in verse 7, it is said that the beast which arises out of the deep (which being the same with that which is described chapter 13:1 is the Roman state, especially as it was under the persecuting emperors) that this beast (I say) shall persecute the two witnesses of God, and their bodies shall lie in the streets of the great cities, whereby in Revelation is meant Rome or the Roman empire.

And hereby also it appears that this term of 42 months mentioned in both places, is not literally to be understood. For the persecution under the Roman Emperors alone, endured so many sabbaths of years, as there are months mentioned in those places, that is, 294 years, as Master Fox expounds it. Now if the other terms mentioned in chapter 11 and 12 of *time and times and half a time*, and if 1260 days are the same as the 42 months, as Bellarmine will needs have it; then by them is not signified Antichrist's reign, neither are they to be understood literally, no more than the 42 months; but in the 11th chapter, the time of the two witnesses preaching, during the time of the aforesaid persecution, and chapter 12, the woman's, that is, the church's living in the desert during the said time.

Howbeit the speech of time and times and half a time may rather be understood (according to Daniel's phrase) of three years and a half, wherein the church of Christ which was at Jerusalem, after it was admonished by a voice out of the sanctuary to depart, and accordingly removed to Pella, was sustained there.[467] For in that place, it is plain that the Holy Spirit speaks not of Antichrist nor yet of the beast, but of the serpent the devil, who seeks the overthrow of the church of Christ among the Jews, and afterwards turns his anger towards the rest of her seed, that is, the faithful among the Gentiles, and to that end stands on the sea shore, from whence he raises the beast with seven heads, etc.

(4) And further I add that if these times mentioned in those places which Bellarmine alleges, did signify the term of Antichrist's reign precisely, and were to be understood literally; then it would follow, that after Antichrist is once revealed, all men that be acquainted with the Scriptures, may precisely define beforehand, the very day of Christ's coming unto judgment: which the Lord notwithstanding will not have known (Mark 13:32), as Bellarmine himself must needs grant,[468] seeing he uses this as the chief argument against those who by *1260 days* understand so many years.

Again, it is incredible, if not impossible, that so many and so great things as they assign to Antichrist, should be effected and brought to pass in so short a time; as Hentenius, a learned papist, does confess, and as has been shown heretofore. For this is an error depending upon the former, concerning the person of Antichrist, and presupposing that Antichrist is but one man. And therefore when we proved that Antichrist is not any one man alone, but a whole state and succession of men, we proved this by consequence, that his reign was not to continue for only three and a half years.

---

[467] See Junius on Revelation 12
[468] Chapter 3 Book 3

And again Antichrist, according to the conceit of the papists, is to reign before the preaching of the two witnesses, and as Bellarmine faith, is to continue one month after their death. Seeing then that the two witnesses preach 1260. days, which, as Bellarmine also says, make three and a half years precisely, how can the term of Antichrist's reign be three and a half years precisely?

Lastly, the Scriptures plainly testify that the Antichrist – who is to be destroyed at the second coming of Christ – was come even in the apostles' time, although he was not revealed by exercising openly a sovereign and universal dominion, until that which hindered, that is, the Roman Empire was taken out of the way. But after the Empire was once dissolved in the West, and the Emperor of the East had lost his right in Italy and Rome, that is, when that which hindered was taken out of the way, then according to the prophecy of 2 Thessalonians 2:8 was Antichrist revealed, succeeding the emperor in the government of Rome, and claiming a universal authority, firstly spiritual, over the whole church in the year 607, and after that temporal, over the whole world, and advancing himself above all that is called God – of all which we have heretofore proved to have been done in the papacy, over three years and a half ago, yea above so many hundred years ago; so that we shall not need to expect another Antichrist, who is to reign for only three and a half years.

And thus you have heard not only Bellarmine's allegations answered, but also his assertion confuted.

(5) Now let us see what Bellarmine can reply – either against our assertion in general, or against the expositions of some Protestants in particular. For whereas we generally affirm – notwithstanding his allegations aforesaid – that Antichrist has already ruled in the church almost a thousand years, Bellarmine besides the slender conjectures of several of the fathers grounded on such prophecies of Scriptures as they could not understand, which are his first argument, he produces six other reasons, no less easy to be

answered. His second argument is, because the Scriptures say that the time of the devil's loosing, and Antichrist's reigning is *brevissimum*, very short, or most short. But how can that be true if Antichrist shall reign a thousand years or more?

For that which he speaks of 1260 years, is the private opinion of some, of which shall be touched afterwards. I answer that the Scriptures nowhere say that Antichrist's reign, or that the time of the devil loosed is *brevissimum*, that is, most short, but only that it is short or small, which we do acknowledge.[469]

Let us then weigh his argument, which may be resolved into two syllogisms. The former is:

- A thousand years or more is not a short time.
- Antichrist's reign is a short time.
- Therefore Antichrist's reign is not a thousand years or more.

Firstly, to the proposition I answer that a thousand years unto the Lord (who speaks in the Scriptures) is a short time. The apostle Peter expressly says, that a thousand years with the Lord are but as one day.[470] Yea, and the whole time from the ascension of Christ until his coming to judgment, is often noted in the Scriptures to be a short time, and in one place it is called *the last hour*.[471] And likewise over 1500 years ago, it was promised that the prophecies concerning the destruction of Antichrist, the second coming of Christ, and end of the world, should within a short time be fulfilled.[472]

To the assumption I answer, that although the time of Antichrist's tyranny seem to belong to them that are exercised thereby; yet it is but short

---

[469] Revelation 17:10 ολιγον; Revelation 12:12 ολιγον καιρον; Revelation 20:3 μικρον χρονον.
[470] 2 Peter 3:8
[471] 1 John 2:18
[472] Revelation 1:1 εν ταχει; Revelation 1:3 ο γαρ καιρος εγγυς, Revelation 22:10 & 20, Hebrews 10:37

in comparison of that time which they shall reign with Christ, and is so called in Revelation 17:10, but yet nothing so short as Bellarmine imagines.

This therefore he proves in the second syllogism:

- The time of Satan loosed is very short.
- The term of Antichrist's reign is the time of Satan loosed.
- Therefore the term of Antichrist's reign is very short.

The proposition he proves by two places in Revelation which affirm his time to be short, but yet nothing so short as the papists imagine: for in the former place of Revelation 12:12, he is said to have but a short time, before he persecuted the church of Christ among the Jews, which was above 1500 years ago. And in the latter place of Revelation 20:3, it is said that he should be let loose for a small time, but this small time begins at the expiration of the thousand years wherein he had been bound, and continues until the time that he shall be cast into the lake of fire and brimstone, in the end of the world.

Now the thousand years expired many hundred years ago, as has been shown. But although the time of Antichrist's reign be called short, yet is it not so short as the time of Satan loosed, and therefore the assumption is false. For however the thousand years expire in the time of Antichrist's reign, yet we are not to begin the reign of Antichrist with the loosing of Satan. For within the thousand years of Satan's imprisonment,[473] Antichrist not only was, but also persecuted those that refused his mark; and yet we are not to confound the time of his persecution, much less of his hottest persecution, with the time of his continuance.

Now the time of the devil loosed, as the papists teach, is the time of Antichrist's most grievous persecution, which was a consequent of men's refusing his mark, and that a fruit of his discovery and acknowledgement,

---

[473] Revelation 20:4

but he was not acknowledged until he came to his full growth, whereunto he attained not at the first. And it is to be thought that the heat of his persecution will be slaked before his end, himself being consumed and wasted by the Spirit of Christ's mouth,[474] and his See impoverished, if not overthrown by the kings of the earth, which before the end of the world, shall not only hate the whore of Babylon (the pope's concubine) but also "shall make her desolate and naked, and shall eat her flesh, and her they shall burn with fire."[475]

(6) Thirdly, he argues from Matthew 24:21, mistaken by some of the fathers, that unless those days (meaning of Antichrist's persecution) should be shortened, and consequently the persecution very short, no flesh could be saved: but how can it be very short if it shall continue a thousand years?

I answer, first, that the tribulation there spoken of, is to be understood of the calamities of the Jews in the siege of Jerusalem, as I have manifestly proven. And secondly, that we are to distinguish between the time of Antichrist's continuance, and the time of his hottest persecution, which Bellarmine confounds; the latter notwithstanding being much shorter than the former. "Fourthly," (says he) "Christ preached only three years and a half, therefore *decet etiam*, it is also fitting that Antichrist be suffered to preach no longer."

Answer:

[1] In this argument, Bellarmine presupposes that Antichrist is but one man, as Christ is, which we have proved to be most false.

[2] He takes upon him to be the Lord's counselor, avouching that it is not fit that Antichrist should preach longer than Christ did: he might have added that it was not fit, or to speak more fitly, not like that Antichrist in the same time should be able to prevail with more than Christ did, and much less

---

[474] 2 Thessalonians 2:8
[475] Revelation 17:16

to pervert almost the whole world in three years and a half; whereas Christ as he was man, could convert but a few of the Jews, etc.

[3] Although Christ in his own person preached but a few years; yet he being the eternal word and wisdom of his father, has ever since the beginning spoken by the mouth of his prophets and ministers, by whose ministry also as it were the breath of his mouth, he shall waste and consume Antichrist.

[4] Neither can it be proven by any show of reason, that Antichrist is to preach just so many years, as Christ our Savior did. Or that he shall in three and a half years subdue by force, I know not how many kingdoms, and convert by preaching, and gather to himself the remnant of the Jews, and all counterfeit Christians, dispersed through so many nations, as a man cannot travel through in three years and a half – not to speak of his repairing Jerusalem, and erecting the temple, and many good morrows, which by many poetic fictions, the papists assign to their devised Antichrist.

His fifth and sixth reasons are not worth mentioning. For the *time and times, and half a time*, as has been shown, belong not to Antichrist's reign, and thereby we understand three and a half years and a half, as also by the seven times, in Daniel 4: seven years, according to the interpretation of the Holy Spirit (expounding, as it seems) times by years in Daniel 11:13.

(7) In the last place, he labors to take away the exceptions which some particular man, as namely, Chytraeus, Bullinger, and the authors of *The Centuries*, make against his former allegations out of Daniel and Revelation, but scarcely touches any one of the six exceptions before mentioned.

[1] For whereas Chytraus answers that the 42 months in Revelation 11 & 13 may not be understood literally for three and a half years, because it is contrary to experience, and besides the apostle affirms that Antichrist shall continue until Christ's coming. Bellarmine replies that he begs the question.

But I answer again as before, that experience shows that the persecutions under the beast with seven heads, continued longer than three years and a half: and when as John affirmed that the Antichrist was come in his time, and Paul foretold that he should after a sort continue (though at the last in a kind of consumption) unto the second coming of Christ, surely their meaning was that he should continue for over three and a half years.

[2] He finds fault with him and Bullinger, who thought that the Holy Spirit mentioning 42 months and 1260 days, by a certain time, meant an uncertain; replying that the number which is meant, is certain, when it consists of great and small numbers mixed. But they speak of the time, and he of the number, and therefore his reprehension is unjust. For although the Holy Spirit does mean no other number than 42 and 1260, yet by the certain time mentioned, that is, months and days, he means an uncertain, which may be as some think 42 sabbaths of years, and 1260 years.

[3] And thirdly, whereas Illyricus, and the other authors of *The Centuries* by *1260 days*, understand so many years; Bellarmine denies that days are put for years anywhere in the Scripture, and yet cannot deny, but that by *390 days* in Ezekiel, is meant 390 years, and by *40 days* so many years, a day for a year, as the Holy Spirit speaks.[476] And likewise Revelation 2:10, by *ten days* is meant ten years, as some of the learned think.[477]

Indeed if any shall by *1260 days* understand (as Bellarmine does) the just time of Antichrist's reign, and also expound them either by 1260 years, as Bellarmine charges some,[478] or by three and a half years, as the papists do; they may be refuted by the reason before alleged, because after the revelation of Antichrist the special time of Christ's coming may according to this exposition be foretold, which notwithstanding shall not come by observation, but suddenly, neither shall precisely be foreknown, as being known only to the Lord.

---

[476] Ezekiel 4:5-6
[477] See Junius on Revelation
[478] Chapter 3

Chapter 9

Answering his sixth demonstration, concerning the end of the world.

(1) The sixth and last demonstration, to prove that Antichrist has not yet come, is taken from the end of the world. But because Bellarmine saw that this could not be made a sign of Antichrist's coming without absurdity (for it is absurd thus to reason: the world has not yet an end, therefore Antichrist is not yet come) therefore he changes the question.

For whereas he propounded this question to be concluded, that Antichrist is not yet come, he concludes that he came not long since. So that for all this demonstration Antichrist may already have come, although perhaps not so long since, as some do imagine. But let us see how he proves that he was not come long since:

- If Antichrist were come long since, then also the world long since should have had an end.
- But the world has not yet an end.
- Therefore Antichrist was not come long since.

The proposition he proves, because Antichrist comes a very little while before the end of the world, and as it were immediately before the second coming of Christ. But this whole demonstration may easily be refuted by this one distinction: for we must distinguish between the coming of Antichrist and his death, between his beginning and his end. Antichrist indeed is not utterly to be destroyed before the second coming of Christ, but this does not prove that therefore he was not come long since.

The apostle Paul does tell us that Antichrist is to be destroyed at the second coming of Christ: notwithstanding both he does insinuate and John plainly professes that the Antichrist which they had heard was to come in the last hour, was already come in his time: and thereupon infers that even then was the last hour or age of the world, which the Holy Spirit calls an hour, that we should not think it long.

(2) Now all the testimonies which Bellarmine alleges, if they were to be understood of Antichrist (as indeed few of them are) do serve to prove that the destruction of Antichrist shall be at the end of the world, which we do freely confess.

But of these places, as some make not for him so the rest are against him. Daniel 7:8-9, 26, Revelation 20:4, and Matthew 24:14 are altogether impertinent. For Daniel speaks not of Antichrist or the last judgment, but of Antiochus and God's judgments on the Seleucidae: John speaks not of the coming of Antichrist or the last judgment, but of the binding and loosing of Satan, and seats of judgment erected for the faithful, as Augustine also expounds.[479] Christ in that place of Matthew speaks not a word of Antichrist's coming or of the end of the world, but of the preaching of the gospel before the destruction of Jerusalem.

The rest of the places make against him, and as he alleges them, against the truth. For first Daniel 12:12, where Daniel (says Bellarmine) after he had said that the kingdom of Antichrist should continue 1290 days, adds: "Blessed is he that expecteth and comes to 1335 days." From whence the papists would infer, that Antichrist having reigned three years and a half, should be destroyed forty five days before the day of judgment. This place, as I have proven, is to be understood of Antiochus.

But suppose it spoke of Antichrist's reign, and end of the world, see what would follow thereof.

[1] First, that the reign of Antichrist is not three years and a half precisely, or 1260 days, but 1290 days. Secondly, that Antichrist shall be destroyed before the end of the world, whereas Paul tells us that Christ shall

---

[479] Augustine, *City of God*, Book 20

destroy him at his appearing, and not 45 days beforehand.[480] Thirdly, then as soon as Antichrist is revealed, men shall be able certainly and distinctly to foretell the very day of judgment, to wit, the 1335 after Antichrist's coming, and 45 after his death: which Christ denies in Matthew 24:36. And lastly, if this were true, then after the coming, or at least after the death of Antichrist, all men would be in expectation of Christ's second coming. And therefore those days will not be (as Christ says) like the days of Noah: neither will his coming be sudden and unlooked for, as he himself says in Matthew 24 if the very day of his coming be known beforehand, and accordingly looked for.[481] But let Christ be true, and all papists liars.

(3) [2] Matthew 24:29 "Shortly after the tribulation of those days, the sun shall be darkened," etc. In this chapter of Matthew, our Savior speaks not at all of Antichrist until the 23rd and 24th verse, which several of the fathers, yea and the papists themselves understand as spoken of Antichrist. "There shall arise false christs, and false prophets, and they shall work great signs and wonders," etc. From whence it appears that Antichrist is not one only man, as Bellarmine says, and that the signs of Christ's coming are to follow the tribulations under Antichrist, which we do confess.

[3] 2. Thessalonians 2:8: "And then shall that outlaw be revealed, whom the Lord Jesus shall consume with the spirit of his mouth," etc., whence Bellarmine would prove that the second coming of Christ shall follow very shortly after the coming of Antichrist.

But we must distinguish between the first coming of Antichrist, and his revelation and acknowledgement. And it cannot be denied, but that there is a great distance between his revelation, and destruction. For he was to be revealed as the apostle says, when that which hindered was taken out of the way, which we have proven to have been done many hundred years since, and consequently that Antichrist appeared long since, howsoever he shall not

---

[480] 2 Thessalonians 2:8
[481] Matthew 24:37-39, 44; 1 Thessalonians 5:2-3

utterly be destroyed until the second coming of Christ. And lastly, we are to distinguish between Christ's consuming him with the spirit of his mouth, and his utter destroying him at his glorious appearance. There are therefore these degrees to be noted between the first coming of Antichrist and his destruction. For after he has come, he shows himself in his colors, and that by degrees, more and more advancing himself, until he comes to his full pitch and height of his Antichristian pride.

After he has come to his height, he is acknowledged, and that by degrees: after he is acknowledged, Christ consumes him by the spirit of his mouth, that is, by the preaching of the everlasting gospel (Revelation 14:6-7).

After this, follows the destruction of Babylon, that is, Rome (Revelation 14:8), effected and brought to pass by the kings of the earth, who assisted the beast until Christ laid him open and consumed him with the breath of his mouth: and after that in the last place follows the utter destruction of Antichrist at the second coming of Christ.

[4] Lastly, 1. John. 2:18: "Children, this is the last hour, and as you have heard that Antichrist cometh," etc., where Bellarmine makes the apostle reason thus:

- We know Antichrist shall come at the end of the world.
- And now we see many petty antichrists, as it were, his forerunners.
- Therefore we know that this is the last hour and age of the world.

But if this reason of Bellarmine's framing were good, we might upon his former grounds conclude thus:

- At the fullness of time, Christ was to come.

- But ever since the beginning there have been patriarchs and prophets, which Bellarmine calls the forerunners of Christ.
- Therefore the fullness of time has been ever since the beginning.
-

But whether shall we say that Bellarmine is so ignorant that he does not know how to make a syllogism, or so shameless as to make the apostle argue sophistically. The apostle's reason is this: when the Antichrist comes it is the last hour.[482] "Now," (says he) "antichrists are come," (meaning by *antichrists* the same with the antichrist, which else where he affirms was then entered into the world, or else there are *4 termini*: four terms in the apostle's argument) "therefore now is the last hour." And if then were the hour of Antichrist his coming, what reason have the papists to restrain his coming, until three and a half years before the end of the world? And thus, as you see, Bellarmine's allegations are either altogether impertinent, or else against himself.

(4) But as I said before, suppose they all spoke of the day of judgment, and end of the world following upon Antichrist, yet none of them joins the end of the world with his coming and birth, but with his death and destruction.

And the like may be said of his allegation from the common consent of the fathers and confession of his adversaries. "For our adversaries," (says he) "confess that Antichrist shall reign," (we say he shall continue) "unto the end of the world, and therefore shortly after his death shall be the end of the world. Yea we further confess, that his destruction shall concur with the consummation of the world: for Christ at his coming shall destroy him."

But this proves not that his coming shall be within three and a half years before the end of the world. For John says that he had come in his time, and

---

[482] 1 John 4:3, 2 John 7

Paul says, he should be revealed when that which hindered was done out of the way, which was done many hundred years ago. Therefore, though his end concur with the end of the world, yet there shall be a greater distance thea Bellarmine imagines, between his coming and the end of the world.

This, Bellarmine foreseeing, perceived very well, that in this demonstration by itself alone, there is no force at all. And therefore he joins it with the fifth, of both which together he says: "An unanswerable demonstration may be made, to prove that Antichrist is not yet come, and that the pope is not Antichrist.

- "For," says he, "if presently after the death of Antichrist the world shall have an end, and Antichrist shall die, after he has reigned but three years and a half; then it follows, that Antichrist shall not appear nor begin to reign until within three years and a half before the end of the world.
- But the pope has reigned longer than three and a half years, and yet the world continues.
- Therefore the pope is not Antichrist."

The vanity of the former demonstration which is made the ground of the last, I have sufficiently shown before: and therefore that which is said of two ciphers in ciphering, the same may be said of these two demonstrations joined together, that $0 + 0 = 0$. For now I will not stand to tell you how the three and a half years, which in the former demonstration were 1260 days precisely, have now grown to 1335. days.

"For Antichrist shall not begin to reign," says Bellarmine, "until within three years and a half before the end, and yet from the beginning of his reign, until the end of the world, shall be 1335 days." So that in Bellarmine's precise account of half a year, 75 days, that is 10 weeks and 5 days, are nothing.

Thus have we answered these six demonstrations, which we have shown to have been far from proving demonstratively, either that Antichrist is not yet come, or that the pope is not Antichrist. Wherefore to conclude, if the papists demonstrations in so weighty a cause, whereupon all popery depends, be such trifling trumpery, as is scarce worth the answering, what shall we think be their ordinary arguments in other causes of less importance. And this was his third principal argument, wherein he has spent seven whole chapters.

Chapter 10
Concerning the name of Antichrist.

(1) Now follows his fourth disputation concerning the name and mark of Antichrist. From the name, he fetches this "unanswerable argument,"[483] as he calls it:

- If the name of Antichrist spoken of Revelation 13 be yet unknown, then is not Antichrist as yet come; and consequently the pope is not Antichrist.
- But Antichrist's name spoken of Revelation 13 is yet unknown.
- Therefore Antichrist is not yet come, etc.

Of this unanswerable argument, there is no part sound, as shall appear. The proposition he proves, because when Antichrist is once come, his name shall be commonly known. This he proves first by a similitude:

- As Christ's name before his coming was unknown, although the prophets had foretold many things concerning Christ, and the Tiburtine Sibyl had prophesied that his name should contain 888.
- But after he was once come, all men know that his name is Jesus.
- So although before Antichrist's coming his name was unknown, yet after he has once come, there will be no more question what his name is, then of the name of Christ, which all even Turks and Jews and Pagans know to be Jesus.

---

[483] *Insolubile argumentum*

Secondly, from a common adjunct of all prophecies, to be doubtful and obscure, until they are fulfilled, as Irenaeus teaches and proves in Book 4, Chapter 43.

For an answer, first I deny the proposition, and the hypothesis whereupon it is grounded, and contrariwise affirm that the name of Antichrist, meaning the name which Antichrist shall impose upon men, spoken of Revelation 13, might be unknown for a time, yea was to be unknown for a long time after his coming. For the name of Antichrist cannot be known as the name of Antichrist, until Antichrist himself be known and acknowledged. But Antichrist himself was not commonly to be known and acknowledged at his first coming. For then he could not be able to seduce many, few or none being so desperately mad as to follow him whom they know to be Antichrist.

First therefore the mystery of iniquity was to work secretly to the seducing of many; afterwards, Antichrist was to be revealed, first, by his manifest appearing and showing himself more plainly and openly; after by his acknowledgement: whereof also there are degrees; first by some particularly; secondly, by whole churches generally; and yet never in this world to be acknowledged of those, that receive and retain his mark.

Again, the name of Antichrist is a mystery, and Antichristianism is a mystery of iniquity: in the whore of Babylon's forehead is written a mystery.[484] And so far is it from the understanding of all to tell the name of the beast, that the Holy Spirit speaking of this name, says, "Here is wisdom, he that has understanding, let him reckon the number of the beast," meaning the number of his name.[485]

(2) In the similitude taken from Christ, there is no likeness, howbeit Bellarmine takes great felicity in comparing Christ with Antichrist. Christ as he was one particular man, so at the time of his circumcision a proper name

---

[484] Revelation 17:5
[485] Revelation 13:18

was given unto him; Antichrist as he is not one particular person (as has been proved) but a state, could not have a proper name given unto him. And accordingly it is said to be the name of the beast, which beast as has been shown, signifies not one particular man, but a whole state. Again, Christ coming to save, his name Jesus the name of the Savior was to be made known, that he might rather be embraced; Antichrist coming to deceive and to destroy, was (according to his devilish policy) to conceal that name whereby he should be known to be Antichrist, least being known he should be forsaken of all.

And as touching the Tiburtine Sibyl,[486] she did not only foretell that the name of Christ should contain the number 888, as indeed the name ιησου, Jesus does: but also sets down certain acrostics, that is, verses, the first letters whereof contain this sentence in Greek, "Jesus Christ the Son of God the Savior," which are also cited by Augustine.[487] But of Antichrist she speaks nothing so plainly. Howbeit she plainly calls Rome *Babylon*, as John does and in the 8th book describing Antichrist, as some think, she says, "There shall be a prince with many heads," (which is to be understood either by a metonymy for his triple crown, or by a synecdoche for the succession of popes) having a name near to *Ponti*, that is, Pontifex the pope.

But to return to my purpose. By this which has been said, you plainly see that there is no similitude between Christ and Antichrist in this behalf, Christ having a proper name; but Antichrist having none, and also you have heard reasons why Christ's name should be well known, whereas Antichrist's was to be obscure and for a long time unknown, or at least not acknowledged.

(3) His other proof touching the obscurity of prophecies before they are fulfilled, proves nothing for him, unless he should add that as before their

---

[486] Book 8
[487] Augustine, *City of God*, Book 18 Chapter 23

fulfilling they are very obscure, so also after their fulfilling they are very plain: which after indeed he adds in the end of the chapter, *Siquidem omnia vaticinia cum impleta sunt, clarissima officiuntur*: "For all prophecies when they are fulfilled become most clear."

I answer that although they become more clear after then before, yet many times they remain dark and obscure to very many. As appears in the prophecies of the Scripture fulfilled in Christ, but not yet understood of the Jews, nor acknowledged to have been verified in Christ. And even as the prophecies concerning Christ are by true Christians easily understood; howbeit to Jews and infidels they remain dark and obscure, because the god of this world has blinded their eyes, that they should not see the shining light of the gospel. So also the prophecies concerning Antichrist, which already are fulfilled in the papacy, howsoever many of them are plainly understood of the true professors; yet to the followers of Antichrist, whom God has given over to strong illusions, that they may believe lies, they seem to be dark and obscure, and not as yet fulfilled.

Notwithstanding, the former part of his assertion we do embrace: that prophecies until they are fulfilled are (for the most part) dark and ambiguous, and herein with Bellarmine we approve Irenaeus' judgment. But hereupon we infer, that therefore the writings of the fathers, who living before the revelation of Antichrist, and expounding the prophecies concerning Antichrist, were most uncertain guesses (as Bellarmine even in this chapter confesses),[488] the prophecies being to them dark and ambiguous, which now since the fulfilling thereof have been more plain and perspicuous: and therefore that it is no arrogance in us which see the event agreeing with the prophecy, to take upon us to expound diverse prophecies concerning Antichrist, the true understanding whereof was hid from the fathers. For if God would have had them plainly known before their fulfilling, surely he

---

[488] Sed nec isti patres voluerunt sententias illas suas, alio loco haberi, quam suspicionum & coniecturarum. Bellarmine. Lib. 5.

would have made them known by those his servants the apostles by whom they were delivered.

And so Irenaeus says, that he would not take upon him certainly to define what this name should be, *Scientes* (says he) *quoniam si operteret manifest praesenti tempore praeconari nomen eius, per ipsum vti{que} editū fuisset, quiet Apocalypsin viderat,* "Knowing that if this name ought in these times to be published, it should no doubt have been declared by him, to whom the revelation was given." Likewise Andreas the Bishop of Caesarea:[489] "The exact account," (says he) "and computation of the number, and likewise all other things which are written of Antichrist, opportunity of time and experience shall make manifest to them that are vigilant. For as some of the doctors say, if it were necessary that this name should manifestly be known beforehand, it should have been revealed by John himself."

(4) Now let us come to his assumption, where he affirms that Antichrists name is yet unknown. We confess that in the Church of Rome this name is either not known as of the ignorant, or not acknowledged as of the obstinate: But in the true church of God, as Antichrist himself is known, so is this name acknowledged.

But let us hear Bellarmine's disputation proving this assumption. *Fatentur omnes* (says he in the beginning of the chapter) *pertinere omnino ad Antichristum verba illa Ioannis* (Revelation 13): "All men do confess that those words of John in Revelation 13 do wholly belong to Antichrist: "And he shall make all both small and great, rich and poor, free and bond, to receive from him a mark in their right hand or in their forehead; and that none should buy or sell, unless he have the mark or name of the beast or number of his name. Here is wisdom: he that hath understanding let him reckon the number of the beast, for it is the number of a man, and his number is 666."[490]

---

[489] Apud. Aretham in Apocalpys.
[490] Revelation 13:16-18

"Now, concerning this number," says he, "there are many opinions. The first of those who think that by this number is signified the time of Antichrist's coming, etc."

But this opinion we do with Bellarmine reject, because it is called the number of his name, and not of the time; and also because Antichrist shall compel all sorts of men to take his name, and the number of his name; which cannot be understood of the time. Thirdly, because Irenaeus reports from those who had seen John face to face, that the name of the beast shall according to the computation of the Greeks by letters which are in it, contain 666.

The second opinion is of those who think Antichrist's name to be Λατεινος or רומיית, of which we will speak anon in his due place.

The third opinion is of many papists who think that his name shall be αντεμος, thereby understanding an adversary, but that is not a name that he shall assume to himself, or impose upon others, but a name rather given him of his adversaries. Neither is it the name of the beast here spoken of.

The fourth of Rupertus, who imagined that by this threefold number 666 is signified, the threefold prevarication of Satan: first in himself; secondly, in our first parents; thirdly in Antichrist.

The fifth of Beda, who supposes that it is a number of perfection, which Antichrist shall challenge unto himself.

But these three opinions Bellarmine rejects, and that worthily. For first, the Holy Spirit says it is the number of the name of the beast: and secondly, this name and number of it, Antichrist causes men to take upon them. The sixth opinion, wherein he rests as the most true, is theirs which confess their ignorance, and profess that this name is not yet known.

(5) To these opinions, many more might be added, but to make short work: the last of these opinions is Bellarmine's, the second is ours, therefore let us consider how he proves his own opinion, and disproves ours. That this name is unknown, Bellarmine would prove by the authority of Irenaeus, as if

he should have said, "This name was not certainly known in Irenaeus' time; therefore not in our time."

I deny the consequence. Irenaeus lived before the fulfilling of this prophecy, as he himself professes and as the truth is: for he lived above 1400 years ago; and as he himself says, the revelation was given to John but a little before his age.[491] "For it was given in the end of the first century, and he lived in the second, and therefore it is more safe, (says he) to wait for the fulfilling of this prophecy, than beforehand to determine anything. For if the Lord would have had this name known in Irenaeus' time, he would have made it known by John himself, to whom the Revelation was given."

But as before the fulfilling of this prophecy, he says, this name was very obscure; so he signifies, that after the fulfilling it should be more plain. And therefore that which he could but guess at in his time, we may now define, time having revealed that truth, which until the prophecy was cleared by the event lay hid: otherwise it shall be lawful for men to reason from the authority of Irenaeus, as Bellarmine does, even unto the end of the world.

But may we then reason thus: this name was not known in Irenaeus' time, therefore it shall never be known? To what end was this prophecy given, if it shall never be understood? Whereas therefore he uses the arguments whereby Irenaeus proves that this name could not be known in his time, to prove that it cannot be known in our time, he is ridiculous. "There are many names," says Irenaeus, "that have this number, therefore it is heard beforehand to tell which is this name." Again, if in Irenaeus' time God would have this known, he would have revealed it by John.

[3] It is dangerous to define beforehand his name, for missing his name, we shall not know him when he comes, and therefore shall be in more danger to be deceived by him. All this we grant. But will Bellarmine need to be so ridiculous, as to conclude the following? *That in Irenaeus' time, men were not able to tell which of those names that contain the number 666 is the name of*

---

[491] Non ante multum temporis, pene sub nostro saeculo. Iren. Lib. 5.

the beast, therefore 1400 years after none shall be able to tell? God would not have it known in Irenaeus' time, therefore he will not have it known now. It was dangerous then before the fulfilling of the prophecy to define what this name should be; therefore it is dangerous now, when the prophecy is expounded by the event, to apply the one to the other.

And what does he infer hereupon? Therefore no doubt the Protestants, who think the pope to be Antichrist, shall be deceived of the true Antichrist, when he comes. But blessed be God that has already revealed unto us the true Antichrist, that knowing him we might avoid him; whereas upon the papists he has sent strong illusions, that they may believe lies, because they loved not the truth that they might be saved (2 Thessalonians 2:11).

(6) Again he proves this name not to be known, because there is great controversy about it, what it should be. But by the same reason he may conclude that few points of religion are yet known, because there are few concerning which there is no controversy. Notwithstanding as in other controversies, the truth is known of those which are orthodox, however others will not acknowledge it: so I doubt not, but that the truth in this matter is known, although some cannot, and others will not, as yet see it. For seeing the hardest matter in this mystery is known, it is not to be thought that the easier is hidden or unknown, especially seeing the knowledge of the one makes the other evident.

The chief thing here to be considered is, what this beast is. For if the beast is known, it will not be hard to tell what his name is, especially if the number of the name is 666. The beast, as appears by the whole context, is, as I have shown, the former beast, which without doubt figures the Roman or Latin state. The name of this beast is Roman or Latin. If therefore this name in the learned tongues contain the number 666 and be such a name, as he to whom all other notes of Antichrist do agree, shall enforce men to take upon them; then without doubt this is the name where of the Holy Spirit speaks: but these properties agree to the name Latin or Roman. For רומיית in

Hebrew (signifying *Roman*), Λατεινος in Greek, signifying *Latin*, and *Romanus* in Hebrew characters, do contain the just number 666, and are besides such names as Antichrist compels all men to take upon them, as has been shown heretofore.

(7) But let us see what Bellarmine objects against this truth. Of those many reasons which we do use, Bellarmine makes a choice of two, as being the easiest to answer, as his manner is; and against them he argues, namely, the conjecture of Irenaeus, and the agreement of the number. But besides these, we produce three other arguments, as you have heard, which together with these make the matter evident.

It is true indeed that Irenaeus besides *Latinus*, produces two other names – Ευανθας, and Τειταν – and seems to prefer the latter of these before Λατεινος. But we build not upon Irenaeus' authority, but upon those reasons, whereon his conjecture is grounded, which are two: the one, because it is the name of that kingdom which is figured under the former beast in Revelation 13:7, whose authority Antichrist was to usurp; the other, because it contains 666: his words are these: "But the name *Lateinos* also comprehends the number 666 *et valde verisimile est*, and it is very likely. For it is the name of that which most truly is called the kingdom. For they are the Latins that now reign." This is in effect is as much as if he had said, this name is very likely, because it is a name containing 666, and is the name of the former beast, spoken of Revelation 13:1, which figures *verissimum regnum*, that kingdom which most truly is called a kingdom, that is the Latin or Roman state.

Yea but this conjecture says Bellarmine, which in Irenaeus' time was of some force, now it is nothing worth: for then the Latins bare the sway, now they do not. For Antichrist as he shall be *Potentissimus Rex*, a most mighty king; so without doubt he shall seize upon the most mighty kingdoms. Whereas therefore the kingdom of the Latins was in those times most mighty, but now otherwise; there was some likelihood then, that he might by subduing them be called *Latinus*, but now there is no such probability.

I answer, the name whereof John speaks is not the name of Antichrist properly the second beast, but the name of the former beast; which name of the former beast, Antichrist the second beast causes men to take upon them. And so *Latinus* is not the name of Antichrist properly, but of the beast, that is, the Latin or Roman state. Neither was it Irenaeus' meaning, that the name of the beast is Λατεινος, because Antichrist was to subdue the Latins, but because the Latins then had *Verissimum regnum*, the most true and sovereign kingdom: and therefore most truly were the beast described Revelation 13:7.

If therefore the Latins then had the greatest kingdom, and were the beast whose authority the second beast, that is, Antichrist was to take upon him (Revelation 13:12), then this conjecture that the name of the beast Λατεινος, which was probable before the prophecy was fulfilled, is now more than probable, the prophecy being verified in the event. And the decay or rather dissolution of the Latin or Roman Empire, before which Antichrist was not to be revealed, is so far from making this conjecture less probable, that it rather confirms it.

Neither do we read in the Scriptures that Antichrist should be a most mighty king, or should cease upon the most mighty kingdoms: only this we read, that he should exercise the power of the former beast, which most fitly agrees to the pope.

As touching the agreement of the number 666, Bellarmine objects firstly that the number agrees not with the names propounded, and secondly, although it did, yet it follows not, that any of these is the name of the beast. That the number agrees not he shows, because Λατεινος, if it is written with a simple iota as it ought to be, it lacks five of that number.

I answer that the ancient Latins used to write and pronounce **i long** by **ei diphthong**; and the Grecians usually express **i long** by **ei**. And it is to be observed, that Irenaeus setting down these two names Ευανθας and Τειταν as containing the number 666, takes it for granted, that Λατεινος may so be written; whereas of Τειταν, he says that it makes that number *if* it is written with diphthong.

Against the name רומיית, that is, Roman, he objects that it is not masculine, unless the last letter signifying 400 is taken away. I answer that collective names in Hebrew are indifferently expressed in either gender. And suppose the name were feminine, yet that hinders not, but that it may be the name here spoken of. For the Holy Spirit speaks of the name of the beast, that is, the Roman state, which elsewhere is called the whore of Babylon, and *foemina*, a woman. And therefore well may the name be feminine.

But although the number agreed (says Bellarmine) yet it follows not that either *Roman* or *Latin* should be the name. First, because neither of them is his proper name, but commune. Neither ought it, seeing it is the name of the beast, which signifies a whole state. Secondly, because many other names make this number: And therefore it follows not that any of these is the name here spoken of, because they contain the number 666. For several authors have noted several other names, as Hippolytus [did], Aretas [noting] seven others, [and also] Primasius, Rupertus, Haymo, and [Platina].

Unto these he adds out of lying Lindanus, *Martin Lauer* (for Luther) in Latin letters, taken (as they never were) for numbers, after the manner of the Greek: out of [Gonebrard] Luther's name in Hebrew, namely: *Lultor*, to which Bellarmine in his wisdom adds *Dabid Chitreiu*, for David Chytraeus, and σαξονικός a Saxon, to signify Luther.

These latter names show the papists to be fraught with malice and void of judgment, forcing these men's names, as they might their own, to this purpose. But we answer that, although there are many names which contain 666, yet notwithstanding, none can be the name here spoken of, unless also it be the name of the beast, that is, the Latin or Roman state, and unless it be such a name, as he to whom all other notes of Antichrist do agree, that causes men to take upon them.

Consider therefore with what conscience Bellarmine would persuade us that any of these may be the name here spoken of, as well as Latin or Roman, seeing first, either of these is the name of the beast, whereas none of those is or can be. Secondly, seeing those are such names as Antichrist will not cause men to take upon them; whereas the pope (whom we have proved to be Antichrist) enforces either of these names upon men, suffering none to buy or sell, or to live among them, unless he profess himself to be a Roman or Latin in respect of his religion. And thirdly, whereas these names agree fitly to him, to whom all other marks of Antichrist agree, many of those do not; and those which do, as κακός οδηγός, an evil guide, which κατ' εξοχήν agrees to the pope, αντεμος, etc. yet cannot be this name, for the reasons before alleged.

And thus I hope this Gordian knot is untied, and this unanswerable argument answered by this. The name of the beast is not yet known, therefore (says he) Antichrist is not yet come.

I answer, even if the name were unknown, yet might Antichrist still have come. But now the name of the beast is known. How far then is Bellarmine from proving by this argument, that Antichrist has not yet come?

Chapter 11
Concerning the mark, which Antichrist shall impose upon men.

(1) Concerning the mark of Antichrist, Bellarmine recites three opinions, unto which he adds a fourth of his own coming. The first of the Protestants, who teach that the mark of Antichrist is some sign of obedience and conjunction with the pope. The second opinion is of some catholic papists, who think this mark to be the letters of Antichrist's name. The third of Hippolytus, and some others, who imagine that this mark of the beast is, not to use the sign of the cross, but rather to detest and abhor it.

The first opinion – namely: of the Protestants – he detests as rash and absurd. The second of the catholics, he rejects as false, which he signifies when he says, they were deceived. The third he would willingly embrace, because it seems to make against us; but the author is counterfeit, and his testimony falsified by Bellarmine. And although indeed he do reject it, as he might well, because it is absurd to feign a privative mark, as if the not using of some mark, were the mark whereof the Holy Spirit speaks; yet he affirms, (such is his blind malice) that herein we are notable forerunners of Antichrist. In the fourth place he adds his own conceit, that Antichrist shall invent a positive or real mark, which as yet is not known, whereby as he would overthrow all the former opinions, so especially he confutes the last. From whence notwithstanding, as if it were true, he would happily infer that we are the forerunners of Antichrist. And this opinion he does confute by two reasons. First, because the mark must be positive; and secondly, because it is as yet unknown. And this is the sum and effect of his whole eleventh chapter.

But what of all this? Or whereunto does all this discourse tend? You will say, to prove that the pope is not Antichrist. He had indeed propounded that question to prove, but in this chapter he concludes nothing for the pope. Only he tells us that there are three opinions concerning the mark, and to them he adds a fourth of his own, and there an end. Other papists when they handle this argument, reason thus:

- Antichrist shall compel men to take the mark of the beast.
- The pope does not compel men to take the mark of the beast.
- Therefore the pope is not Antichrist.

Which argument if he had used, and had also made good the assumption, he should have said something to the purpose. But Bellarmine concludes no such matter, *Nec enim ausus est, nec potuit*. For well does he know, that from this mark of the beast we conclude the affirmative, namely, that the pope is Antichrist.

(2) How then does he argue? surely it is not easy to tell. For after the sophister's guise, he hides his conclusion, that he may more easily deceive. But so far as I can guess, either by resolving the discourse itself, or by conferring the same with the former chapter, whereunto he seems to refer us, he would seem to reason thus:

- If Antichrist's mark is not yet known, then is not Antichrist yet come.
- But Antichrist's mark is not yet known.
- Therefore Antichrist has not yet come: and consequently the pope is not Antichrist.

The proposition he omits, and so takes it for granted: although in truth there is no necessity of the consequence. For as we said before of his name, so now we say of his mark: that after Antichrist is come, his mark might be unknown, yea was for a time to be unknown. Otherwise he should not be able to enforce his mark upon many, few or none being so desperately wicked, as knowing his mark, to suffer themselves by the same to be branded to destruction; as all they are, who do receive and retain it (Revelation 14:9-10).

And further I add, that although this mark be known to very many of those who have the mark of God,[492] yet to them that are branded with this mark of the beast, and do retain the same, that is, who live and die papists, it neither is, or shall be known, or at least not acknowledged of them during this life. And therefore no marvel, though Bellarmine confesses his ignorance on this behalf.

(3) But let us see also how he proves the assumption, namely: that the mark of the beast is not yet known. Indeed by this reason:

- If neither that be the mark of the beast which the Protestants teach, nor yet that which the Catholics imagine (so many of them as take upon them to know what this mark is) then assuredly this mark is not yet known.
- But neither is that the mark which the Protestants speak of, nor yet that which the catholics have supposed.
- Therefore this mark is not yet known.

As for the papists, we confess that either they know not, or at the least acknowledge not this mark, for if they did, the most of them would refuse to take it. Wherefore leaving them to Bellarmine's discretion, whether to be confuted or allowed; let us consider whether that be the mark, which the Protestants have supposed, or not.

The heretics of this time (says Bellarmine) teach that the character of Antichrist is some sign of obedience and conjunction with the pope of Rome. But what this sign is, they do not express after the same manner. Bullinger understands by the mark the chrism, wherewith young ones are

---

[492] Revelation 9:4

anointed in their confirmation. Bibliander says that it is the profession of the Romish or popish faith. Chytraeus to these adds the oath of fidelity, which many are compelled to swear to the pope: as also the priestly unction which is received in the head and the hand, impressing (as the papists speak) *Characterem indelebilem*: Finally to fall down before images, and the host, and to be present at masses for the dead. *Sed facile est* (says he) *has nugas refutare*. But it is easy to refute these toys.

But before I come to answer his trifling cavillations, I think it needful first to refer the reader to the former book, where I shown what this mark is, and that this mark which is but one in substance, is variously expressed and testified; and therefore that there is no opposition in the opinions of the Protestants, concerning this matter, all these notes, which they mention, belonging to the mark of the beast.[493] And secondly, to deliver briefly the popish conceit concerning this mark.

For the papists imagine that the character is a visible mark of Antichrist's name, which the followers of Antichrist shall have imprinted in their foreheads, and carry as a sign in their hands, that it may be as it were their warrant to buy or sell. And so Bellarmine (to omit others) writes also of the name and the number. "The proper name of Antichrist," (says he) "must be shown for a token of all that buy or sell." To which purpose he approves the judgment of Rupertus, who says, that Antichrist's name is such a one as he shall glory in, *Adeo vt jubeat inscribi in frontibus hominum*, Insomuch that he shall cause it to be written in the foreheads of men. And again, the beast (whose number this is) shall command all merchants that they use this number for a sign or token in their contracts.

But who could be so gross as to imagine that princes and magistrates, and men of all sorts, would ever suffer themselves to be branded as it were with Antichrist's visible mark? or if that were Antichrist's practice, who should not be able to discern him? Why, their ordinary gloss could tell them

---

[493] Book 1 Chapter 8 Sections 4-5

that the mark is received in the forehead by confession, and in the right hand by operation, as we also hold. Antoninus also and Lyra teach that character *est determinatus modus viuendi secundum legem alicujus, quo à caeteris distinguuntur*; a character or mark is a certain manner of living according to the law of any, whereby men are distinguished from others: which also agrees with our judgment. Again, the Scriptures often make mention of marks and seals, which cannot without absurdity be understood of visible marks.[494]

(4) Now let us see how easily this trifler is able, according to his vain brag, to refute those toys of ours. His reasons are two: the former, because that which we deliver concerning the mark, agrees not with the words of the text: which he shows by four instances. First, because the text speaks but of one character, we speak of many. We answer, that as of the lamb, so of the beast also there is but one character in substance, although the same by various means may be variously expressed and testified; that is, subjection to the pope as their head, and the acknowledgment of the See of Rome, and of the pope's supremacy, etc. And this mark (to answer his second instance also,) is common to all, as being enforced upon all sorts of men without exception.

Hear the words of their law:[495] *Subesse Romano pontifici, omni humanae creaturae declaramus, dicimus, definimus, and pronuntiamus omnino esse de necessitate salutis*: "For every human creature to be subject to the pope of Rome, we declare, affirm, determine, and pronounce, that it is altogether of the necessity of salvation." See more in Book 1 Chapter 8, § 6 and 7.

"Thirdly," says he, "the Scripture shows this character to be such a one, as may indifferently be carried either in the right hand or in the forehead.

---

[494] Ezekiel 9, Revelation 9:4 & 7:2 & 2:17; 2 Timothy 2:19
[495] Extr. de maior. et obed. C. vna sancta.

But none of these marks which the Protestants mention are such. The chrism is received in the forehead, and not in the hand," etc.

The Scripture says thus in Revelation 13:16. "And he causeth all, both small and great, etc., that he may give them a mark on their right hand, or else upon their foreheads." That is, by his usurped dominion and tyranny, he shall make all sorts of men subject unto him, and in testimony of their subjection, to receive his mark on the forehead by profession, or in the right hand by practice and operation. Of the carrying of this mark, and the carrying of it indifferently either on the forehead, or in the hand, the scripture speaks not. The mark is subjection unto him, which (as has been said) is variously expressed and testified.

"Fourthly, the Scripture says that none in the kingdom of Antichrist shall be suffered to buy or sell, unless he have this mark: but how many (says he) are there within the dominion of the pope, who having none of these marks, do buy and sell, as namely the Jews?"

I answer that Antichrist was to sit in the church of God, and to tyrannize over Christians. Now of all those that profess the name of Christ, the pope suffers none where he has to do, either to buy or sell, except he has his mark. See the Bull of Martin V, annexed to the council of Constance, where express and straight charge is given, that whosoever does not live in subjection to the pope, and communion with the Church of Rome (meaning such as Wycliffe and Hus) shall not be suffered to buy or sell, or to enjoy the comforts of human society. Whereas therefore the pope permits to the Jews that which he will not permit to the professors of the gospel of Christ: that, as it shows his greater opposition to the servants of Christ, then to the enemies of Christ the Jews; so it reveals him to be Antichrist.

(5) His second reason is thus concluded:

- If all these things, which the Protestants mention, were used in the Catholic Church before the coming of Antichrist, then

- none of them belong to the mark of Antichrist, (for otherwise Antichrist should have learned them from the church).
- But all these things, as namely: chrism and the rest, which the Protestants mention, were used in the catholic church before the year 607, that is, before the coming of Antichrist, according to the opinion of the Protestants.
- Therefore none of these belong to the mark of the beast.

First I answer to the proposition, that although these things had been used in the catholic church before the revelation of Antichrist, yet that hinders not, but that now they may appertain to the mark of the beast. For we doubt not to affirm that before the revelation of Antichrist there were many corruptions crept into the church, both in doctrine and in the worship of God (the mystery of iniquity more and more working, even from the apostles' times, unto the revelation of Antichrist) which corruptions Antichrist was to retain with increase.

If therefore the seeds of Antichristianism, which were sown before Antichrists appearing, were signs of his approaching; the same being as it were grown up, confirmed and increased, may without absurdity be said to belong to the mark of Antichrist already come. Especially if we consider the diversity in using them since the revelation of Antichrist and before.

For there was not in the catholic church a universal subjection to the pope as the head, until he by much ambition and contention obtained the supremacy, and was called *the universal bishop*, and *head of the universal church*, which he could never obtain until the year 607. Seeing then there was not a universal subjection to the pope before that time, these things if they had been used at all, could not be used as signs thereof; as since they have.

Neither were they imposed before and enjoined upon all by the laws of the pope, as since they have; so that the cause of using them now, is not the example of the ancient church, but the authority of the pope's law, enjoining and commanding them. Therefore, although these things had been used in the Church before the year 607, yet now they may appertain to the mark of the beast. And therefore the connection of the proposition, is first to be denied. But now if these things were not used in the first 600. years, will not he then in confuting those toys, show himself a mere trifler?

(6) But let us consider the particulars. And first, that chrism was used before the year 606, he proves by the testimonies of Tertullian, Cyprian and Augustine. I answer that these fathers speak of the anointing with oil used in the sacrament of baptism, which also without warrant of the Scriptures is retained among the papists. But of the chrism of salvation, which the papists make the element of their counterfeit sacrament of confirmation, whereof there is no institution in the Scriptures, no word, no element, these Fathers speak not. The ceremony of imposition of hands, with prayer for the confirmation and strengthening of those, which before had been baptized, was indeed used in the primitive church: neither is it altogether misliked of us, although not much used among us, because it was so much abused by them. But this ceremony was done without unction or chrism: for further proof whereof see Dr. Fulke's answer to the Rhemists: Acts 8:17.

And therefore notwithstanding that ancient practice of the Church, this Chrism used in confirmation, may belong to the mark of the beast. And rather because the papists make their confirmation with Chrism, not only a sacrament, but also a most necessary and principal sacrament – so necessary as that they have set it down as a law, that no man is to be esteemed a Christian without it. *Nunquam erit Christianus nisi confirmatione episcopals fuerit Chrismatus*:[496] "He shall never be a Christian, who is not confirmed with chrism by a bishop." So principal, as that they prefer it before baptism, affirming that it is *maiore veneratione venerandum*:[497] with greater veneration to be reverenced.

---

[496] De consecrat. dist. 5. C. vt iciuni.
[497] De consecrat. dist. 5. C. de. his vero.

Now if it be a privilege peculiar unto Christ the author and bestower of grace, to ordain sacraments of grace, then must it needs be accounted a practice Antichristian, if any man shall take upon him to ordain a sacrament, and not only to obtrude the same upon all as necessary to salvation, but also to prefer it before that excellent sacrament of baptism ordained by Christ himself. Therefore as the ordaining and enforcing of this sacrament upon men is a note of Antichrist, so those which do not only receive it when they are young, but also retain it when they are old, remaining in the communion of the church of Rome, may be said to have the mark of the beast.

(7) Secondly, that to adhere to the Roman Church was a mark of a true Catholic before the year 606, he proves by the authority of Augustine, Ambrose and Victor Vitensis.

But we speak of the church of Rome that now is, that is, the *apostate* church of Rome: he argues of the ancient church which was *apostolic*. Indeed, while the church of Rome did cleave unto Christ, so long might it be a note of a good Christian to cleave unto it, although these testimonies do scarcely prove it. But after that church became apostatical and adulterous, as appears by their fundamental heresies, and horrible idolatries, and consequently of a faithful church became an harlot, and of the church of Christ the synagogue of Antichrist: it has been the mark of an Antichristian to live in the communion of that church.

Besides this great difference between the present and the ancient state of the church of Rome, there is also great odds in the manner of adhering or cleaving thereto. Then, as other churches did cleave to the church of Rome, so did the church of Rome cleave to them: now it acknowledges no church besides itself. Then the church of Rome was accounted but a part of the catholic church, and so a man might be a good Christian although he were not of the church of Rome. Now the church of Rome alone must be accounted the catholic church; and consequently he that is not a member of that church, must not be taken for a catholic or true Christian. For when the pope got the title of universal bishop, or head of the universal church, then the church whereof he was head, was accounted the only catholic and universal church.

Hereunto agrees that gloss, *Constat ecclesiam ideo esse vnam, quia in vniuersali ecclesia est vnum caput supremu, cui omnes de ecclesia obedire tenentur Scil. Papae*:[498] "It is evident that the church is therefore one, because in the universal church there is one supreme head, whom all that are of the church are bound to obey." And agreeably thereunto says a late writer, whose books were published at Venice in the year 1588. *Non potest quis se Christianum fateri, qui curae Papae dicit se non subesse*:[499] "No man may profess himself to be a Christian, who does not confess himself to be subject to the pope's cure or charge." And therefore in the conclusion of his book he professes himself to be *Mancipium S. R. E.*, the bond servant of the holy church of Rome, *Non ignorans* (he says) *haud possehaberese deum patrem, si sanctam vniuersalem Romanam ecclesiam non habuerit matrem*, "knowing that a man cannot have God to be his Father, unless he has the holy universal church of Rome to be his mother."

Seeing therefore the church of Rome is become the whore of Babylon, as has been proven, and the synagogue of Antichrist; and seeing the pope compels all men to cleave to the church of Rome, suffering none to buy or sell, or to enjoy any benefits of human society, which profess not themselves to be members of the church of Rome, it follows that this cleaving to the apostate church of Rome, or living in the communion thereof, belongs to the mark of the beast.

(8) Thirdly, as touching the oath of obedience and fealty made to the pope of Rome, Bellarmine proves that it was used in the time of Gregory the

---

[498] Clementin. Lib. 5. ad nostrum in gloss.
[499] Rod. Cupers 127. num. 29.

Great, and therefore before the year 606, as appears in the epistles of Gregory.[500] I answer that, although before the year 606, the bishops of Rome took more upon them than became the ministers of Christ, yet Bellarmine is not able out of all antiquity to allege one example of such an oath of fealty and allegiance imposed by the pope upon foreign bishops, and much less upon kings and princes, as all catholic bishops, as they call them, priests, graduates, princes and potentates are compelled to swear unto the pope of Rome.

That one example, which, as it seems, is all that he can allege, of an oath taken not long before the year 606 is little to the purpose. For it is not an oath of obedience and allegiance to the pope, but of faith and religion towards God, conformable to the faith and religion then professed by the bishop, and church of Rome. For it is the oath of a certain bishop who swore to renounce his former heresies, and to profess and maintain that faith and religion, which then the bishop and church of Rome did profess: which oath in effect is no otherwise to be understood, than if a minister among us, being reclaimed from popery or some other heresy, should take an oath before a bishop, that while he lives, he will profess and maintain that religion which is now professed and established in the church of England, and other reformed churches; which is not to swear allegiance to them, but the like allegiance with them unto Christ.

(9) Fourthly, the anointing of priests, we confess to be as ancient as the priesthood of Aaron, from whence they profess they have received this Jewish ceremony; which together with the sacrifices, priesthood, and ceremonies of the law, are abrogated by the sacrifice and death of our Savior Christ. And why then do they not as well retain circumcision, the sacrifices of bulls and goats, and other ceremonies of the Levitical priesthood, that they might more plainly show themselves, whiles they seek to be the apes of the

---

[500] Lib. 10, Epist. 31.

Jews, to be as indeed they are, according to the censure of Paul in the epistle to the Galatians, apostates from Christ.

But as their priesthood itself is Antichristian, whereby the Levitical priesthood and many Jewish ceremonies are retained, as though Christ had not put an end to them, whereby Christ is denied to be our only priest, whereby Christ himself (as they say) is daily offered, to the disgrace of his own sacrifice, as though that once performed had not been sufficient; to the overthrow of his human nature, which they hold to be in many places at once invisible and incircumscriptible [incapable of limitation], without quantity and dimension, and consequently nobody; to the disparagement of his divine excellency, while every shaveling priest takes upon him by breathing out a few words after a magical manner to create his maker, and when he has done to offer him as a sacrifice to the father, every sacrifice being inferior to the sacrificer; to the deifying of a piece of bread consecrated to most sacrilegious idolatry; as I say, their priesthood itself is Antichristian, so their unction, whether of bishops on the head, or of priests on the hand, undoubtedly belongs to the mark of Antichrist.

And although they were able to show some practice hereof in the church before the year 606, yet this hinders not, but that this priestly unction may belong to the mark, because as I said, some corruptions were before the revelation of Antichrist crept into the church, which by him were to be retained with increase and maintained, as also because this ceremony is used not by authority of their example, but as received from Moses by the authority of the ceremonial law, as though it were not abrogated by Christ, and as imposed upon the church by the law of the pope.

And lastly because it is a ceremony belonging to such a sacrificing priesthood, as was not known in the primitive church. But as I suppose they are not able to produce any sufficient testimony or authentic proof to declare the use of this ceremony in the primitive church, which some of them impute to the rudeness, and unsettled estate of that time.[501] For whereas he alleges two testimonies of Nazianzen, both places are to be understood figuratively, of consecration to the ministry. For as appears by the testimony of Innocent III,[502] this ceremony of anointing was not used in the Greek Church, whereof Nazianzen was, but rejected as Jewish, until he imposed the same upon them, about the year 1200.

(10) As touching the fifth: sacrifices of praise we offered for those that died in the Lord; but no propitiatory sacrifices, such as their masses be, were offered for them. The oblations for the dead, whereof Augustine speaks,[503] prove not that mass, were used as propitiatory sacrifices for the quick and the dead. Unless therefore he can prove that they had before the year 607, masses as superstitious and idolatrous as since, the frequenting of masses may now belong to the mark of the beast, which before did not.

(11) Adoration of images and of the eucharist, may most fitly be said to belong to the mark of the beast. For those that are made drunk with the cup of the whore of Babylon's fornications, that is, which are besotted with the idolatries of the Church of Rome, are the same with those that receive the mark of the beast. But the adoration of images and of the eucharist, is notorious idolatry or spiritual fornication; and therefore those that are besotted with these idolatries have received the mark of the beast. And as touching the worshiping of images, it is most plainly forbidden and condemned in the Scriptures, and councils, and writings of the fathers, who lived in the first 600 years.

The wine of this fornication, wherewith all sorts have been made drunk, was first set abroach to the world in the second Council of Nice, about the year 789. For further proof whereof read Bishop Jewel in his 14th article

---

[501] Pighius
[502] De sacra vnctione C. cum venisset.
[503] *Lib. de hares*. C. 53. See Dr. Fulke. in Revelation 14:13. s. 5. contra. Rhemists

against Mr. Harding. And the like may be said of the adoration of the eucharist, which is a consequence of the elevation of the sacrament and transubstantiation, neither of which were used or heard of in the first 600. years, as the same Jewel proves in Article 75.10. And in Article 8, he shows that the adoration of the sacrament cannot be warranted by any commandment of Christ, nor by any word or example of the apostles or ancient fathers, but that it is a thing lately devised by Pope Honorius about the year 1226. But let us weigh his proofs.

That images were worshiped he proves by the testimony of Jerome, who in the life of Paula, speaking of her zeal and devotion in visiting those places, where our Lord Jesus had been conversant; he shows how at length she came to the sepulcher and kissed the stone, which the angel had rolled away from the mouth of the sepulcher, and licked the place where Christ's body lay: and seeing that very cross (as was supposed) whereon Christ was crucified, *Prostrata ante crucem quasi pendentem Dominum cerneret adorabat*, Falling down before the cross she worshiped the Lord, as if she had now seen him hanging on the Cross.

I answer that this practice was not common, but peculiar to her; and to her not usual, but only at that time, and in that place: neither did she worship the cross (as the papists do the images of that Cross, *cultu latriae*: with divine worship) but seeing the cross whereon Christ was crucified, and being ravished with the memory of his death, she falling before that cross, worshiped Christ.

Now that the adoration of the eucharist was also in use before the year 606, he proves by the testimonies of Ambrose and Augustine. Ambrose's words are these, *Itaque per scabellam terra intelligatur, per terram caro Christi, quam hodie quoque in mysterijs adoramus, et quam Apostoli in Domino Jesus, vt supra diximus, adorarunt:*[504] "Therefore by *the footstool* let us understand the earth, and by *the earth* the flesh of Christ, which at this day also we adore in

---

[504] *Lib. 3. de spiritu S. chap. 12*

the mysteries, and which the apostles adored in the Lord Jesus," as we said before.

But it is one thing to adore and honor Christ in his sacraments, as the ancient Christians and we do: and another thing to adore the sacrament, as if it were Christ himself, as the papists do, deifying a piece of bread, and adoring it with such a worship as indeed does not belong (I say not to the man Christ, but) to the humanity of Christ, whereof alone and not of the deity the bread is a sacrament: For the bread is a sacrament of the body of Christ crucified, and the wine of his blood shed.

But if Bellarmine would have read but five or six lines further, he should have found a better testimony against their adoration of saints and images than this was for the adoration of the sacrament. For Ambrose proving that the Holy Spirit was to be adored, because he is adored that according to the flesh was borne of the Holy Spirit: *Ac ne quis hoc deriuet (says he) ad Mariam virginem: Maria erat templum dei, non deus templi, et ideo solus ill adorandus qui operabatur in templo*: "And lest any should derive this to the virgin Mary, Mary was the temple of God, not God of the temple; and therefore he alone is to be adored who did work in the temple."

Augustine[505] – understanding by the footstool mentioned Psalm 99:5 the flesh of Christ – says, *Ipsam carnem nobis manducandam ad salutem dedit. Nemo autem carnem illam manducat nisi prius adorauerit*: "He gave his flesh itself to be eaten by us to salvation, but no man eats that flesh unless he has first adored it." Here Augustine speaks no more of the sacrament or of the bodily eating of the flesh, than Christ himself does in John 6, and therefore this allegation is impertinent; or if it were not, yet is it one thing to adore the flesh of Christ, and another thing to adore a piece of bread, which by the testimony of Christ John 6, and of Augustine, is proven not to be turned into the body of Christ, because both do signify that the wicked do not eat the body of Christ.

---

[505] On Psalm 99

To conclude therefore – whereas Bellarmine argues thus: these things were used before the year 606, therefore they belong not to the mark of the beast. – the sum of my answer is this: that they were not used in the first 600 years: and again, if they had been used then, yet they may belong to the mark of the beast now, for the reasons before alleged.

Chapter 12
Of the generation and nation of Antichrist.

(1) The Jesuit's fifth disputation is concerning the generation and nation of Antichrist, whereof he shall come, and of which he shall especially be received. From whence as he vainly supposes, is gathered a most evident demonstration, that the pope is not Antichrist:

- For Antichrist shall be received of the Jews for their Messias, and consequently he is to be a Jew both by nation and religion.
- But none of the popes since the year 607 have been received by the Jews as their messiah; neither has any one of them been a Jew either in nation or religion.
- Therefore the pope is not Antichrist (or rather as he ought to conclude from the premises): therefore not any one of the popes is Antichrist.

For in all this disputation Bellarmine presupposes that to be true, which we have proved to be most false, that Antichrist is but one singular person, and accordingly reasons, as if we held that this or that pope were the Antichrist.

We hold indeed that every pope for his time, as he is the head of the catholic apostasy, so is *an antichrist*; but *the Antichrist* is the whole row and order of them from Boniface III downward. If therefore Bellarmine argues upon a false supposition, we are likely to have but a simple demonstration of it. But let us examine his disputation.

Before he proposes his proposition, as the basis or ground of his demonstration, he deals with us as cunning tradesmen, who being desirous to utter their bad wares at a good price, first, show those that are worse, that the naughtiness of the worse may commend and set forth those that be not so bad.

So he brings forth various opinions concerning the generation of Antichrist, and first those that are false and absurd, as namely, that Antichrist should be borne of a virgin by the operation of the devil, as Christ was borne of a virgin, by the operation of the Holy Spirit. This opinion is propounded by the author of the treatise concerning Antichrist, falsely ascribed to Augustine.

Secondly, that the devil himself is Antichrist, who shall feign himself to have taken flesh of a virgin, as Christ truly did; which is the conceit of Hippolytus: upon whose counterfeit authority the papists in other points concerning this controversy, do so much rely.

Thirdly, that Antichrist shall be a true man, but also a devil, by the incarnation of the devil; even as Christ, who is God, by incarnation became man. "This opinion," (says Bellarmine) "Origen thought to be possible."

These opinions show into what absurdities men do fall, when they will need to compare Christ with Antichrist, as the papists in many things do.

Fourthly, that Nero who died above 1500 years ago, should come again in his own person to be Antichrist.

(2) But these wares are all so corrupt, that Bellarmine will not for his credit sake commend them unto us. And therefore he makes a second show of such opinions as are more probable, namely: that Antichrist shall be borne in fornication and not in marriage, which is the opinion of Damascene and some others.

And secondly, that he shall be borne of the tribe of Dan, which is the judgment of twelve of the fathers, and other approved authors among the papists; and generally of all papists almost besides Bellarmine himself. But although these opinions are, as he says, very probable, and the latter commended by a whole jury of ancient writers, yet because they cannot be proved out of the Scriptures, he will not put them into our hands, as though he meant to warrant them. So that now we must think that we shall be well dealt also, and that no corrupt or counterfeit stuff shall be commended unto us, but that which tends towards and is warrantable by the word of God.

But what say you Bellarmine, cannot this opinion that Antichrist shall be of the tribe of Dan, be proved out of the Scripture? What say you then to those three places of Scripture, which are to this purpose usually alleged in the Church of Rome? The first is Genesis 49:17: "Dan shall be a serpent in the way," etc. The second is Jeremiah 8:16: "The neighing of his horses was heard from Dan." The third is Revelation 7, where 12,000 of every tribe being sealed to salvation, the Tribe of Dan is left out, because Antichrist was to come from that tribe.

To the first of these places, Bellarmine answers with us that the prophetic blessing of Jacob, was verified in Samson, who was of the tribe of Dan: and that Jacob meaning in these words to bless Dan, his meaning cannot without absurdity be perverted to the signification of a curse.

And I add, that they might with as good reason allege that Antichrist shall be of the tribe of Benjamin, of whom it is said, verse 27, that he shall ravin as a wolf. Jeremiah undoubtedly speaks not of Antichrist, nor yet as Bellarmine says, of the tribe of Dan, but of Nebuchadnezzar, who was to come by the coast or country called Dan, to destroy Jerusalem, as Jerome rightly expounds. "Why Dan is omitted in Revelation 7, it is not well known," says Bellarmine, "especially seeing as Ephraim also – which was one of the greatest tribes – is left out."

But here Bellarmine prevaricates, and by trifling, betrays the truth. For it is not true that Ephraim is left out: for seeing Manasseh is mentioned in verse 6, we must, by *the tribe of Joseph* mentioned in verse 8, understand the tribe of Ephraim. Nevertheless, this may truly be said, that there are other causes of this omission, then that which is alleged concerning Antichrist. For else we may say as well, that Antichrist should come from the tribe of Simeon because he is not mentioned in the blessing of Moses in Deuteronomy 33.

The truth is that where the Holy Spirit numbers the twelve tribes and mentions Levi,[506] which for the most part is not reckoned among the twelve tribes, because it was scattered among them all; someone of the other tribes is left out, otherwise, where twelve are named, thirteen should be reckoned. The mentioning therefore of Levi, is the cause why someone of the rest is not expressed, but either comprehended under another that is mentioned, as Simeon under Judah (Deuteronomy 33), Ephraim and Manasseh – being two several and great tribes under Joseph (Deuteronomy 27:12, Ezekiel 48:32) – are altogether omitted, as Dan in Revelation 7.

Now Dan seems to be omitted rather than any other, because that was the first tribe which fell from God unto idolatry: and for the same cause (as some think) the genealogy of that tribe is omitted in the first book of the Chronicles.

(3) These opinions therefore, though countenanced with the authority of the fathers, Bellarmine dares not deliver as matters of truth, because they cannot be proven out of the Scriptures. This in truth is the cause why we reject all the fancies of the papists concerning Antichrist, wherein they differ from us, because that although many of them were also the opinions of the ancient writers (who could but guess at the meaning of prophecies not then fulfilled), yet they cannot be proved out of the word of God, wherein Antichrist is sufficiently described.

This liberty therefore, which Bellarmine lawfully takes unto himself in rejecting the testimonies of the fathers in this point not warranted by the Scriptures, must in equity also be granted unto us. For upon the same principle or ground which Bellarmine here sets down, we reason against the popish conceits after this manner:

---

[506] As Revelation 7

- Those opinions concerning Antichrist which cannot be proven out of the Scriptures, are not to be held as certain truths, or believed as matters of faith, although they have the testimony of the fathers.
- But all the popish conceits concerning Antichrist, are such as cannot be proved out of the Scriptures.
- Therefore none of the popish conceits concerning Antichrist are to be received for certain truths, though several of them have the testimony of the fathers.

(4) Now let us hear in the third place what those things are which Bellarmine would have us take upon his word for certain and sound in this point. "There are two things," says he, "most certain: one that Antichrist shall come for the Jews especially, and shall be received by them for their messiah. The other, that he shall be born of the nation of the Jews, and shall be circumcised, and shall at the least for a time observe the sabbath."

On which two points the proposition of the syllogism before rehearsed does consist, which Bellarmine thought to set out as true, by setting by it other opinions more absurd then it is. But although there are degrees of falsehood in all these opinions, yet all of them are false, as being grounded upon this false supposition, that Antichrist is but one singular man. And secondly, by the same reason that moved Bellarmine to reject the former opinions, may these also be rejected, namely, because they cannot be proved out of the Scriptures; but contrariwise may be disproved thereby.

For Antichrist shall sit in the temple of God, that is, shall reign in the church of Christ, and shall be an apostate, and the head of the apostasy, as Bellarmine confesses, and therefore not the head of the Jews (who cannot be said to make an apostasy before they be called) but of backsliding Christians.

Again, Antichrist is one of the seven heads of the beast mentioned in Revelation 17, that is, of the Roman state, having his seat in Babylon, that is, in Rome, in the government whereof he succeeds the emperor, who while he ruled in Rome, hindered the revelation of Antichrist, as it has been shown heretofore out of Revelation 17:13 and 2 Thessalonians 2. All this sufficiently proves that Antichrist was not to be a Jew, either by nation or religion, but a Latin or Roman. This name with the mark thereof, he causes all sorts of men to take upon them.

And lastly, for as much as the papists themselves hold the calling of the Jews, it would be known whether they shall revolt, after their calling from Christ to Antichrist, or whether they shall be called after the destruction of Antichrist, or during the time of Antichrist's reign, which shall be as they say, the term of three years and a half precisely, or 1260 days. But they themselves deny that the Jews shall revolt after their calling, or that they shall be called in the time of Antichrist's reign, and that they shall be called after the destruction of Antichrist, which shall not be before the end of the world, it is absurd.

(5) But let us see how he proves these things which he says are most certain and sure, and from whence he draws his most evident demonstration. First that Antichrist shall be received of the Jews for their messiah, he proves by testimonies of Scripture, by authority of fathers, and by reason.

Out of the Scripture, he produces two testimonies, the former John 5:43, which place I have heretofore freed from the corruptions of the papists, showing that our Savior Christ does not speak absolutely, "Another shall come," but conditionally, "*If* another shall come," and therefore does not foretell what they were afterwards to do, but tells them what in respect of their present disposition they were ready to do, if another should come in his own name unto them, not sent of God. [2] Neither does he speak definitely of Antichrist, but indefinitely of any false teacher. [3] He speaks of those Jews, to whom he speaks, who could not be the receivers of Antichrist, unless he had come over 1500 years ago.

(6) His second testimony is 2 Thessalonians 2:10-11. "Because they received not the love of the truth that they might be saved: therefore God shall send them the efficacy of error that they may believe lies," etc. These words he understands of the Jews, who because they received not Christ shall therefore be seduced by Antichrist. But the place is plain enough to those who will understand.

The apostle, immediately before these words says, that Antichrist shall prevail with them that perish, because they received not the love of the truth that they might be saved. And immediately after these words – "Therefore God shall send them the efficacy of error, that they may believe lies" – he adds that all might be judged or condemned that have not believed the truth, but have taken pleasure in unrighteousness. In these words the Apostle does not go about to define of what Nation or people Antichrist shall be received: but having described Antichrist as by other arguments, so in the last place by this effect of seducing, now he describes the followers of Antichrist, who shall be seduced of him not by their nation, but by their condition before God. And also clears the justice of God in giving them over to be seduced to their destruction.

The followers of Antichrist are described by their condition before God, that they are reprobates, or such as perish, according to Matthew 24:24, that it is impossible that the elect should finally be seduced by him, which is set down, not so much to be a note whereby to discern Antichrist, as to signify the estate of those that follow him, whom before he had described, that they are such as perish, and that worthily.

For as I said, in the next words he clears the justice of God, after this manner:

- On such as have not received the love of the truth that they might be saved, nor believed the same, but have delighted in

unrighteousness, the Lord sends justly the efficacy of error, that they may believe lies, that they may all be condemned.
- But the followers of Antichrist are such as have not received the love of the truth, that they might be saved, nor believed the same, but have delighted in unrighteousness.
- Therefore the Lord justly sends upon them strong illusions, that they may believe lies, that all such as believe not the truth, but delight in unrighteousness, may be condemned.

This is the discourse of the apostle, concerning the followers of Antichrist, which cannot with any show of reason be restrained to the Jews, unless it may be said that they alone are such as perish; that they alone have not received the love of the truth that they might be saved; that they alone have not believed the truth, etc. for he says, that all might be condemned, etc. For it is certain that as Antichrist, which in this chapter is described, is not the head of the Jews, but of counterfeit Christians; so the Jews (as they are Jews) are not the followers of Antichrist here described.

Antichrist is the head of the apostasy or revolt from Christ, and consequently the head of apostate Christians (1 Timothy 4:1). Antichrist shall sit in the temple of God, that is, shall rule and reign over the church of Christ. Antichrist was to sit in Babylon, that is, Rome, and therein was to succeed the emperors who, while they ruled in Rome, hindered the revelation and dominion of Antichrist. All of these points, as they do fit the pope, so they do prove that the papists are the followers of Antichrist, and have received the name and mark of the beast. And hereof there can be no doubt, if this description also agrees unto them, as most evidently it does. For seeing as they are the apostate Christians described (1 Timothy 4:1, 3), certain it is, that they have not received the love of the truth, that they may be saved.

That strong illusion is sent upon them that they might believe lies, etc. it appears plainly in their written vanities, which they call unwritten verities, in their legends, portuises, and festivals fraught full of incredible lies, in their ridiculous dotages and devout superstitions, wherein they plainly show themselves to be besotted and made drunk with the whore of Babylon's cup of fornications, and to be given over to believe untruths. That they will not believe the truth, appears by their manifold gross errors, from which they will not be reclaimed And that they delight in iniquity appears by their doting upon the doctrine and religion of Antichrist, which as there it is opposed to the truth, so before is called *the mystery of iniquity*.[507]

This description therefore of the followers of Antichrist, ought to be an admonition for all papists to renounce that religion of Rome, if they would not be in the number of them that perish: and a caveat for all Christians, who professing the true religion, have no true love thereof, but are ready to accept and embrace the religion of Rome, lest this heavy judgment of the Lord fall upon them, that because they have not received the love of the truth to their salvation, the Lord sent upon them strong illusion, that they believe lies unto their destruction.

(7) Yea, but (says he) this place cannot be understood of Christians, but of the Jews, for he says that Antichrist shall be sent to them who would not receive Christ, which is true of the Jews, but untrue of Christians. The Apostle speaks of those that receive not the love of the truth that they might be saved, which may be verified of unsound Christians (as the Rhemists themselves on this place do grant) that is, of all those who content themselves with a bare profession of the faith, having neither a true faith, nor yet a sound love of the truth.

A sound Christian does not only profess the name of Christ, but also has some good understanding and knowledge of the truth, and withal an assent thereto, in which two, namely knowledge and assent, consists the historical, or dogmatical faith: and not only a knowledge and assent (for so much the

---

[507] Verse 12, verse 7

devils have) but also a love and liking of the truth; and not only that (for even hypocrites and temporary believers may attain to a love and liking of the truth for some temporary respects) but also a special application of the promises of the gospel unto himself, and particular apprehension of Christ his merits, whereby he is received of the believer to justification and salvation.

Now the papists are such as profess Christ, but indeed receive him not, nor yet the love of his truth that they might be saved. And therefore this place is verified of them. For does any man, I beseech you, receive Christ or believe in him, who does not believe that Christ is his Redeemer and Savior? But if you are a papist, you must not believe that Christ is your Redeemer and Savior; you must sing *Magnificat*, but you may not say with Mary that your soul rejoices in God your Savior, nor with Paul that Christ has loved you, or given himself for you (Galatians 2:20). Must you believe that Christ is thy Savior and redeemer? Then you must believe that you are redeemed by Christ, and shall be saved by him. Must you believe that you have redemption by Christ? then you must also believe that by him you have remission of sins (Ephesians 1:7, Colossians 1:14). "But this to believe without special and extraordinary revelation, is damnable presumption," says the papist. Therefore they profess Christ, but they receive him not.

Nay, they are so far from receiving Christ by a justifying faith, that they might be saved, that they have not so much as the historical faith, which consists in knowledge of the truth and assent thereto. For the most of them have no knowledge, pleasing themselves in their implicit faith: under which name gross and palpable ignorance is commended in the laity of the church of Rome. And the rest assent not to the truth, but set themselves against it. So that whereas all the faith which they profess themselves to have, is but that faith which is also in the devils, yet they have not even that little which they do profess. But the apostle (says Bellarmine) speaks in the preterite tense, which have not received the love of the truth, etc. not in the future: therefore this speech cannot be understood of any other but those who before the apostle wrote this, had refused to believe the preaching of Christ and his apostles, that is to say, the Jews.

Answer: The apostle speaking both of the sin of the Antichristians, and of their punishment, which presupposes their sin going before, he expresses their sin in the preterite tense, which is to be referred not to the time of the Apostles writing, but to the time of their punishment. Antichrist shall be received of those that perish. But why shall they perish? Because they have not received the love of the truth, etc. But this appears more plainly in verse 12: "God shall send them strong illusions to believe lies, that all may be condemned, οι μη πιστευσαντες τη αληθεια αλλ ευδοκησαντες εν τη αδικια, that have not believed, that is, that shall not have believed the truth, *Qui non crediderint veritati*, but have delighted, that is, but shall have delighted in iniquity, *Sed acquieverint in iniustitia*."

Confer with this place, Mark 16:16: "Go preach the gospel says our Savior Christ, to every creature, baptising them;" (as it is in Matthew 28:19)[508] ο πιστευσας και βαπτισθεις σωθησεται ο δε απιστησας κατακριθησεται: "He that hath believed and hath been baptized shall be saved" – that is, shall have believed, and shall have been baptized – "but he that hath not believed, that is, shall not have believed, shall be condemned." Otherwise, if Bellarmine will needs urge the preterite tense, as though the apostle meant that Antichrist should be received only of those who before that time had rejected the truth, he must with all hold, that Antichrist shall be received in the end of the world of those who died over 1500 years since.

(8) To these testimonies of Scripture, he adds the authority of several fathers, who supposed that Antichrist was to be received of the Jews, and accordingly expound the place alleged out of 2 Thessalonians 2:10-11.

Answer: So they held that Antichrist should come from the tribe of Dan, and accordingly expounded some places of Scripture, which no man now unless he will be too ridiculous, can understand of Antichrist. Therefore as

---

[508] *Qui crediderit & bap tizatus suerit &c.*

Bellarmine in that point answered a whole dozen of fathers, so may I answer here with as good reason, that although this opinion might seem probable to the Fathers in their time, living before the revelation of Antichrist, yet now there is no probability in it, seeing it cannot only not be proved out of the scripture, but as you heard, is confuted both by the Scripture and the event.

(9) Let us therefore in the third place consider his reason: Antichrist shall without doubt join himself first and chiefly to those who are ready to receive him: But the Jews are ready to receive him, not the Christians nor the Gentiles, therefore Antichrist first and principally shall join himself to the Jews. First to the proposition I answer, that Antichrist shall join himself not to any whatsoever, but to those in the Church that are ready to receive him. For as Cyprian truly notes:[509] "They are the servants of God whom the devil troubles, and they are Christians whom Antichrist impugns," *Ne{que} enim quaerit illos, quos iam subegit, aut gestit evertere quos iam suos fecit*: "For he seeks not those whom he has already subdued, or desires to overthrow those whom he has already made his own, the enemy and adversary of the church: whom he has estranged and kept forth of the church, them he neglects and passes by as captives and overcome: those he assaults, in whom he perceives Christ to dwell."

If therefore Antichrist be led by the spirit of Satan, then no doubt he shall pass by both Jews and infidels, and set himself εις τον ναον του θεου,[510] that is, both in the Church of God, and against it, that the unsound he may seduce, and the sound he may persecute. The assumption stands on two parts: [1] affirmative, that the Jews are ready to receive Antichrist. [2] Negative, that the Christians and Gentiles are not ready to receive him.

The former he proves, because the Jews do yet look for their messiah, who shall be a temporal king, such a one as Antichrist shall be. But this reason is built on false suppositions. First, that Antichrist shall be one

---

[509] Epistle 1. Lib. 1
[510] 2 Thessalonians 2:4

particular man, which we have proved to be false. Secondly, that Antichrist shall profess himself to be the messiah of the Jews, which as it has been disproven out of the Scriptures, so can it not with any color of reason be proven out of the same.

For as has been shown, Antichrist is the head of the catholic apostasy or apostate Christians, sitting in Babylon, that is, Rome, professing herself the church of God, being one of the seven heads of the Roman state, succeeding the emperours in the government of Rome, etc. Thirdly, as Antichrist shall not be such a one as the expected messiah of the Jews: so there is no necessity that there should such a one come to the Jews, as they expect.

The second part also of his assumption is false. For although sound and constant Christians are not ready to receive Antichrist, but always have been ready to resist him even unto the death; yet unsound and backsliding Christians, who embrace not the love of the truth that they might be saved, either are as ready to receive Antichrist, as they are apt and prone to decline from the truth (a fearful caveat to those which wax weary of the gospel) or already have revolted from Christ to Antichrist, and have received the mark of the beast.

"Yea, but Christians," says he, "do not expect Antichrist, as the Jews do. The Jews look for him with joy, as for their messiah, but the Christians with fear." I answer, as true Christians look not at all for the expected messiah of the Jews to be Antichrist, but acknowledge him that has come.

So papists, but that they cannot see the wood for trees, might instead of looking for Antichrist, look upon him.

(10) The second thing which Bellarmine delivers concerning Antichrist for a certain truth, is, That Antichrist shall be a Jew both by nation and religion; that is, he shall be a born a Jew, he shall be circumcised, he shall be an observer of the Jews' sabbath, and other Jewish ceremonies. But how is this certain truth proved? Indeed from the premises. For the Jews will not

receive one for their messiah, that is not a Jew born, nor circumcised. Nay, it is not to be doubted, but that as the Jews look for their messiah out of the family of David; so he will feign himself to be of the tribe of David, although indeed he be of the tribe of Dan.

But this popish conceit, built upon their own vain imaginations, needs no answer. For seeing I have overthrown their former assertion, whereupon this is grounded; therefore this building of itself falls to the ground.

- "Whosoever," (says he) "shall be received of the Jews for their messiah, he shall be born and circumcised a Jew."
- But Antichrist shall be received of the Jews for their messiah, as has been proven.
- Therefore Antichrist shall be born a Jew," etc.

The proposition is not altogether true, for the Herodians received Herod for their messiah, and thence had their name.[511] But I will not stand upon that. The assumption I have already disproven, showing that Antichrist was not to be received of the Jews for their messiah, and therefore there is no validity in this argument.

In the next place therefore for want either of reason, or authority of Scripture, he props up this tottering wall with testimonies of fathers; but such as either himself before has rejected, or else in this question may by the same reason be little regarded. "The twelve fathers," (says he) "who affirmed that Antichrist shall be of the tribe of Dan, do therefore hold that he should be born a Jew." But he himself has told us that we are not to believe them, because their opinion cannot be proved out of the Scriptures, and therefore by the same reason, neither they, nor the rest are to be believed in this point, which has no ground in the word of God.

---

[511] Epiphan. lib. 1. de haeresi Iudaeor. 7.

And thus his most evident demonstration has come to nothing. For although the Jews receive not the pope for their messiah, but rather esteem of him as of another Pharaoh, and also apply unto him all that is spoken either of Antichrist, as the papists say, or of the type of Antichrist, Antiochus, as we say (Daniel 7 and 11).[512] This hinders not, but that the pope may be Antichrist. Yea, this may be some inducement to persuade us, that if those things which be spoken of Antichrist, or his type, may in the judgment of the Jews, who are no parties, be applied properly to the pope: that then the pope is that Antichrist, that in Daniel is figured, and in other places of Scripture not unlike to that figure described.

---

[512] Rabbi Levi Gershon (Gersonides)

Chapter 13
Of the seat or See of Antichrist.

(1) Our adversary's sixth disputation is concerning the seat or See of Antichrist, which is concluded in this syllogism:

- Antichrist shall sit at Jerusalem, and not at Rome.
- The pope sits at Rome, and not at Jerusalem.
- Therefore the pope is not Antichrist.

The proposition, concerning which all the controversy is, is first proved by testimonies of Scriptures, and afterwards defended against our objections. His κατασκευή or proof stands on three testimonies of Scripture.

The first is Revelation 11:8, where John says that Enoch and Elijah shall be slain by Antichrist in Jerusalem: "And their bodies shall lie in the streets of the great city, which is called spiritual Sodom or Egypt, where our Lord also was crucified."

But what if John speaks neither of Antichrist, nor of Enoch and Elijah, nor of Jerusalem? that he speaks not of Antichrist, it may be doubted. For in verse 7, he says that the beast which ascends out of the deep (which seems to be the former beast described in the beginning of chapter 13) shall kill the two witnesses. And in verse 2, it is said that the court of the temple should be given to the Gentiles, and that they should tread upon the holy city for 42 months, which is the time allotted to the persecution of the beast with seven heads in Revelation 13:5.

Besides, the papists teach that Antichrist shall be the prince of the Jews and counterfeit Christians, therefore by their own doctrine, this persecution of the Church by the Gentiles, should not be the persecution under Antichrist. And that Enoch and Elijah are not here spoken of, it has been shown before: and thirdly, that the Holy Spirit does not mean Jerusalem, I have heretofore proven.[513]

But suppose that John did speak both of Antichrist, as it seems he does not, and also of Jerusalem, which I am sure he does not. Yet notwithstanding, it does not follow that wherever the witnesses of Christ are put to death by him, or by his authority, that there should be his principal seat. Whereas therefore Bellarmine argues thus:

- Where the two witnesses are put to death, there is the seat of Antichrist.
- At Jerusalem, the two witnesses are put to death.
- Therefore at Jerusalem is the seat of Antichrist.

I answer first to the proposition, that it being generally understood, is false: if particularly, then Bellarmine's argumentation is not a syllogism, but a paralogism. And to the assumption I answer negatively, and that answer I have heretofore made good, proving that not Jerusalem is here meant, but *civitas Romana* (the city and empire of Rome) which everywhere in Revelation is called *the great city*, wherein, and by authority whereof, our Lord was crucified. See the first book, chapter 2, § 16 & 17.

(2) His second testimony is, Revelation 7. 16. whereunto I have answered before in the second chapter of the first book, §. 18. But as from that place he would prove that Rome is not the seat of Antichrist, so by another argument which he adds, he proves that it is Jerusalem. For says he, If Antichrist be a Jew, and profess himself to be the messiah and king of the Jews, then no doubt he will sit in Jerusalem: but the former of these I have disproven in the former chapter, and therefore further answer needs not.

---

[513] Book 1, Chapter 6, Section 17

Yea, but four of the fathers avouch that Antichrist shall sit at Jerusalem. Although they did, yet Bellarmine has taught us that we are not bound to believe them, unless their assertion can be proven out of the Scriptures. And yet of these four fathers which he alleges, Lactantius does not speak of Antichrist. Jerome and Theodoret, where they deliver their own judgment,[514] do not affirm that he shall sit in the temple at Jerusalem, but in the churches of Christ.

(3) His third testimony is 2 Thessalonians 2:4, in so much that he sits in the temple of God. Of which words there be many expositions says Bellarmine: some by *the temple of God* understand the minds of the faithful, in which Antichrist shall sit after he has seduced them, which interpretation agrees fitly to the pope, who only sits as it were a god in the minds of men, prescribing laws to bind the conscience, and that with guilt of mortal sin, as they speak.

Others expound these words of Antichrist and his whole people,[515] who is therefore said to sit *in templum Dei*, because Antichrist shall profess himself with his people, to be the true church of God, which also most fitly agrees to the pope and church of Rome, which vaunt that they alone are the catholic church; and that all others professing the name of Christ which are not subject to the pope, or acknowledge not themselves members of the church of Rome, are heretics or schismatics.

Others by *the temple*,[516] understand the churches of the Christians, which Antichrist shall make subject to himself. The which as we proved it to be the most true exposition, so does it properly agree to the pope of Rome.

Others, by *the temple of God*, understand the temple of God at Jerusalem, wherein Antichrist shall sit, and this (says Bellarmine) is the more common, more probable, and more literal opinion. I doubt not but that it is an opinion

---

[514] Jerome ad Algas. 9. 11. Theodoret. in 2. Thess. 2. & Epitom. 1. Anselm.
[515] Augustine, *City of God*, Book 20 Chapter 19
[516] Chrysostom, etc.

more plausible to the papists, who care not what they hold concerning Antichrist, so long as it does not agree to the pope.

But of these three things which Bellarmine avouches in commendation of this conceit, two are false, and the third is to no purpose. For neither is this exposition more common among the ancient fathers than that other, which by *the temple* understands the churches of the Christians, which heretofore we have shown to have been the judgment of Theodoret, Jerome, Chrysostom, Theophylact, Oecumenius, etc.[517] And although it were the more common exposition, yet that would not prove it to be more true, for truth goes not by voices, neither is to be weighed by multitude of suffrages, but by weight of reason.

Neither is it more probable, for if the temple shall never be reedified, as has been shown, then is there no probability that Antichrist should sit in it. Neither were that material, though it were more literal, unless the literal were usual. For in all the epistles by the temple of God is meant *the church*, and there is an usual metonymy between the words which signify either the assembly, or the place of the assembly. So ναος, which signifies the place, is often used for the assembly or church: and *ecclesia*, that is, church, is often used for the place.[518] Neither can the temple erected by Antichrist be truly called the temple of God.

"Yea but," says Bellarmine, "in the Scripture of the New Testament, by *the temple of God* are never understood the churches, that is to say, the temples of Christians."

The more absurd is he to understand this place of a material temple, contrary to the usual acceptance of the word in the writings of the apostles. The apostle therefore by *temple*, does not not a material temple of wood and stone, but a spiritual temple compact of living stones: and by sitting in the temple, not a corporal gesture, for Antichrist is to sit there as God, that is, he

---

[517] Book 1 Chapter 4 Section 15
[518] 1 Corinthians 3:16-17, 2 Corinthians 6:16, Ephesians 2:21, Revelation 3:12

is to rule and reign in the church of God, as if he were a god upon earth. But of this whole matter, see more in the first book, chapter 2. § 13, 14 & 15.

(4) Now let us come to his disproof of our assertion, who hold that Antichrist shall sit not at Jerusalem but at Rome, and in Rome professing herself the church of God.

Firstly, by a fond cavillation [objection] wherein he greatly pleases himself, he seeks to drive us to an absurdity. "For," (says he) "if Antichrist shall sit in the church of God, and if the pope be Antichrist, then the church wherein the pope sits is the true church. And consequently the Protestants and all others that are not of that church, are out of the church, etc."

This cavil is to be resolved into three syllogisms:

- Antichrist sits in the Church of Christ.
- The pope of Rome is Antichrist.
- "Therefore," says Bellarmine, "the pope sits in the true church of Christ."

But he might as well conclude thus:

- He that professes the name of Christ is a Christian.
- The papist, the Anabaptist, the Familist, etc., all profess the name of Christ.
- Therefore the papist, the Anabaptist, and the Familist are all true Christians.

But has not Bellarmine learned so much logic as not to foist into the conclusion, that which is not contained in the premises? The word *true* is not contained in the premises, and therefore sophistically thrust into the conclusion.

For Antichrist may sit in the church, although not in the true church. Generally the church of Christ signifies the company of Christians, that is, of those that profess the name of Christ. But as of Christians, some are only in title and profession, some indeed and in truth: so of churches, some are only in title and profession churches of Christ, others are his true churches.

Now Antichrist he was to be an apostate, and the head of the catholic apostasy: therefore the church whereof Antichrist is the head, although it be in title and profession a church of Christ, as being a company of them that are christened, and profess the name of Christ: yet it is but an apostatical church; a church which of a faithful city is become an harlot; and of the true Church of God, the whore of Babylon. But may not this absurdity rather be returned upon the papists, who by *the temple of God* in 2 Thessalonians 2:4 understand that temple which Antichrist shall build at Jerusalem?

- Antichrist shall sit in the temple of God, says the apostle.
- Antichrist shall sit in that temple which himself shall build at Jerusalem, says the papist.
- Therefore that temple which he shall build at Jerusalem shall be indeed the temple of God.

Whereas in truth according to their own conceits, it were rather to be called *the temple of the devil*. If any man object that it might after a sort be called *the temple of God*, because the temple of God did stand there, and because Antichrist will pretend to make it to the honor of God, whereunto the former temple was erected, I answer by the like reason the church of Rome may be called *the church of God*, because once it was a true church, and still is in title and profession the church of Christ – although in truth it is but little more *the church of Christ* than Antichrist's imaginary temple at Jerusalem would be *the temple of God*.

(5) His second syllogism which is inferred upon the former is this:

- If the pope sits in the true church of God then the church of Rome is the only true church (for the church of Christ is one as Christ is one).
- But the pope sits in the true church of God, as was proven in the former syllogism.
- Therefore the church of Rome is the only true church of Christ.

First, I answer to the proof of his proposition:

- The catholic and invisible church of Christ is one sheepfold under one shepherd Christ; but particular and visible churches are more than one, as the church of Corinth, the church of Rome, the seven churches in Revelation, and all the churches of the Gentiles mentioned in Romans 16:4, and therefore the church of Rome, although it were a true visible church, yet were it but a particular church, and therefore not the only true church.
- But now the church of Rome is not a true visible church of Christ, but the whore of Babylon, an adulterous, idolatrous, and apostate church, which once was Rome, as Petrarch says, now Babylon; once Bethel, now Bethaven; once the church of Christ, now the synagogue of Antichrist, as has been proven.
- And therefore, there being no truth either in the proposition, or the assumption, I answer the proposition in this way: although the pope did sit in the true church, yet it does not follow that therefore the church of Rome is the only true church, and the assumption by this – that the pope does not sit in the true church – and therefore there is no show of reason in this cavil.

(6) His third syllogism is inferred upon the second:

- If the church of Rome be the only true church, then those which are not members of this church, whereof the pope is head, as namely the Protestants, are out of the church.
- But now (say I) the church of Rome is so far from being the only true church, as that it is that Babylon (Revelation 18:4), from which we are commanded to separate, if we will be saved: there being no salvation in that Church for those that receive and retain the mark of the beast (Revelation 14:9).
- Therefore this also is a fond and sophistical cavil.

Notwithstanding, as the adulterous and apostate state of Israel under Jeroboam and Ahab, so the church of Rome under the pope, may be called the church of God, in respect both of some notes and signs of a visible church, as the administration of some sacraments and profession of the name of the Lord, and also of some relics and remainder, as it were the gleanings of the invisible church.

In Israel, although an apostate and idolatrous state, the sacrament of circumcision was retained: so in the church of Rome, the sacrament of baptism. The church of Israel professed Jehovah to be their God, although they worshiped him idolatrously: so the church of Rome professes the name of Christ, but exceeds Israel in idolatry. In Israel, even under Ahab the Lord had reserved 7,000 who never bowed their knee to Baal, and so we doubt not, but that in the corruptest times of popery, the Lord has reserved some who have not received the mark of the beast.

And as the church of Sardis was still called *the church of Christ*, although grievously fallen from Christ, because they still professed the name of Christ, and retained no doubt the sacrament of baptism, and had among them some few names that had not defiled themselves: so I confess with Calvin, that the church of Rome may be called a church of Christ, both in respect of some vestigia and outward notes of a visible church, as administration of baptism, and profession of the name of Christ, and some secret relics of the invisible church, which have not bowed their knees to Baal.[519]

But that which is said to the church of Sardis, may most justly be avowed to the church of Rome. "Thou hast a name that thou livest, but indeed art dead"[520] – Thou professest thyself to be the church of Christ, but art the synagogue of Antichrist:[521] thou art called the church of Rome, which once was famous for her says, but art the whore of Babylon, the mother of all the fornications, and abominations in the Christian world.

(7) Here Bellarmine objects two things: If there remains in the church of Rome but ruins and relics of a true church, then the church may be destroyed, and the truth has lied, who says that the gates of hell shall never prevail against it.

Answer: The catholic and invisible church of Christ, which is the whole company of the elect, can never fail. But visible and particular churches which consist of hypocrites many times and unsound Christians (which are in the visible church, but are not of the invisible) as the greater part, may fail and fall away, although not one sound Christian that is of the invisible church does fall away.[522] As the lamentable experience of the church of Israel severed from Judah, the examples of Corinth, Ephesus, and many other famous Churches, which were planted by the apostles.

Again says Bellarmine: "If the church is destroyed, and the ruins remain in popery, then the papists have the church, although decayed and ruinated, but the Protestants have no church: not entire, for the entire church is ruinated; not ruinated or decayed, for the ruins are among the papists. What

---

[519] Revelation 20:4
[520] Revelation 3:1
[521] Revelation 3:4
[522] 1 John 2:19

have they then? A new building, which because it is new, is none of Christ's, and therefore who sees not, that it is safer to live in the church decayed, then in no church at all?"

But in this cavil there is not so much as any show of reason, unless he takes that for granted (which we do most confidently deny, and they are never able to prove) that the Church of Rome not only is the true church of Christ, but also the only true church. For otherwise the church of Rome may fall, and yet the catholic church of Christ may stand, yea, shall stand, maugre the force of Antichrist, and malice of Satan himself.

And as for the church of the Protestants, it is no new building, as Antichrist vaunts, but is a part of the catholic church of Christ, reformed and renewed according to the word of God, and the example of the primitive church: even as the Church of Judah under Josiah, was no new building, but the old frame, as it was under David, renewed and reformed according to the law of God.

(8) The exceptions which he takes against our arguments, concluding that Rome is the seat of Antichrist, I have for the most part taken away before.[523] It shall suffice therefore now, to answer those which before were not touched. That Rome is the seat of Antichrist we prove, because it is mystical Babylon, situated on seven hills, and having dominion over the kings of the earth, etc. Bellarmine – among other answers before refuted – says that by *mystical Babylon* we are to understand heathen Rome, not Rome christened, because John speaks of that Rome which had dominion over the kings of the earth, and which is said to be drunk with the blood of the saints and martyrs of Jesus.

I answer, that although these notes agreed not to popish Rome, yet we might understand the apostle thus, that that city which then had dominion over the kings of the earth, and then persecuted the saints, is called Babylon:

---

[523] Book 1 Chapter 2

because it was to be the seat or See of Antichrist. But now these notes agree also to popish Rome, both in respect of dominion usurped more insolently over the kings of the earth by the pope, then by any emperor, and in regard of most cruel persecution of the saints of Christ, as before has been shown.

(9) Again, whereas we prove that Antichrist shall sit in the church of God because the apostle says "he shall sit in the temple of God," and also affirms that this cannot be understood of the Temple of Jerusalem, which now is utterly destroyed, and is no more to be reedified, as Daniel testifies in chapter 9 verse 27.

He answers that Daniel would say something that he does not say: either that the temple should not be reedified until a little before the end of the world. But Daniel does not say until a little before the end: but as their own translation reads, *Vs{que} ad consummationem and finem perseverabit desolatio*, "the desolation shall continue until the consummation and end;" or as Jerome says, *Vs{que} ad finem mundi*, "unto the end of the world;" or as others, *Vs{que} ad consummationem eam{que} praecisam*.

As it is said of Michal (2 Samuel 6:23) that she had no child until the day of her death. And of Joseph, that he knew not Mary until she had brought forth her first begotten son (Matthew 1:25), and of Christ, that he will be with the faithful until the end of the world (Matthew 28:20). Not that Michal at her death, or a little before had children; not that Joseph ever knew Mary; nor that Christ will ever forsake the faithful, so that this word *until* in the Scriptures signifies rather perpetuity than cessation before the time, which seems thereby to be limited.

Whereas therefore Daniel says that the temple should lie desolate until the end and consummation of the world, it is as much as if he had said, that it should never be reedified. Or if that were not Daniel's meaning, then he must say, that although the temple should be built again, yet as it was desolate before it be built, so afterward the abomination of desolation, that is, Antichrist or his image, should remain in it to the end.

Yea, but the primitive church believed that the temple should never be built again, and held this assertion of the papists as a Jewish fable. And as touching the abomination of desolation,[524] it has been shown that our Savior Christ by a metonymy understands thereby the armies of the Romans, who in respect of their paganism were abominable, and in regard of their effect desolations, such as brought upon Jerusalem the final destruction and desolation. Daniel says *per alam detestationum desolantem* by a synecdoche for *per legiones* etc. as Isaiah 8:8.

Or lastly, this must be Daniel's meaning, that the temple shall never perfectly be reedified, but that the reedifying is to be begun, and that in the temple so begun, Antichrist shall sit. Thus shamefully, the wilful patrons of error stick not to draw the Scripture to their fancies, not caring to conform their judgment to the Scripture. Daniel in that place speaks not a word of Antichrist, nor yet of Antiochus his type, but of the utter desolation and final destruction of Jerusalem by the Romans. And of this desolation, according to their own translation, he says that it should continue to the end and consummation: that is, (says Bellarmine) "the temple shall never perfectly be built again, but yet it shall be built again, and in it being so built, Antichrist shall sit."

Built how? Is it like that Antichrist, who shall according to their conceit be the most mighty prince and monarch in the world, that he, I say, will suffer that temple which he chooses for his chief seat, to be unbuilt? Or that so great and so proud a monarch will sit in a temple without a roof or unfinished, professing the same also to be his principal seat? Why but Christ says, the destruction of the temple should be such as that one stone should not be left upon another; and Daniel says according to their own translation, that this desolation of the temple should continue to the end. How then can his meaning be, that it should be reedified – either in whole or in part?

---

[524] Luke 21:20 & Matthew 24:15

The stories also of the church[525] do testify that as Daniel and our Savior Christ had foretold the final destruction and desolation of Jerusalem, so when Julian the Apostate, desiring to convince the preaching of our Savior of untruth, endeavored by the Jews to re-edify the temple, the Lord – to verify his word – would not suffer it to be built either in whole, or in part, but by a fearful earthquake overthrew the foundations, by fire from heaven burnt the tools of the work-men, by wind and tempest scattered the lime and mortar, and by fire proceeding out of the earth burnt the workmen as they digged.

Jerusalem and the temple were types of the church of Christ. Therefore when by the preaching of the gospel to all nations the church of Christ was planted among the Gentiles, the city and temple were to have an end, as our Savior has prophesied in (Matthew 24:14), then shall be the end, to wit, of the city and temple of Jerusalem: which being once overthrown by the legions of the Romans, should according to Daniel's prophecy remain desolate until the end of the world, or as our Savior foretold in other words, that Jerusalem should be trodden underfoot of the Gentiles, until the times of the Gentiles be fulfilled.[526]

(10) Lastly, whereas Theodore Bibliander proves by the testimony of Gregory the Great that Antichrist was to sit in the church,[527] and to exercise an universal dominion over the same, because Gregory says that John of Constantinople challenging the title of *universal bishop*, therein was the forerunner of Antichrist. And secondly, because he says that an army of priests were prepared for Antichrist, thereby signifying that he should be a prince of priests.

Bellarmine answers that the contrary is to be inferred upon Gregory's words. For the forerunner must not be equal to him, whose forerunner he is, but less and inferior. If therefore John of Constantinople, who was the

---

[525] Socrat. li. 3 c. 20., Theodores li.3 ca.20, Sozomus li.5 cap.ult
[526] Luke 21:24
[527] Lib. 4, Epist. 38

forerunner of Antichrist, challenged the title of *universal bishop*, Antichrist himself shall challenge greater matters, and shall advance himself above all that is called God.

But I reply that, although the pride and ambition of John of Constantinople was very great and Antichristian, yet it was not to be compared with the incredible insolence and pride of the Antichrist of Rome. John of Constantinople sought a superiority over all other Bishops, but challenged not that height of authority and sovereignty which the popes since have usurped, not only over bishops and ecclesiastical persons, but also over the kings and monarchies of the earth. Neither has the Antichristian pride of the pope rested here, but as I have shown heretofore, in some things he matches himself with Christ, in some things he advances himself above him, and above all that is called God.[528]

To the second, Bellarmine answers that it was not Gregory's meaning that priests as they are priests belong to the army of Antichrist, but as they are proud. "But hence it does not follow," says he, *Antichristum fore principem sacerdotum, sed fore principem superborum*: "that Antichrist shall be the prince of priests, but that he shall be the prince of proud men: shameless, and yet ridiculous."

Does it not follow, that if he is the prince of priests as they are proud, that he is the prince of proud priests, such as the whole hierarchy of Rome consists of? It follows therefore upon our arguments, notwithstanding all his cavils, that Antichrist was to have his chief seat in Rome, and in Rome professing herself the church of God, but being indeed the whore of Babylon.

---

[528] Book 1 Chapter 5

Chapter 14
Concerning the doctrine of Antichrist.

(1) Our adversary's seventh disputation is concerning the doctrine of Antichrist. "For whereas it is certain," says Bellarmine, "that there are four principal doctrines of Antichrist, none whereof is taught by the pope; therefore it follows necessarily, that the pope is not Antichrist."

I answer that there are more doctrines of Antichrist that false prophet than four, among which those two doctrines of devils which are mentioned by the apostle in 1 Timothy 4 as notes of that catholic apostasy, whereof Antichrist is the head, are to be numbered, forbidding marriage, and commanding abstinence from meats. But yet not all these four are the doctrines of Antichrist, and those which are, do not unfitly agree to the pope, as shall appear in the particulars, which we are to examine in order. For from these four doctrines, Bellarmine fetches four arguments.

The first is that:

- Antichrist shall deny Jesus to be Christ, and consequently shall oppugn all the ordinances of our Savior, as baptism, confirmation, etc. and shall teach that circumcision, the sabbath, and other ceremonies of the old law are not yet ceased.
- But the pope does not deny Jesus to be Christ, nor bring in circumcision instead of Baptism, nor the Sabbath instead of the Lord's day, etc.
- Therefore the pope is not Antichrist.

The proposition – and so also the assumption – has two parts, the former concerning the denial of Christ itself, the second concerning the consequents thereof.[529] Of the former, I have sufficiently spoken heretofore:

---

[529] Book 1 Chapter 4 Sections 6-8

proving evidently that as Antichrist was to deny Christ, so the pope does not in deed only, but in word also and doctrine, although not openly directly and expressly (for Antichrist was not to be an open and professed enemy), yet covertly, indirectly, and by consequence. And of such denying of Christ, Bellarmine himself in this chapter understands John to speak in the place by him alleged for the proof of his proposition.[530]

(2) But perceiving that this expression will not clear the pope of Antichristianism he affirms that Antichrist is to deny Christ simply, and openly, and by all means. This bold assertion, I have hereto sufficiently disproved, when I proved that Antichristianism is as the apostle calls it, a mystery of iniquities; and that Antichrist is a covert and disguised enemy who under the name and profession of Christianity denies, yea oppugns, Christ and his truth.

But let us weigh his reasons. The first whereof has all his weight from such assertions as we have before proven to than vanity itself: and it is thus concluded:

- He that is shall in nation and religion a Jew, and shall be received of the Jews for their messiah shall oppugn Christ, and teach that our Christ is not the messiah.
- But Antichrist shall be in nation and religion and shall be received of the Jews for their messiah, as before has been shown.
- Therefore he shall oppugn Christ openly, etc.

I answer first to the proposition and assumption jointly, that there is no necessity nor yet likelihood that there should come to the Jews such a one as they expect; and yet Bellarmine everywhere takes this for granted. But the

---

[530] 1 John 2:22

assumption I have proved heretofore to be a new fable,[531] and therefore further answer is superfluous.

3 The second argument is gathered out of 1 John 2:22: "Who is a liar, but he that denieth Jesus to be Christ, and this is Antichrist." For all heretics (says he) are called *antichrists*, which any way deny Jesus to be Christ. Therefore the true Antichrist himself shall simply and by all means deny Jesus to be Christ. And this is proven because by the heretics, the devil is said to work the mystery of iniquity, because they deny Christ covertly, but the coming of Antichrist is called a *revelation*, because he shall openly deny Christ.

I answer first, that John in that place speaks neither of the body of Antichrist in general (as elsewhere in his epistles the word ι αντιχριστοι is used) nor of the head of that body in particular, who is most worthily called ο αντιχριστος the Antichrist; but of some other members of that body, that is to say, of those antichrists or heretics of that time, as Cerinthus and others, who denied the divinity of Christ; and denying the Son, did consequently also deny the Father, for he is the Father of the Son, as appears plainly by that which follows in the text ουτος εστιν ο αντιχριστος ο αρνουμενος τον πατερα και τον υιον: "This is that Antichrist that denieth the Father and the Son."

Secondly, the difference between the petty antichrists and the grand Antichrist, is not in respect of the covert and open denial of Christ; or if there be a difference to be made in this behalf, it is in this, that diverse heretics and petty antichrists, such as Simon Magus and some others, have denied Jesus to be Christ more plainly and directly, which the grand Antichrist according to his greater cunning and efficacy of deceit (coming as the apostle says, εν παση απατη της αδικιας, in all deceivableness of iniquity)[532] was to deny more cunningly and covertly. But the difference is

---

[531] Chapter 12
[532] 2 Thessalonians 2:10

both in respect of the apostasy and opposition against Christ, and also in regard to the ambition and advancing of themselves.

The apostasy and opposition may be considered either in respect of the parts and points wherein it consists, or in respect of the parties which make it. In both respects, the apostasy and opposition of the petty antichrists is but particular, that is, of few men in few things: but the apostasy and opposition of the grand Antichrist is more catholic and general, that is, in the most parts of Christianity, and of the greatest part of Christendom.

Likewise, the ambition of petty antichrists is to seek preeminence with Diotrephes in particular churches, and over some other men.[533] But the grand Antichrist claims an universal sovereignty over all men, and a double monarchy over all the world: and not contented to advance himself above all other men, even kings and emperors, and that by many degrees; but in many things also matches himself with Christ the King of Kings, and in some things advances himself above him. Yea, but this difference between the small Antichrists and the great Antichrist is proven, because by the small Antichrists or heretics, Satan is said to work the mystery of iniquity, whereas the coming of Antichrist is called a revelation.

The mystery of iniquity (2 Thessalonians 2:7) is Antichristianism, or that Antichristian apostasy from Christ mentioned in verse 3, which is therefore called a mystery of iniquity, because it being a devilish opposition unto Christ, is cunningly cloaked under the profession of Christ. This mystery as it was a working in the apostles' time in the heretics and petite antichrists by degrees: so was it more fully wrought and accomplished in Antichrist himself, the head of the catholic apostasy: under whom it deserved so much the more to be called the mystery of iniquity, as it masked under more glorious shows and visards of outward profession, and shrouded itself under the name and title of the catholic and only true visible church.

---

[533] 3 John 9: ο φιλοπρωτευων αυτων

The mystery therefore of iniquity, which in the former part of this Antithesis is appropriated unto heretics, does indeed most truly belong to Antichrist himself; and therefore if it be called a *mystery* because it is a covert and cunning denial of Christ. Then under the grand Antichrist, Christ shall be most cunningly denied, when he is most gloriously professed.

Now Antichrist is said to be revealed, when the head of the Antichristian body is manifested, and of this revelation there be degrees; the first his showing of himself in his colors, by challenging and usurping an universal supremacy and sovereignty over all the world; and secondly his acknowledgement after he was come to his full growth, of which we have heretofore spoken. It appears therefore that Antichrist was not to deny Christ plainly and openly; and consequently, that the first part of his proposition (whereupon the latter is inferred) is false.

(4) The latter part of his proposition is that Antichrist shall abolish all the ordinances of Christ, and in their stead, bring in the ceremonies of the Jews, as circumcision instead of baptism, and the Jewish sabbath instead of the Lord's day. But how is this proven? because he shall openly deny Christ, and shall in nation and religion be a Jew. But as both these assertions have been proved false: so are we to think of this which is inferred upon them.

For seeing he was to be a disguising hypocrite, and his religion a mystery of iniquity: it cannot be thought that he sitting in the temple of God; and professing the name of Christ, should abolish all his ordinances; but rather that he would deprive and corrupt them, and take away the right use thereof, by devilish doctrines, by superstitious idolatries, by mixture of Jewish and heathen ceremonies. But both the parts of his proposition he seeks further to prove by testimonies of fathers, and by reason. The testimonies of the fathers in this question deserve no further credit than as they conspire with the prophecies of Scripture, and agree with the event. But let us examine them severally.

First Hillary is alleged as though he testified, that whereas the Arians affirmed that Christ is not the son of God by nature, but only by adoption: the Antichrist shall teach that he is not so much as the adoptive son of God. But if you read the place, you shall find that Hillary applies the speech of John in 1 John 2:22 to those heretics who professing Christ to be their Savior, but denying him to be the natural Son of God, and consequently denying him to be Christ, affirmed that he is the adoptive Son of God: and therefore infers out of that place of John, that they cannot avoid, but that they are Antichrist. Wherefore the Antichrist, of whom Hillary speaks, confesses the name of Christ; neither does he deny him openly and directly, but indirectly and by consequent.[534]

The next authority of Hippolytus is counterfeit,[535] and the testimony here alleged as currant (that the mark of Antichrist shall be *nego baptismum, nego signum crucis*: "I deny baptism, I deny the sign of the cross"), heretofore has been rejected by Bellarmine himself, and refuted as false in chapter 11, where he has taught that there is but one mark of the beast, and that not a privative (as this is) but a positive mark, which is not yet known.

Thirdly, he alleges Augustine,[536] as though he affirmed that Antichrist should suffer none to be baptized. Yet Augustine speaks not of Antichrist, but of the devil, and affirms, that even then when the devil shall be loosed, many shall be added to the church: and that the devil himself being loosed, shall not be able to hinder baptism, but surely so valiant shall be both the parents for the baptizing of their children, and also those which shall then first believe, that they shall overcome that strong one being unbound. The speech of Jerome on Daniel 11, if it deserves credit, it must be taken either as a prophecy itself, or else a true exposition of Daniel's prophesy in verses 21 and 22. But Jerome was no prophet.

---

[534] Lib. 6. *De Trinit.* Fol 102
[535] De consummat. mundi
[536] Augustine, *City of God*, Book 20 Chapter 8

And Daniel's speech undoubtedly is to be understood of Antiochus Epiphanes, to whom this exposition (if it were good) should literally agree. But Antiochus did not rise of the Jews, neither did he feign himself to be the prince of the covenant. And for further answer, and better understanding of the place, read Polanus on Daniel 11.[537] If Sedulius affirm as Bellarmine cites him, that Antichrist shall restore all the ceremonies of the Jews, his speech is incredible, for many of them cannot be observed but in the Temple, which shall never be reedified. If he speak of many, it may be verified of the pope, and of some other heretics, who notwithstanding have not openly denied Christ.

Gregory in the same place which Bellarmine alleges, does affirm that Antichrist shall have in reverence not only the Sabbath day, but also the Lord's day; which cannot stand with such an open denial of Christ as Bellarmine imagines.[538] His words are these: *Qui veniens diem Sabbati atq dominicum ab omni faciet opere custoderi*: "Who when he comes (speaking of Antichrist) shall cause the Sabbath day, and the Lord's day, to be kept from all work." And of this, there may better reason be given, then of the other, because (as has been proven) Antichrist was to be a pretended Christian.

(5) These were his authorities; now let us weigh his reason, which is thus concluded. In whose time the public service of God, and divine sacrifices shall cease by reason of the vehement persecution, he shall openly deny Christ, and shall abolish all his ordinances, and instead of them, bring in Jewish ceremonies: But in Antichrist's time, by reason of the vehement persecution, the public service of God, and divine sacrifices shall cease; therefore, etc.

I answer by distinction: if by *the service of God*, he means the true worship of God, then the proposition is untrue. For in the papacy, the true public worship of God, by reason of the vehemency of persecution has

---

[537] Polanus on Daniel 11:21-22, in 2 Thessalonians 2
[538] Lib. 11 Epist. 3

ceased, and yet the pope does not openly deny Christ and abolish his ordinances, although he do vilely deprive them, and mingle them not only with Jewish, but also heathen ceremonies.

If by *the public service* and *divine sacrifices*, he meanes generally any service of God, although superstitious, any sacrifices although idolatrous (such as is the sacrifice, of the mass) then the assumption is false: for such superstitions and will-worships do best beseem Antichrist.

But of this argument concerning the persecution of Antichrist, we have spoken before in chapter 7.

(6) This may suffice for an answer to his proposition and the proofs thereof. Whereas therefore he assumes that the pope does not deny Christ, etc. I answer: if he means a direct denial in open profession, that the pope may be Antichrist, although he does not so deny Christ.

If he means a denial of Christ in deed and in truth, although covertly, indirectly, and by consequent, I have heretofore proved that he does so deny Christ, not only in word and doctrine, as he is a false Prophet, but also in deed and fact, as he is a man of sin, denying him in his life, and as he is an adversary, not only denying, but also oppugning Christ and his truth. See Book 1, Chapter 4, Sections 6-8.

(7) The second doctrine of Antichrist, says Bellarmine, is to affirm himself to be the true Christ. From whence he gathers his second argument:

- Antichrist shall affirm himself to be Christ.
- The pope does not affirm himself to be Christ.
- Therefore the pope is not Antichrist.

That Antichrist being *hostis & amulus Christi*, (that is, an enemy of Christ opposed unto him, in emulation of like honor) shall indeed challenge unto himself those offices, prerogatives, and authority which properly belong to Christ (which in effect is as much as if he should say, I am Christ) we deny not: and withal avouch that the pope of Rome does so affirm himself to be Christ. But that Antichrist shall openly and in so many words expressly affirm that he is the Christ or Messiah of the world, that we deny to be agreeable to that Antichrist, who is described in the word of God. For Antichrist was to be a dissembling hypocrite, as has been proved, and his religion is a mystery of iniquity cloaked under the profession of Christianity. Neither could he seduce so many Christians, if he should plainly and openly profess himself to be the true Christ.

But let us see how Bellarmine proves that Antichrist shall openly and expressly name himself Christ. Indeed out of John 5:43: "If another come in his own name, him will you receive," "Where," says he, "our Lord seems of purpose to have added these words (in his own name) foreseeing that the Lutherans and Calvinists would say, that Antichrist shall not come in his own name, but in the name of Christ as being his vicar."

But I have heretofore proved, that Christ in this place does not speak absolutely another shall come, but conditionally, if another shall come, nor definitely of Antichrist, but indefinitely of any false prophet that should come in his own name, not sent of God.

Neither does it follow that if Antichrist shall come in his own name, that therefore he will profess himself to be Christ. For all false prophets come in their own name, because they are not sent of God, and yet the most of them have not professed themselves to be Christ. And it is plain that our Savior Christ in this place makes an opposition between himself and every false prophet in this respect, that he came unto them in the name of his Father, that is, not taking upon himself this honor to be our prophet and priest, without authority and commission from God, but sent from the bosom of his Father, and yet was not received of the Jews. *But if another*, meaning any other false prophet, *should come unto them not in the name of the Father, but in his own name*, that is, having no commission or authority from God, such a one should be embraced of them.

And further we are to consider, that Christ, professing himself to be the Messiah, seems to deny that he came in his own name, (for he signifies that false prophets come in their own name, but he came in the name of the Father) therefore to come in his own name, signifies to come of himself, without any calling or commission from God. And therefore our adversaries cannot with any show of reason conclude out of this place, that Antichrist shall profess himself to be Christ. And yet this is all the proof which he can bring out of the Scriptures.

Yea, but though the Scriptures teach no such matter, Yet some of the Fathers affirm, that Antichrist shall profess himself to be Christ. Yea, but Bellarmine has told us, that we are not to give credit to such conjectures of theirs, as having no ground in the word of God. For how could they, being no prophets, certainly foretell such things of Antichrist without book, that is to say, without warrant of the Scriptures. And whereas he adds what these fathers affirm – that he shall be received of the Jews for their messiah, and therefore shall profess himself to be the messiah – I answer, that in like sort a dozen of them affirmed that Antichrist should come of the tribe of Dan, whereof notwithstanding there is no probability.

(8) To the proposition therefore, I answer that Antichrist was not plainly and openly to profess himself to be Christ, but to challenge the office and authority of Christ, which is in effect although indirectly and by consequent, as much as if he said I am Christ. To the assumption I answer, that although the pope does not plainly and directly say, I am Christ, but forbears the name of Christ, as Caesar did the name of a king: yet notwithstanding, in that he challenges the office and authority of Christ, it is as much in deed and in truth, although indirectly and by consequent, as if he made himself Christ, Christ being a name of office. For certainly whosoever professes himself to

be the foundation, the head, the husband, and lord, etc. of the universal church, he makes himself Christ, even if he abstains from the name.

For who is the head and Lord, etc. of the universal church, but Christ? Who has authority to ordain sacraments, to prescribe laws to the conscience, to deliver doctrines and articles of faith as necessary to salvation, to forgive the sins of the quick and the dead? Who is the Prince of Priests, the great Priest after the order of Melchizedek, the Pastor of Pastors, the King of Kings, and Lord of Lords, by whom kings and emperors do reign, who has authority to command the angels, to bestow the kingdom of heaven on whom he pleases. Finally, unto whom is all power given in heaven and in earth, but only to Christ?

But the pope does challenge all this to himself, and much more, as has been shown.[539] He indeed is the foundation, the head, husband and Lord of the universal church, etc. And to conclude, if you respect his nature, *Atque ac Christus Deus est ens secundae intentionis, compositum ex Deo & homine*:[540] As well as Christ he is God, an essence of the second intention, compounded of God and man: if his office, *vnctione Christus est*, he is by anointing Christ, having the very same office which Christ had when he was upon the earth. And therefore if this be a property of Antichrist to leave unto our Savior the name and title of Christ, and to take to himself the dignity, office, and authority of Christ, it cannot be avoided but that the pope is Antichrist.

(9) The third doctrine of Antichrist (says Bellarmine) is this: "He shall affirm himself to be God, and will require that he may be worshiped as God." From whence he reasons thus:

- Antichrist will affirm that he is God, and will be worshiped for God.

---

[539] Book 1 Chapter 5
[540] Bellarmine, *De Pontif. Rom.* Lib. 5, Cap. 4

- The pope of Rome does not affirm himself to be God, neither would be worshiped as God.
- Therefore the pope is not Antichrist.

The proposition is proven out of 2 Thessalonians 2:4, so that he sits in the temple of God, showing himself as though he were God.

Answer: The meaning of the apostle's words is thus much: that Antichrist shall sit in the temple of God, as God, that is, he shall rule and reign in the church of God, as if he were a God upon earth, showing himself not so much by words as by deeds, that he is a God. Or as the vulgar Latin edition and English translation of the Rhemists do read, *tanquam sit Deus*: as though he were God.

And thus Chrysostom, Theophylact, and Oecumenius, expound this place. Chrysostom says: "He says *showing himself*, he said not, *saying*, but endeavoring to show, for he shall work great works, and shall show forth wonderful signs." and the word αποδεικνυντα: *showing*, as Beza observes, is answerable to the Hebrew *Moreh* – *faciens se apparere, prae se ferens*, or as we say, *taking upon him as if he were a God*.

It is not therefore necessary that Antichrist should in word plainly and openly profess himself to be God: it is sufficient, if in deed and behavior he takes upon him as if he were a god. As for example, if he shall be content to be acknowledged, saluted and called *God*. If he shall cause, nay, if he shall but willingly suffer himself to be worshiped as God, if he shall challenge unto himself those titles, attributes, and works which are proper and peculiar to the Lord.

But Bellarmine perceives that this place in this sense may fitly be applied to the pope, and therefore he contends that it is not sufficient that Antichrist should indeed show himself to be God (as the pope does) but that he shall *openly* name himself God, and that he shall usurp, not only some authority of

God (as the pope does) but also the very name of God. And that he says is proved out of these words of the apostle in 2 Thessalonians 2, in so much that "he sitteth in the temple of God, showing himself *tanquā sit Deus*, as though he were God." Where says he Paul does not only affirm that Antichrist shall sit in the temple (for we also sit in temples, and yet are no antichrists), but also expounds his manner of sitting, namely that he shall sit as God: to whom alone a temple is properly erected. And this he says is more clearly set down in the Greek text: for it is not said ως Θεός: *as God*, but οτι εστιν θεος: *that he is God*. But in this cavil are contained several errors:

[1] By *temple*, which as we have proved, signifies the church of God, he understands a material temple, which should be built at Jerusalem.

[2] By *sitting in the temple*, which signifies his reigning in the church, he understands the corporal gesture of sitting in that material temple.

[3] By his *sitting in the temple of God as God*, which signifies his ruling over the church as if he were God, he understands thus much, that the material temple should be erected and consecrated to his honor, as if he were God. As though that temple which should be erected to his honor, as if he and no other were the true God, were called of the apostle *the temple of God*: or as though he pretending himself to be the messiah of the Jews sent from God, would not also pretend the building of that temple to the honor of God.

[4] Whereas he says that the Greek text has not ως but οτι, it is plain that the text has both. "In so much that he sitteth in the temple of God ως θεον as God, showing himself οτι εστιν θεος, that he is God." Now Antichrist may sit in the temple of God as God, and by his deeds and demeanor bear the world in hand that he is a god upon earth, and yet not profess himself openly and plainly to be God.

(10) And in this sense (to come to his assumption) does this place properly agree to the pope of Rome, who sits in the temple of God as God, that is, rules in the church of God as if he were a God upon earth: and in his

behavior and course of life, takes upon him as if he were a God and so would be reputed of others.

For first in their own law the pope is not obscurely called *God*.[541] The Canonists call him *Dominū Deum nostrum Papam*, Our Lord God the pope. But for further proof of this point, I refer you to the former book, chap. 5 §. 6. etc. where I entreated of the Antichristian pride of the pope.

To which former testimonies I will add one practice of the pope in his great year of jubilee, when as in solemn procession he is carried in a seat of gold upon noble men's shoulders (his god of bread being carried before him upon a hackney as his attendant) and at length comes to the gates of paradise, which he beats open with a golden hammer, at which time he is worshiped of all sorts present as a God, from whom they expect indulgence, remission of sins and eternal life, according to his large promises made to all those which shall come to Rome to celebrate the jubilee. In a word, he is *numen quoddam visibilem quendam Deum pre se ferens*, a certain divine majesty showing himself to be a certain visible god.

The premises therefore considered, together with my allegations in the place before named,[542] this argument may be returned upon our adversary after this manner:

- Whosoever sits in the temple of God as God, that is, rules and reigns over the church as if he were a god upon earth, and declares himself either by word or deed that he is God – for example, if he shall challenge unto himself those titles, attributes and works which are proper unto God, and shall be willing to be saluted, acknowledged and adored as God – he undoubtedly is Antichrist.

---

[541] Dist. 96 c. satis euidenter
[542] Book 1 Chapter 5 Sections 6 & 7

- But the pope of Rome rules over the church as if he were a god upon earth, and declares himself both by word and deed that he is God, challenging unto himself those titles, attributes and works which are peculiar unto the Lord, etc., as has been proven.
- Therefore the pope is Antichrist.

"Yea, but the pope," says Bellarmine, "does not declare himself to be God, for he acknowledges himself to be the servant of the Lord." He might as well conclude that the pope never calls himself *regem regūterrae, ac Dominū Dominorum*, the king of the kings of the earth, and Lord of Lords, because he acknowledges himself *seruū seruorū Dei*, the servant of God's servants. Neither does his verbal profession oversway his real practice.

But he should have remembered that the second beast which is Antichrist (Revelation 13:11), as he speaks like the dragon belching out blasphemies against God, so he has two horns like the lamb, and as a dissembling hypocrite imitates in some things the humility of Christ. And therefore that the pope could not be such an Antichrist as is described in the Scriptures, unless he were a hypocrite, who does by open profession pretend himself to be the servant of God, when as in truth he advances himself against him. And yet this is all that our adversary alleges to prove his assumption, that the pope does not show himself to be God.

(11) "The fourth and last doctrine," says the Jesuit, "is this: he shall not only affirm that he is God, but that he only is God, and shall oppugn all other gods, both true and false, and shall suffer no idols."

But this absurd conceit of the papists, is not only repugnant unto the truth, but also contradictory to their own doctrines concerning Antichrist. For is it credible either that a mortal man shall affirm himself alone to be the true God, and none but him. Or if he shall so affirm of himself that

Christians and Jews – and all the world almost – will acknowledge and worship him as the only true God?

Again, the Antichristian seat is figured by the whore of Babylon, which because of her own idolatry is called a whore, and because she infects all nations that adhere unto her with her idolatries and superstitions, she is said to make them drunk with the cup of her fornications, and also to be the mother of all the fornications, that is, idolatries of the earth. Yea, and the papists themselves expound Daniel 11:38, where Antiochus Epiphanes is described as an idolater as properly spoken of Antichrist.

And do not themselves teach that Antichrist shall profess himself to be the messiah of the Jews, and consequently that he is sent and anointed by God? Now if he shall profess himself sent from God, shall we think that he will say there is no God besides himself? Or if he being but a mortal man, shall say there is no God besides himself, may we not well think that either they will hiss at him as a fool, or stone him to death as a blasphemer? Nay, do not themselves teach that he shall be in religion a Jew, an observer of the Sabbath, and other Jewish ceremonies? And do they not allege Jerome to prove that Antichrist shall feign himself to be the chief of the covenant, and a chief maintainer of the law and testament of God?[543] And are not his *two horns like the lamb* expounded by some approved authors among them, of the two testaments which he shall seem to profess?[544]

(12) But let us see how this wise conceit is proved: indeed by testimonies of the Scriptures and the fathers.

Out of the Scripture he alleges two places, the former being 2 Thessalonians 2:4: "Who is extolled above all that is called God, or worshiped." As if he should say, "Antichrist shall be advanced above all that is called God, or that is worshiped, therefore he shall avouch that he alone is

---

[543] In Daniel 11
[544] In Revelation 13

God, and will suffer no other God either true or false to be worshiped besides himself." I deny the consequence.

For firstly, Antichrist may advance himself above all that is called God, or that is worshiped, and yet suffer, yea require them to be worshiped. Jupiter was supposed among the heathen to advance himself above all other gods, and yet suffered them to be worshiped as gods. Antichrist the second beast, advances himself above the image of the former beast, which is the empire renewed,[545] whereon he sits as the rider death upon a beast, and yet requires the same to be worshiped.[546] The pope advances himself above angels, kings, and princes, who are called *gods*; above the saints, the host, the cross, and whatsoever σεβασμα is in the church of Rome, and yet requires them all to be worshiped.

Secondly, Antichrist may advance himself above or against all that is called God, or is worshiped, and yet not profess himself to be the only God. For so Antiochus Epiphanes advanced himself against every God, yea, against the God of gods (Daniel 11:36), and yet he was never so mad as to profess himself the only God.

Thirdly, seeing Antichristianism is not open atheism, but a mystery of iniquity; and Antichrist is described in the Scriptures as an hypocrite and pretended Christian, we may be assured that although in deed and in truth he shall advance himself against God, and against Christ our Savior, and list up himself above all that is called God, or that is worshiped; yet he shall profess himself to be the servant of Christ, and a worshiper of God.

Fourthly, the words of the text do not ascribe to Antichrist so great an extolling of himself as the Jesuit imagines.

For first he is called a *man of sin*, and *son of perdition*, and therefore we are to conceive of such an advancement of himself, as is incident to a mortal and wretched man.

---

[545] Revelation 13
[546] Revelation 17

Secondly, he is said to extol himself above all that is called God, or that is worshiped. By *all that is called God*, we are to understand all to whom the name of God is communicated, as to angels in heaven, to kings and princes on earth. And of this advancing above kings, we are rather to understand this place, because afterwards it is said that the Roman Empire hindered Antichrist's advancing or revealing himself.

And by σεβασμα, we are to understand anything which is worshiped as God, or wherein God is worshiped. Such in the church of Rome are the host, the cross, the saints, and their images and relics. Above all of these, a man may advance himself (as the pope does) and yet may acknowledge some other god besides himself.

Thirdly, the greatest height of pride that is incident to any creature whatsoever, is not to seek to be above God, for that cannot be imagined, but to be as God. And indeed the height of Antichrist's pride and advancing of himself, is noted in the words following, ωστε: "in so much that he shall sit in the temple of God as God."

Whosoever therefore being but a mortal man, shall advance himself above all that is called God and worshiped, insomuch that he shall sit in the temple of God as God, that is, rules in the church of Christ as if he were a God upon earth, he is to be deemed Antichrist (that is *aemulus Christi*, one that would feign to be equal to Christ) although he neither professes himself to be the only God, who only is to be worshiped, neither yet abolishes all other worship of God both true and false.

And if in this sense this place does properly agree to the pope, as indeed it does, then can it not be avoided but that he is Antichrist.

(13) The second testimony which he alleges to prove this fond conceit is Daniel 11:37: "neither shall he care for any of the gods, but shall rise against all." I answer, Daniel in this place speaks not of Antichrist, and he of whom

he speaks was an idolater, and therefore this allegation is altogether impertinent.

As touching the first, it is evident that Daniel from verse 21 of that chapter to the end, does most plainly and properly describe Antiochus Epiphanes. For howsoever in this place Bellarmine would prove by the authority of Jerome, that these words are to be understood of Antichrist, and not of Antiochus,[547] yet in another place when part of this verse is objected by some Protestants as sitting the pope, he tells us plainly that Daniel speaks *ad literam*: literally of Antiochus, who was a figure of Antichrist.

Secondly, he of whom Daniel speaks was an Idolater, and establisher of Idolatry. So far was he from professing himself to be the only true God, or suffering none to be worshiped besides himself. For if he speaks of Antiochus Epiphanes (as most certainly he does), it may easily be proven both by the history of the Maccabees, and by other stories, that he was both an idolater himself, and an enforcer of idolatry upon others. See 1 Maccabees 1:50, 2 Maccabees 6:2, etc. Polybius also testifies that in sacrifices and honoring the Greek gods, he surpassed other kings which went before him, as might appear by the Olympiaeum at Athens, and the images about the altar at Delos.[548] This Jerome also avouches, and Bellarmine confesses.

But of whomsoever Daniel speaks, he does plainly describe him in the next verse to be an idolater.[549] And it is a world to see what silly shifts the Jesuit makes to avoid this truth. For first he reads the words thus: "And he shall honor the God *Maozim* in his place." Secondly, he omits the words following ("the God which his fathers knew not, he shall honor with gold," etc. which most plainly specify his idolatry who is here described) and busies himself wholly in giving a false interpretation to the God *Maozim*. "The God Maozim," says he, "signifies either Antichrist himself, and then the meaning is he shall honor himself, that is, cause himself to be worshiped: or

---

[547] Book 3 Chapter 21
[548] Apud Athenaeum.
[549] Daniel 11:38

else it signifies the devil whom Antichrist being a sorcerer shall worship in secret, which interpretation he prefers before the other." And therefore this place does not prove that he which is here described shall be an idolater.

(14) I answer first, that although either of his interpretations of the God Maozim were true (as neither is) yet the one hinders not, and the other proves that he which is here described is an idolater.

For let the word *Maozim* signify what it may, yet the words following plainly convince the party here described of idolatry, the God which his fathers knew not he shall worship with gold. And if the God *Maozim* signifies any but the true God, and if also the words are so to be read as Bellarmine reads them: "And he shall honor the God *Maozim*, and the God whom his fathers knew not, he shall worship with gold and silver," etc. then by these words, the idolatry is increased.

[1] For first it is said, that he shall worship the God Maozim according to Bellarmine's reading, whereby is not meant as he says the true God, nay he says to make Christ the God *Maozim*, it is intolerable blasphemy.[550] And therefore first in these words is signified an idolater, and secondly it is added, that the God also which his fathers knew not he shall worship, where again his idolatry is most plainly noted.

[2] But indeed Bellarmine's interpretation is merely false, and that which he infers thereupon, altogether absurd. The God *Mahuzzim* signifies the God of fortitudes, that is, the most mighty or almighty God, which title as it is proper to the Lord, as Jeremiah calls him יְהוָה עֻזִּי וּמָעֻזִּי "Jehovah, my strength and fortitude." And likewise David in Psalm 31:5, so may it not be ascribed to any other. And therefore it is a senseless imagination, that Daniel by *the God of fortitudes* would signify either Antichrist himself, a wicked and wretched man, or the father of Antichrist the devil.

---

[550] Li. 3 Ca. 21

And further, as touching the former interpretation, it seems to be absurd, that when Daniel according to his reading says, he shall worship the God Maozim, his meaning should be, that Antichrist should worship himself, as though he that worships, and he that is worshiped were one and the same. And then in like sort in the latter clause, by *the God which he shall worship, which his fathers knew not*, we must absurdly understand himself.

For whereas he cavils at the word *worship*, and says, we must read *glorify*, as though Daniel's meaning were, that Antichrist should glorify himself, and cause himself to be worshiped, it is certain that the vulgar Latin (which he prefers before the Hebrew, and which by the Council of Trent he is bound to stand to) has *venerabitur*, shall worship: and himself both in the second clause of the verse, he reads according to the vulgar *colet*, shall worship: and in his second interpretation, which he says is the better, he does so read and understand the word. His first interpretation therefore, that the God Maozim should signify Antichrist himself, is sottish and absurd.

(15) Let us therefore consider whether the second, which he prefers before the other, is any better. "In the second place," says he, "it may be said, which pleases me better, that Antichrist shall be a magician or sorcerer," (such as very many popes of Rome have been), "and that according to the manner of other magicians, he shall in secret worship the devil," (as several of the popes have done homage unto him) "by whose help he shall work wonders, and that he is called the god *Maozim*."

Answer: Whereas Bellarmine prefers this exposition before others, it seems he has forgotten the question which he took upon him to defend, namely, that Antichrist shall not be an Idolater. For if he shall be a worshiper of the devil, and also of a God whom his fathers knew not, I hope by this exposition he shall be proven an idolater. But let us see what he further alleges to prove this exposition, which although it be false (for Daniel here neither speaks of Antichrist, nor yet of the devil) yet it makes against himself. Indeed, *Maozim* as he supposes is not the name of God, but of a certain strong and secret place, in which shall be the chief treasures of Antichrist, and wherein he shall worship the devil.

For it follows in Daniel, that he shall fortify *Maozim* with a strange God whom he knew, and surely מָעוֹז *Mahoz* signifies as well fortitude as a tower or place of munition. His meaning then is, that the devil is here called the God Maozim, because Antichrist shall worship him in a certain tower, which if it were true, he should rather be called *the God Maoz*, but Daniel speaks in the plural number, the God of fortitudes or munitions, signifying according to the Hebrew phrase, the most mighty and strong God, *Deum summiroboris*, as Tremellius reads.

And whereas he says it follows that he shall fortify Maozim with a strange god whom he has known, I answer, that there is no such matter in the original text, which word for word is thus: "And he shall do to the munitions of *Mahuzzim* with a strange god," that is, he shall commit the munitions of *Mahuzzim*, that is, Jerusalem and the cities of Jewry to a strange god.

"Yea, but," says Bellarmine, "one of these interpretations (either that Antichrist is the god *Maozim*, or if he be any other (for he dare not now say it is the devil), he shall not be worshiped of Antichrist, but secretly and in a most hidden place), one," says he, "of these interpretations must be good, or else there will be a repugnancy in Daniel's words. For if he cares for no God, how shall he publicly worship idols? yea, rather if he cares for no God, how shall he worship any privately? For it is more likely that he who is an atheist, and cares for no god indeed, will in Machiavellian policy worship some god publicly, although privately he cares for none."

And it more fits the disposition of Antichrist to be secretly an atheist, and openly an idolater, than contrariwise although Bellarmine here does hold the contrary.

(16) But now perhaps you expect that, having freed this place of Daniel from Bellarmine's corruptions and depravations, I should open unto you the true meaning thereof, and show how this prophecy was fulfilled in Antiochus, who in many things was a type of Antichrist. "And the king," says the angel in verse 36 (or this king *hamelech*, that is, Antiochus Epiphanes, of whom I have all this while entreated, namely, from verse 21), "he shall do what he will, his will shall be to him for a law;" wherein he might seem to be a lively figure of the pope, of whom it is said, *Sic volo, sic iubeo, slat pro ration voluntas*: And again, *Iudicium{que} est pro lege suum*. And this was the ground of all his actions, willfully following in all things his own will. Then more particularly the angel describes his actions, both in respect of religion and policy.

His actions tending to irreligion (of which only we are now to speak) are first summarily comprised in verse 36, and afterwards more fully expressed. The sum is this: that he should alter and abrogate all the religions of the Syrians, as well the false religions of the idolaters, as the true religion of the Jews. The abrogation of all the religions of the Syrians is here called the magnifying himself עַל above or against every god, whose worships he did put down. The profanation of the Jewish religion ordained by the true God, the God of gods, is here signified by speaking great and swelling words against him, which we are to understand of his blasphemous edicts to abolish the whole religion of God:[551] both of which we see performed by Antiochus Epiphanes (1 Maccabees 1:43, 46, etc.) The same things are again repeated in verses 37 and 38.

First, as touching the gods and religions of the Syrians in general, whether true or false, he says in verse 37 that unto the gods of his fathers he shall not attend, neither will he listen to the desires of women: that is, as some expound, his wives, who entreated the continuance of those religions whereunto themselves were addicted, so that neither the reverence of his

---

[551] 1 Maccabees 1:43, 46; 2 Maccabees 6:2

fathers, nor the love of his wives could stay him from following his own will in abrogating their religions, neither will be regard any of the gods – namely: of the Syrians – because he will magnify himself against all, in abrogating the religions of them all, whether true or false. And more particularly concerning the true religion of the true God, he says in verse 38 וְלֶאֱלֹהַּ, מָעֻזִּים.

And as touching the God *Mahuzzim*, that is, the God Almighty, and there he pauses, in his place he will honor, even a God whom his fathers knew not, will he honor with gold and with silver, with precious stones and with jewels; and (verse. 39.) he shall commit the munitions of Mahuzzim, that is, of the Almighty unto a strange god, that is, he shall deal so despitefully with the God of Israel, the Lord of Hosts, that having abrogated his worship and religion, he shall set up in the temple of God the idol of Jupiter Olympius to be worshiped (as it is recorded in 2 Maccabees 6), who was a god whom his fathers knew not, that is, acknowledged not, nor worshiped. For the Syrians worshiped Apollo and Diana.[552]

And the munitions of *Mahuzzim*, that is, Jerusalem and other cities of Jewry, which had been as it were the munitions and cities of God, he committed them to the tuition of a strange god, namely, Jupiter Olympius. The same prophecy in effect was before delivered in Daniel 7:25. and 8:11. By conference of these places with this in hand, it is manifest, that by *the God Mahuzzim*, is meant the true God.[553]

(17) This prophecy therefore, being meant of Antiochus Epiphanes, and fulfilled in him, cannot properly belong to Antichrist or any other. Notwithstanding as in some other things, so in the premises, Antiochus may not unfitly be thought to have been a type or figure of Antichrist – in so much that both the ancient fathers have understood these prophecies of

---

[552] Strabo, geograph., lib. 16
[553] See Tremellius in Daniel 7 & 8

Antichrist, and many also of the late writers (besides the Jews) have applied the same particularly to the pope.[554] For besides that it is most true of the pope, that he does what he will, seeing he is subject to no law, and no man may say to him, "Sir, why do you do so?"

The rest also after a sort may be verified of him, that both he sets himself against the idols of the Gentiles, and also has abrogated the true worship of God. And that instead of Christ the Almighty God, he has set up in his churches, besides many other idols, the abominable idol of the mass, a god which his fathers, the first bishops of Rome knew not, which notwithstanding he honors with gold and silver, and precious stones, and has committed the churches, cities, and countries of Christendom, to the tuition and patronage of various saints, who as they are indeed, so are they called by Paulus Ionius, a popish bishop, *the tutelary gods of the papists*.[555]

(18) And these were his testimonies of Scripture. In the next place, for want of better proofs, he flies to the authority of the fathers as his last refuge, as though they testified that Antichrist shall not be an idolater, nor one that will suffer idols.

But I answer, that the fathers do either speak of the idols and idolatry of the Gentiles only, and in that sense their speeches are verified in this behalf of the pope, who neither honors nor suffers the idols of the Gentiles; or else if they speak of all idols and idolatry in general, when they say *Idola seponet* as Irenaeus, or *idololatriam non admittet* as Hippolytus, or *idola odio habebit*, as Cyril, or *ad idololatriā non adducet ille*, as Chrysostom, they deserve such an Antichrist as in this behalf is better than the pope. But indeed as the pope is, so Antichrist in the Scriptures is described to be an idolater, as has been shown.

---

[554] Legi non subiacet vlli.
[555] Hist. lib. 24 in fine.

(19) Having thus doughtily proved this Popish conceit, the Jesuit proceeds to the disproof of our assertions and expositions of some places of Scripture, and especially that of 2 Thessalonians 2. Our assertion concerning the doctrine of Antichrist, he says, is only built upon the Scriptures falsely expounded by new glosses. "In token whereof," says he, "they allege not one interpreter or doctor for them."

But this is a malicious slander, witness this place which he mentions 2 Thessalonians 2, where we prove by the consent of many of the fathers that by *the temple* is meant the church of God, and that in the church of God Antichrist was to be revealed, after the Roman Empire, which hindered, was taken out of the way, etc. Our assertions concerning Antichrist, are grounded on the prophecies of Scriptures expounded by the event, which is the best expounder of prophecies.

And with our assertions, the opinions of the fathers agree, where they are consonant to the Scripture and the event. Contrariwise, the assertions of the papists concerning Antichrist, as they are repugnant to the Scriptures and the truth of the event: so are they wholly grounded either upon the uncertain (and many times misalleged) conjectures of the fathers, who were no prophets, and therefore, not being able to foresee the event, did not many times understand the prophecies, or else on the blind conceits of popish writers, who being deceived with the efficacy of illusion, and made drunk with the whore of Babylon's cup of fornications, were given over to believe lies. And whereas our writers expounding those words of the Apostle in 2 Thessalonians 2:4 ("who is lifted up above all that is called God," or "that is worshiped") do apply the same unto the pope upon very good and sufficient proofs, and from thence do plainly conclude the pope to be Antichrist (for evidence whereof, I refer the reader to the fifth chapter of my former book). He culls out some straggling sentences out of someone of the least sound writers of our side (as their manner is), which he may best hope to answer. As though we had no more, nor no better arguments to prove, that the pope advances himself above all that is called God, or that is worshiped, then these two: First, because he professes himself to be the vicar of Christ: And secondly, whereas Christ subjected himself willingly unto the Scriptures, the pope challenges authority to dispense with the Scripture.

Howbeit, the former of these two reasons he depraves, and the latter he is not able to satisfy. For Illyricus' reason to prove that the pope advances himself above all that is called God, is not because he makes himself the vicar of Christ, but this, because he – vaunting himself to be the vicar of Christ – does notwithstanding usurp greater authority, than the son of God claimed unto himself, of which, that which Bellarmine alleges as a second reason, is by Illyricus added as a proof; whereunto Bellarmine is not otherwise able to answer, than by impudent and shameless denial, either that Christ subjected himself to the law and word of God, or that the pope takes upon him to dispense with the Scriptures, or that any catholic (meaning popish) writer has said, that he may dispense with divine precepts; both which notwithstanding I have heretofore proved by many instances and most evident allegations. See the first book. chapter 5, §. 10.-12.

For that which he adds of Christ's subjecting himself to the prophecies, and not to the precepts, as though Illyricus had spoken of the one in his proposition, and of the other in the assumption, it is partly false and partly ridiculous, and indeed not worth answering.

Chapter 15
Of the miracles of Antichrist.

(1) We are now come to the eighth main argument, which Bellarmine uses to prove that the pope of Rome is not Antichrist; because indeed those things which the Holy Spirit in the Scriptures has foretold concerning the miracles of Antichrist, do not agree to the pope and church of Rome.

For concerning the miracles of Antichrist, the Scriptures (says he) mention three things: [1] that Antichrist shall work many miracles, [2] what manner of miracles they shall be, and [3] there are recorded examples. Of all which points I have entreated heretofore, proving from Bellarmine's own grounds, that the pope is Antichrist.[556]

And first that many signs and wonders should be wrought by Antichrist and his adherents, which they call miracles, the Scriptures testify, the event has proven, and we do confess. And secondly, that all these signs and wonders, however he and his followers do boast of them, and in respect thereof contemn the true professors: yet are as the apostle says, lying signs and wonders, both in respect of the ende, which is to seduce and to confirm lies, and in respect of the substance, which is counterfeit.

For whereas Bellarmine adds that they are also called lying signs in respect of the efficient and author of them, which is the father of lies, according to whose power Antichrist was to come, who as some of the fathers affirm, was to be a notable magician or sorcerer. This seems to be somewhat far-fetched, unless we will take the word ψευδους to be masculine (as none does).

Notwithstanding, because the apostle ascribes the working of these miracles to the power of Satan, we will trace him in his own steps, not doubting to apply this note also to the pope and church of Rome, seeing it

---

[556] Lib. 1, cap. 7

cannot be doubted, but that as very many not only of their clergy, but even of their popes, have been notable magicians and sorcerers: so also very many of the miracles in the church of Rome, have been the operations or illusions of the devil.

As for their clergy, who does not know that there have been few learned men among them, who have not been known, or at the least suspected, to be conjurers, and skillful (as some call it) of the black art. But as touching the popes, because it may seem incredible that any known magician or sorcerer should be advanced to the Apostolic See, as they call it; therefore it may be thought, that the sorcery and witchcraft of the most of them, who indeed were sorcerers, was hidden and unknown.

Notwithstanding, even in their own writers, there are over twenty popes recorded as known magicians and sorcerers, several of whom gave themselves wholly to the devil, that in them the prophecy of the apostle might be fulfilled, namely: that they might come to the papacy by the help of the devil, or as the apostle speaks in 2 Thessalonians 2:9, that their coming might be according to the efficacy of Satan. And as this happened often, so especially about those times wherein Antichrist in the papacy had in a manner come to his full growth, that is to say, in Sylvester II and Gregory VII, and all the popes between them, who were a sort of infamous sorcerers. And therefore if any miracles have been wrought by such popes, (as Saunders brags of many signs and wonders wrought by Gregory VII) we need not doubt, but that as themselves were magicians and sorcerers, so their signs and wonders were wrought by the power of the devil.[557]

(2) And thus Bellarmine through all the causes shows the miracles of Antichrist, to be lying signs and wonders. But to what end, I beseech you, does all this discourse serve? Will Bellarmine conclude from hence that the pope is not Antichrist, either because there are no miracles in the church of

---

[557] Demonst. 20

Rome, which was the first point, or because those miracles which they have, are not lying signs and wonders, which was the second? If this were his ende, why then does he not from this proposition, as it were his groundwork, assume and conclude after this manner:

- By Antichrist and his adherents many signs and wonders shall be wrought (which they call miracles) as the Scripture testifies.
- By the pope and his adherents many signs and wonders have not been wrought which they call miracles.
- Therefore the pope is not Antichrist.

But Bellarmine dares not reason thus, seeing as the papists brag of nothing more than of their signs and wonders, which they call miracles. And therefore from this ground I have heretofore inferred the contrary. For if it be a peculiar note of Antichrist and his adherents in these latter times to work many signs and wonders, which they call miracles: then can it not be avoided, but that the pope of Rome is Antichrist, and the church of Rome the Synagogue of Antichrist, seeing they alone do brag of miracles. See the first book, chapter 7, Sections 1 and 2.

Secondly, why does he not reason thus?

- By Antichrist and his followers, lying signs and wonders shall be wrought.
- But by the pope and church of Rome, there have been no lying signs and wonders wrought.
- Therefore the pope is not Antichrist.

Indeed this would Bellarmine have the simple reader gather from his words, and that is the drift of all that discourse. But this he could not assume and conclude, because his own conscience does tell him that which all the world knows: that their church is full of lying signs and wonders, which they call miracles. Therefore from Bellarmine's own ground I reason thus:

- If it be a peculiar note of Antichrist and his synagogue in these latter times to work many lying signs and wonders, then it must be confessed that the pope is Antichrist, and the church of Rome the synagogue of Antichrist, because among them are many lying signs and wonders.
- But the first is testified in the Scriptures.
- And therefore the latter cannot be denied, seeing I have proved that the church of Rome is full of lying signs and wonders, which notwithstanding they call miracles. See the first book, chapter 7, Sections 3-7.

(3) It is plain therefore, that of those three things which Bellarmine observes out of the Scriptures concerning the miracles of Antichrist, the two first do fitly serve to prove the pope Antichrist. Neither will the three examples of Antichrist's miracles which Bellarmine sets down in the third place, disprove the same. For of these three examples, to wit, first that Antichrist, or at least his ministers, shall make fire to come down from heaven in the sight of men. Secondly, that he shall put life into the image of the beast, and cause it to speak. Thirdly, that he shall feign himself to die, and to rise again.

The first two (which indeed belong to Antichrist) do fitly agree to the pope (as has been shown in the first book, chapter 7, from the 8th section to the end of the chapter). The third does not belong to Antichrist. From whence notwithstanding, Bellarmine argues thus:

- The third miracle of Antichrist (says he) is, that he shall fain himself to die and to rise again, for which miracle especially the whole world almost shall admire him.

- But never did any pope feign himself to die and rise again.
- Therefore the pope is not Antichrist.

I answer to the proposition, that no such miracle in the scripture is assigned unto Antichrist, but that it is a fond imagination of the papists, which by some of them, and namely by Bellarmine himself is propounded more fondly, to wit, that Antichrist shall fain himself to die, and by the help of the devil shall rise again.[558] For if his death is only counterfeit, then he shall not need the devils help to raise him. Notwithstanding, they would ground this miracle upon those words in Revelation 13:3: "And I saw one of his heads as it were wounded to death, but his deadly wound was healed, and all the world wondered after the beast."

I answer, that in these words the Holy Spirit speaks not of Antichrist, and that he of whom he speaks, does not feign himself to die, and rise again. As touching the first of those two beasts described in this chapter, the former is not Antichrist, but the latter. The former which is described up to verse 11 is the Roman Empire, especially under the persecuting emperors, as has been shown, every part of that description fitting the same. And that the latter beast signifies Antichrist, it is in a manner confessed of all.

Hear what Bellarmine says in the beginning of his tenth chapter,[559] speaking of Revelation 13:16-18, which are spoken concerning the second beast, *Fatentur omneo* (says he) *pertinere omnino ad Antichristum verba illa Ioannis* (Apoc. 13) *& fuciet omnes pusillos cum magnis, etc*: "All men confess that those words of John in Revelation 13 – *And he shall make all both small and great, etc.* – do wholly appertain to Antichrist."

And in this very chapter how does Bellarmine prove: [1] that Antichrist shall work great signs, because it is said in verse 13: *& fecit signa magna*: "and he wrought great signs." [2] That many of the signs of Antichrist shall be

---

[558] Lib. 3, *De Pontif. Rom.* cap. 5
[559] Lib. 3, *De Pontif. Rom.* cap. 10

fantastical, and only in appearance, because it is said in the same verse, that he causes fire to descend in the sight of men. [3] That Antichrist shall cause fire to come down from heaven, and make the image of the beast to speak, because it is so prophesied of Antichrist in verses 13 and 15.

Now if this is confessed, that the latter beast is Antichrist, then can it not be truly affirmed that the former beast is Antichrist, unless we may say that the former and the latter are one and the same. But that cannot be truly said. For of the latter, John says, "And I saw αλλο θηριον: another beast." (verse 11). If it is another, then is it not the same, and the great difference in the descriptions of both, does show that they are different beasts: the one arising out of the sea has ten horns; the other arising out of the earth has two horns like the lamb. The latter exercises the power of the former, and that in his sight causes men to worship the former beast, whose deadly wound was healed,[560] makes an image to the former beast which had a deadly wound, and lived (verse 14). Therefore the second beast which signifies Antichrist, is not that beast which had the deadly wound and was cured thereof, nor yet the head which was so wounded.

(4) Again (to come to that objection which Bellarmine makes unto himself, and does not satisfy), this miracle and the two first do not belong to one and the same subject. If therefore the two first concerning fire and the Image, belong to Antichrist, then this does not; or if this do, then the other two do not – but all confess, that those two do belong to Antichrist, therefore this does not.

Hereunto Bellarmine would seem to answer that the former beast signifies either the Roman Empire, or the multitude of the wicked, and that one (that is to say the chief head thereof) which seemed to die and rise again, is Antichrist. "For, says he, "Antichrist shall be the chief and the last head of the wicked, as also of the Romans."

---

[560] Revelation 13:12

The second beast signifies either Antichrist himself, according to Rupertus, or the ministers and preachers of Antichrist, according to Richardus and Anselmus. And therefore these three miracles belong either to Antichrist alone, or to him and his ministers. In which answer of Bellarmine, we see that proverbial speech verified, that *great is the truth, and it shall prevail*,[561] seeing as the force and evidence of truth has expressed from him in this place a confession that overthrows the popish concerning Antichrist, and manifestly proves the pope to be Antichrist. Namely, when he confesses according to the true interpretation of the ancient interpreters and fathers of the Church, that the beast with seven heads is the Roman Empire, and that Antichrist is one of those seven heads – as also elsewhere he has confessed that the whore of Babylon is the city of Rome.[562]

From hence therefore it follows that Antichrist shall be the head, not of the Jews, but of the Romans, that his chief seat or See shall be, not Jerusalem, but Rome, that the name of the beast is Roman or Latin, that Antichrist is not one particular man, no more than the other six heads of the Roman Empire, but a state of government, as the kings were one head, and the consuls another, and the emperors but one head, and the popes and papacy but one head, and lastly, that the head of the beast or Roman Empire, which is Antichrist, can be no other but the pope of Rome.

For of these seven heads, John says that in his time five of them were fallen, one was, and another was not yet come. These five which were fallen, were the five first, namely: kings, consuls, decemviri, tribunes, and dictators. The head that then was – beyond question – was the emperors, who were the sixth head; the seventh (which is of the popes) was not yet come.

Which then of these seven heads does signify Antichrist? surely none of the five first, for they were past before John's time; nor the sixth, which is the state of emperors, for that then was, and Antichrist was not yet come, and as

---

[561] 1 Esdras 4:35
[562] Revelation 13

the papists confess, that was it which hindered the revelation of Antichrist, and therefore was to be done out of the way before Antichrist could be revealed.[563]

It remains therefore that the seventh head (which is of the popes) is Antichrist. For as touching the imperial state renewed in the West, the Holy Spirit plainly says that the beast which was, and is not, though it be, as being but the image of the old empire, is the eighth, and is one of the seven; that is: in name and title it is the same with the sixth, as images bear the names of those things which they do represent. If therefore Antichrist is one of the seven heads of the Roman state (as undoubtedly he is, and as our adversary here confesses) then can it not be denied, but that the pope, who is the seventh head, is Antichrist.

(5) The other interpretation, that the beast with seven heads does signify the whole multitude of the wicked, is senseless and absurd. For if the beast be the universal company of the wicked, what is the world, which in verse 3 is said to wonder after the beast? What are all the kindreds, tongues, nations which are made subject to the beast in verse 7? Who are all those inhabitants of the earth that do worship him? Does not the Holy Spirit plainly say in verse 8 that they are those whose names are not written in the book of the lamb; that is to say, the company of the wicked and reprobates? When as Bellarmine therefore says, that this beast signifies either the Roman Empire, or the whole company of the wicked, we may add, but it does not signify the whole company of the wicked.

It remains therefore that it signifies the Roman state, whereof Antichrist is a head. But although Antichrist be one head of the seven, yet it does not follow, that the head which was as it were wounded to death, is Antichrist, but rather the estate of Emperors which then was. For albeit the beast with seven heads does signify the Roman state in general, yet in that place it

---

[563] 2 Thessalonians 2

seems to be described as it was subject to the sixth head, in the 17th chapter, as it is renewed and subjected to the Antichristian state.

For the beast (which he there speaks of) which was, and is not though it be, was after to arise, and being the eighth in order, was in name one of the seven: on which beast as also upon those waters, that is, nations whereof the old empire did arise, the whore of Babylon (whereby is meant the Antichristian state) sits, that is, rules and reigns as a queen.

(6) And that it may appear that there is no necessity that we should understand this wound of Antichrist, let us consider what wounds the Roman state had received, and was cured thereof. First therefore, by the death of Julius Caesar, and the civil wars thereupon ensuing, the Roman Empire received as it were a deadly wound, and yet recovered it so again, as that in Augustus and some of his successors, it flourished more than ever before. And this, some think to be the wound of the beast which was cured, whereof the Holy Spirit here speaks, describing the beast by that which was known to have been done in the Roman state.

The second wound which the Roman Empire received, was at the death of Nero, in whom the stock of the Caesars ended, which being cut off, the succession of the imperial crown was uncertain, and by the uncertainty of succession the like desolation threatened to that empire, which happened to the Greek monarchy after the death of Alexander the Great – the empire being left as a prey for the mightiest.

Neither was this wound cured until Vespasian obtained the empire. For after Nero, Sergius Galba seized upon the empire, and enjoyed the same but seven months and seven days. And albeit to establish the succession, he had adopted Piso, yet was he murdered by Marcus Salvius Otho, who succeeded him, and Otho after three months and five days was slain by Vitellius, who also after eight months was deposed and put to an ignominious death by Vespasian, in whom the empire which since the death of Nero had been *incertum & vagum*, as Suetonius says, was established, and as it were cured of the former wound, which several learned men think to be understood in this place. Others rather expound this deadly wound of the dissolution of the Empire in the West, Augustulus; being overcome by the Goths, and the Empire in the West lying void until Charles the Great, in whom this wound was after a sort cured. Therefore although Antichrist be one of the heads of this beast, yet seeing he is but one of the seven, and the Holy Spirit speaks of this empire especially, as it was ruled by the sixth head, that is to say, the emperors; there is no necessity, nay, no probability that by the head which was wounded we should understand Antichrist, especially seeing Antichrist is afterwards described at large, and that by these notes among others, that he causes men to worship the former beast, whose mortal wound was healed (verse 13), and causes an image to be made to the beast which had the deadly wound (verse 14), which as appears also by the image, was the Roman state under the emperors; for thereof the empire renewed is an image.

(7) But now suppose that Antichrist were this head which was wounded and cured as he is not, yet how does it follow that therefore Antichrist shall feign himself to die and rise again, seeing he speaks not of a particular man's death and resurrection, as the papists imagine, but of the wounding and curing of a state signified by the head.

Neither does he speak of death and resurrection, but of wounding and curing. Neither is the wound and the cure counterfeit and feigned, but the wound is truly inflicted and truly cured. Such, as was both the wound of the Roman Empire, either at the murder of Julius Caesar, or death of Nero, or vanquishing of Augustulus; and also the cure in Augustus, in Vespasian, and as Bellarmine elsewhere says, in Carolus Magnus:[564] "If therefore neither Antichrist be spoken of in this place, nor yet he who is spoken of, does feign himself to die and rise again; how is it proven from these words that Antichrist shall feign himself to die and rise again?"

---

[564] 2 Thessalonians 2

Chapter 16
Of the kingdom and battles of Antichrist.

Concerning the kingdom and battles of Antichrist, we read four things in the Scriptures, says Bellarmine:

> (1) That Antichrist – arising from a most base estate – shall by fraud and deceit obtain the kingdom of the Jews.
>
> (2) That he shall fight with three kings, to wit, of Egypt, Libya, and Ethiopia, and having overcome them, shall possess their kingdoms.
>
> (3) That he shall subdue seven other kings, and by that means shall become the monarch of the whole world.
>
> (4) That with an innumerable army he shall persecute the Christians in the whole world, and that this is the battle of Gog and Magog.
>
> – Seeing as none of these agree with the pope, it follows manifestly that he can by no means be called Antichrist.

To these four points I will answer, first jointly to them all, and then severally to everyone. For whereas Bellarmine says, that these four things are read in the Scriptures concerning the kingdom and battles of Antichrist, I answer, that not any one of these four is to be found in the Scriptures, and therefore that this argument as it is the last, so of least force, and that his disputation standing now as it were on the tilt, he seems to draw of the lees. Notwithstanding the three first he would feign father upon Daniel, as though he in chapters 7 and 11 had prophesied such things concerning Antichrist.

But I answer, that these prophecies had, and according to Daniel were, to have their complement before the coming of the Messiah, and therefore that the papists may as well with the Jews expect the coming of their messiah, as still to expect the fulfilling of these things in their imaginary antichrist, the counterfeit messiah of the Jews.

Seeing as I said, these prophecies were to be fulfilled before the coming of Christ: and seeing the Jews do still wait for their messiah, because with the papists they will not acknowledge these prophecies (which were to have their complement before the coming of the messiah) to have been fulfilled before the incarnation of Christ. The occasion of which error of the papists (whereat the Jews also do stumble) has been an erroneous interpretation of some of the Fathers, who understand whatsoever is spoken of the kingdom of the Seleucids and Lagedae, that is, the kingdom of Syria and Egypt (so far forth as it tyrannized over the people of God the Jews) figured by the two legs of the image, chapter 2, and the fourth beast with ten horns, chapter 7, they understand (I say) as spoken of the Roman monarchy. And consequently whatsoever is spoken of the little horn in chapters 7, 8, and 11, whereby Antiochus Epiphanes is most plainly described, they expound it of Antichrist.

(2) But the learned of our times have made it clear, although the papists shut their eyes against the truth, that by the two legs of the image, and by the fourth beast, is not to be understood the Roman Empire, and by the little horn not Antichrist properly, but Antiochus Epiphanes.

For these things which are recorded of the two legs in chapter 2, and of the fourth beast in chapter 7, do not only fitly, but also properly and only agree to the kingdom of the Seleucids and Lagedae. And those things which are written of the little horn, do wholly and properly belong to Antiochus Epiphanes, as the papists themselves cannot deny.

Porphyry – that learned, though malicious enemy of Christianity – perceived Daniel's prophecies in chapters 7, 8, 11, and 12, which the papists understand of Antichrist, so fully and perfectly to agree to Antiochus Epiphanes, that he caviled against the prophecies of Daniel; affirming that they were written not before hand of Daniel, but after the fulfilling of them by someone that lived in the times of Antiochus Epiphanes.

For so Jerome wrote of him:[565] *Contra prophetam Danielem doudetimum librum scribit Porphyrius, notans eum ab ipso cuius inscriptus est nomine esse compositum, sed à quodam qui temporibus Antiochi, qui appellatus est Epiphanes, fuerit in Judea,* and *non tam Danielem ventura dixisse, quam illum narrasse praeterita.* And after, *tanta enim dictorum fides fuit, vt propheta incredulis hominibus non videatur futura dixisse, sed narrasse praterita*: "So fully and plainly is Antiochus deciphered in the prophecy of Daniel, that the author of that book seemed to Porphyry to have written a story of Antiochus Epiphanes, rather than a prophecy."

(3) As for Antichrist, he is not once mentioned or meant in all the prophecy of Daniel the which I deliver, not as though I thought, that those things which the papists expound concerning Antichrist, could not for the most part be fitly applied to the pope: for not only diverse protestants arguing from the papists own grounds, have out of Daniel proved the pope to be Antichrist: but also the Jews, and namely Rabbi Levi Gerson [Gersonides], whom Bellarmine cites in chapter 12, expounds all those things in Daniel 7 and 11 which the papists understand of Antichrist, as spoken of the pope of Rome, whom he calls *another Pharaoh*.

And most true it is that, excepting Antiochus Epiphanes, these prophecies do best fit the pope of Rome. And therefore I willingly grant that, which both old and new writers have affirmed that Antiochus Epiphanes may be said to have been a type of Antichrist. A *type* I say, not in all and every particular (as though whatsoever can be said of Antiochus, the like may be said of Antichrist), but in some principal matters, in respect whereof he is a type.

---

[565] Praefatione in Daniel

Solomon the king of peace, David the kingly prophet, the high priests, which by offering sacrifices made atonement for their brethren, Joshua the deliverer of the people, were types of Christ. And yet it would be a ridiculous, if not a blasphemous course, to apply to Christ whatsoever is recorded of Solomon, David, the high Priests, or Joshua.

Neither is this without cause set down by the Schoolmen as a rule of Divinity, that *theologia symbolica non est argumentutina*. For those things which properly are spoken of Antiochus, cannot properly be understood of Antichrist, (if at all) but only allegorically, and allegories prove not: and that force which they seem to have in proving, is not to prove the same particular, but the like: for allegories are similitudes without notes of likeness. If therefore it were scarce a good argument in divinity, from a type or allegory to prove the like, because *similia claudicant*: then must it needs be a senseless argumentation from a similitude, to conclude not the like, but the same particular, seeing *nullum simile est idem*, no like is the self-same.

The principal matters which are recorded of Antiochus are these: that he was an enemy to God, and a persecutor of his church, an advancer of himself above or against every God;[566] or as the apostle speaks, one that was ruled by no law, but his own will, having a mouth speaking presumptuous things, and such like: which as they are recorded of Antiochus, so are they by the Apostles applied to Antichrist, and do most fitly and properly agree to the pope. But if we shall apply to Antichrist those things which were proper to the person of Antiochus, and in respect whereof he was not a type of Antichrist, and from thence shall infer not the like, which were too much, for like things are not like in all things, but the same particular which was proper to his person, we shall be ridiculously absurd.

As for example, if we shall say that Antichrist shall by craft attain, not to his kingdom, but to the same kingdom of Syria, because Antiochus did so: that Antichrist shall fight with the kings of Egypt, Libya and Ethiopia,

---

[566] Daniel 7:8

because in Bellarmine's conceit Antiochus did so, and such like particulars; then may we by as good right affirm, that Antichrist shall immediately succeed in the kingdom of Syria his brother Seleucus Philopater, for that is expressly noted in Daniel 11:21 "and in his place," etc. and consequently, that he shall be the son of Antiochus Magnus, that he shall be an hostage at Rome before he be king, as Epiphanes was: that he shall make three expeditions into Egypt, and in his return homeward every time shall he afflict the land of Jewry; especially in the second expedition, when being hindered by the ships of Chittim, that is the Romans, he wrought his malice upon the Jews (Daniel 11:30), and all the rest of the particulars, which properly belong to the person of Antiochus, all which Daniel does so fully and particularly describe, that he has seemed to some which knew not with what spirit he did write, to have written a story rather than a prophecy of him in chapters 7,8, 11, and 12.[567]

(4) But now let us examine severally the particular instances from whence Bellarmine would prove that the pope is not Antichrist. From the first he argues thus:

- Antichrist arising from most base estate (*ex humilimo loco*) shall by fraud and deceit obtain the kingdom of the Jews.
- The pope of Rome did not arise from a base estate, neither did he obtain the kingdom by fraud and deceit.
- Therefore the pope is not Antichrist.

The proposition is after his manner proved out of Daniel 11:21: "And in his place shall stand a vile person, and they shall not give unto him the honor of a king, but he shall come secretly, and obtain the kingdom by fraud."

---

[567] Josephus, *Antiquities*, lib. 12 cap.6

I answer first, that Daniel speaks not of Antichrist: and secondly, that this proposition is not true of him of whom Daniel speaks, and therefore that this allegation is both impertinent and untrue.

That Daniel speaks not of Antichrist, it shall appear out of Daniel himself. For Daniel speaks of him that immediately in the kingdom of Syria succeeded Seleucus Philopater. For so he says, in his place, who was described in verse 20 "shall stand up a vile person," meaning thereby Antiochus, who κατ' εξοχήν is called Ἐπιφανής, but properly as Polybius calls him Ἐπιμανής, unto whom that which is cited out of the 21st verse, and all the rest of the chapter unto the end, does wholly and properly agree.

(5) For the better understanding of this place and the rest of Daniel, we are to know, that excepting one prophetic comfort of the resurrection in chapter 12, his whole prophecy is of those things which happened within less than 700 years, that is to say, from the taking of Jerusalem by the Chaldeans, unto the final destruction thereof by the Romans: and his prophecy concerns those kingdoms which should in the meantime be in the world.

And those are either such terrestrial kingdoms unto whose tyranny the Jews were subject before the coming of the Messiah, or else the spiritual kingdom of Christ (the Messiah and king of the Jews) before which all the former kingdoms were to have an end (Daniel 2:4, 35 and 7:11 & 26-27). The time whereof, as also of the desolation of Jerusalem, is foretold in chapter 9:25-27, according to which time this Messiah and king, is by the wise men acknowledged to be born in Matthew 2, and his kingdom by John the Baptist the forerunner of Christ, was said to be at hand (Matthew 3:2), and in like sort preached our Savior Christ (Matthew 1:15) and his apostles (Mark 10:7). Christ also a little before his death confessed that he was a king, and in his death his title was the king of the Jews.

After his death and resurrection he professed that all power was given him in heaven and in earth, and thereupon ascended into heaven, and sits at the right hand of God: which is noted in Daniel 7:13 that after Christ the son of man was come into the world, he went unto the ancient of days, and to him was given power, glory, and kingdom, that all people, nations and tongues should serve him. Of both these sorts of kingdoms, Daniel entreats in chapters 2 and 7. And as touching the terrestrial kingdoms which tyrannized over the Jews before the coming of Christ in the flesh, they are noted to be four: the first of the Babylonians, the second of the Medes and Persians, the third of the Macedonians, the fourth of the Seleucids and Lagidae.

And of these four Daniel prophecies, either jointly of all together, or severally of some of them. In the second and seventh chapters, of them all together, resembling them in the second chapter by an image, the golden head whereof figures the Babylonians, the breast and arms of silver the Medes and Persians, the belly and sides of brass, represent the Macedonians, his legs of iron, and his feet, part of iron, and part of clay, resemble the Seleucids and Lagidae: and in the seventh chapter, the same four kingdoms are figured by four beasts, the Babylonians by a lion, the Medes and Persians by a bear, the Macedonians by a leopard, the Seleucids and Lagidae, by the beast with ten horns.

(6) Severally, he prophecies either of the Babylonian monarchy, or of the rest. His prophecies concerning the Babylonian monarchy, which also were fulfilled in his time, are set down in chapters 4 and 5. Of the three other, and especially of the last (because that especially was to afflict the people of the Jews) he prophecies again in the 8th and 11th chapters. In the 11th chapter, to omit the rest, the angel promises in verse 2 to declare the truth; that is, the true and proper sense and meaning of the aforesaid visions concerning the three kingdoms which yet remained, recorded in chapters 2, 7, and 8. And first as touching the kingdom of the Medes and Persians, he

mentions but four kings, because the rest did nothing memorable against Judah (verse 2).

In the third verse, he prophesies of Alexander the Great, the mighty monarch of the Greek, and of the division of that empire into four principal parts in verse 4, which before was foretold in chapter 8:22. Of this division, Jerome writes thus:[568] *Quo (sc. Alexandro) tricesimo secundo aetatis suae anno mortuo in Babylon, surrexerunt pro eo quatuor duces eius, qui sibi imperium diuiserunt. Aegyptum enim Ptolemeus Lagi filius tenuit*, etc: Alexander being dead in Babylon at age 32, there arose in his stead four of his captains, who divided the empire among them. For Ptolemy Lagides held Egypt, Philip who also is called Arideus, the brother of Alexander held Macedonia. Seleucus Nicanor, held Syria and Babylon, and all the kingdoms of the East. Antigonus ruled over Asia Minor.

These four kingdoms were by mutual conflicts reduced to two under Seleucus Nicanor, and Ptolemy Lagides, from whom did spring the kingdom of the Lagidae and kings of Egypt in the south, and of the Seleucids or kings of Syria and Babylon in the north. These two used to contend for Judea, which lying in the midst between them, became a prey to the conquerors, and was grievously afflicted by them. These two are the two legs and feet of the image in chapter 2, and also the fourth beast with ten horns in chapter 7, for of these two kingdoms there are ten kings reckoned, which tyrannized over the people of the Jews, especially the tenth horn; that is, Antiochus Epiphanes, who arose in the end of the kingdom of this beast, namely, over the Jews (Daniel 8:23). For in his time the people of God were freed from the tyranny of the Seleucids by Judas Macchabaeus.

(7) These ten horns which successively tyrannized over Jewry are mentioned in order in this 11th chapter. First Ptolemy Lagides (the first horn) who is called in verse 5 *the King of the South*, that is of Egypt, who

---

[568] In Daniel 8

shortly after he had gotten Egypt, invaded Judea, and surprised the city of Jerusalem on a sabbath.[569] Secondly, Seleucus Nicanor (the second horn) the mightiest of the princes of Alexander, as he is described in the same fifth verse. For although Ptolemy for a time held Judea, yet after it was agreed upon that Seleucus should have Syria and therein Judea.

He succeeded Antiochus Soter (the third horn) so called, because he expelled the Frenchmen out of Asia, whose son Antiochus Theos (the fourth horn) to confirm a league between him and Ptolemy Philadelphus King of Egypt, took in marriage Berenice, the daughter of Ptolemy Philadelphus, according to that prophecy of the two legs, consisting of iron and clay mingled together, that they should mingle themselves together in the seed of man, but they should not cleave together, even as iron cannot be mixed with clay (chapter 2:43), for even so it follows verse 6. For however they had combined themselves together by marriage, yet this conjunction held not, and they which had any hand in it shortly after died. For Antiochus Theos had a former wife yet living named Laodice, by whom he had Seleucus Callinicus, and Antiochus Hierax. This Laodice, to avenge this despite, poisoned her husband Antiochus Theos. Her son Seleucus Callinicus (the fifth horn) slew Bernice, her child, and her train, and Ptolemy Philadelphus shortly after this marriage ended his life.

But in his place (verse 7) did arise his son Ptolemy Evergetes (the sixth horn) proceeding from the same roots with Bernice (that is, her brother) who to avenge the death of his sister, made war with Seleucus Callinicus, and overcame him, and having caused himself to be crowned king of Syria, returned with much spoil, and many captives into Egypt; and being stronger then Seleucus Callinicus, he held the dominion of Syria for many years.[570] But the sons of Seleucus Callinicus – to wit, Seleucus Ceraunus, and Antiochus Magnus – raised war (verses 5 & 10). First Seleucus Ceraunus

---

[569] Josephus, *Antiquities*, lib. 12 cap.1
[570] Polyb. li. 5. Appian. in Syria. Ioseph. l. contr. Appian. Vers. 10.

against Ptolemy Evergetes, and they both being dead about the same time, Antiochus Magnus against Ptolemy Philopater, the son of Evergetes.

Of him (I mean Antiochus Magnus) the angel prophesies unto the 20th verse: to wit, of his battles first with Ptolemy Philopator, and those sometimes prosperous, whereby he recovered Syria (verse 10), sometimes adverse, whereby he lost the same again (verses 11-12). Whereupon Ptolemy – being lifted up – became the seventh horn, and killed many of the Jews, for which he shall not prosper (verse 12). After, of his battles and victories against Ptolemy Epiphanes son of Philopater (verses 13-15). Of his afflicting the lande thereby that is Jewry (verse 16) as being the eight hour: of his giving his daughter Cleopatra to Ptolemy Epiphanes to mingle the iron and the clay (according to the prophecy, chapter 2), therein pretending peace and friendship, but intending by her his destruction, although in vain, she joining with her husband against her father (verse 17). Of his expeditions into the islands of Greece, and conquering them. Of his wars with the Romans, which brought shame upon him, they making him to sit down with dishonorable conditions (verse 18). Of his ignominious ende, namely in a Barbarian tumult for sacrilege (verse 19).

In his place succeeded his son Seleucus Philopater (the ninth horn) one who did pill and poll his subjects by great tributes and exactions, and sent to empty and exhaust the treasury and temple of Jerusalem: and having set free his brother Antiochus Epiphanes, who was an hostage at Rome, and instead of him sent his own son Demetrius, was shortly after poisoned by Heliodorus, suborned by Antiochus Epiphanes (verse 20).

(8) "Now in his place," (says the angel in verse 21) "shall stand a vile person," etc. that is, in the kingdom of Syria, a vile person shall succeed Seleucus Philopater as the tenth horn, which cannot be understood properly of any other but of Antiochus Epiphanes, who in the rest of the chapter to the end, is most fully and plainly described.

For firstly he entreated of his coming unto the kingdom, secondly of his affairs afterwards, and lastly of his end. Of his coming unto the kingdom he says, that having no right of succession (for Demetrius was the heir) nor lawful election, by flattery and fraud attained to the kingdom, pretending himself (as Richard IIII did) to be the tutor and protector of the young Prince Demetrius, and administrator of the kingdom during the minority and absence of Demetrius, who had been sent in his stead as an hostage to Rome.

Wherefore Daniel in this place speaks not of Antichrist, unless we may say, that Antichrist was to be the immediate successor of Seleucus Philopater, which is ridiculous; yea, and Bellarmine himself confesses elsewhere, that in this latter part of the chapter, Daniel speaks of Antiochus literally, who was a figure of Antichrist.[571] This place therefore does not prove Bellarmine's proposition, namely: that Antichrist – arising from a most base estate – should by fraud obtain the kingdom of the Jews.

Neither does this proposition sit Antiochus, who is here described; neither is it agreeable to the description itself. For neither did Antiochus arise from most base estate, for he was son to Antiochus the Great, and brother to Seleucus Philopater. Neither does Daniel say so, but only that נִבְזֶה – a vile or despised person – should succeed Seleucus Philopator; which is to be understood not in respect of his base estate and condition, but of his base manners and vile conditions, in regard whereof the Holy Spirit calls him, although a great king's son, *vile and contemptible*.

And so is every wicked man, though mighty in the world, a vile and despised person in the eyes of the godly (Psalm 15:4): "The wicked man is vile in his eyes." And as Solomon says: The wicked man is an abomination unto the righteous."[572]

---

[571] Lib. 3 cap. 21
[572] Proverbs 21:27

Such an one was Haman in the eyes of Mordechai,[573] and Jehoram the wicked king of Israel, in the eyes of Elisha.[574] So that it was not the base condition, but the vices and base conditions of Antiochus that made him vile, in respect whereof Polybius called him Ἐπιμανής. So is Seleucus Philopater in verse 20 in the vulgar translation called *Vilissimus*, because of his base polling of his people, and not because he did arise from base estate.

Wherefore it is evident that Daniel speaks not of Antichrist in this place, and that he of whom he speaks, did not arise from a most base estate, as Bellarmine would bear us in hand; unless it be a most base estate to be the son of a mighty king, who for his greatness was called Antiochus the Great.

(9) But will you see with one view the absurdity of this popish argument. He proves from this place that Antichrist shall arise from a most base estate, and shall by deceit obtain the kingdom of the Jews. But (say I) Daniel speaks not of Antichrist, but of Antiochus Epiphanes. Yea but Antiochus was a type of Antichrist. Be it that he was a type not only in some other things, but also in this particular; yet from hence we must infer not the self-same particular which is proper to the person of Antiochus, but the like, and that by way of allegory only, which were but a sleight argument to prove so weighty a controversy in divinity.

Whereas therefore he infers from hence not the like (namely: as Antiochus obtained his kingdom by fraud: so shall Antichrist obtain his) but the very same particular, (namely: as Antiochus obtained the kingdom of the Jews, so shall Antichrist obtain the same kingdom of the Jews) his argument is ridiculous: and yet this is not all the absurdity of this argument. For when as from the likeness of Antichrist to his type, he would prove that Antichrist shall arise from base estate, this assertion is not true of the type itself.

Yea but Jerome says that this place may better be understood of Antichrist, *Qui consurgere habet de modica gente id est de populo Iudaeorum*, etc.

---

[573] Esther 3
[574] 2 Kings 3:13-14

"Who is to arise of a small nation, that is, the people of the Jews," etc., and Daniel compares Antichrist because of his base beginning to the little horn in chapter 7.

I do not deny that Antichrist's beginning might be base; but yet neither can the testimony of Jerome, nor does that allegation out of Daniel prove it. For Jerome's testimony in this case, if it ought to be of weight with us, it must be taken either as a prophecy, or else as a fit exposition of Daniel's prophecy, as I have said heretofore. But Jerome was no prophet; neither does he fitly expound Daniel, who speaks plainly, not of Antichrist, but of the successor of Seleucus Philopator.

And it is a wonder that Jerome – one of the most learned of the fathers – should in so easy a matter be overseen. For seeing as he confesses that the former part of the chapter is to be expounded of the Seleucids, and that in the 20. verse is described Seleucus Philopator, for so he says on those words {*Et stabit in loco eius vilissimus*} *Seleucum dicit cognomento Philopatorem, filium magni Antiochi*, he speaks of Seleucus, surnamed Philopator, the son of Antiochus the Great.

It is therefore most plain, that when Daniel says, and in his place shall stand a vile person, he speaks of the next successor of Seleucus Philopator, meaning Antiochus; even as in the 20th verse after he had spoken of Antiochus Magnus, he says, "and in his place shall stand up a sender forth of an extortioner," meaning Seleucus. Neither does Daniel say anywhere that Anchrist, or he of whom he speaks, shall arise of a small nation, meaning thereby the Jews: that which he speaks *de modico populo* (verse 23) is to be understood properly as Jerome himself expounds it, according to the literal, that is, the proper sense, of the small company wherewith Antiochus surprised Egypt. Neither can there be any such allegorical sense, as he seems to frame.

Neither does Daniel by the little horn mean any other but Antiochus Epiphanes, who may not unfitly in several things be said to have been a type of Antichrist. For the terrible beast with ten horns, does not signify the Roman state as the papists would have it, but the kingdom of the Seleucids and Lagidae: and by the ten horns, not the ten kings whereof John speaks in Revelation 17, among whom the Roman Empire was to be divided; but ten of these kings, namely: three Lagidae, and seven Seleucids, which tyrannized or ruled over the people of God.

The tenth, that is to say, the last of them that had dominion over Judea was, not Antichrist, but Antiochus Epiphanes, who in cruelty towards the people of God surpassed all that went before him.

(10) This I speak not as though this exposition did much hinder our assertion; for others which have held the same, have applied those things which are spoken of the little horn, unto the pope. And surely if this fourth beast were the Roman state, and the horns the rulers thereof, and the tenth or last horn Antichrist, then is it hereby very likely that the pope is Antichrist, seeing as hitherto he is the last that has ruled in Rome, and shall according to the papists own conceit continue to the end.

But the truth is that the description of the fourth beast does not agree to the Romans, but to the kingdom of the Seleucids.

[1] For this fourth beast was a kingdom which was to have an end before the coming of the Messiah and his kingdom (Daniel 7:11, 26-27). So had the kingdom of the Seleucids, so had not the Romans.

[2] This fourth beast warred with the Jews, tyrannized over them, and hindered their religion and worship of God at Jerusalem, not only before the coming of Christ, but also before the purging of the temple, and restitution of religion by Judas Maccabaeus (Daniel 7:25-27). So did the Seleucidae, so did not the Romans.

[3] Of the fourth beast there were but ten horns, that is Princes that ruled over Judea, which is most true of the Seleucids and Lagidae; but of the Romans, after they had once obtained the dominion of Jury, there were many more then ten that ruled over the holy land. If any say the Roman

Empire is figured in Revelation 17 by a beast with ten horns, I answer, that the ten horns whereof John speaks in Revelation 17:12 are ten kings, among whom the Roman Empire was to be divided, who succeeded not one another in the same kingdom, but were rulers of so many several provinces or kingdoms at the same time. But these ten horns tyrannized over the same kingdom of the Jews successively, as they are particularly described in chapter 11. And further, he that in Daniel is supposed by the papists to be Antichrist, is one of the ten horns, but in John is not.

[4] That which is spoken in Daniel of the tenth horn does fitly and wholly agree to Antiochus Epiphanes, who was the tenth and last king of that kingdom, that ruled over Judea, but the same things cannot in like sort be applied to the tenth prince of the Romans.

[5] By conference of that which is written of the little horn in chapter 7 with those things which are more plainly recorded of Antiochus in chapter 8:23, etc., and chapter 11:21, etc., to the end of the chapter, it appears evidently, that he and no other is that little horn.

For whereas Daniel in the 7th chapter had described three kingdoms besides the Babylonian, which should tyrannize over the Jews by three beasts: in the 8th chapter, he figures the same three kingdoms by two beasts. For the kingdom of the Medes and Persians which before was resembled by a bear, is here signified by the ram with two horns: the kingdom of the Macedonians and Seleucidae, which before were represented by two several beasts, are here figured by the goat buck, containing them both; for both the Macedonians and Seleucids were Javan, that is, the Greeks (Daniel 8:21).

And as in the 7th chapter, the kingdom of the Macedonians was signified by a leopard which had four heads: so here it is said, that after the great horn signifying Alexander the Great was broken off, there grew four horns instead thereof, meaning the four princes among whom the Macedonian monarchy was divided.

The fourth kingdom figured in chapter 7 by the beast with ten horns, is here signified to be that kingdom which was chiefly erected by one of those four horns, namely Seleucus, that is, the kingdom of the Seleucids: and from him, namely in the end of their kingdom over the Jews, came forth a little horn, that is, the king with the impudent face, chapter 8, verses 9 & 23, which is Antiochus Epiphanes, who was the tenth horn of the fourth beast. And in the 11th chapter, without figures of beasts, the same three kingdoms are described, the same ten horns reckoned up, and the same tenth horn is more particularly deciphered.

[6] The people pushed at and oppressed by these horns, is Daniel's people, the people of the Jews yet remaining and inhabiting in *Tzeby*, that is in Jewry and Jerusalem, not only before the desolation of Jerusalem, but also before the reformation under Judas Maccabaeus. But Antichrist, if we will believe the papists, shall be the counterfeit messiah of the Jews, neither shall he afflict the Jews, but by them the Christians, and that in the end of the world, etc.

[7] The times of afflicting the people of God assigned to the little horn, do precisely agree to the persecution under Antiochus. But these times are variously to be reckoned, in respect either of the beginning, or the end of the account.

For as touching the beginning, we reckon either from the defection and revolt of the people wrought by Menelaus the priest, in the year 142, the sixth month, and sixth day, unto the restitution of religion, in the year 148, and 25th day of the ninth month, and this space is 2300 days (that is 6 years, 3 months and 18 days), foretold in Daniel 8:14.

Or else we reckon from the pollution of the temple, and erection of the new altar, and abolishing of the daily sacrifice, to wit, in the 145th year of the Seleucids, on the 15th of Kislev, variously in respect of the end, namely: either to the restitution begun by Judas Maccabaeus, in the 25th of the same month of Kislev, in the year 148, which space is called a time and times, and parcel of time, that is, three years and ten days.[575]

Or if we read a time and times and half a time, we may reckon unto the time of that victory which Maccabaeus and the Jews had against the armies of Antiochus, whereby his instauration [renewal] of religion was secured and confirmed, and Antiochus' armies were expelled out of Jewry, which as Josephus notes,[576] was done after three years and six months. Or if we reckon to the time that Antiochus – having heard of these and some other overthrows of his armies after his own discomfiture and slight from Persepolis – was stricken by the hand of God, and promised all good things to the Jews, it is 1290 days; if to his death, 1335.[577]

By all of these considerations, it appears that Daniel by the fourth beast understands not the Roman monarchy, but the kingdom of the Seleucids and Lagidae, nor by the tenth horn Antichrist properly, but Antiochus Epiphanes.

(11) Thus much therefore may suffice to have spoken of his proposition: now let us briefly consider the assumption. "The pope," (says he) "arises not from a base estate, neither by deceit obtains his kingdom."

As touching the former I answer:

[1] That although it were false of Antiochus, yet is it true of the pope, whether you consider the mean estate of the first bishops of Rome, or the base birth and obscure parentage of various popes. For that which Bellarmine alleges in commendation of the primitive religion, and ancient church of Rome, is but a vain flourish, nothing appertaining to this purpose.

[2] That the pope has not attained to his kingdom by fraud and deceit, Bellarmine had rather it should be taken for granted, then once called in

---

[575] Josephus, *Antiquities*, Lib. 12, chapter 6, 1 Maccabees 1:57, 1 Maccabees 14:52, Daniel 7:25, Daniel 12:7
[576] Josephus, *The Jewish Wars*, lib.1 cap.1
[577] Daniel 12:11-12

question: and therefore cunningly passes it over with silence. But if this were set down in the Scriptures as a badge of Antichrist, to attain to his greatness by fraud and deceit, I would make it manifest, that never in any estate more deep policy, and devilish deceit has been used then in the See of Rome, whereby they have obtained their supremacy, and maintained their sovereignty over the Christian world.

Yea their whole religion of popery and mystery of iniquity, seems to be naught else but a pack of policy devised by worldly men to deify the pope, and to enrich the popish clergy. For whereunto else I beseech you tended their indulgences and pardons, their jubilees, their doctrines of merits and supererogation, their purgatory, their trentals of masses, and prayer for the dead, their pilgrimages and adoration of saints, images, and relics, their licenses and dispensations, their thunderbolts of excommunication, their oath of allegiance and fealty imposed on princes and potentates, subjection to the pope enforced upon all sorts, as absolutely necessary to salvation, their willful depravations of Scriptures, forgeries of canons, counterfeit donations of Constantine and others, to prove the double supremacy of the pope?

Whereunto tended his often maintaining of quarrels among Christian princes, his wars enjoined them for the recovery of the holy land, but that they being by these means weakened, might be the more easily subdued unto himself, his Crusades, and promises of heaven, to all those that sight such battles as like him? Have not their clergy come to their riches, and the pope to his greatness by these and such like means?

But because the coming to his greatness by fraud and deceit, is not set down in the Scriptures as a note of Antichrist, unless it be by way of type and allegory in Antiochus, I will therefore let it pass; only let me put you in mind that the prophecy of Peter in the former respects is performed in the pope and clergy of Rome, who by feigned words make merchandise of men's souls through covetousness. And this was Bellarmine's first instance.

12 His second argument is thus to be framed:

- Antichrist shall war with three kings, to wit of Egypt, Libya, and Ethiopia; and having overcome them, shall possess their kingdoms.
- But the pope of Rome has not warred at any time (he should say, shall not war, and that is more than he is able to prove) with the Kings of Egypt, Libya, and Ethiopia, neither having vanquished them, has possessed their kingdoms,
- Therefore the pope of Rome is not Antichrist.

And in this argument Belarmine does so greatly please himself, that after an insulting manner he breaks forth into these brags: *Hoc autem maxim refellit insaniam haereticorum*, etc: "This especially refutes the madness of heretics, who make the pope Antichrist. For let them say if they can, when the pope has killed the kings of Egypt, Libya, and Ethiopia," etc.

What would this Thraso do, do you think, if he had any good argument against us, that thus insults upon a mere dotage? For where does the Scripture say that Antichrist shall sight with the kings of Egypt, Libya, and Ethiopia, and that having vanquished them, he shall possess their kingdoms? Indeed, in Daniel. In the 7th chapter of Daniel, speaking of the ten horns of the fourth beast, he says (verse 8): "I considered the horns, and lo, the last horn came up, a little one among them, and three of the former horns were plucked up before it." And after (verse 24), expounding the same words, he says: "And the ten horns are ten kings of that kingdom, after whom shall arise the last (namely of the ten) diverse from the rest, and he shall abase three kings."

But this allegation is impertinent. For I have shown that this fourth beast is the kingdom of the Seleucids and Lagidae; that the ten horns are those ten kings of that kingdom which tyrannized or ruled over Jewry; that the tenth or last of them that tyrannized over the Jews, was Antiochus Epiphanes, who is therefore called little before his coming to the crown, because of his unlikeness to be king. Firstly, because he was the third and youngest son of Antiochus Magnus, his elder brother Seleucus having also a son called Demetrius. Secondly, because he was to be a perpetual hostage at Rome. For whereas other hostages, which Antiochus the great gave to the Romans, were to be changed every third year, he was to be a perpetual hostage. And thirdly, because of his vile and base conditions.

Now whereas it is said that three horns were to be plucked up before him, we are by those three horns to understand three kings, not of others, and those also various kingdoms, as of Egypt, Libya, and Ethiopia; but three kings that successively had ruled before him in the same kingdom usurped over the Jews, as being expressly called three former horns, namely: of the ten (verse 8).

Yea but Antiochus was a type of Antichrist. It cannot be proven that he was a type in this point, or if he were a type in this, we may not infer the same particular as Bellarmine does, for then those three kings mentioned in Daniel, must be revived again, that Antichrist may make them away, but the like might be inferred, namely: that as Antiochus Epiphanes to make himself a way to the kingdom, did make away his brother and two others that went before him, so it is not unlikely that this should be an Antichristian practice.

It is well known that Gregory VII, who resembled Antiochus in many things, to make himself a way to the papacy, made away six of his predecessors by poison. And it is an ordinary practice among the cardinals of Rome that aspire to the papacy, now and then to minister an Italian fig to their popes, that you may not marvel that there have been nine popes in the time of Queen Elizabeth's reign, of whom the three next predecessors of the present pope Clement VIII were so suddenly plucked up before him – namely: Urban VII, Gregory XIV, and Innocent IX – that I suppose their names have been heard of few among us.

(13) *But Daniel 11 perhaps will prove Bellarmine's assertion.* That allegation will prove nothing but Bellarmine's willful blindness. He says that in 11:43, Daniel explains who those three kings are: "He shall stretch out his hand over countries, and the land of Egypt shall not escape, and he shall pass through Libya and Ethiopia," as Bellarmine reads it, but according to the Hebrew, the Lubim and Cushim, that is, the Libyans and Ethiopians, shall be in his passages or voyages. From this, Bellarmine infers that Antichrist shall kill three kings, namely: of Egypt, Libya, and Ethiopia.

Answer: [1] Daniel speaks not of Antichrist but of Antiochus, as I have manifestly proven.

[2] Although Antiochus were granted to have been a type of Antichrist herein, yet the same particular which is proper to the person of Antiochus, may not be applied to Antichrist. For then we must dream that the world and the kingdoms thereof, must be brought again just to the same pass wherein they were when Antiochus reigned, and the same kings to be revived.

But something similar might be applied, that as Antiochus, in Bellarmine's conceit, suppressed three kings, so Antichrist should be a suppressor of kings, which is true of the pope: who besides various kings deposed by his means, has also depressed four emperors at the least, as Bellarmine himself confesses.

[3] Daniel in this place is so far from mentioning three kings slain by Antichrist according to Bellarmine's conceit, that he neither speaks of Antichrist, nor of three kings, nor of the killing of any one king, but only of Antiochus' spoiling of Egypt, having in his company the Libyans and Ethiopians.

Whether therefore this argument of Bellarmine does reprove our madness, or rather prove his folly, let any indifferent arbiter be judge. Now if Jerome or any other of the fathers have let fall any such thing, we are to esteem it as an excrement of theirs, which we are to pass by, rather than with the *Cacovorae* the papists, to gather it up as fit food for their souls.[578]

(14) And the like answer we frame unto his third argument, which is not grounded upon the Scriptures; but upon the bare conjectures of some of the fathers. For where is there in all the Scriptures any word of this which Bellarmine says he reads in the Scriptures, that Antichrist shall subdue seven other kings, and by that means shall become the monarch of the whole world? Indeed, Lactantius and Irenaeus say so. But I never took their writings before to be the scriptures. Why then Jerome, says so upon Daniel 11:24, where Daniel speaks of Antiochus' dealings in Egypt, that he did that which his forefathers never did: *Nullus Iudaeorum absque Antichristo in toto vnquam or be regnauit.*

These are Bellarmine's Scriptures. But where do the Scriptures indeed say that Antichrist shall subdue seven of the ten kings? Nay, the contrary may rather be gathered out of the Scriptures. The ten horns whereof Daniel speaks, were ten kings which successively reigned over Judea, as has been shown. And although Antiochus Epiphanes might help away three of his next predecessors, yet he could not hurt the other six (for there were but nine besides himself) which were all dead and gone before he came to years. Yea, but this opinion of the fathers is plainly enough deduced out of Revelation 17:12, where we read: "And the ten horns which thou sawest, are ten kings; these have one mind, and they shall give their power and authority to the beast."

No marvel though some of the papists call the Scripture a nose of wax, seeing they can frame and fashion it at their pleasure, and give unto it what sense they list. Does John speak of Antichrist's either killing three, or

---

[578] [*Cacovorae*: A bird that devours the excrement of birds. Downame's footnote follows:] Cacouora, auis quaedam est apud Indos, quae alterius auis [assencla] est: cuius vescatur excremētis. Scalig. de subtil.

subduing seven? Or does John speak of the same ten horns whereof Daniel does?

Daniel speaks of ten kings which were to be dead and gone before the coming of the Messiah; John speaks of such as in his time had not yet attained to their kingdom (verse 12). Daniel speaks of ten kings of the Seleucids and Lagidae which succeeded one another; John, of ten kings among whom the Roman Empire was to be divided, who also were to have their kingdom together with the beast. Daniel tells us what the little horn, which was one of the ten, should do to three of the other nine, without mention of the rest; John shows what all the ten horns should do to Antichrist, which is none of the ten horns, but one of the heads of the beast. If therefore Bellarmine can prove from hence that these are the same ten horns spoken of in Daniel, and that Antichrist shall kill three of them, and subdue the other seven, he may hope to prove anything,

But what other Scriptures has he? Indeed, Chrysostom and Cyril. For Chrysostom on 2 Thessalonians 2 says that Antichrist shall be a monarch, and shall succeed the Romans in the monarchy, as the Romans succeeded the Greeks, the Greeks succeeded the Persians, and they the Assyrians. And Cyril says that Antichrist shall obtain the monarchy which was the Romans.[579]

I answer that for substance, these fathers held the truth. For what monarch has there been in the West these five or six hundred years, besides the pope, who calls himself *King of Kings* and *Lord of Lords*, to whom all power is given in heaven and in earth, who has as they say, the double monarchy both of spiritual and temporal power; who indeed is Lord of the whole earth, in so much that he takes upon him authority to dispose of the new found world?[580] And that he succeeds the emperors in the government of Rome, as it becomes Antichrist, who is the second beast (Revelation 13)

---

[579] Catech. 15
[580] Alexander VI

and the seventh head of the beast (Revelation 17) whereof the emperor was the sixth, I shall not need to prove.

(15) There remains the fourth argument: Antichrist shall persecute the Christians throughout the world with an innumerable army, and this is the battle of God and Magog: but this agrees not to the pope, therefore the pope is not Antichrist. I answer to the proposition, that no such thing can be proved out of the scripture. He alleges Ezekiel 38 and 39, and Revelation 20:7-10. But Ezekiel speaks not of Antichrist, nor of the persecution of the Christian Church by him. But having foretold the restitution of the Jews from the Babylonian captivity in chapter 37, and also prophesied of the coming of Christ; in those chapters he foretells of the afflictions and troubles which the people of the Jews should sustain in the meantime, to wit, after their return out of captivity, before the coming of the Messiah, and also, denounces the judgments of God against the Seleucids, who were the kings of Syria and Asia Minor, and their adherents, who should be the chief enemies of the church, and people of the Jews after their return.

For *Gog* signifies Asia Minor, having that name from Gyges the King thereof. Magog is Hierapolis the chief seat of idolatry in Syria, built by the Scythians, and from them has that name. So that by *the land of Magog*, we are to understand Syria, and by *Gog*, Asia Minor.[581] And the rest of the peoples that are named in Ezekiel, were such as assisted the Seleucids (who were the kings of Syria, and Asia Minor) in their wars, either as their subjects, or as their friends, or as their mercenary soldiers.

And for as much as the princes and people of Syria and Asia Minor were the most grievous enemies of the Jews, by whom they sustained the chiefest calamities after their return before the coming of Christ, therefore by an usual speech in the Jewish language, the mortal and deadly enemies of the church, are called *Gog and Magog*. And in this sense John the Divine uses

---

[581] Plin. lib. 5 cap. 23

these names, *Gog and Magog*, to signify the enemies of the church, meaning not the same enemies whereof Ezekiel speaks, but the like enemies of the church, which should afflict the true Christians, as Gog and Magog afflicted the Jews.[582]

Neither does John in this place speak of the persecution of Antichrist properly, but of Satan (after he was loosed), his inciting the enemies of the Church to battle, and of God's judgments against them, signified by fire. And so much shall suffice to have answered to this argument.

For after so long a treatise I will not trouble the reader with the ten several opinions which Bellarmine recites concerning Gog and Magog, neither yet with any further answer to his cavillations and exceptions against some of the arguments of several Protestants, which he thought were more easy to answer: seeing in the former book I have sufficiently cleared those arguments whereby the pope is more evidently proved to be Antichrist.

Neither is the controversy between us, whether every argument that has been produced by everyone, does necessarily conclude the pope to be Antichrist. That discourse therefore being rather personal than real, I let it pass.

---

[582] Ad Tremellius & Junius in Ezekiel 38-39

Chapter 17
Being the conclusion of the whole treatise.

Having therefore both by sufficient arguments manifestly proved that the pope is Antichrist, and by evidence of truth maintained the same assertion against the arguments of the papists, let us now consider in the last place, what conclusions may upon this doctrine be necessarily inferred for our further use. For first, if this be true – that the pope is Antichrist, as I have proven; and the church of Rome that now is, Babylon the Synagogue of Antichrist – then all other controversies between us and them, may be easily decided: their chief ground being the authority of their church, and of the Apostolic See.

(1) For then it is to be presumed, that those doctrines which are peculiar to the pope and Church of Rome, are the errors of Antichrist; yea, and as the apostle calls them, *doctrines of devils*.[583]

(2) If the Romish church is Antichristian, then our separation from it is warranted, yea, commanded by the word of God, and all returning to it forbidden (Revelation 18:4): "Come out of her my people lest, partaking with her in her sins, you partake also in her punishment."

(3) If the pope is Antichrist, then those that embrace that religion, and join themselves to that church, acknowledging the pope to be their head, receive the mark of the beast. And those that do receive the beast's mark (especially after he is revealed) shall drink of the wine of God's wrath, and shall be punished with fire and brimstone before the holy angels, and before the Lamb (Revelation 14:9). This therefore must serve as a serious admonition, and necessary caveat both to reclaim all tractable papists, and to

---

[583] 1 Timothy 4:2

confirm all wavering and unstaid Protestants. The former, as they tender their salvation, so to come out of Babylon: The latter, as they will avoid their endless confusion, to keep out of Babylon. For not only to retain the mark of the beast willfully after he is discovered, but to revolt from the profession of the truth unto Antichristian religion. It is also is a fearful sign of reprobation. For it is impossible that the elect should finally be seduced by Antichrist (Matthew 24:24).

And the apostle Paul observes that Antichrist shall effectually deceive them that perish with all deceitfulness of iniquity, because they have not received the love of the truth, that they might be saved. And therefore God shall send them strong delusions, that they should believe lies, that all they might be damned which believed not the truth, but delighted in unrighteousness (2 Thessalonians. 2:10-12). Wherupon Chrysostom also writing, has these words: "Antichrist prevails with castaways or such as perish." And Jerome likewise:[584] "They shall be seduced," (says he) "by the lies of Antichrist, who are prepared unto perdition."

But on the other side, those who renounce the pope and church of Rome, and rise from the grave of Antichristianism and popery, and follow our Savior Christ in the sincere profession of the truth. "Blessed and holy are they for they having part in the first resurrection, shall be freed from the second death."[585] And howsoever they are esteemed of the followers of Antichrist, as heretics and schismatics, which are to be persecuted with fire and faggot, yet are they happy in their life whiles they join with Christ against Antichrist, for such are called, *elect* and *faithful*, and *redeemed out of the world*;[586] and they are also blessed in their death, dying in the quarrel of Christ against Antichrist,[587] for of those specially does the Holy Spirit speak in Revelation 14:13: "Blessed are those that die in the Lord," etc.

---

[584] Ad Algasiā quest. 11
[585] Revelation 20:6
[586] Revelation 17:14
[587] Revelation 14:4

(4) If the pope is Antichrist, then those that are found to be resolute Antichristians, that is recusant papists; but especially Jesuits and seminary priests, which are sent to reconcile men unto the pope and Church of Rome, that is, (as has been proven) to set on them the mark of the beast, and consequently to brand them to destruction, and all such as seek to pervert and seduce others, ought not to be favored or spared in a Christian commonwealth.

Firstly, because they are limbs of Antichrist, and therefore by the commandment of God, we should do to them as they have done to us (Revelation 18:6). Secondly, because they are enemies to God, and traitors to Christian princes. They are enemies to God, not only because they themselves are idolaters, and consequently such as hate God (Exodus 20:5), but also because they labor to withdraw others from the true worship of God, unto superstition and idolatry, and therefore in no case ought to be spared (Deuteronomy 13:5, 8). They are traitors also to Christian princes, being sworn vassals to the pope, their capital enemy. For he esteems all Christian princes that do not acknowledge him to be their head, as schismatics or heretics. And as he tends (so often as he dares) to proceed against such four ways, namely: by excommunication, deposition, depriving them of their temporal goods and possessions, and raising war against them,[588] so all papists acknowledging the pope's supremacy, do hold both that he has authority so to proceed against Christian princes, and also that in his definitive sentence he cannot err.[589]

And therefore, if they put not in execution the sentence of their holy father, it is not for want of treasonable will, and rebellious affection towards their prince, but for lack of means and opportunity. As for example, when Pius V had sent his bull of excommunication against our late sovereign queen of happy memory, therein deposing her from her crown, and

---

[588] Antonin. sum. part. 3. tit. 22. cap. 5. §. 11.
[589] Antonin. sum. part. 3. tit. 22. cap. 5. §. 10

absolving her subjects from their allegiance towards her,[590] it is most certain, that whatsoever many hollow hearted papists pretended, yet few of them did acknowledge her for their lawful queen; and many of them thought it a meritorious work to take away her life. And surely if not their persons, then much less ought their Antichristian religion, the mystery of iniquity, be tolerated in the church of Christ. For what fellowship can there be between light and darkness? or what agreement can the temple of God have with idols?[591]

(5) If the pope is Antichrist, and his church Antichristian, then can there be no reconciliation between us and the church of Rome, we being, as often has been proven, the true church of God. For what agreement can there be between Christ and Antichrist? Such neuters therefore show themselves to be nullifidians and political atheists, who would persuade men that both we and they are the true church of Christ, and that the difference between us being in words rather than in substance, may easily be composed. But they might as well say that there is but a verbal difference between the gospel of Christ, and the doctrine of Antichrist.

(6) Lastly, if the church of Rome, which because of her largeness, calls herself the catholic, that is to say, the universal church, is notwithstanding the synagogue of Antichrist, then what infinite thanks do we owe to our good and gracious God, who has not suffered us to be carried away with that catholic apostasy, as it were an universal deluge, but has gathered us into the ark of his true church, making us with the rest of his true professors his peculiar people?

It remains therefore that, seeing God has been so gracious to us, we should not be unthankful to him, but rather should walk worthy our calling,

---

[590] Cupers. pag. 182. num. 8.
[591] 2 Corinthians 6

as it becomes the children of the light, adorning the profession of the glorious gospel of Christ, by a godly conversation; to the end that by the plentiful fruits of righteousness and true holiness, we may glorify God our heavenly Father, stop the mouths of our adversaries, and gather assurance unto our own souls, of our justification and salvation by Jesus Christ our blessed Lord and Savior, to whom with the Father and the Holy Spirit, be all praise and thanksgiving, both now and evermore.

Amen.

FINIS

Appendix – The Historic Reformed Doctrine of the Papal Antichrist

That the pope is the Antichrist is a Protestant, Reformed, and confessional doctrine. The Westminster Confession of Faith states: "There is no other head of the Church, but the Lord Jesus Christ; nor can the Pope of Rome, in any sense, be head thereof; but is that Antichrist, that man of sin, and son of perdition, that exalteth himself, in the Church, against Christ and all that is called God."[592] (WCF 25.6)

Martin Luther said that the papacy was: "nothing else than the kingdom of Babylon and of very Antichrist. For who is the man of sin and the son of perdition, but he who by his teaching and his ordinances increases the sin and perdition of souls in the church; while he yet sits in the church as if he were God? All these conditions have now for many ages been fulfilled by the papal tyranny."[593]

John Calvin stated: "But to conclude this point in a few words: I deny that See to be Apostolical, wherein nought is seen but a shocking apostasy — I deny him to be the vicar of Christ, who, in furiously persecuting the gospel, demonstrates by his conduct that he is Antichrist — I deny him to be the successor of Peter, who is doing his utmost to demolish every edifice that Peter built — and I deny him to be the head of the Church, who by his tyranny lacerates and dismembers the Church, after dissevering her from Christ, her true and only head."[594]

---

[592] <https://www.fpchurch.org.uk/about-us/what-we-contend-for/a-protestant-witness/the-pope-in-scripture/> [Accessed 11/28/2023]

[593] <https://www.semperreformanda.com/creeds/the-reformers-on-who-is-the-antichrist/> [Accessed 11/27/2023]

[594] <https://reformedbooksonline.com/topics/topics-by-subject/roman-catholicism/historic-quotes-on-the-papacy-being-the-antichrist/> [Accessed 11/27/2023]

John Knox "Yea, to speak it in plain words; lest that we submit ourselves to Satan, thinking that we submit ourselves to Jesus Christ, for, as for your Roman kirk, as it is now corrupted, and the authority thereof, whereon stands the hope of your victory, I no more doubt but that it is the synagogue of Satan, and the head thereof, called the pope, to be that man of sin, of whom the apostle speaks."[595]

Wilhelmus a Brakel declared: "**Question:** Who is the antichrist? **Answer:** With all Protestants we reply: The pope of Rome. The papists deny this strongly."[596]

Thomas Manton: "Now in this temple of God he sitteth as an officer and bishop there, as I before explained it: and whereas other princes are said to reign so many years, the Pope is said to sit so long. It is his sedes, his cathedral or seat. And again, here he is said to sit as God, that is, as God incarnate, for Christ is the true and proper Lord of the church; none should reign there but he. And the name of this man of sin is not Ἀντίθεος [Antitheos], but ἀντίχριστος [antichristos]; not one that directly invadeth the properties of the supreme God, but of God incarnate, or Christ as Mediator: he sitteth negatively, not as a minister, but positively as supreme lord upon earth, whom all must adore and worship, and kings and princes kiss his feet. In short, he usurpeth the authority due to Christ."[597]

Thomas Cranmer said: "Whereof it followeth Rome to be the seat of Antichrist, and the pope to be very antichrist himself. I could prove the same by many other Scriptures, old writers, and strong reasons."[598]

---

[595] <https://www.semperreformanda.com/creeds/the-reformers-on-who-is-the-antichrist/> [Accessed 11/27/2023]

[596] <https://reformedbooksonline.com/topics/topics-by-subject/roman-catholicism/historic-quotes-on-the-papacy-being-the-antichrist/> [Accessed 11/27/2023]

[597] <https://www.covenanter.org/reformed/2015/8/17/sermon-four-2-thess-24> [Accessed 11/27/2023]

[598] <https://www.semperreformanda.com/creeds/the-reformers-on-who-is-the-antichrist/> [Accessed 11/27/2023]

Francis Turretin: "Lest we seem to assert these facts for no reason, it must indeed now be shown that all the marks by which the Antichrist is described in Scripture converge only on the Roman pontiff. By our so doing, no honest person will be able to examine these marks closely without easily observing them reflecting, as if in a mirror, the pope himself."[599]

J.A. Wylie: "The following demonstration is rested on no narrow basis. Its two postulates, like two posterns, admit us into the edifice, but they are not its foundations. The whole economy of redemption, and the whole course of history are the broad substructions on which the argument is based and built up; and the author humbly submits that it cannot be overturned, or the conclusion arrived at set aside, without dislocating and shaking the structure of both revelation and providence. The same line of proof which establishes that Christ is the promised Messiah, conversely applied, establishes that the Roman system is the predicted apostasy. In the life of Christ we behold the converse of what the Antichrist must be; and in the prophecy of the Antichrist we are shown the converse of what Christ must be, and was. And when we place the Papacy between the two, and compare it with each, we find, on the one hand, that it is the perfect converse of Christ as seen in His life; and, on the other, that it is the perfect image of the Antichrist, as shown in the prophecy of him. We conclude, therefore, that if Jesus of Nazareth be the Christ, the Roman Papacy is the Antichrist."[600]

---

[599] <https://www.iconbusters.com/iconbusters/htm/catalogue/turretin.pdf> [Accessed 11/27/2023]

[600] <https://reformedbooksonline.com/topics/topics-by-subject/roman-catholicism/historic-quotes-on-the-papacy-being-the-antichrist/> [Accessed 11/27/2023]

www.ingramcontent.com/pod-product-compliance
Lightning Source LLC
Chambersburg PA
CBHW030326010526
44119CB00027B/389/J